RECLAIMING THE
AMERICAN LIBRARY PAST:
WRITING THE WOMEN IN

INFORMATION MANAGEMENT, POLICY, AND SERVICES

Peter Hernon, series editor

RECLAIMING THE AMERICAN LIBRARY PAST: WRITING THE WOMEN IN

Suzanne Hildenbrand
Editor

Ablex Publishing Company
Norwood, New Jersey

Printed in the United States of America

Library of Congress Cataloging-in-Publication Data

Reclaiming the American library past : writing the women in / Suzanne Hildenbrand, editor.
    p. cm.—(Information management, policies, and services)
    Includes bibliographical references (p.   ) and index.
    ISBN 1-56750-233-4 (cloth).—ISBN 1-56750-234-2 (pbk.)
    1. Women in library science—United States—History.
I. Hildenbrand, Suzanne, II. Series.
Z682.4.W65R43   1996
020´.082—dc20   95-43839
                                                   CIP

Ablex Publishing Corporation
355 Chestnut Street
Norwood, New Jersey 07648

Contents

Preface

Geraldine Joncich Clifford

The essays in *Reclaiming The American Library Past: Writing the Women In* contribute along several dimensions to the new scholarship on a profession and public service of vital importance for well over a century to American literacy, culture, and invention. Their authors add to the individual and collective biographies of women who have founded and administered diverse institutions and taught succeeding generations of librarians. The worksites of influential women such as Anne Carroll Moore, Josephine Rathbone, and Grace Hebard, like the nameless paid and volunteer staff who have served as unrecognized catalogers and children's librarians, have varied. They range from the pioneering libraries and library schools of the settled East–including Brooklyn and the Harlem, Times Square, and Morningside Heights neighborhoods of Manhattan–and historically Black Howard University to the numberless small towns of the West. They include the raw "A & M" colleges of Arkansas, Utah, New Mexico, and similarly neglected centers of local and regional enlightenment about which Georgia Higley writes in "College, Community and Librarianship: Women Librarians at the Western Landgrant Colleges." These latter venues turn out to have valuable archives for researching women's social history, as Higley and Joanne Passet capably demonstrate.

However, as Suzanne Hildenbrand argues in her chapter, "From The Politics of Library History to the History of Library Politics," in order to advance the historiography of librarianship beyond the *her*story phase of feminist scholarship, it is necessary to do more than introduce female contributors into the saga. Rather, the ideological foundations and structural operations of differentiated gendered experience also need to be revealed and explained. Comparative analyses of male- and female-intensive professions can edify, as can tracing "objective" characteristics like income, autonomy, and other elements of status and power as an occupation moves from the province of one sex to that of the other. The contributors to *Reclaiming The American Library Past* expose several linkages and similarities between librarianship and other formerly male activities such as nursing, charity work (social welfare), clerking, and, especially, schoolteaching. The "domestic imperative" shaped public expectations, colored career opportunities, and set the reward structure for all of these occupations, as well as for the new home economics, which was first invented as academic employment for women scientists and as an alternative "career" path for college-educated women.

Several of the early librarians discussed in this volume, including Jean Blackwell Hutson, Charlotte Baker, Ida Kidder, Mary Wright Plummer and Dorothy Porter Wesley, were educated in normal schools and had stints as teachers. Like other former teachers who prepared for alternative occupations, librarians sometimes paid for their library training with their teaching earnings. Also, over the history of librarianship in America, many librarians have collaborated with teachers as school librarians or offered in-service instruction in children's literature or related subjects. Julia Brown Asplund's work in establishing travelling libraries and then the New Mexico Library Extension Service, which provided books for school children in Spanish and in English, was a landmark effort in an impoverished state. The shared histories of teaching and librarianship are further illustrated in C.C. Williamson's 1921, Carnegie-sponsored attack on most library schools: It is remarkably like the indictments of normal schools and teachers colleges made by university professors of education in the same period. The library, hospital, and social work agency also have their own versions of what David Tyack calls the "pedagogical harem:" the male principal and his women teachers. More recently, female occupations have wrestled with the appearance of their "aides"—sub-professionals, paid or volunteers, whose supervision theoretically promises higher status for the professional, but whose labors may actually so confuse or dilute the essence of the professional service as to contribute to de-professionalization and de-skilling.

The powerful image of woman's fields as socially approved versions of "mothering," of women professionals being engaged in the conservative (if not reactionary) work of cultural reproduction and social homemaking, has contributed both to the silencing and the blaming of library women at the historian's hands. The "piety and purity" ascribed to middle-class women, which helped ease their way into library work, also made them vulnerable to the historian's charges of repressed "ladies" leading the puritanical censoring of the library's educational and recreational offerings to America's reading public. These propensities of the earlier historiography help explain why the chapters written for this volume by Glendora Johnson-Cooper (on the "African-American Historical Continuity: Jean Blackwell Huston and the Schomburg

Center for Research in Black Culture"), Clare Beck ("Adelaide Hasse: The New Woman as Librarian"), Anne Lundin ("Anne Carroll Moore: 'I Have Spun Out a Long Thread' " and Clara Sitter ("Librarian, Literary Detective and Scholar: Fannie Elizabeth Ratchford") explicitly identify their subjects as reformers, troublemakers, or "new women," and why the other contributors' chapters speak to the issue of "agency" in one or another guise. In "Since So Many of Today's Librarians are Women . . .;" Women and Intellectual Freedom in U.S. Librarianship, 1890–1989 Christine Jenkins offers a fine-grained analysis of the prevailing studies of misconceptions about women librarians' roles in defense of intellectual freedom.

A major theme unifying these essays is how gender shaped career-building in librarianship. Images of selfless messianic advocacy and service, "vocation" rather than career, have persisted in the forms of low wages and the value ascribed to "psychic rewards," as they also have done in other female-intensive occupations—as Joanne E. Passet details in "You Don't Have to Pay Librarians." Nonetheless, the possession of higher education, women's growing participation in wage labor with demographic and industrial change, and the examples of male advances in librarianship and other professions together nourished careerism among women librarians. Given the relatively flat structure of the occupation, the stingy public funding that supported the libraries that employed most women librarians, and the small size of most libraries, opportunities for promotion in librarianship were limited. Movement into administration was the obvious choice for the ambitious librarian, especially given the low status of certain library specializations, like the children's services of which Anne Lundin writes. Male specialties and work sites were somewhat "off limits" to women and even inexperienced men were given preference as library administrators. As Barbara Brand notes in "Pratt Institute Library School: The Perils of Professionalism," breakthroughs were reserved for the "exceptional" woman, a requirement not imposed on male librarians. Moreover, a pronounced tendency described in studies of women managers in business—as preferring to exercise "power-with" rather than "power over"—characterized as least some women library administrators. Oregon State University's Ida Kidder ("Mother Kidder"), described her own relationships with her subordinates as being between peers, and Fannie Ratchford served morning and afternoon tea to her staff in the Rare Books Library at the University of Texas (Austin). The dubiety of such an ideology in the normally competitive world of the professions was compounded by the changing status of volunteer library staff and their proliferation when the historic underfunding of library budgets was institutionalized by tax-limitation legislation, as Cheryl Malone shows in "Women's Unpaid Work in Libraries: Change and Continuity."

Historians of women's occupations—from traditional unpaid housewifery to being the "office wife," from mothering in the family to pediatric nursing—share something of a dilemma with their subjects. As Christine Jenkins summarizes the subjects' problem in the specific case of librarians, women in librarianship continue to negotiate their way between the expectations of them as women and as librarian, and these stereotypes have a direct or indirect effect on all members of the female-intensive profession of librarianship. Because most serious students of women's experience are, like all the authors in this collection, themselves women, they become members of another female-intensive profession. As such, their enterprise remains marginal, their motives often taken lightly, their intellectual integrity and conceptual creativity doubted. If there is any remedy, it would seem to be persistence in accumulating both the illustrative case studies and broader theoretical research that the history profession in general will have need of in time—when gender will no longer be able to be considered a parochial, political, or neurotic interest of feminist scholars, but rather an essential conceptual tool of all historical research.

—University of California, Berkeley

chapter 1

Women In Library History: From The Politics of Library History To The History of Library Politics

Suzanne Hildenbrand

INTRODUCTION

Library history, or the written record of the library past, distinct from actual past events, is more influenced by library politics than by mainstream historiography. The two major, and mutually reinforcing, features of library politics are its dominance by a largely male elite within a profession that is mostly female and the marginal place of the library in American society. Both have contributed to the invisibility or, worse, the scapegoating, of women in traditional library history.

In recent years library feminists have challenged these politics and have sought a new history that reflects the centrality of women to American library development. They have articulated the role that library history plays in maintaining male dominance in the field, and have urged the historical exploration of that dominance. Their publications show a range of perspectives: from recognizing the politics of library history to seeking the history of that politics, from identifying the problem as the exclusion of women to identifying it as the subordination of women.

1

The new body of work not only reflects many of the trends in contemporary historiography, including the historiography of women, and trends in women's studies generally, but also reflects the pitfalls of these approaches. This chapter traces the effort to build a better and more accurate library history. It begins by examining the inadequacies of traditional library history and then examines alternate models found in women's history. Finally, it offers a sampling of the new library history that holds the promise of a "liberating past."[1]

TRADITIONAL LIBRARY HISTORY

Dominant groups manage memory and myths,[2] and that management is crucial to their dominance or control of contemporary resources. These groups create systems that "explain and order the world" in a way favorable to themselves and reserve for themselves the power to name and define.[3] Because women have been poorly represented in dominant groups, it's not surprising that women are so frequently invisible or written out of history.

The invisibility of women in written history has a negative impact on women while sustaining male dominance. It denies women recognition of their role in the development of human culture, it deprives them of role models and it impedes the development of women's history. Human culture is seen as a male product when women are absent from the record of human achievement; girls and women too often conclude that no women can achieve. In each generation a few intrepid persons struggle to establish women's claim to a historical role and are surprised to discover that although others have done the same work in earlier generations, it has been forgotten or lost. This "cruel repetitiousness" accounts for why there is so little progress in the historiography of women.[4]

While all the foregoing holds true for library women, their situation is both different and worse. While women represent 80 percent of the professional library workforce, they are underrepresented in the elite or dominant group. This imbalance exaggerates the need of the library elite to manage myth and memory in order to both distance itself from the non-elite and to scapegoat it. Not surprisingly then, the same elite male minority that dominates the field also dominates the writing of its history as authors, journal editors, and reviewers and readers for publishing houses.[5] Equally unsurprising is the poor treatment of women in library history. Marginalized in the production of library history, women were invisible or trivialized in that history. More surprising is the extent to which library women have contributed to this process.

Recent research on male librarians shows a widespread unease at being identified with "women's work" and possibly being seen as insufficiently masculine.[6] Library history offers examples of efforts to create an all male or mostly male professional institution within the profession.[7]

Scapegoating of contemporary women, rendering them responsible for the problems of librarianship, is easier when there is little literature showing the contributions of early women librarians. Denial of the contributions of women supports the longstanding myth that women are responsible for library failures, real or imagined. (This myth is common in all female-intensive occupations. It is often held, for example, that it is all those women teachers who are responsible for the failure of the schools to teach reading.) Low salaries, small budgets, and the poor image of librarians have all been attributed to the large number of women in librarianship. Even in the '90s, women librarians have been blamed for the public library's failure to attract a wider readership.[8]

Historian Gerda Lerner pointed out that women often collude in their oppression and this is evident in librarianship also. (The author who blamed women for the failures of public libraries was a woman.) Both women and men in librarianship, ever conscious of the marginality and low status of their occupation, strive to present a professional image to the world and this is likely to mean a masculine image. This attitude supports historical research in areas such as the management of large libraries, a seemingly more masculine and more professional activity than children's services or rural librarianship.

An obvious corollary to this equation of masculinity with professionalism is the drive to recruit more men. Library literature over the years shows numerous examples of efforts to recruit men as well as to place men in top positions, particularly in the larger and more scholarly libraries. Again, recruitment of men is a characteristic of other female-intensive fields where upgrading or professionalization is also identified with masculinization. While this strategy is not likely to achieve greater male participation, it does tend to silence women.

Ironically, the professional history that reinforces library leadership is a history sadly out of step with contemporary historical writing. The library history created by and under the sponsorship of a male minority resembles the traditional patriotic narrative in United States history, a history that has been under steady assault throughout most of this century. The continuing allegiance of library historians to this earlier style perpetuates a history isolated from mainstream intellectual and historiographic currents (weak in explanatory power) unable to illuminate major topics, and weak in explanatory power.

Where nation building was the goal of the patriotic narrative, profession building has been the goal of the traditional library history.[9] Like the patriotic narrative, the library narrative was Whiggish and celebratory and assumed that the good of some—a white male elite—represented the good of all. Accounts at variance with this chronicle of success went unwritten as these did little to advance a uniform view of professional development. Institutional development was stressed, and little attention was paid to context or to populations.

A major force in the erosion of the patriotic narrative in U.S. history was the "new social history." However, this new history, now decades old, has had little impact on the writing of library history. Social history emphasizes history "from the bottom up", offering a methodology, often quantitative, that permits access to those who left no written record of their own. In keeping with recent societal trends towards a greater inclusiveness, this social history could be adapted to library history to make the latter more accurate. Failure to adapt methods that permit access to the anonymous, humbler folk of another age limits library historians to studies of the privileged individuals who left significant written records. These privileged individuals tend to be men who held directorships or similar positions.

Social history also legitimates the study of topics previously overlooked by historians. Childhood, for example, is not dismissed as a biological unfolding, but instead is seen as a social construct, different in different contexts and therefore a valid subject for historical investigation.

However, despite the many excellent studies of the history of the child and childhood, and the fact that children's services are the "classic success" of American libraries,[10] the history of children's services has been all but ignored in library history. Children's librarians remain "invisible women,"[11] and although this is the most female intensive speciality in librarianship, little is written about women as a factor in the origins, growth, or status of children's services. If treated at all, the emphasis is rather on the happy story of the growth of children's services or the expansion of the professional narrative to include it.

While the history of different ethnic and racial communities flourishes today, this too is an area that is inadequately treated in traditional library history. Library history offers some work on people of color who are librarians, but it has yet to show a serious attempt to integrate different aspects of identity as has been done in several historical monographs on other female intensive professions, such as Darlene Hine's exploration of nursing *Black Women in White* (1989.)[12]

Study of the gay and lesbian past is currently receiving considerable attention. While there have been publications on gay and lesbian library service, library history lags again. However, the American Library Association was the first professional organization to have a gay and lesbian caucus, suggesting an early significant lesbian and gay presence in librarianship.[13] In addition library history offers numerous examples of "Boston marriages" or female couples.[14]

Another area of importance, scarcely touched on in library history, but receiving growing attention in general history, is the question of women and reading. The reader is the most elusive character in library development, yet works such as Kate Flint's *The Woman Reader* (1993)[15] and the collection *Gender and Reading* (1986)[16] show that this topic can be the subject of meaningful historical investigation.

The isolation of library history from social history and similar trends has insured the continuation of the professional narrative and its political benefits, but has meant a sacrifice of explanatory power. Although there has been some modest revisionist work tying the establishment of libraries to the needs of the ruling class for a docile but trained body of workers, generally library historians have eschewed explanation and rigorous causal analysis in favor of description.

Library historians have too often been content to rely upon official sources and prescriptive material, rather than investigating social context or political settings.

Social history is often identified with the study of large processes, such as industrialization, but telling the story with a focus on one social group. There are many similar processes that need a telling, or an explanation, from the women librarians' perspective, including the simultaneous professionalization and feminization of librarianship.

Critics from within library history have long lamented the failings of the field, but they themselves have failed to probe the political roots of those failings. By identifying such problems as the use of library history as "indoctrination" in library education programs, the emphasis on telling the story of "strong and determined leaders" who build a "distinguished institution"[17] and isolation from mainstream historical writing, critics have highlighted the symptoms but avoided an analysis of the causes and consequences. Not surprisingly, this criticism has had little impact. Although the first major critical essay on library history, by Jesse Shera, appeared in 1945, similar criticism echoing similar concerns was still being written decades later.[18]

In summary, the narrow focus of library history, celebrating white male leaders and their institutions, reflects the politics of library history. It has forestalled the development of a realistic library history in step with contemporary historiography and fails to show the centrality of women to library development.

HISTORIANS OF WOMEN AND LIBRARIANS

Discouraged by the traditional library history, those seeking a liberating and more accurate history of librarianship might reasonably expect to turn to historians of women. Unfortunately, these scholars have shown little interest in the so-called women's professions: nursing, elementary school teaching, and librarianship. Instead, they have preferred, particularly in the 60s and 70s, to study women pioneers in so-called male professions or radicals and working-class women. Many of these first historians of women in the "second wave" of feminism had a background in labor history, and this encouraged them to dismiss teachers, nurses, and librarians as agents of the capitalist class engaged in pacifying the workers. Many also had participated in consciousness raising groups, and this experience led to a view of women in the so-called women's professions as victims of "false consciousness." In addition, long years of study at universities where schools of nursing, education, social work and librarianship were generally objects of academic condescension further devalued women in these professions and perpetuated their stereotype as unworthy subjects of historical research.

The situation of women librarians is, if anything, somewhat worse than that of nurses and teachers, largely due to the political realities of the place of the library in American culture; the institutions with which teachers and nurses are associated have a higher profile than libraries. Linked to such major national dramas such as racial desegregation and health reform, schools, hospitals, and health care institutions have attracted much national attention from policy makers, politicians, and the large number of persons using these institutions. They also attract attention from feminists who have long devoted a significant portion of their agenda to education and to women's health issues.

Policy and feminist concerns not only place a spotlight on educational and health care institutions, they also cause a re-examination of the role of the practitioners. Health economists ask why nurses can't deliver some of the services traditionally provided by doctors, and feminists demand an expanded role for women in medicine generally. In education, feminists demand a non-sexist environment for children and emphasize the need for adequate role models for girls. This latter supports the entry of women into positions usually filled by men in the school hierarchy. Parents and policy makers, recognizing the importance of preparing girls for a lifetime of paid employment, may also support these demands.

Libraries have no similar link to high-profile national policy issues, despite the attempts of librarians to create these links. Nor do libraries have obvious ties to the feminist movement, although individual librarians have been active as participants in that movement. For policy makers, the general public, and feminists, library collections have been of greater interest than the people who work in libraries. In this, libraries resemble museums or zoos more than schools or hospitals. The lesser degree of interaction between professional and client in zoos, museums, and libraries compared to that in schools and health care facilities may account for the lesser interest in the professional role within these institutions. Thus the women professionals in libraries who fight for gender justice wage an isolated struggle.

In addition to the marginalization of librarians in American life, librarians are often seen as handmaidens to historians. In this century, as many historians have been Librarian of Congress as have librarians. If the library is the laboratory of the humanist, the librarian is all too often the bottle-washer in that lab. Just as doctors do not write histories of nursing, historians of women, with few exceptions, have avoided library women's history.

The most notable of these exceptions is Dee Garrison, whose work still dominates the historiography of women in librarianship. Her revisionist monograph *Apostles of Culture: The Public Librarian and American Society, 1876–1920* (1979)[19] offers the fullest treatment of the topic and has been widely cited and reviewed. Although a self-styled feminist, she accepted without question the view that women were responsible for the failure of the public library to develop a vigorous clientele and an expansive future. "Female dominance of librarianship did much to shape the inferior and precarious status of the public library as a cultural resource; it evolved into a marginal kind of public amusement service."[20]

Garrison arrived at this conclusion by an over-reliance on prescriptive sources, a common problem among early historians of women. That is, she relied on what people, including women librarians, said about women and librarianship without examining these comments in their context. It is now widely recognized that the entry of women into any new field, such as librarianship, is often justified politically and strategically by linking the new activity to some aspect of women's supposed biological natures or traditional roles. Thus, patience, a characteristic frequently attributed to women, was held by many to suit them to librarianship. (It is still said by some that compassion and other supposed womanly characteristics suit women to the practice of medicine.)

Ironically then, the only serious treatment of women in library history by a historian of women, Garrison, goes beyond the traditional library history, which merely ignored women for the most part, and blames them for the supposed failures of the public library.

TRENDS IN THE HISTORIOGRAPHY
OF WOMEN: *HER*STORY

Even though library women have received scant or negative attention from historians of women, it is important for those pursuing an accurate and women-centered history of librarianship to examine the evolution of women's history in recent years. Several stages, offering differing models of women's historiography, have appeared, each with its strengths and weaknesses.

Scholars in women's studies have enumerated stages in the evolution of women's studies and the problems characteristic of each stage. Historian Joan Wallach Scott traces the development of history through the early women's history or *her*story phase (distinguished from *his*tory) with its two types: contributions or compensation,* and women's culture. Eventually both types of *her*story are challenged by a gendered history that analyzes the interdependent roles of women and men.[21] Philosopher of science Sandra Harding documented the evolution from feminist empiricism, featuring acceptance of the dominant tradition, to the feminist standpoint, calling for a woman-centered discipline, to postmodernist feminism, with its skepticism about the very categories of analysis which themselves are increasingly found to be gendered.[22] Sandra Coyner of the National Women's Studies Association described the evolution in historical writing as "a move from an early interest in how women have been oppressed through time, to a concern for the world women created for themselves

---

*Although many treat the compensation and the contributions phases separately, they are considered together here due to the relatively small amount of library women's history.

... (and a displeasure with the notion that women are always victims of oppression) ... and now to a critique of the error of looking at women's own world without seeing the patriarchal contexts in which women" lived.[23]

The earliest phase of *her*story, the compensatory or contributions stage, emphasizes that women too participate in history. Limited goals prevail, such as seeking to establish or validate the female subject. The compensatory stage is a minimalist, antidiscrimination approach in which there is no real challenge to the discipline or its institutions. In science, Harding points out that in this early empiricist stage, authors emphasize that it isn't science, but *bad* science, that is under attack.[24] The only real problem identified is that women have been left out or have not received proper credit for their contributions. All that is really needed to make it right is to find the foremothers and tell their stories. In women's library history there is a significant body of biographical work that highlights the contributions of individual women, compensating for the absence of a strong women's presence in traditional library history. The professional narrative is accepted.

The biography that is itself such a prominent feature of this phase of *her*story is vulnerable to criticism. As add-ons to the existing research, individual biographies may be easily overlooked or ignored. Furthermore, the achievements of any individual life are vulnerable to challenges that the subject came from a privileged background, enjoyed male sponsorship, or doesn't represent women's typical experience. Then too, compensatory history usually accepts the traditional narrative, calling only for more inclusiveness. It seems unlikely that a history that can lead to a better future—a liberating past—can be built upon the traditional structures, even when women are added.

The other major approach to telling *her*story is the women's culture model, where emphasis is almost totally on woman and her so-called separate sphere. Authors often depict women as the architects of this sphere which gave them "a space of their own, an autonomy."[25] Strengths are made of circumstances usually deplored as limitations, and the authors often assail the tendency to judge all humanity by one, inevitably male, standard. This approach is usually viewed as a reaction to the view of woman as victim emphasized in the typical "contributions" or "compensations" historiography, where authors often stress how women have been discriminated against or exploited. Historian Estelle Friedman has seen the separate space that women experienced as a place to develop skills that would be useful in a larger sphere.[26] The women's culture model also gives the reader a greater understanding of the motivations and satisfactions of the historical actors in a particular milieu.

However, criticism of the women's culture model has also been strong, often emphasizing the unmistakable tendency to "romanticize women's subordinate position."[27] It can also promote a kind of essentialism, as it stresses that women in their separate sphere possessed better values than when contaminated by male standards in the larger world.

These criticisms are especially relevant to the use of a women's culture model in librarianship where there has historically been such a discrepancy between the education required of the workforce and the material rewards it received. Authors may find cultural consolations an especially appealing explanation under such circumstances, but the professional implications are unfortunate.

It is not only the women's culture approach that is under attack today, however. The entire *her*story model has stimulated ever-increasing amounts of criticism, even from those who acknowledge its role in establishing woman as a subject and in adding immeasurably to our knowledge of women's lives in earlier times. Joan Wallach Scott faults *her*story for tending to sustain the idea of a separate sphere with its relentless emphasis on women and women alone, and also for a somewhat overly enthusiastic acceptance of what earlier women said or did.[28]

Although early women's history drew much of its value from social history—notably its methodology, validation of subjects, and challenges to traditional political history—it also became obvious that there were limits to what social history could offer to those seeking a more accurate historical picture of women. Social history "assumes gender difference can be explained within its existing frame of explanation," such as demographics or economics, and women are simply fitted into the larger scheme.[29] Furthermore, much social history was Marxist inspired, and as Marxism seemed to collapse intellectually as well as politically, the *her*story influenced by this tradition also lost credibility.

Scott concluded that the *her*story phase fostered by social history produced contradictory trends that were equally unsatisfactory. While contributions or compensation history was "too integrationist," subsuming women under a larger framework, the women's culture model of *her*story was too separatist![30]

Another significant problem faced by *her*story scholarship is that, despite its high quality and huge volume, it has made almost no impact at all on mainstream history, being basically an add-on or specialty and creating a kind of female ghetto for historians of women. Traditional issues occupy the leaders of the historical profession, and they rarely see the need to integrate women's experiences in a course on, for example, the French Revolution. That task can be left to the overworked women's history specialist.[31]

These criticisms are highly relevant for library women in pursuit of a more accurate and liberating history. As in general history, much good work has been done on the history of women in librarianship, but none of it has made an appreciable impact on mainstream library history, which continues to reflect the tired professional narrative. Library women's history is merely an add-on and this is an intolerable situation in an occupation where women are 80% of the workforce. A way must be found to make the experiences of women central to library history.

TRENDS IN THE HISTORIOGRAPHY OF WOMEN:
GENDERED HISTORY

Gendered history or, as one of its leading proponents describes it, gender as a "category of historical analysis"[32] has emerged in recent years as a major trend in historical writing. To some it now seems that history that omits "gender as process" appears to "belong to an older historiographical moment."[33] Gendered history reflects an increasingly common view in women's studies that the position of women in society cannot be understood without reference to the position of men, a perspective captured in sociologist Barbara Reskin's call to "bring the men back in."[34]

The need for this approach was seen by historian Natalie Zemon Davis in 1976 when she wrote:

> It seems to me that we should be interested in the history of both women and men, that we should not be working only on the subjected sex any more than a historian of class can focus exclusively on peasants. Our goal is to understand the significance of the *sexes*, of gender groups in the historical past. Our goal is to discover the range in sex roles and in sexual symbolism in different societies and periods, to find out what meaning they had and how they functioned to maintain the social order or promote its change.[35]

Gendered history permits an approach to large questions such as the persistence of inequality. Gender studies assume that relations between women and men "are a primary aspect of social organization," and that "differences between the sexes constitute and are constituted by hierarchical social structures."[36] Joan Wallach Scott urged a study of gender systems to understand better woman as subject and to reconnect the study of women to traditional politics. Gendered history recognizes as politics all relationships that involve distributions of power and also accepts gender as "a primary way of signifying relationships of power."[37]

A history that exposes "the often silent and hidden operations of gender that are nonetheless present and defining forces in the organization of most societies"[38] would yield a truer women's history than a history that emphasizes the great achievements of early women. The gendered approach holds out the promise of "transformation" sought by many scholars in women's studies[39] so that we may move from the distorted and partial narratives of the past to a more complete understanding.[40]

Library history offers an increasing number of examples of this approach, and it is through the use of this approach that issues like the origins of the "dual career structure" identified by Alice I. Bryan in 1952 can be investigated[41]: the mechanisms by which male dominance in the profession were established and are maintained.

In this phase of historical writing there is less justification by reference to the politics of library history or to how women have been written out or mis-represented—the justification that was so common in *her*story. Instead, there is an investigation of the history of library politics for the origins and durability of inequity.

The gendered approach to the study of women in history has its critics, par-ticularly among those skeptical of the postmodern thought from which it draws much intellectual sustenance.[42] Scott, for example, has been criticized for a ten-dency to reduce history to "the perception of meaning."[43] Indeed, many charge that postmodern history and its offspring, gendered history, bring the end of his-tory or its deconstruction. To some it seems a "descent into discourse."[44] More significant for those who seek a "liberating" history is the criticism that the sort of extravagant theorizing favored by many authors of gendered history alien-ates non-academic feminists, thereby threatening an alliance necessary for meaningful change. Others argue that there is still much to learn from *her*story and we should not abandon the search for women's past so quickly.

LIBRARY *HER*STORY

The nature, rate, and development of women-centered research since the "sec-ond wave" of feminism emerged in the 1960s have varied from discipline to discipline, largely dependent on the resistance encountered.[45] Resistance within librarianship has been significant, delaying development of these studies. Nev-ertheless, a significant body of historical writing has been produced, largely by library women and women library educators. The different women's studies perspectives are all in evidence, although they appear to be less clearly se-quential in librarianship than in other disciplines. This overlap of stages may stem from the later start in the field, so that those writing library women's his-tory have had the opportunity to observe several types of historical scholarship in other fields.

The following selective overview of the literature on women in library his-tory will focus on similarities between it and women's studies scholarship, es-pecially women's history.

The compensation or contributions phase of library *her*story is dominated by biographies both individual and collective. Many of the recent studies, building on a rich vein of literature now reaching back some decades, make an explicit statement about the politics of library history: Women have been left out and that needs to be corrected. Where there is no such foundation of earlier works, there is no such statement. The contrast is especially clear in comparing the lit-erature on prominent early women educators with that on the founders of ser-vices to children.

Nancy Becker Johnson's recent dissertation "Sarah C.N. Bogle: Librarian at Large" told us, "The history of the profession, when viewed through standard sources or histories of library school education, is seen as an activity directed by men," thus depriving women of role models. Insisting that materials on "women who led the profession *are* available," she asserted women's "role in the development of library education and library science [is] unacknowledged."[46] Becker Johnson draws on decades of feminist research in history, and in library history on the pioneering biographic work of Laurel Grotzinger.

In her groundbreaking monograph *The Power and the Dignity: Librarianship and Katharine Sharp* (1966),[47] Grotzinger noted the paucity of biographic work in librarianship, listing the handful of full-length studies available, all of men. Grotzinger did not directly address the question of why biographies of women were missing as Becker Johnson did 30 years later. Instead Grotzinger focused on the story of Sharp, an energetic woman who was overworked and underpaid and finally driven from librarianship by these factors. By the 1980s, Grotzinger took a more overtly feminist position in an article entitled "Biographical Research on Women Librarians: Its Paucity, Perils and Pleasures,"[48] in which she described the peculiar absence of women "greats" in library reference tools and linked this absence to discrimination against women in the profession.

Still solidly within the compensatory stage of the *her*story tradition, studies of groups of librarians take a collective or demographic view of the lives of these women. Clearly showing the influence of trends in social history, these studies are more ambitious than individual biographies, reaching for generalizations on the kind of women who entered library service in a given period and in a given place.

Joanne Passet has been a leader in taking this approach. In *Cultural Crusaders: Women Librarians in the American West, 1900–1917* (1994),[49] Passet concluded that myths and oversimplifications obscure women's role in library development. Her western library women resembled the reforming New Woman of Progressive America in other fields: social work, public health, and education. Passet identified more than 300 professionally trained women librarians in the 11 western states during the period studied and analyzed common elements in their lives. Through her judicious use of their personal papers, Passet also allows us to see them as individuals and gain some understanding of what their lives were like.

In an earlier article " 'The Rule Rather Than the Exception': Midwest Women As Academic Librarians, 1875–1900" (1986)[50] Passet exploded the myth that late 19th century academic librarians were male professors put out to pasture. From the 1870s on, academic librarians in the states Passet studied were increasingly likely to be women. Passet's landmark work influences both the thinking about the subjects investigated, and the methods used in library history.

A similar approach is taken by James Carmichael in "Atlanta's Female Librarians, 1883–1915." (1986)[51] Neither the New Woman of Passet's findings nor the exploited wretch of Dee Garrison's *Apostles of Culture*, Carmichael's library women were "southern ladies" who wielded power in the traditional way: from behind the scenes and with smiling indirection. Unfortunately, while Carmichael celebrates the power of these women, his own article makes it all too clear that they had that power because no able men were available to work at the salaries offered.

A final example of collective biography is only marginally *her*story, as it resembles the professional narrative more than any distinct type of women's history. The 1990 dissertation by Sybille A. Jagusch entitled "First Among Equals: Caroline M. Hewins and Anne C. Moore. Foundations of Library Work with Children,"[52] offers profiles of Hewins and Moore and briefer sketches of eight others who developed modern American and, indirectly, international library service for children during the period 1880–1906. Yet Jagusch is not analytic and she does not explore the lack of literature on this major area of librarianship—hers is only the third full-length study of the origins of children's work—nor does she explain the importance of this field to women and why they were drawn to it. She does observe in passing that women of the period had few career options. Moore, for example, had hoped to read law and was supported in this aspiration by her indulgent father. However, after the deaths of her parents and sister-in-law she became a housekeeper for her brother, escaping to library work upon his remarriage.

This brief sampling of recent biographic studies of library women illustrates some of the findings from women's history generally. While a necessary and important part of the history of women in American librarianship, introducing us to a variety of long-forgotten women, these studies are, as has been noted about compensatory studies in general history, insufficient to change the canon, transform the professional narrative, or provide a liberating past. They can be, and indeed to large degree have been, overlooked by mainstream historians of librarianship. The major individual biographies are not clearly representative of more than one person's story. Their subjects are exceptional, owing much of their success to privileged backgrounds and male sponsorship. Sharp, for example, was a disciple of Melvil Dewey, and after leaving librarianship went to work for him at the Lake Placid Club.

In addition, the areas where the most biographic work has been done are those with which the authors are most familiar. Both Becker-Johnson and Grotzinger are library educators and write about historic women in library education. Studies of individual women identified with other professional areas and with other personal identities are needed. The collective portraits offer hope of a greater degree of explanatory power. As the work of James V. Carmichael shows, however, explanations that are valid for women in one place and time may be less valid elsewhere. Hence greater numbers of these studies are required also. In order to explain the interaction of opportunity and personality, biographic studies need greater emphasis on both the context of opportunity and of the subject's individual development.

Library women's history offers numerous examples of the women's culture model of *her*story. Stung by repeated depictions of library women as exploited and victimized, these writers present an invaluable picture of early library women as active agents, choosing their work and making valuable contributions in the face of enormous obstacles. They show the involvement and the satisfactions that library work brought to women as they contributed to their communities' development.

The role of women in sponsoring libraries, especially as members of women's clubs, has stimulated much literature of the women's culture type. The first two works considered might easily be seen as contributions to history if not for their emphasis on how a uniquely "woman's" agenda led to library development. These works are "Founding Mothers: The Contributions of Women's Organizations to Public Library Development," by Paula D. Watson (1994)[53] and the earlier "Women and Libraries" (1986) by historian Anne Firor Scott.[54] Watson shows both the importance of the role women working in groups had in founding public libraries and how this force has been slighted or denigrated in standard treatments of the public library by male historians. Years before, Scott had chided library historians for overlooking the role of women's clubs and urged them to give club women "a high place on your agenda."[55] Scott also stressed that self-improvement was the initial pursuit of the club women, but this pursuit also brought educational and recreational opportunity to their communities.

Watson found that in addition to library development, the activities of the club women contributed to "an awakening feminine political consciousness, since it involved women in such a high degree of organized political advocacy and ultimately resulted in fairly large-scale female participation in appointive political office on library boards and commissions."[56] This nicely illustrates historian Friedman's view of the importance of women's "separatism."

Not all library founders were club women, however, as shown by an early unpublished dissertation, "The New England Mill Girls: Feminine Influence in the Development of Public Libraries in New England, 1820–1860," by Elfrieda B. McCauley (1971)[57]. McCauley illustrates the role in fostering cultural activities, especially libraries, for these farm women, who spent a few years before marriage in the mills. Despite the rigors of long days at the looms and crowded conditions in their boarding-houses, these women enjoyed a number of "liberating advantages,"[58] many of their own invention. They forced existing libraries such as the mechanics libraries and the counting house libraries to accept them as readers, and several eventually became librarians of various small collections after their service in the mills. As a pioneering study, with almost no previous work to build on, there is little explicit observation on the politics of library history. But this work is a landmark study of how women's culture, as developed in essentially middle class rural Protestant families, was kept alive even under conditions of extreme drudgery and how this culture promoted libraries.

Professional library women have also been placed within the women's culture tradition. In "Reconceptualizing Women's History: Anne Hadden and the California County Library System," (1992)[59] Denise Sallee states her motivation clearly as she assails Garrison and others for a history "centered around the inequity of women's position in American libraries and the lack of respect given to them by society." These historians "emphasized the exploitative nature of librarianship for women"[60] and overlooked the real satisfaction enjoyed by many library women. Hadden's professional life revolved around the development of library service in a frontier environment and featured such challenges as delivering books on horseback to the residents of rural Monterey County. A member of a large Anglo-Irish immigrant family, Hadden's personal life was centered on the lives of her siblings and their children. Sallee, like Passet, identifies her subject as a typical "New Woman" of Progressive America and insists that the California county library system of the period was full of similar women who were strong, autonomous "agents of their own history."[61]

James Carmichaels' work, including the article already cited and his later "Women in Southern Library Education, 1905–1945," (1992)[62] celebrates the achievements of women even though a "most pervasive factor acting in favor of the predominance of women in southern librarianship was the cult of southern womanhood . . . and the perception of library work as part of 'women's spheres.' "[63] One especially interesting feature described is the willingness of these white Protestant women to reach out to other communities such as Jews and Blacks. Like Sallee, Carmichael views his subjects as agents, determining their own course in life to large degree and eagerly choosing traditional domestic roles—and abandoning librarianship—when the opportunity arose.

Criticized in general history as conservative and supportive of the status quo, the women's culture model seems especially ill-suited to a liberating history of a profession. The emphasis on psychic rewards when low salaries and poor working conditions have been a problem in modern librarianship is puzzling. Much of this women's culture literature in librarianship features women who did not depend exclusively upon the library for their support. The club women and the mill workers clearly had other means of support, and Carmichael stresses that the early southern women librarians he studied left for marriage at rates higher than did librarians elsewhere. While Hadden evidently supported herself, she had access to the resources of her securely middle-class family in the service of her career. For example, her doctor brother accompanied Hadden on one memorable foray in 1922 into a wilderness area and his film of the expedition was later used to further the work of county librarians.

Still, even acknowledging this limitation, it is clear that the women's culture model does help to explain to the modern reader what library development meant to these early women library founders and workers. This work, more than many of the compensatory or contributions biographies, reveals personal motivation and satisfaction and helps clarify the origins and growth of the profession.

However, the weaknesses identified in *her*story in general history apply to library *her*story as well. Women's role in library development cannot be understood in isolation. It would hardly be possible to write a military history of the United States by examining the lives of the enlisted personnel only. The policy decisions, the structural features of the library world, are not much influenced by those "in the ranks." So while library *her*story has introduced us to many interesting women in our past and their varied work and motivations and has shown us a collective picture of who the librarians were in various settings and periods, it has not retold the story of American library development in a way that fully illuminates women's roles. We must understand what shaped the library systems and who ran them to understand women's place in them.

TOWARD A GENDERED HISTORY OF LIBRARIANSHIP

A growing number of library authors have recognized that there is no possibility of an accurate library history without an examination of the place of men as well as that of women within librarianship. Biographic works are less common here than in *her*story and there is more analysis than description. If the tendancy among authors of *her*story was to assail earlier historians for omission or denigration, the authors of gendered library history avoid such recrimination generally and make their political statement in the choice of their topic. They choose those topics that will "help to understand the significance of the *sexes*, of gender groups in the historical past."[64]

Not surprisingly many articles examine the creation of a male elite in the profession either through the selection of men for, or the exclusion of women from, the top spots. In "Men in a Feminized Profession: The Male Librarians, 1887–1921," (1993)[65] Joanne Passet examines the demographic characteristics of the men who graduated from library education programs. Men were destined for leadership, regardless of their condition. One male program director wrote in a reference letter that although the candidate lacked initiative and confidence and was "more or less nervous" he "ought to be at the head of his own library."[66] Although Passet claimed the stereotype of the male librarian as a man who had failed in an earlier career or who was rendered physically or mentally incapable of other employment is wrong, some of her evidence offers support for this view.[67]

Passet identified about 8,000 graduates, of whom only 3.4% were men. The number and percentage of men enrolled increased over time, as in the earliest period it was common for men to become directors with no library training at all.

An earlier article, by Nancy O'Brien, entitled "The Recruitment of Men Into Librarianship Following World War II," (1983)[68] described the effort to recruit men for administrative posts in the postwar period. American Library Association President Ralph A. Ulveling, in an interview with the *New York Times* in

1945, described library personnel problems and stressed the "especially strong demand for administrators, particularly men."[69] According to O'Brien, recruitment literature well into the 1960s "attempted to attract more men by offering them security and quick advancement, yet reassured women that they still had the opportunity to rise to the top ranks."[70]

Methods of excluding women were varied and often linked to noble positions or reformist causes that were hard to challenge. These included concern for the health of the workforce or upgrading the profession. In an article entitled "The Sexual Politics of Illness in the Turn of the Century Libraries" (1990)[71] Rosalee McReynolds explores the relationship between the emergence of a largely male directorate and the view, encouraged by the psychiatric establishment, that mental work was dangerous to the female constitution. Melvil Dewey and a variety of other library leaders, including some women, justified greater income and responsibility for men on the basis of a presumed female fragility, even though they had examples of robust women in their own circles. McReynolds attributes the vague symptoms reported on in the library press to what is today called "burnout," afflicting those with high responsibility and low autonomy; a condition which, not surprisingly, characterized library women more than library men.[72] She does note, however, that some female weakness may have come from the typically wretched working conditions.

In an essay entitled "Women in Library Education: Down the Up Staircase," Mary Niles Maack (1986)[73] noted the impact of elevated standards, specifically the movement of library education into the university, on women in library education. It had a devastating effect on their careers, and led to diminished opportunities for their female successors. Not exactly unintended, this outcome was one way to achieve what library education reformer C.C. Williamson had urged. In a confidential report in 1921 he recommended, "consideration be given to the need of checking the feminization of library work."[74] Maack's article offers clear evidence that the impact of reforms can be quite different for women and men.

Men were not only in the top positions, they were also in the better paying and more prestigious specialties. In her "Sex-typing in Education for Librarianship, 1870–1920," Barbara Brand (1983)[75] examined the emergence of two specialties: legislative reference service and children's services. The former, a male specialty, was founded by Charles McCarthy, a historian, and it enjoyed considerable status. The children's services specialty emerged at about the same time, but despite its undoubted success, has never been highly regarded in the profession. That fact is clearly reflected in the level of salaries in this specialty.

A much earlier work directly confronted the most difficult issue of all, feminization. Sharon B. Wells' "Feminization of the American Library Profession, 1876–1923," an unpublished but often cited 1971 thesis,[76] investigated the correlates of women's entry into the profession. Since feminization is usually presented as a negative event, it is important to see it documented as accompanying an accelerated library professionalization movement, rising educational standards, and rapid growth in number and type of libraries. This simultaneous feminization and professionalization of librarianship yielded much bigger library systems, with more varied services, over which men were more likely to preside than were women.

The harshest criticism of the theoretical foundations of gendered history has little relevance for the gendered history that has appeared in librarianship. The studies described are typical in their focus on political realities and the ideological support for them. The elaborate linguistic analysis which can undermine alliances with nonacademic women is missing. More relevant, however, is the observation that there is still much to be learned about library *her*story. There are still many early library women to identify and study, including women of different races and ethnicities and lesbian women. An historical analysis of readers and of children's services from a women's perspective is also needed. So while gendered history makes a valuable contribution it cannot substitute for a continuing investigation of library *her*story in all its phases.

CONCLUSION

Despite numerous obstacles, the foundation for a modern history of librarianship has been established. Various trends, reflecting similar developments in women's studies, women's history and the political realities of librarianship are evident. While much additional work is needed in library *her*story, an overview of modern Amrican librarianship from a gendered perspective is a much-needed next phase.

With that project, the long route will have been traversed: from the politics of library history or the recognition that male dominance of librarianship is the cause of women's omission from library history to the history of library politics, or the recognition that the major task for library historians is an investigation of how the gendered structure of librarianship came about. Then a modern history of librarianship, reflecting the intellectual currents of our times, more inclusive and more accurate—and potentially liberating—will have begun.

ENDNOTES

[1]"Liberating Our Past" was the title of a panel at the 1982 meeting of the Library History Round Table. The papers presented were subsequently published in *The Journal of Library History* 18 (Fall 1983). Implicit in the call to liberate the past is the belief that such a history will stimulate a better future for women and men in librarianship.

[2]Mary Douglas, *How Institutions Think*, (Syracuse: Syracuse University Press, 1982), p. 112.

[3]Gerda Lerner, *The Creation of Feminist Consciousness: From the Middle Ages to Eighteen-Seventy*, (New York: Oxford University Press, 1993), p. 5.

[4]Ibid., p. 281.

[5]For a discussion of library history as a specialty of male faculty see Roma Harris, Gilliam B. Mitchell and Carol Conley, "The Gender Gap in Library Education," *Journal of Education for Library and Information Science* 25 (Winter 1985), p. 170. Nine of the 15 chairs of the Library History Round Table since 1980 have been men. The journal devoted to library history has been continuously edited by men since its founding.

[6]James V. Carmichael, "The Male Librarian and the Feminine Image: A Survey of Stereotype, Status, and Gender Perceptions," *Library & Information Science Research* 14 (Oct–Dec 1992): 435.

[7]For example, the attempt, which ended in disappointment, to develop a program attractive to men at the newly founded library education program at the University of Chicago. John Richardson, *The Spirit of Inquiry: The Graduate Library School at Chicago, 1921–51.* (Chicago: American Library Association, 1980), 60. Also see p. 28. Additionally, Dewey's ill-fated American Library Institute had an all-male board and would have been disproportionately male due to selection criteria. Dee Garrison, *Apostles of Culture: The Public Librarian and American Society, 1876–1920.* (New York: Free Press, 1979), pp. 156–158.

[8]Carol Hole, "Click! The Feminization of the American Public Library," *American Libraries* (December 1991): 1076–79.

[9]This discussion collapses many different streams of historiography into one, termed the patriotic narrative. For a view of the complexity of the tradition see John Higham, "The Future of American History," *Journal of American History* 80 (March 1994): 1289–1309.

[10]Robert D. Leigh quoted in Sybille A. Jagusch, "First Among Equals: Caroline M. Hewins and Anne C. Moore. Foundations of Library Work With Children" (PhD dissertation, University of Maryland, 1990), p. 4.

[11]Margo Sasse, "Invisible Women: The Children's Librarian in America," *School Library Journal* 19 (January 1973): 21–25.

[12]Darlene Hine, *Black Women in White: Racial Conflict and Cooperation in the Nursing Profession 1890–1950* (Bloomington: Indiana University Press, 1989).

[13]Wayne A. Wiegand and Donald G. Davis, eds. *Encyclopedia of Library History* (New York: Garland, 1994), "Gays and Lesbians in Library History," by Polly J. Thistlethwaite. p. 325.

[14]For example, *An Independent Woman: The Autobiography of Edith Guerrier.* (Amherst, MA: University of Massachusetts Press, 1992), p. iv, or John Neal Waddell,

"The Career of Isadore G. Mudge: A Chapter in the History of Reference Librarianship," (PhD dissertation, Columbia University, 1973) p. 99.

[15]Kate Flint, *The Woman Reader, 1837–1914.* (New York: Oxford University Press, 1993).

[16]Elizabeth A. Flynn and Patrocinio P. Schweickart, eds. *Gender and Reading: Essays on Readers, Texts and Contexts* (Baltimore: Johns Hopkins University Press, 1986).

[17]John Calvin Colson, "The Writing of Library History, 1876–1976," *Library Trends* 25 (July 1976): p. 13.

[18]Jesse Shera, "The Literature of American Library History," *Library Quarterly* 15 (January 1945): 1–24.

[19]Dee Garrison, *Apostles of Culture: The Public Librarian and American Society, 1876–1920* (New York: Free Press, 1979).

[20]Ibid., p. 174.

[21]Joan Wallach Scott, "Gender: A Useful Category of Historical Analysis," in her *Gender and the Politics of History* (New York: Columbia University Press, 1988), pp. 18–24.

[22]Sandra Harding, *The Science Question in Feminism* (Ithaca, N.Y.: Cornell University Press, 1986), pp. 24–28.

[23]*Transforming the Knowledge Base: A Panel Discussion at the National Network of Women's Caucuses* ([New York]: National Council for Research on Women, 1990) p. 8.

[24]Harding, p. 25.

[25]Linda Gordon, *U.S. Women's History,* (Washington D.C.: American Historical Association, 1990) p. 7.

[26]Estelle Friedman, "Separatism as Strategy: Female Institution Building and American Feminism, 1870–1930," *Feminist Studies* 7 (Fall 1979): 512–529.

[27]Gordon, p. 7.

[28]Ibid., pp. 20–21.

[29]Ibid., p. 22.

[30]Ibid.

[31]Scott, pp. 30–31.

[32]Scott, "Gender: A Useful Category of Historical Analysis."

[33]Linda K. Kerber, "Women's History for the 90s: Problems and Challenges," in *New Viewpoints in Women's History: Working Papers from the Schlesinger Library 50th Anniversary Conference, March 4–5, 1994*. Ed. by Susan Ware. (Cambridge, MA: Schlesinger Library, 1994) p. 30.

[34]Barbara F. Reskin, "Bring the Men Back In: Sex Differentiation and the Devaluation of Women's Work," *Gender & Society* 2 (March 1988): 58–81.

[35]Natalie Zemon Davis, "Women's History in Transition: The European Case," *Feminist Studies* 3 (Spring-Summer 1976): 90.

[36]Scott, "Women's History," p. 25.

[37]Scott, "Gender," p. 48.

[38]Scott, "Women's History," p. 27.

[39]Minnich.

[40]Elizabeth Minnich, *Transforming Knowledge*, (Philadelphia: Temple University Press, 1990).

[41]Alice I. Bryan, *The Public Librarian*, (New York: Columbia University Press, 1952), p. 86.

[42]For a discussion of this issue see Chapter 6 "Postmodernism and the Crisis of Modernity" in Joyce Appleby, Lynn Hunt and Margaret Jacob, *Telling the Truth About History*, (New York: Norton, 1994).

[43]Ibid, footnote, p. 226.

[44]Bryan D. Palmer, *Descent into Discourse: The Reification of Language and the Writing of Social History*, (Philadelphia: Temple University Press, 1990).

[45]Sandra Harding, ibid. note, p. 33.

[46]Nancy Louise Becker Johnson, "Sarah C.N. Bogle: Librarian at Large," (PhD Dissertation, University of Michigan, 1991), pp. 14–15.

[47]Laurel Grotzinger, *The Power and the Dignity: Librarianship and Katharine Sharp*, (New York: Scarecrow, 1966).

[48]Laurel Grotzinger, "Biographical Research On Women Librarians: Its Paucity, Perils and Pleasures," in *The Status of Women in Librarianship: Historical, Sociological and Economic Issues*, Kathleen Heim, ed. (New York: Neal–Schuman, 1983).

[49]Joanne E. Passet, *Cultural Crusaders: Women Librarians in the American West, 1900–1917*, (Albuquerque: University of New Mexico, 1994).

[50]Joanne E. Passet, " 'The Rule Rather Than the Exception': Midwest Women as Academic Librarians, 1875–1900," *Journal of Library History* 21 (Fall 1986): 673–692.

[51]James V. Carmichael, "Atlanta's Female Librarians, 1883–1915," *The Journal of Library History* 21 (Spring 1986): 376–399.

[52]Jagusch, Ibid.

[53]Paula D. Watson, "Founding Mothers: The Contributions of Women's Organizations to Public Library Development," *Library Quarterly* 64 (July 1994): 233–269.

[54]Anne Firor Scott, "Women and Libraries," *Journal of Library History* 21 (Spring 1986): 400–405.

[55]Ibid., p. 401.

[56]Watson, p. 265.

[57]Elfrieda B. McCauley, "The New England Mill Girls: Feminine Influence in the Development of Public Libraries in New England, 1820–1860" (D.L.S. thesis, Columbia University), 1971.

[58]McCauley, p. 312.

[59]Denise Sallee, "Reconceptualizing Women's History: Anne Hadden and the California County Library System," *Libraries & Culture* 27 (Fall 1992): 351–377.

[60]Ibid., p. 372.

[61]Ibid.

[62]James V. Carmichael, "Women in Southern Library Education, 1905–1945," *Library Quarterly* 62 (April 1992): 169–216.

[63]Ibid., p. 208.

[64]Davis, quoted above on page 17.

[65]Joanne E. Passet, "Men in a Feminized Profession: The Male Librarians, 1887–1921," *Libraries and Culture* 28 (Fall 1993): 385–402.

[66]Ibid., p. 397.

[67]For example, she cites the director of one program, asking the author of a reference for a male applicant if the latter had "any physical defects" or had "tried other lines [of work or study] and failed." Ibid., p. 395.

[68]Nancy Patricia O'Brien, "The Recruitment of Men into Librarianship, Following World War II," in *The Status of Women in Librarianship: Historical, Sociological and Economic Issues*, ed. Kathleen M. Heim (New York: Neal-Schuman, 1983), pp. 51–66.

[69]Ibid., p. 56.

[70]Ibid., p. 63.

[71]Rosalee McReynolds, "The Sexual Politics of Illness in Turn of the Century Libraries," *Libraries & Culture* 25 (Spring 1990): 194–217.

[72]Ibid., p. 211.

[73]Mary Niles Maack, "Women in Library Education: Down the Up Staircase," *Library Trends* (Winter 1986): 401–432.

[74]Ibid., p. 409.

[75]Barbara E. Brand, "Sex-typing in Education for Librarianship, 1870–1920," in *The Status of Women in Librarianship: Historical, Sociological and Economic Issues.* ed. Kathleen M. Heim (New York: Neal-Schuman, 1983) pp. 29–49.

[76]Sharon B. Wells, "Feminization of the American Library Profession, 1876–1923" (Master's thesis, University of Chicago, 1971).

part   one

Personalities and Programs

chapter 2

African-American Historical Continuity: Jean Blackwell Hutson and the Schomburg Center For Research in Black Culture

Glendora Johnson-Cooper

Today's multi-cultural agenda has fostered an increased interest in African American history and culture. Simultaneously, appreciation for collections devoted to this subject has grown. Who are the visionaries behind the collections? Why did they choose this profession? How did they manage, in some cases, to institutionalize these invaluable, yet at times unappreciated, repositories of information? Why are these collections important? These are questions worthy of exploration and they are the motivation behind my examination of the professional life of Jean Blackwell Hutson, former Curator and Chief of the Schomburg Center for Research in Black Culture.

The Schomburg Center is one of the most comprehensive research centers in the world for the study of people of African descent. Located in Harlem, New York, the center provides print and non-print research materials, public programs, exhibits, art and artifacts, publications, and a scholars-in-residence program, all devoted to the documentation of achievements of African people throughout the diaspora. The center is named in honor of Arthur Alphonso

Schomburg, an historian, lecturer and bibliophile who strengthened the early collection through the addition of his private library. Born in 1874 in Puerto Rico of African and German parents, Schomburg spent his life gathering materials that documented the accomplishments of people of African descent. His lifelong quest for dignity and respect for African peoples refuted the uncorroborated scientific theories of his day regarding African-American racial inferiority.[1]

Schomburg's interest in African culture and history can be traced back to his native Puerto Rico. As a young student, he was told by one of his teachers that "the Negro had no history." This callous remark left a profound impression upon Schomburg—and he dedicated his life to disproving it.

Schomburg's biographer Elinor Des Verney Sinnette traced his interest in history back to his participation in a multi-racial youth club in San Juan, Puerto Rico.[2] Schomburg's white clubmates were well-versed in the history of their ancestors and this caused him to question and search the origin and achievements of his own.

By the time the New York Public Library (NYPL) purchased Schomburg's collection in 1926 with a $10,000 grant from the Carnegie Corporation, it had grown to include between 5,000 and 6,000 books, 3,000 manuscripts, 2,000 etchings, and several thousand pamphlets.[3]

The seed that Schomburg planted as a bibliophile was nurtured and cultivated by Jean Blackwell Hutson for more than three decades. A little-known leader within American librarianship, she was the individual responsible for developing the vision of the important institution that Schomburg's collection could (and would) one day become. In order to actualize this vision, she set out to raise the consciousness and support of the local and national community, as well as of leaders and other key people within the city and throughout the world. The results of her efforts are extraordinary, especially in light of the racism and sexism she had to contend with throughout her career.

During her tenure, Hutson initiated four major accomplishments which have assured the center's survival and development. They are:

1. The creation of the Schomburg Corporation, a non-profit organization dedicated to generating financial support for the purchase, conservation, and preservation of materials for the Schomburg Center;
2. Planning, design, funding, and construction of a new, enlarged physical facility in which the center is currently housed;
3. Implementation of an archival preservation program through support of the National Endowment for the Humanities (NEH); and
4. Transferal of the center from the branch libraries of the NYPL to the Research Libraries Division.

Her administrative adroitness, Afrocentricism, dedication, and professional expertise offer us insight to and an increased understanding of an important part of the history of American librarianship.[4]

YOUNG, GIFTED, AND BLACK

Jean Blackwell Hutson describes herself as a precocious child, full of inquisitiveness. She was born in Summerfield, Florida, on September 3, 1914, to Sarah Myers Blackwell and Paul Blackwell. Sarah Blackwell was an elementary school teacher by profession and Paul Blackwell a commission merchant who bought and sold crops on a consignment basis. She remembers being very jealous of her mother's work, resenting the nightly lesson plans, grading of papers, and other tasks that took her mother away from her.

Physically, Sarah Blackwell was fragile and she received little medical care during her late-life pregnancy. She was 38 years old when she had her first and only child. Doctors had actually predicted that the baby would be stillborn, but Jean arrived yelling, three months premature, as her father was preparing a tiny wooden box to bury her in. In her own words, she has been talking since.

When she was 4 years old, she and her mother moved to Baltimore, MD, to be close to medical treatment her mother required for kidney trouble. Relatives in Nebraska assisted with medical expenses during this separation from her husband. Jean's memories of Paul Blackwell are sparse as they spent little time together. His business commitments prevented him from relocating with his family. Speculation is a large inheritance was his primary reason for marrying Sarah Meyers. Jean Blackwell Hutson described her father as a person possessed of good fortune. According to her, he once owned the land on which the Waldorf Astoria Hotel in midtown Manhattan stands. He reportedly left the deed with a reprobate lawyer, never to be seen again by Paul Blackwell. While he often made considerable sums of money, it never seemed to remain in his possession long.

Premature children often suffer a host of medical problems. For Jean Blackwell Hutson, her stomach was not completely formed at birth. She should have spent time in an incubator, but African-American children weren't given that kind of attention then. She developed allergies, anemia, and rheumatism, which caused her to spend a good deal of time as an outpatient at the Harriet Lane Clinic of the Johns Hopkins Hospital. Recuperative periods were spent reading and studying. She remembers being very bright and teaching herself to read by the early age of four. She credits her early progress to a childhood very different from that which children experience today. Other than reading, she had few distractions and little competition for her time and soon read and absorbed most of the European classics. This early start is what instilled in her a love of books and knowledge. She was tested by the Baltimore School System and identified as having the highest IQ of the children in her age group. One of the disadvantages of being so bright was that she always finished her schoolwork before everyone else and asked for more; she felt her zeal to learn actually antagonized many of her teachers.

She grew up receiving positive exposure to African-American culture. Her mother knew Frederick Douglass and was very active in the Baltimore Branch of the NAACP. Her uncle was an acquaintance of Booker T. Washington and

C.A. Phillip Randolph. From a young age she was fortunate to have never internalized feelings of racial inferiority. Her image of both herself and her people was positive, in spite of daily exposure to racism. Educated in predominantly black elementary and high schools, she developed a knowledge of Black history, a strong sense of cultural pride, and a keen interest in African-American literature.

"Separate but equal" was the nation's prevailing school doctrine. Maryland's educational system was segregated by law, as were most states until the 1954 Brown vs Board of Education Supreme Court decision that ruled discrimination in education was unconstitutional.

One of the advantages of her upbringing, in her opinion, was the fact she had African-American teachers who took an interest in her development. Among her memorable teachers were Mrs. Norma A. Williams Marshall, her kindergarten teacher, mother of the late Supreme Court Justice Thurgood Marshall; Yolanda DuBois, daughter of W.E.B. DuBois; and May Miller, daughter of pioneer, black historian Kelly Miller. The foundation of race consciousness and pride they instilled in her served her well throughout her adult life.

Graduating as her high school valedictorian, Hutson went on to attend the University of Michigan on a partial academic scholarship. Her initial ambition was to be a psychiatrist, so she selected an undergraduate major of pre-medicine. She chose Michigan partially because of the financial assistance she was offered, but also because she understood the value of attending an institution with high academic standards.

At the University of Michigan, as on most predominantly white college campuses, African-American students were not allowed to live in the student dormitories; instead, they were housed in a segregated "Negro House." Through the help of the Detroit Branch NAACP, she challenged the university's segregated housing policy in a legal suit. She did this in addition to her involvement with the American Student Union, a student-run organization concerned with civil rights issues. Hutson continued her civil rights activism during summers in Baltimore where her mother remained an active member of the NAACP and the Urban League. Mr. Edward Lewis, then Executive Director of the Baltimore Urban League, suggested Hutson would be happier at a more liberal, eastern college such as Barnard in New York City. Simultaneously, her mother was pressuring her to transfer back home because she was too involved in what she viewed as radical activities. The fact that she was becoming more politically active and less religious frightened her mother. She bowed to pressure from all sides and in her senior year transferred to Barnard College where again, as in Michigan, housing was segregated. Arrangements were made for her to live in the International House which actually housed graduate students.

Leaving the University of Michigan forced her to reevaluate her educational plans and reach the decision to attend library school. She also changed her major to English. The switch from pre-medicine to librarianship was predicated upon her limited financial resources. The stock market crash of 1929 and the ensuing Depression eliminated the prospect of money being available for four more years of medical school. With the country still in the throes of the Great Depression, she felt pressure to be practical. Money was scarce, unemployment was high, and job security was a major factor in making career decisions. She knew she had only enough money to finish an undergraduate degree and one year of professional school.

Reflecting upon her options, she thought of her enjoyment of libraries throughout her education. Librarianship was a profession of status in her eyes. She recalled the librarians she had known, her love of reading, books, and knowledge, and decided upon librarianship. A second variable in this decision was the fact that librarianship represented a deviation from teaching, the profession of choice for most of her friends. Teaching has long been a respectable, secure choice for college educated blacks. At that time, it represented one of the few professions blacks had entry to because of the traditionally segregated educational patterns. Financially, librarianship was not particularly attractive, though it did offer job security, an important consideration.

In 1935, after graduating from Barnard College, she entered the Columbia School of Library Service. (She had been denied entrance to the Enoch Pratt Library Training School and convinced that the real, though unexpressed, reason was race, she brought a lawsuit against Enoch Pratt, which was litigated by the Baltimore Branch of the NAACP. Though she moved on, the case was continued by Louise Kerr, who eventually won the suit.) Jean Blackwell Hutson graduated from Columbia in 1936 with a Master's Degree in Library Service. Continuing her education, in 1941 she was awarded a teacher's certificate from Teachers College of Columbia University.

EARLY PROFESSIONAL CAREER

Sometime prior to graduation from Columbia, Franklin Hopper, Chief of Circulation for New York Public Library (NYPL), addressed a group of perspective graduates and urged them to apply for employment at NYPL. Jean Blackwell Hutson accepted his offer at face value, and she went to NYPL and applied for work. She was politely told they presently had their quota of "Negroes." African-American librarians were only employed at the 135th Street Branch, and the only way a new one was hired was through death or retirement. While relating this experience to a friend at a social gathering, she was overheard by an Urban League official who later confronted Hopper about the incident. Needless to say, Hopper was described as one very embarrassed "liberal."

After her rebuff by the NYPL, she sent employment inquiries across the country. She was interviewed for a position at Talladega College, in Talladega, AL, and appeared ready to accept an offer from President Buell Gallagher. Further reflection upon his conversation concerning "the decrease in campus lynchings," however, caused her some serious misgivings. It was while she was mulling over the Talladega offer that she received a telegram from NYPL to report to work. She was to replace Catherine A. Latimer, who was taking a maternity leave. Latimer was the first professional African-American librarian employed by the NYPL.[5] At that time, the Division of Negro Literature, History and Prints (as it was then called) was housed on the third floor of the old 135th Street Branch of the NYPL.

It was during this first, brief stay at the Division of Negro Literature, History and Prints that Jean Blackwell Hutson angered Arthur A. Schomburg. Though cataloged by the Dewey Decimal System, Schomburg kept his books, which he knew intimately, arranged according to color and spine height. Hutson, being the efficient and conscientious librarian she was, thought it would be much better to arrange the books by the Dewey Decimal System so others could gain access through the card catalog, and she did so. Needless to say, this infuriated Schomburg, who couldn't locate a thing as a result of her reorganization, and consequently forbade her to come near the materials again. She was barred from having any access to the third floor collection, much to her dismay. Until this happened, she and Schomburg had had a friendly relationship. He never forgave her, however, and she was subsequently moved from the special collection to branch work by Ernestine Rose, Branch Manager. Her first trip to the Schomburg lasted less than one year!

Ernestine Rose, a strong proponent of racially integrated staffs, liked and appreciated the fact Hutson was willing to challenge the issue of segregation. Jean Blackwell Hutson was a self-possessed woman of strong convictions who was not easily intimidated. This attitude got her transferred to the 124th Street Branch Library under the supervision of a white librarian resistant to the concept of integration. She worked at the branch for almost a full year before her supervisor even spoke to her. From 1936–1948 her career was rather eclectic. She worked as a circulation librarian at various NYPL branches and spent some time as a school librarian in Baltimore at the Paul Lawrence Dunbar High School.

In 1941, she married Andy Razaf, a man of royal Madagascan descent. She and her husband moved to Englewood, New Jersey, and she applied for New Jersey state certification as a school librarian. After an overly long waiting period, she contacted state officials regarding their lack of response. They reminded her she was "colored," and that the segregated Asbury Park schools were one of the few areas in which Negroes could work. Since there were no vacancies there, they could do nothing for her. She persisted, however, and received both the certification and the opportunity to be one of the first African Americans to work in a predominantly white area. The New Jersey schools' segregated employment policy was quite similar, in her view, to that of NYPL, and its injustice made her equally angry. Between 1941–1948, she returned to NYPL, commuting between New York City and her Englewood, New Jersey,

Photo reprinted with the permission of the Schomburg Center for Research in Black Culture.

A community reading group led by Jean Blackwell Hutson.

home. Because of her ability to work well with diverse people and because her job performance was always exceptional, she became a troubleshooter for the system, going into areas and handling situations the average librarian couldn't. She recalls working at the 145th and 160th Street Branches. More and more the branches were having to serve African Americans as a result of their growing numbers within the city. This growth spread throughout the boroughs. Yet, in spite of all the rapid change, NYPL still had not integrated its staff, and so was unable to send qualified African-American professionals into areas where they were needed.

A forthright person, she spoke to the NYPL administration about their personnel practices. She felt she was not being promoted like her peers and was not being advanced through the system. The administration was surprised and shocked by her outspokenness. They basically placated her, responding that she was young, she was moving rapidly in spite of how she felt, and her concerns were not valid. Shortly after the confrontation, however, she was moved to the Main Library on 42nd Street as a special assistant to the chief of the circulation department. In 1948, she was made supervising librarian at the Woodstock

Branch, where she became very involved with the Puerto Rican population. Her childhood exposure to and appreciation of her own culture helped her to accept and appreciate the culture of other ethnic groups. After a brief eight months at Woodstock, she was again called back to the 135th Street Branch, this time as Acting Curator of the Division of Negro Literature, History and Prints.

FROM 135TH STREET BRANCH LIBRARY
TO SCHOMBURG COLLECTION

The Schomburg Center for Research in Black Culture's inception dates back to the establishment in 1925 of the Division of Negro Literature, History and Prints within Harlem's 135th Street Branch Library.

When the branch was opened in 1905, Harlem was predominantly wealthy and white.[6] The influx of African Americans to Harlem began around 1910 when there was a mass exodus from the South. With the United States on the brink of World War I, there was a demand for increased industrial production that precipitated a shortage of labor. African Americans filled that labor shortage, leaving the segregated South for the opportunities of the North and its promise of equality. By 1920, New York's black population had increased to 150,000, a conservative estimate, as compared to 50,000 at the turn of the century.[7]

The 135th Street Branch was under the supervision of Ernestine Rose who was chosen to manage the branch with the specific purpose of adapting the library to meet the needs of Harlem's increasing African-American population. Rose had successfully worked with ethnic populations in other parts of New York. She was equally successful, in a very short time, in turning the 135th Street library into a heavily used branch and thriving community cultural center. Rose served as Branch Manager from 1920–1942. One of her most significant achievements was an integrated staff. "Rose racially integrated her staff in Harlem at a time when it was not common for there even to be black librarians, and still less common to have a biracial staff."[8] Hutson recalls "she insisted on equal pay for all. The money might have been meager, but it was equally meager for blacks and whites."

Along with the dedication of Rose and her staff, the Harlem Renaissance was a major factor in the development of the library. A literary and intellectual movement of a fairly short time span, the Harlem Renaissance has been given various dates of duration ranging from as early as 1917 to as late as 1935. Claude McKay, Langston Hughes, Countee Cullen, Jessie Fauset, and James Weldon Johnson represent but a few of the writers and lecturers who frequented the 135th Street Library for both formal and informal gatherings. The branch was the hub of serious activity throughout the 1920s with Arthur A. Schomburg as a major motivating force.

Historians cite four important factors that contributed to the creation of the Harlem Renaissance:

1. The migration of blacks from the South to the North;
2. The growing visibility of African-American communities and their increased interest in black life and culture;
3. The presence of black World War I veterans who refused to accept second-class citizenship after fighting for democracy on foreign soil; and
4. The increase of race riots, which mirrored a new black militancy in response to rising American racism and intolerance.[9]

The Harlem Renaissance coincided with the economic "boom" of the 1920s. Jobs were plentiful and people were living well. Many historians agree the stock market crash of 1929 signaled the end of the movement and brought about a drastic decline of artistic activities, jobs, and financial stability. The Renaissance further represented a period in which African Americans sought to both discover and reclaim their sense of self. Schomburg, in 1925, expressed the feeling of the period well in his statement:

The American Negro must remake his past in order to make his future. Though it is orthodox to think of America as the one country where it is unnecessary to have a past, what is a luxury for the nation as a whole becomes a prime social necessity for the Negro. For him, a group tradition must supply compensation for persecution and pride of race the antidote for prejudice. History must restore what slavery took away, for it is the social damage of slavery that the present generations must repair and offset.[10]

Race consciousness produced a great number of prolific poets, writers, artists, and musicians. Throughout this period, the formulation of the value of African-American culture was driven by an acknowledgment and exploration of the African past. Though centered in Harlem, the Renaissance was felt outside New York City. Washington, D.C., as well as Chicago, Memphis, Philadelphia, and other major urban areas with large, growing black populations, also provided environments that nurtured artists.

This same growth in black populations created an increased demand for library materials by and about African Americans at the 135th Street Branch Library. Community interest generated such a high demand for these materials that they began to deteriorate rapidly. Limited funds for the branch and the fact that many titles were out of print and irreplaceable caused Ernestine Rose to sound a community alarm regarding the collection. Her concerns were immediately answered by a group of Harlem citizens including Schomburg, who had already loaned a large portion of his collection to the branch; writer James Weldon Johnson; intellectual and educator Hubert Harrison; and John A. Nail, a prominent black realtor.[11] These forward-thinking individuals formed a committee to oversee the care and protection of special materials. One of their first actions was to remove from circulation the rare, irreplaceable titles, thus hopefully prolonging their lives and making them available to more people. They approached the NYPL administration about creating a separate, non-circulating reference collection of materials by and about African Americans. Their intention to create a "Negro Collection" focused attention on the branch's need for such materials, and almost immediately gifts and loans from private collectors began to pour into the center.

On May 8, 1925, a separate reference collection was created and the New York Public Library's Division of Negro Literature, History and Prints officially opened. The collection's mission was "to preserve historical records of the Negro race, promote racial pride and consciousness, provide information to everyone relative to the accomplishments of the Negro and make it available for research."[12]

According to Ernestine Rose, the Division's Negro Collection "should properly become one of the largest and most valuable in the country."[13] Almost immediately though, the collection proved inadequate. Ernestine Rose knew Arthur A. Schomburg was interested in selling his collection and she knew the 135th Street Branch would be an appropriate home. She wrote L. Hollingsworth Wood, president of the National Urban League, to encourage him to purchase Schomburg's collection for the division. NYPL would not commit funds for this purchase even though private collectors were pressuring him to sell. Early in 1926, Schomburg, being very selective about where his materials would ultimately be housed, offered his collection to the New York City Office of the National Urban League.[14] Without adequate space, staff, or funds to maintain the collection, the Urban League had to decline his offer. It is from discussions stimulated by the league's rejection that arrangements were made for the NYPL to apply to the Carnegie Corporation for a grant to purchase the collection for the 135th Street Branch. The transaction was officially completed in the summer of 1926. The price paid for the collection, $10,000, was not considered fair nor representative of its value; it was a token payment at best. African-American books and documents to this day still remain underpriced and have only recently begun to appreciate in value. According to the 1926 report of the NYPL, the collection included 2,932 volumes, 1,124 pamphlets, and numerous valuable prints and manuscripts.[15] An undated inventory by Schomburg, however, indicates that his collection of 3,338 bound volumes, added to the 1,886 already in the collection, brought the total bound volumes to 5,224. These discrepancies are attributed to the fact that NYPL did not process the entire collection immediately upon receipt.[16]

Among the most prized items in Schomburg's collection when it came to the library were:

> A copy of *Juan Latino's Latin Verse* (Granada, Spain 1573). Remembered as incumbent of the chair of poetry at the University of Granada during the reign of Philip V and spoken of as the "best" Latinist of Spain in his day, Latino had not been thought of as a Negro for gen-

erations. Schomburg reminded scholars that Juan Latino was a full-blooded African Negro. The poet's verse on the return of the Spanish prince from the battle with the Turks at Lepanto (published twenty years before the first of Shakespeare's writings) was an exhibit of Negro accomplishment.

The work of America's first Negro poet—Jupiter Harmon's *Address to the Negroes in the State of New York* (1787).

Manuscript poems and early editions of the works of Phyllis Wheatley, slave girl.

The autobiography of Gustavus Vassa, which led to Granville Sharp's attack on slavery in the British colonies.

Copies of the almanacs (1792 and 1793) compiled by Benjamin Banneker, the Negro whose unusual abilities were employed by Thomas Jefferson and others.

The sermons of Lemuel Haynes, the Negro who served as pastor of a white church in Rutland, Vermont, for thirty years following the Revolutionary War.

The scrapbook of Ira Aldridge, who won fame in Europe as a Shakespearean actor during the nineteenth century.

Clotel, or the President's Daughter: A Narrative of Slave Life in the United States, the first novel by an American Negro.[17]

The newly acquired collection was placed under the charge of Catherine A. Latimer. She had the responsibility of integrating Schomburg's materials, plus the existing collection, into the New York Public Library system. She remained with the 135th Street Branch as reference librarian until her death in 1954.[18]

In 1932, a second gift from the Carnegie Corporation enabled the library to hire Schomburg as curator. He held this position until his death in 1938. Two years following his death, the Negro Division was renamed the Schomburg Collection of Negro History, Literature and Prints in his honor.

In 1938, after Schomburg's death, Dr. Lawrence D. Reddick became curator. The collection's mission remained the same with added civic and cultural dimensions. Dr. Reddick created the annual Honor Roll in Race Relations Awards. The library expanded its public programs and played a more active role in the Harlem community. A national focus was adopted and programs became more diverse. The Schomburg became actively involved with the NAACP and the National Urban League. In 1940, the New York City Board of Estimate and Apportionment appropriated funds to construct a new library. The Schomburg Collection occupied the entire top floor of the new 135th Street Branch, then the newest and finest branch building in the system. The library's basement auditorium became home and training ground for the American Negro Theatre, from which came such performers as Frederick O'Neal, Hilda Simms, Sidney Poitier, Rosetta LeNoire, and Harry Belafonte. The collection further served as a primary reference source for writers Langston Hughes and Richard Wright, as well as a center for black scholars involved in the Works Projects Administration (WPA) efforts.

Dr. Reddick's departure from the Schomburg in 1948 was precipitated by what he perceived as a lack of commitment to the collection on the part of the NYPL. By his reasoning, the collection should receive one-eighth of the Branch System budget as "Negroes" represented one-eighth of New York's population. He accused NYPL of cheating the Schomburg and made the unfortunate mistake of giving the administration a deadline to come up with the one-eighth portion. He went even further; utilizing the strong community base he had built, he set up a picket line of community supporters around the branch to pressure the administration to concede. All these events converged around budget appropriation time and highly embarrassed the library administration. The situation was resolved by Dr. Reddick being asked to resign. Jean Blackwell Hutson, in her capacity as troubleshooter, was sent to talk and "reason" with Dr. Reddick, to no avail. NYPL fired Reddick and drafted Dr. Dorothy Williams from the 42nd Street Branch to replace him, much to Dr. Williams' dismay. She viewed the reassignment as a demotion and appeared to dislike the fact she was moved from the 42nd Street Branch where she had been quite satisfied. In spite of these feelings, Dr. Williams in her short four-month stay conducted a survey and reevaluation of the collection's role. The survey resulted in a set of recommendations that served as guidelines for the collection's growth and development for the following two decades.[19] Dr. Williams additionally advised that the community activist posture taken under Dr. Reddick be abandoned for a research and reference focus.

DECADES OF GROWTH

In 1948, Jean Blackwell Hutson was temporarily appointed to the Schomburg Collection of Negro History, Literature and Prints. She succeeded Dr. Dorothy Williams who was granted a six month leave of absence. Hutson's temporary appointment turned into a 32-year administration.

At the time she was appointed to the Schomburg, she was happily assigned to the Woodstock Branch of the NYPL as supervising librarian, working successfully with the rapidly growing Puerto Rican community. She remembers being told by the NYPL to return to the Schomburg to "keep the Negroes quiet." She found this ultimatum insulting, objectionable, and infuriating. She mulled over the library's directive with a former Columbia Library School faculty member who gently reminded her that she was a child of the depression and as such, she ought to know better than to jeopardize a job for any reason. Having been brought back to reality by this advice, she prepared herself for her next career move.

Her first decade at the Schomburg was relatively peaceful, with collection maintenance and assessment her focus. With Dr. Williams leaving a strong collection development policy in place, efforts could be focused on processing the four storerooms of acquisitions that had accumulated since the retirement of Catherine Latimer. She recalls causing some commotion with her staff for requiring them to inventory the collection. It had been over 20 years since the task had last been undertaken. She viewed knowing exactly what was in the collection as critical. In addition to organizing the stored materials, considerable time was spent publicizing their contents to appropriate community groups who were unaware of the collection's rich resources. She and librarian–cataloger Kathleen Hill spent time organizing and cataloging the manuscripts and materials of such important acquisitions as the papers of the Negro Writers Project, *The Negro in New York*, and the papers of the National Negro Congress.

The Schomburg's community base and support, which had reached a high under Dr. Reddick, eroded with his firing and required her attention. She fully understood the importance of a positive relationship with the African-American community; it represented the collection's major constituency. Together with Langston Hughes, a close friend and supporter of the Schomburg, she planned a series of public programs that drew old supporters back and attracted a host of new ones.

Next to organizing the collection, one of her most challenging goals was to secure additional funds for acquisitions. During Dr. Reddick's tenure, support had been forthcoming from the General Education Fund, a private foundation to which she again made application. Her request for support was denied, but denied in such a way it caused NYPL to increase the collection's meager budget. Dr. Channing Tobias, Educational Director of the Phelps Stokes Fund and her contact at the General Education Fund, stressed the fact that the collection was a responsibility of the NYPL and that it was about time they became accountable and committed enough to provide the support needed.[20] His rejection letter pointed a finger of negligence at NYPL and forced them to acknowledge their obligation to the collection. Since its initial acquisition, the Schomburg had received minimal attention and support from the administration. Further, being a research collection, its needs were quite different from the branches.

Though acquiring funds was always quite difficult, Hutson remembers, in the early years, the helpfulness of Mary Brady, then executive officer of the Harmon Foundation, which supported Negro artists through grants. Funds from the Harmon Foundation were extremely helpful in carrying on the Schomburg's mission.

Although hiring was centralized, Hutson had a great deal of influence over employment decisions. A controversial issue that continually arose was the Schomburg's policy of hiring only African Americans. Hutson was always sensitive to the community's apprehension of whether a white person could appreciate, value, and respect the materials housed in the collection and its mission.

Photo reprinted with the permission of the Schomburg Center
for Research in Black Culture.

Jean Blackwell Hutson with noted author, Langston Hughes.

The precedent to maintain an African-American staff was established in the collection's early years when segregation was an accepted way of life and Arthur A. Schomburg served as curator. In today's context Schomburg would be thought of as a Nationalist. Schomburg believed strongly, I maintain, in the principle of Kujichagulia (self-determination). Kujichagulia is a commitment to the principle and practice of African Americans defining, defending, and developing themselves instead of being defined, defended and developed by others. Kujichagulia demands that African Americans build their own lives in their own image and interests, and construct through their own efforts institutions that house African-American aspirations.[21] Kujichagulia is one of the Seven Principles of Nation Building that Dr. Maulana Karenga prescribes as the minimal moral value system African people need to live by in order to rescue and reconstruct their history and humanity.

While she understood Schomburg's concerns and philosophy, she chose to take a different approach. Because the library administration thought of the Schomburg as a staff "dumping ground," she reluctantly changed the hiring policy. She selectively added some whites to her staff, but always remained sensitive to the African-American community's feelings of distrust. For her, hiring whites represented a way to attract additional bright, promising people to work on behalf of the institution.

African Americans, like many whites, internalize the message of "black inferiority" perpetrated by the majority culture. Hence, it was difficult to attract the "brightest and best" black professionals. In many cases their feeling was that in order to get ahead, they couldn't be associated with a struggling black institution. From an institutional perspective, the Schomburg had as staff members many bright, conscious African Americans with strong personalities who were outspoken and proud to be part of the institution. Often individuals like these were placed at the Schomburg to move them outside the system.

The historic 1954 Supreme Court Decision on school desegregation had a profound impact upon the collection. Much of the research for the case was done at the Schomburg with the staff actively participating. Initial joy at the victory was overshadowed by the suggestion from the library administration that the Schomburg Collection might no longer be needed due to the fact that Negro history would now be integrated into the general collection. Publicly, Hutson understood the unique role of collecting, preserving, and documenting the historical record of African-American people would always be needed, and she confidently reassured her staff they need not worry about becoming obsolete or unnecessary. She personally did not foresee integration happening as willingly as the administration suggested. She did not expect a change in law suddenly to remove the racism and hatred society had harbored for generations toward "Negroes." Integration would merely help facilitate what the Schomburg did and hopefully allow them to generate additional supporters and credibility. Privately, however, she worried about a continued commitment from the NYPL. Would they view this landmark decision as a convenient reason to cease their already inadequate commitment to the Schomburg? She shared her concerns with Robert Kingery, a friend of the Schomburg who was chief of the Preparation Division of NYPL. In response to her concerns, he arranged to have the G.K. Hall Company film and publish the catalog of the Schomburg. To Jean Blackwell Hutson, the appeal of publishing the catalog was the visibility it would give the collection. Politically, it would be more difficult for NYPL to get rid of the Schomburg should they decide to take that course of action. Surprisingly, *The Dictionary Catalog of the Schomburg Collection of Negro Literature and History* sold well to libraries throughout the U.S., Europe, and Africa. The decision proved to be more forward thinking than anyone could have realized. What was undertaken as a philanthropic gesture proved to be a sound economic idea. Editions of the catalog were published through 1976 when it was replaced by the annual publication *Bibliographic Guide to Black Studies*.

INSTITUTIONALIZATION

The 1954 Supreme Court Decision on school desegregation, the 1955 Montgomery Bus Boycott, the sit-ins, freedom ride movements, and civil rights demonstrations thrust the world's attention on African Americans. Anger stemming from generations of discrimination, oppression, disinterest, and outright bigotry came to a head in the late 1960s with the manifestation of the "Black Power" movement. The term *black power* was coined to symbolize the belief that it was time to shift the balance of power. Blacks wanted to control their own communities, relinquish second-class citizenship, and lay claim to the freedom, justice, and equality that had thus far eluded them. On college and university campuses throughout the country this growing concern and unrest created a cry for Black Studies or Afro-American Studies curricula. African Americans wanted to see themselves and their history included in curricular offerings and they wanted American society to learn of, value, and accept their many contributions.

Unlike the quiet and uneventful 1950s, the 1960s created a thirst for information on the "black man" from a cultural, historical, educational, psychological, philosophical, and economic perspective. The argument can be made that the foundation for building an "institution" rather than a "collection" was laid during this decade. Scholars, writers, and the African-American community rediscovered the Schomburg and its use skyrocketed. Increased use brought the deteriorating conditions of the collection to the community's attention. Demonstrations were held at the Schomburg decrying the neglect from the NYPL. The escalating use created a set of problems very similar to those which led Ernestine Rose and her committee of concerned Harlem residents to form the original reference collection. This time, as done earlier by Rose, an alarm was sounded. Again, the institution had a body of concerned supporters who helped address the critical issues of survival, maintenance, and preservation.

The renewed interest in African-American history allowed Hutson two fortuitous professional experiences. A former Schomburg page, Joseph Borome, became librarian at Columbia University. He additionally taught Black History at City College of New York. During his years at City College he established the tradition of having the director of the Schomburg Collection lecture at the college in an adjunct capacity. Hutson had previously been offered an adjunct teaching position at the college but had declined the offer citing her assumed dislike of teaching. Forced to retire due to a heart condition, Borome prevailed upon Hutson to accept the adjunct professorship, in spite of her apprehensions. Her relationship with City College lasted from 1962–1971. The demand for Black Studies grew along with insistence by its supporters of departmental status as well as a call for a more radical approach which Hutson did not support. She resigned, exasperated with the pressure from radical forces and in spite of the growing popularity of the Black History course and the fact it had become a requirement by the New York City Board of Education. Though Borome had pressed her into teaching, she ended up savoring the experience as well as growing professionally.

Hutson was regarded as "a doyen of black librarianship. She was respected nationally and internationally for her extensive knowledge of books and related materials concerning peoples of African descent."[22] This respect and expertise earned her an invitation from the late Kwame Nkrumah, then president of Ghana, to assist in the development of their Africana collection. Nkrumah, as well as other African and Caribbean leaders, had participated in library-sponsored discussions of the worldwide struggle for freedom by African peoples. They greatly admired and appreciated the Schomburg's mission. Nkrumah's invitation, an honor, took her to Africa as the Assistant Librarian in charge of Africana at the University of Ghana from 1964–1965.

She describes her time spent in Africa as very liberating. In America, as a 50-year-old African-American woman, she felt ashamed of being an old lady. In Africa, the tables turned; there she was revered and sought after. She relates the experience as the first time in her life she was accepted as a person without regard to race. The time spent in Africa was fulfilling professionally as well for she fought and won the battle to make the Africana collection inclusive of Africans in the diaspora as well as on the African continent, no minor achievement.

Through assistance from the late Whitney Young of the National Urban League, Hutson got the opportunity to return to Africa to attend the First World Festival of Negro Arts in Dakar, Senegal, in April 1966. Her mission was to acquire some publications for the Schomburg she had identified during her travel to Ghana in 1964. While at the festival, she came to the attention of *Ebony* magazine writer Ponchita Pierce, who wrote one of the first national stories on the collection titled "Schomburg's Ailing Collection," in the October 1967 issue. *Ebony* staff writer Allen Morrison, who relied upon the collection for much of his research, had long been unsuccessful at convincing the editors to feature a story on the collection. The *Ebony* article focused on inadequate funds and support for the Schomburg and charged the NYPL with treating the collection as a "stepchild." White institutions have historically had little interest in collecting and preserving African-American history and culture as a major part of their mission and purpose. Dr. Julius Block of Queens College charged the administration with diverting federal and private funds earmarked for the Schomburg. Few could dispute his summary of why the NYPL took such an unappreciative attitude: "Part of the reason is because it is a collection of Negro material and is housed in Harlem. As such, it has not received the kind of professional services and financial support to which it is entitled."[23]

Hutson corroborates this statement by acknowledging the Schomburg was always thought of as a "backwater" by the library administration. In addition to receiving inadequate funding, the Schomburg was usually sent the worst staff people, people with no ambition, commitment, or interest in their work. She attributes this holdover attitude to the 1950s and the early part of the 1960s when there was little respect for Black Studies. Fortunately, the consciousness of the late 1960s and 1970s turned things around and earned a more respectable place for African-American Studies as well as the Schomburg. In her mind, because of her Afrocentric perspective, she never felt the collection inferior or a "backwater." During the opportunities she had to be away from the collection, she was able to spend time reflecting on its future and creating a vision of how she wanted to see the collection grow. In her mind, the Schomburg was much more than a "collection." It was a national treasure, an "institution" established for the broad public purpose of documenting, presenting, and preserving African-American culture and history. To her, their mission was permanent not temporal. It became clear to her that for the collection to grow, the community would have to accept responsibility for maintaining it and resources would have to be identified for acquisitions, preservation, and other needs. Dr. Carleton Sprague Smith, who had known Arthur Schomburg and witnessed the collection's early development, shared her concerns. They discussed the problem in Africa and agreed to meet further upon return to the United States. It was in Africa, however, that the seed was planted to charge the community to develop an endowment for the collection. She needed only the right opportunity to share her vision with the Harlem community.

The right opportunity presented itself in February 1966 when she was presented an award by the New York branch of the Association for the Study of Negro Life and History for her years of dedicated service. Professionally, she was active in and drew support from the Association for the Study of Negro Life and History and the African Studies Association. It was these organizations, not the American Library Association, that expressed an interest in her important mission. The American Library Association basically avoided dealing with African Americans and didn't demonstrate an interest in representing all of its members until the 1960s.[24] While graciously accepting this award, she shared with the community the fact that the collection was in grave danger. Materials were deteriorating at an alarming rate due to increased public usage, air pollution, lack of environmental control, and overcrowding. The collection needed help if it was to survive, and survival was critical. The dignity of the African past was important. She urged the Association as well as the African-American academic community to become involved. Educator–psychologist Dr. Kenneth B. Clark, who also received an award on the same program as Hutson, stated, "Accepting an award for past behavior is making a commitment for the future."[25] Dr. Clark took a leadership role and established the Schomburg Endowment Fund.

Her cry for help was taken very seriously and many others responded immediately. Groups of concerned individuals began attacking the problem on several fronts. Some met with NYPL regarding improvements the administration could make, others sought greater financial support for the collection on the local and state level as well as with private individuals and foundations. Concerned professional groups tapped their membership for contributions for the collection.

A financial turning point manifested itself in the North Manhattan Library Project, which generated additional funds through 1973.[26] The project provided support for additional staff and acquisitions.

With multiple fund-raising events under way simultaneously, it became evident that coordination of all the volunteer activities was needed. Informally in 1968 and officially in 1971, all fund-raising activities were brought under the direction of a not-for-profit corporation known as the Schomburg Collection of Black History, Literature and Art, Inc.—called the Schomburg Corporation for short. The corporation's mission was to "raise funds for the conservation and preservation of materials in the Center, to solicit and purchase new materials, and work toward the construction of a new facility to adequately house the collection and provide sufficient space and services for scholars and other users."[27]

Stanton Biddle, in his article "A Partnership in Progress," identifies preservation, administrative status, and financing as the three major problem areas for the collection. Jean Blackwell Hutson saw these problems on a larger scale as challenges to be overcome to effectuate the institutionalization of the Schomburg Center.

With the Schomburg Corporation in place, it immediately tackled two critical issues: preservation and the design of a new, state-of-the-art facility. A three-phase program was planned which would include new facilities for: (a) the Schomburg Research Library and Archives, (b) the Schomburg art and artifacts collection, and (c) the Countee Cullen Regional Branch Library.[28] The new facility would include all those amenities prerequisite for special collections such as temperature and humidity control, adequate fire–sprinkler systems, air filtration system, appropriate lighting, and storage space, as well as viewing and listening areas to support audio visual materials. The corporation worked cooperatively with NYPL administration and local political officials to secure eventually land and financing for this long-term project which was finally completed in the spring of 1991.

While this plan would speak to providing a proper home for future acquisitions, it didn't address the severe deterioration already in progress with existing materials. The fact that the collection was part of the branch system rather than the research libraries, where preservation is a major concern, excluded the Schomburg from appropriate NYPL conservation and preservation programs. This major oversight began to receive some attention in 1967 when the Schomburg received a grant from the Ford Foundation to support an archival preservation program.[29] The grant provided for microfilming of rare books, restoration of materials through lamination, and de-acidification. This grant led to the development of an ongoing program which eventually gave users access to thousands of materials previously unavailable due to their poor condition. Cooperation between the corporation and library administration led to a series of matching preservation grants from the National Endowment for the Humanities (NEH). National figures led the matching funds campaign for the institution, giving it greater visibility and response. The acquisition of the prestigious NEH grants drew assistance and contributions from individuals, community groups, fraternities, sororities, college students, and others who took seriously the challenge to become responsible for their own historical record. By the late 1970s, the worst preservation problems had been brought under control, with plans in place to address future crises.

The fact that the Schomburg Collection came to the library without an endowment resulted in it being placed administratively with the Branch Libraries rather than the Research Libraries. The accumulated deterioration of the collection was testimony to the fact that city funds were woefully inadequate. Though a cooperative relationship was maintained with the Branch Library administration, the collection was obviously misplaced. On May 1, 1972, the Schomburg Collection was finally acknowledged as a major research center and moved within the Research Libraries Division of the NYPL, "forty-seven years, almost to the day, after its founding."[30] At the same time, Jean Blackwell Hutson was promoted from curator to chief. Once this transfer was made, it was agreed that the term "collection" no longer adequately defined the operation, nor were the terms "literature" and "history" reflective of the diverse resources housed there. The official name of the institution became the Schomburg Center for Research in Black Culture.

Specific advantages of joining the Research Libraries Division included:

1. Greater access to other supportive research materials;
2. The opportunity to work within an administrative structure that understood problems unique to research collections;
3. Interaction with peers who share similar problems and concerns as the Schomburg staff;
4. An increase in status within the public library system;
5. Greater visibility of the collection through inclusion in additional bibliographic databases;
6. Initiation of a study of the future directions of the Schomburg as well as a thorough documentation of its past history; and
7. Access to a staff conservation consultant.

For nonprofit institutions, funding is the eternal challenge. Hutson describes it as certainly one of the most critical issues during her tenure. Next to the infusion of NEH dollars, one of the most significant sources of funding was and is support from the New York State Legislature. Legislative support has allowed the center to maintain longer hours, hire more staff, maintain preservation, and increase acquisitions. State Senator Sidney von Luther provided the first grant in 1973 and his support was continued by Senator Carl McCall, Assemblyman George Miller, and the Black and Puerto Rican Legislative Caucus.

A direct mail, national fund-raising campaign under the leadership of Mrs. Ralph Bunche and Drs. John Hope Franklin and Robert Weaver raised matching funds for two National Endowment for the Arts (NEA) grants. An annual fund-raising dinner was initiated as well as a quarterly journal, which is mailed to donors and national educational institutions. A 1972 NEH grant literally gave the institution's holdings a new lease on life by enabling staff to clear up a cataloging backlog of nonbook materials.

In 1973, the National Cash Register Corporation developed a proposal to convert extensive vertical file materials to microfilm. Vertical file materials included clippings from non-black periodicals, newspaper clippings, broadsides, programs, playbills, leaflets, pamphlets, newsletters, book reviews, and other types of ephemera. The file dates back to 1925 and provides a wealth of important information.

LATER YEARS

From 1972–1980 Hutson served as Chief of the Schomburg with the institution in high gear, moving closer to the reality of occupying its new facility. The new building was designed to "reflect and reinforce the culture and work of African people throughout the world."[31] It was to house the archival and library collections, and a future project was scheduled to renovate the old 135th Street structure to provide an auditorium, art collection, and meeting space.

Ironically, when the new building opened in 1980, Hutson was denied the opportunity to bask in the joy of her accomplishment. Her friend of 20 years, Dr. Kenneth Clark, then member of the New York State Board of Regents, worked to have her transferred from the Schomburg back to the Central Research Library at 42nd Street on the basis of incompetency. He claimed that Hutson ran the Schomburg as if it existed for the exclusive use of "Negroes" only. The rift between the two centered around the acquisition of some Marcus Garvey, Universal Negro Improvement Association (UNIA) papers. A drug prevention–rehabilitation program was given access to a vacant apartment in Harlem which was once occupied by a former secretary or treasurer of the UNIA. Detailed records and documentation of the UNIA were left in this apartment. The papers were discovered by the drug program participants who sold them on the streets for one dollar per page or some equally ridiculous figure. Upon learning of this, Hutson immediately contacted the library administration and requested financial assistance to buy these historical documents for the Schomburg's collection. Armed with $10,000 provided by an anonymous donor, she took to the streets to consummate the transaction with little thought for her personal safety. Her fearlessness was testimony to how well known and respected she was in the Harlem community. The speed with which events happened did not allow her to confer with professional associates. She was driven by the desire to save an authentic piece of historical documentation. When Dr. Clark, who was also a close family friend, learned of her success, he was furious. He considered the papers stolen goods and felt she should not have negotiated with "junkies" for "hot items." He accused her of being dishonest and using poor judgement, and he never forgave her. As best she can understand the situation, there was some resentment at how adeptly she handled the situation and the fact she did not confer with him. Not content merely to be angry, Dr. Clark used his considerable influence with the library administration to remove her from the Schomburg. Unaware of how upset Dr. Clark was, initially, she did not connect his anger with the sudden offer from the administration of a new position at the 42nd Street library. She simply refused it and thought it odd they would make such an offer at the time that they did. When the administration approached her a second time, it came as an ultimatum. Again, she found herself forced to change professional positions against her will just to keep her job. The pain of being denied the opportunity to observe, first-hand, the institutional progress she had long worked for and to continue to work where she chose was great.

Hutson sought the advice of her minister, Rev. Moran Weston, pastor of St. Phillips Church, who advised her to talk with Dr. Anna Hedgman, a pioneer worker with the Harlem YWCA. Dr. Hedgman gathered four other outstanding African-American women who became known as the Group of Five. In addition to Dr. Hedgman it included Harriet Baltimore Brown, a Brooklyn librarian; Ellen Craft Dammond, a pioneer in personnel practice; and an unidentified fourth member. This Group of Five orchestrated a community protest in hopes of keeping Hutson at the Schomburg. They met with the chief of the NYPL as well as branch librarians. They published community protests in the New York Amsterdam News and the New York Voice. She found the situation sad and uplifting at the same time. Never before in her life had she been so humiliated and embarrassed as she was by Dr. Clark's unsubstantiated charges of incompetency. At the same time, she was overwhelmed by the outpouring of community support. She had no idea she was appreciated and revered by so many. The community support, however, was not enough to keep her there. It did cause the library to compromise and give her an office at the Schomburg where she worked one day per week.

The irony of the situation was that the library thought they were honoring her by promoting her to the 42nd Street library, but for her, it was a slap in the face. She had worked the greater portion of her professional life institutionalizing the Schomburg, and she would never be able to enjoy one of her proudest accomplishments—the completion of the new facility.

From 1980 to her retirement in 1984 she supervised collection development in African and African-American Studies. She acknowledges enjoying her new responsibilities to a degree, but her heart was at the Schomburg.

As Hutson reflects upon her life, she feels she was extremely fortunate. Things always seemed to fall into place for her. Her years at the Schomburg were difficult, yet fulfilling. She had key people in her corner who supported and respected her, plus the goodwill of some influential people. She had her share of personal and professional tragedies that deeply wounded her. She never chose to dwell on her sorrow and was always thankful she had her work to inspire her. Admittedly, her work was the center of her life, which is not to suggest her family life was not important.

Hutson credits Andy Razaf as the individual who had the greatest influence upon her life. Razaf, son of the Crown Prince of Madagascar, greatly broadened and enriched her life through travel and knowledge of African culture. Interestingly, her professional life molded her personal life.

As to her weaknesses or shortcomings, she confesses to having an inner arrogance she trusted intuitively which sustained her through turbulent times. Self-reliant, she was always pleased with her performance because she always gave her very best. She was attentive to all patrons, regardless of their stature. She took a lot of ridicule from people about the illegitimacy of Black or African-American Studies and feels proud she defended it and stood her ground. Its legitimacy is evidenced today in the current multi-cultural initiatives.

The Schomburg, according to Hutson, is a monument to the African-American community. In her words, she "took Mr. Schomburg's vision and developed it from what she learned from others."

MAINTAINING THE VISION

Much ground was gained through the process of successfully addressing the issues of expansion of funding sources, establishment of preservation efforts, and the transferal of the collection to the Research Libraries Division. The alarm Hutson sounded to the community ensured the collection a continued life. The challenge for those who follow is to maintain the collection and increase its community outreach, resources, programs, and acquisitions. At the heart of maintenance and growth is the issue of money. For an institution to survive on a long-range basis, it must have a healthy and committed financial lifeline. To augment their aggressive grantsmanship efforts, the Schomburg Society for the Preservation of Black Culture was created to allow concerned individuals, organizations, corporations, and institutions an opportunity to help ensure the Schomburg's future. The annual fund-raising efforts have attracted celebrities the likes of Susan Taylor, Harry Belafonte, Arthur Ashe, Lloyd Richards, Betty Shabazz, Wole Soyinka, and a host of others who wish to see the center survive and thrive into the 21st century.

The Schomburg annually serves more than 70,000 visitors and handles over 40,000 telephone inquiries with a staff of more than 70 people. Each year its mission and programs become more international in scope. The collections now house in excess of 5 million items. In April 1991, the institution celebrated its 65th year of commitment to documenting African-American history. Its expanded facilities now include the 360-seat Langston Hughes Auditorium and the original library space on the northwest corner of 135th Street and Malcolm X Boulevard, the newly renovated 1905 Stanford White Building. An exhibition hall, study area, gift shop, and a refurbished American Negro Theatre are all now accessible to the public. The institution bursts year-round with a wide spectrum of educational programs in celebration of African-American history and life. The center remains a popular meeting place for professional and community groups. A thriving exhibition, publication, and Scholars-in-Residence program round out its offerings.

The Schomburg Center for Research in Black Culture stands today as a living legacy to the vision of Arthur A. Schomburg. Jean Blackwell Hutson perpetuated that vision through her work, her dedication, her foresight and her commitment. For this she is to be honored and remembered.

ENDNOTES

[1]Elinor Des Verney Sinnette, *Arthur Alfonso Schomburg: Black Bibliophile & Collector* (New York: New York Public Library and Wayne State University Press, 1989), p. 1.

[2]Ibid., pp. 13–14.

[3]Arna Bontemps, "Special Collections of Negroana," *Library Quarterly*, 14 (July 1944): 187.

[4]This paper is based on an interview with Jean Blackwell Hutson (November 19, 1990) and several subsequent telephone conversations.

[5]Sinnette, *Arthur Alfonso Schomburg*, p. 132.

[6]Celeste Tibbets, *Ernestine Rose and the Origins of the Schomburg Center* (New York: New York Public Library, 1989), p. 18.

[7]Roi Ottley, *New World A-Coming* (New York: Arno Press, 1968), p. 35.

[8]Tibbets, *Ernestine Rose and the Origins of the Schomburg Center* (New York: New York Public Library, 1989), p. 20.

[9]Margaret Perry, *The Harlem Renaissance: An Annotated Bibliography and Commentary* (New York: Garland Publishing, 1982), pp. xvii–xviii.

[10]Alain Locke, ed., *The New Negro* (New York: Atheneum, 1974), p. 231.

[11]Sinnette, *Arthur Alfonso Schomburg*, p. 134.

[12]Ibid.

[13]Tibbets, *Ernestine Rose and the Origins of the Schomburg Center* (New York: New York Public Library, 1989), p. 22.

[14]Sinnette, *Arthur Alfonso Schomburg*, p. 136.

[15]"Report of the New York Public Library for 1926," *Bulletin of the New York Public Library*, 31 (4) (April 1927).

[16]Sinnette, *Arthur Alfonso Schomburg*, p. 99.

[17]*Dictionary Catalog of the Schomburg Collection of Negro Literature & History* (Boston, Massachusetts: G. K. Hall & Company, 1962), p. iv.

[18]Allen Kent, Harold Lancour, and Jay E. Daily, eds., *Encyclopedia of Library and Information Science* Vol. 26 (New York: Marcel Dekker, 1979), p. 356.

[19]Elinor Des Verney Sinnette, W. Paul Coates, and Thomas C. Battle, eds., *Black Bibliophiles and Collectors: Preservers of Black History* (Washington, D.C.: Howard University Press, 1990), p. 72.

[20]Ibid., p. 76.

[21]Maulana Karenga, *Kawaida Theory: An Introductory Outline* (Inglewood, CA: Kawaida Publications, 1980), p. 45.

[22]Schomburg Center for Research in Black Culture, *Jean Blackwell Hutson: An Appreciation* (New York: New York Public Library, 1984), p. 5.

[23]"Schomburg's Ailing Collection," *Ebony*, 22 (12) (October 1967): 56.

[24]Mary Lee Bundy and Frederick J. Stielow, eds., *Activism in American Librarianship, 1962–1973* (New York: Greenwood Press, 1987), p. 15.

[25]Sinnette, Coates, & Battle, *Black Bibliophiles*, p. 76.

[26]Stanton F. Biddle, "Partnership in Progress—The Schomburg Center for Research in Black Culture," *Crisis* (December 1978), p. 334.

[27]James A. Drayton, "The Schomburg Corporation," *Crisis* (February 1978), p. 69.

[28]Biddle, "Partnership in Progress—The Schomburg Center for Research in Black Culture," *Crisis* (December 1978), p. 334.

[29]Ibid., p. 335.

[30]Ibib., p. 336.

[31]Sinnette, Coates, & Battle, *Black Bibliophiles*, p. 79.

chapter 3

College, Community, and Librarianship: Women Librarians at the Western Land-Grant Colleges

Georgia M. Higley

When one realizes the opportunity of an agricultural college to influence life, life at the fountain head, youth, there is no place in the world more inspiring than such a library . . . The library ought to be a place that by its very spirit teaches the students harmonious relation to surroundings. Like everything else about the college, the library ought to realize that the young people attending it are learning to live and that it has a duty in teaching them this great lesson which can not be shirked.

—"Requisites of an Agricultural College Library,"
Ida Angeline Kidder

In many ways, the involvement of women in American librarianship has paralleled the western land-grant college movement, and there was a great deal of cross-influence between the two. Based on democratic, pluralistic, and utilitarian values that reached their height of influence in the middle of the 19th century, the land-grant colleges not only provided women with the opportunity for academic study and technical training (they were among the first coeducational institutions of higher learning in the country), but the opportunity for a significant professional career as well. The libraries of these nascent institutions, particualrly those in the western states, offered women librarians opportunities for professional development and advancement. Many of these women librarians were given the chance to influence the growth of both library and college.

This chapter explores the relationship between the western land-grant college movement and women in librarianship. By looking at the history of the movement and of the specific colleges during their formative years, and focusing in particualrly on the roles of different women library administrators during this period, it attempts a broader understanding of the implications of their work toward modern librarianship and American higher education.

THE LAND-GRANT COLLEGE MOVEMENT

The land-grant college movement was a product of two emerging forces of early 19th-century America: popularization of scientific education, and recognition of the importance of agriculture and industrialization for the country's development. More and more during this period, practical education was equated with technological expertise, particulary in the areas of agriculture and mechanics.

Since at least 1850, there has been popular support for governmental involvement in the provision of such education. In November 1851, an early plan for an agricultural university was published in the Illinois *Prairie Farmer*, and a convention at Granville, Illinois, that same year promoted the concept of specialized education for the agriculturalist and engineer:

> *Resolved*, That, as the representatives of the industrial classes, including all cultivators of the soil, artisans, mechanics, and merchants, we desire the same privileges and advantages for ourselves, our fellows, and our posterity, in each of our several pursuits and callings, as our professional brethren enjoy in theirs.[1]

Jonathan Baldwin Turner, a Yale-educated teacher at the Illinois College in Jacksonville, spoke for the movement in the February, 1852, *Prairie Farmer*, citing the need for an educational institution to "apply existing knowledge directly and efficiently to all practical pursuits and professions in life, and to extend the boundaries of our present knowledge in all possible practical directions."[2] He advocated what became known as the "Common Man's Bill of Rights," an idealistic expression of what later became the federal government's more pragmatic land-grant plan. It was characterized by a concern for:

1. Educational opportunity for all citizens;
2. Practical education for practical professions;
3. Knowledge gained through experimentation and research;
4. Research and education molded for regional needs; and
5. Community outreach.

The passage by Congress of the Morrill Act of 1862 (also called the Land-Grant College Act) was the first important legislation produced by the land-grant college movement; it signified a national commitment to democratic education by allocating federal monies (earned through the sale of public lands) for the specific purpose of supporting agricultural and mechanical education. Justin Morrill, the Congressional sponsor of the bill, declared his intention "to offer an opportunity in every state for a liberal and larger education to large numbers, not merely to those destined for sedentary professions, but to those much needing higher instruction for the world's business, for industrial pursuits and professions in life."[3] Other bills supporting land-grant colleges followed, including the Morrill Act of 1890. All bills supporting land-grant college development gave states the right to determine how best to establish a local institution:

> The general wants and local conditions were very different in the different States and for the best use of this fund there must be much variety allowed in the *details*, although all the colleges should be the same in spirit and essentially of the same grade, that is—*colleges*, in which science and not classics should be the leading idea.[4]

By 1893, all western states and territories beyond the Mississippi had established land-grant institutions tailored to the needs of their local communities. (*See* Appendix A.)

The land-grant colleges affected American education far in excess of the funds allocated for their support. In 1930, Eugene Davenport, Dean of the College of Agriculture of the University of Illinois, best expressed the continued legacy of the land-grant colleges:

> Perhaps the greatest single service rendered by the colleges in the early days was a sympathetic nursery for science and for the scientific spirit; that is, the inductive method of study. Sometimes I have spoken of these colleges as wet nurses for science when nobody else would harbor the foundling, and the language is hardly too strong. That such public-supported institutions are by nature public-service institutions gradually developed as logical corollary to the reason for their existence. The idea that research, education, even formal, is mainly for the public welfare in which the student, instead of being the end product of all educational effort, is a means to an end, gradually evolved as the logical, if not the inevitable consequence of publicly supported institutions of higher learning.[5]

To meet public needs, land-grant institutions developed curricula for subjects never before considered academic; often teachers had little or no professional training. The study of agriculture, the initial focus of the land-grant colleges, had no recognized science or body of literature. Likewise, the mechanical arts curriculum concentrated on practical training and lacked scientific research. Curricula were modified as funding and materials permitted; experimental stations addressed the specific problems of farmers and engineers in the surrounding locale. As the land-grant colleges developed in scope, specialization, and substance, they established themselves as community resources for scientific experimentation and technical expertise. Curricula developed in response to the particular needs of their region and state.

Coeducation at land-grant institutions originated in the West. In general, colleges "established early usually waited a long time for the admission of women; those established later were coeducational from the start or changed in the course after a few years."[6] Western colleges usually mirrored public sentiment by including women as instructors and students. That women took advantage of coeducational training opportunities is evident by the number of women who preferred coeducational schools over women's colleges: "Women in coeducation schools increased from 3,044, in 1875, to 19,959 in 1900 (a sixfold increase), whereas students at women's colleges increased only from 9,572 to 15,977."[7] In September 1862, two months after the Morrill Act became law, the Iowa Agricultural College (chartered in 1856) became the first land-grant college to enroll women from its inception, and others soon followed its example. As Edward Eddy pointed out, "It remained for the land-grant movement to give genuine acceptance to the notion that women could and should study on the same campus as men."[8]

Unlike many of the eastern land-grant colleges, western institutions were seldom formed from already existing institutions and programs; in several cases, the land-grant college represented the first institution of higher education in the state or territory. Often the vicitims of political squabbles and rivalry, many land-grant institutions were located in remote areas, with few amenties and shoestring budgets. Ethnic differences, religious controversy, and general impoverishment also affected the land-grant colleges.[9] However, despite their modest beginnings, land-grant colleges were imbued with the service, educational, and outreach ideals that were the foundation of the movement. Due to local conditions, the establishment of land-grant colleges was experimental; few models existed on which to base curricula, develop requirements, and recruit faculty.

Typically, financial restrictions, together with the problems of remote locations, poor facilities and undefined curricula, made it difficult for adminstrators of western land-grant colleges to attract qualified faculty and staff and develop programs. Frank S. Kedzie, Dean of Applied Science at Michigan State Agricultural College, gave a typical picture of early land-grant education:

> There was never anything comaprable in a State educational effort to the hardships endured by the students and faculty in those pioneer days. An early founded denominational college in the Middle West, such as Oberlin, had nothing on the Michigan State Agricultural College so far as hardships were concerned. Oberlin had the advantage of carrying forward the work with her students with a well-known and generally accepted classical curriculum. At Michigan State Agricultural College there was doubt from the beginning as to what studies should be offered, how long the student should remain under instruction and whether a degree should finally be granted him.[10]

It was not until the 20th century that the western land-grant colleges were able to address these issues.

LAND-GRANT COLLEGE LIBRARIES

Libraries of land-grant colleges mirrored institutional development, but evolved more slowly, limited by the lack of funding for collections and staff, the lack of qualified personnel to maximize available resources, and a lack of recognition within the university hierarchy. The degree to which college administrators included libraries in their initial land-grant curricula varied widely; some failed to recognize the need to establish a library until the book collection grew too large to be ignored, while others used the library as an early advertisement for the school.

For example, Hiram Hadley, President of New Mexico Agricultural College, publicized the library in an 1891 issue of the *Rio Grande Republican*, setting as a goal the quick acquisition of 20,000 volumes for the book collection.[11] In addition to the general library, each department at the college had technical libraries for classroom use, "calculated to increase the usefulness of the library by making it more accessible to the students while engaged in special lines of work."[12] The Board of Regents set annual appropriations for the library and requested donations of primary sources concerning the early history of the territory. The subsequent contributions became the nucleus of one of the library's most important special collections, the New Mexico Collection.

At the Agricultural College of Utah, the importance of the library to the new college is well-documented. The library is listed in early publicity as a "means of illustration" for the fields of instruction together with the experiment station, horticulture grounds, and workshops.[13] In March of 1890, months before the college opened, a benefit concert was held for the library.[14] With an initial appropriation of $1,500, the library began with 1,500 "carefully selected" volumes, a collection which, despite the fact that the college initially excluded the study of liberal arts from its curriculum, was made up of books of that were humanistic rather than scientific in content. From then on, financial support for the library was dependable, with yearly appropriations.

More typical was the University of Arkansas where the library is first mentioned in a resolution passed by the board of governors in 1872 stating the "reading room which had been opened in town and supplied with periodicals at considerable expense was so far from the university as to be of questionable benefit to the faculty and students."[15] This embryonic collection was housed within a single bookcase. Library appropriations were undependable at best at Arkansas; no appropriations are recorded from 1880 to 1895.

Initially, some student literary societies had better library collections than the land-grant colleges themselves. At the Oregon Agricultural College, for example, the first library associated with the college was a collection of 600 volumes

gathered by the Corvallis Library Association and given to the student Adel-
phian Literary Society in 1880. The society made the collection available for
use by students and faculty until it was officially transferred to the college, establishing the college library, which was managed by students until 1898.[16] The
recollections of one student librarian from the early 1890s proved the library
was not considered a priority of the university administration: "Along about
Christmas time somebody asked me what I was doing and I told them I was arranging the library. I think it was one of the faculty who asked me and his reply
was, 'Thunder, I didn't know we had any library.' "[17]

In his Plan for Industrial Education, Jonathan Turner specifically mentioned
the importance of building an industrial literature if reform education was to
succeed:

> I should have said, also, that a suitable industrial library should be at once pro-
> cured, did not all the world know such a thing to be possible, and that one of the
> first and most important duties of the professors of such institutions will be to
> begin to create, at this late heur [sic], a proper practical literature, and series of
> text books for the industrial classes.[18]

In Arthur Klein's 1930 *Survey of Land-Grant Colleges and Universities*,
Charles Harvey Brown, Director of the Iowa State University Library and author of the library section of the *Survey*, listed five functions basic to all land-
grant college libraries:

1. Assist in the instruction of all students by supplying reading material
   and adequate facilities;
2. Provide for and aid research through availability of source material;
3. Keep faculty current in developments in their field, particularly important in scientific disciplines;
4. Encourage general reading by faculty and students; and
5. Participate in extension services of the college and provide information to persons beyond the campus.[19]

These functions emphasize the importance land-grant librarians placed on research and extension service. In many western states, land-grant college libraries were the only sources for information on agriculture and mechanical
arts; thus, despite the paucity of their collections, they were a major resource
for the practical disciplines.

Funding for libraries was scarce until well into the twentieth century; on the
average, only campus dormitories were more poorly funded.[20] Financial restrictions, remote locations, and poor facilities made it difficult for western
land-grant institutions to attract qualified individuals as librarians. Recognition
of the importance of trained library professionals grew slowly at land-grant institutions. The first librarians were usually professors with part-time responsi-

bilities for the book collection or students working their way through school, and only as the college curriculum grew was recognition given to the need for a full-time staffperson to oversee library operations. Eventually, college administrators realized the necessity of having a librarian in charge of the library. Klein's 1930 survey affirmed the impact a librarian can have at land-grant institutions: "One dean, shortly after the reorganization of a library, stated that the greatest incentive to improvement in the instructional work in his college, and the marked progress in this work, were due to the influence of the librarian."[21] However, the degree of training and experience librarians brought to their positions varied widely.

Librarians at most land-grant institutions were not financially recompensed for their efforts, and salaries of librarians were usually much lower at these land-grant institutions than at other institutions. As a result, fewer librarians at land-grant colleges had professional training than at other academic institutions; this was particularly true before 1900, when both librarianship as an academic profession and land-grant college development were in their infancy. Even as late as 1927, more librarians at land-grant institutions did not have bachelors degrees than at other institutions (22.5% versus 12.3%); in nine of the 69 land-grant institutions surveyed, individuals were hired as librarians who had neither library training nor experience.[22] The land-grant institutions in the western United States were particularly vulnerable to this phenomena. But, however scarce the resources, libraries, like their institutions, had the ambitious agenda of giving practical expression to land-grant ideals. The western land-grant colleges found their best library employees from one of the chief populations to benefit from the land-grant movement: women.

WOMEN LIBRARIANS AT LAND-GRANT COLLEGES

Although initially considered a male profession, by 1910 more women were entering librarianship than men (*See* Table 3.1).[23] Librarianship offered women the opportunity to advance in a professional career, a rare possibility in the late nineteenth century, and the western land-grant institutions in particular offered them significant and challenging positions, if not pay. Of the 22 land-grant institutions west of the Mississippi, 15 are known to have had at least one woman responsible for the library prior to 1930. (*See* Appendix B.) It is unclear whether or not a woman served in the position of chief librarian in any of the other seven during this period; despite the existence of institutional histories for each of these colleges, identification of their librarians is difficult to determine (which is probably indicative of the status of the library on these campuses at this time). In any case, many women undoubtedly worked at some level in the libraries of all of the colleges.

All women librarians were involved to some degree in the issues of service, funding, library expansion, and collection development. Most were the first

Table 3.1.   Women in Librarianship, 1870–1930

Year	Number of Women	Percent of Profession
1870	43	20.0%
...		
1910	5,771	78.5
1920	13,337	88.3
1930	26,785	91.4

women adminsitrators on campus, and were certainly among the small minority of women in faculty positions. Each interpreted her role in promoting land-grant ideals differently, influenced by local conditions, her professional training, and personal motivation. While some viewed their position as custodial in nature, others considered themselves pioneers in college library development, managing successfully to advance their positions within the institution, the local community, and the state as well as affirming the role of the librarian in progressive education.

The First Women Librarians

It's difficult generalize about the first women librarians at the western land-grant colleges, because in each case the position of librarian depended on the particular institutional attitudes, personalities, and local conditions of the college. Most of the first librarians were already affiliated with the college in some way (either as alumni, donors, or faculty) before they became librarians; few were deliberately recruited from library schools or other land-grant colleges. As a group, their background and degree of library training varied greatly, as did the details of their specific positions. Although there are broad patterns to be discerned in their history—it seems clear, for instance, that library management skills were usually of secondary importance in the hiring of chief librarians— the nature of the subject makes it useful to consider some of the unique situations of individual librarians.

Grace Raymond Hebard served as librarian at the University of Wyoming from 1894 to 1919 in addition to her other duties as secretary of the Board of Trustees and professor of political economy. Hebard was a formidable political force on campus through her influence on the Board and was a vigorous advocate of women's rights, but she had no formal training in librarianship. Her early academic education was particularly suited to a land-grant college; in 1882, from the State University of Iowa, she received the first B.S. in civil engineering conferred upon a woman.[24] Her academic interests were wide-ranging: she passed the Iowa bar, earned a Ph.D. in political science, and became a noted, if controversial, Wyoming historian. Her longevity as librarian is attributed to her knowledge of campus politics, her success as a college administrator, and her natural affinity for management and public service.

At Kansas State Agricultural College, different professors served in the dual capacity of teacher and librarian from 1863 to 1894. Julia Pearce was the first librarian to have no teaching responsibilities; she was also the first woman to serve as director of the library, coinciding with the construction of the college's first library building. University records indicate she was an 1890 graduate of the college, initially employed as a stenographer at the President's Office before becoming assistant librarian in 1892. She did not receive any formal training until 1894—*after* she became librarian—when she was "allowed Leave of Absence for six weeks to attend a library school."[25] Despite her lack of experience in librarianship, she was given faculty rank, a status that was retained by her successors.

There is some confusion as to who was the first librarian at the Agricultural College of Utah. Several sources cite Sara Godwin Goodwin as the first librarian in 1890; others give Lettie C. Richman as the first librarian in 1892.[26] According to the school's catalog, Richman was an elocutionist instructor and librarian for the years 1892–1893, followed by Clare Kenyon in 1894–1895, also a teacher of elocution and a librarian; however, no records exist concerning their library activities. Goodwin was a member of the first faculty of the college, an instructor of music, and also served on the Board of Trustees of the college for the 1896–1897 academic year. Beginning in the fall of 1897, Goodwin resumed her teaching responsibilities and is listed in the college catalog as "Librarian and Instructor of Music." With Goodwin, a tradition began at the college. Although most of the presidents of the college were Mormon, the librarians were not. Goodwin was a member of the influential St. John's Episcopal Church, and was married to one of the wealthiest men in Logan. Little is known about Goodwin prior to her arrival in Logan, particularly regarding her educational background.[27] Her appointment as college librarian was apparently the result of her family's influence on campus and within the community.

At several western land-grant colleges, women were hired as librarians only to find that they had other duties assigned to them. Estelle Lutrell, hired in 1904 as librarian at the University of Arizona at Tucson, found she was also expected to teach English. However, despite the dual responsibilities given Lutrell, the university president was proud to announce in the 1904 annual report that "a trained librarian has been put in charge of the growing collection of books, the care of which has been too long imposed upon a man already overburdened with other duties."[28] The librarian taught literature in the Department of English until 1922 when teaching responsibilities were finally removed from the position. Lutrell received a B.A. from Canton University of Chicago in 1887 and a B.A. in literature from the University of Chicago in 1896. As a student she had worked as a library assistant (1894–1896) and as assistant librarian in the campus biology library (1897–1899) before accepting a position as cataloger at the John Crerar Library in Chicago (1900–1903). Thus, while having little formal schooling in librarianship, Lutrell had practical experience in library operations prior to her work at the University of Arizona.

Reprinted with permission from the Special Collections and Archives, Utah State University.

Librarian Sara Godwin Goodwin surveys the room from her post behind the circulation desk in the rear of the cramped library at Utah Agriculture College.

Charlotte Baker became a librarian through circumstance rather than by design. In January 1890, she graduated from the New York State Normal College for teachers at Albany, but soon after suffered the first of a series of tuberculosis attacks.[29] While recuperating in Colorado, she studied at Colorado Agricultural College, intending to become a high school math teacher; however, as she wrote, "during that winter [1893] I had an opportunity to teach and broke down again. Then I knew I could never earn my living in an occupation that required constant use of my voice."[30] The following fall, she entered the training class of the Denver Public Library under the guidance of the dynamic John Cotton Dana and remained at the library until the summer of 1900, working as a cataloger in addition to taking teacher training courses in literature. In 1899 the president of New Mexico College at Messila Park (three miles from Las Cruces in a Spanish-American community with few amenities), Frederick W. Saunders, asked Katharine Sharp, Dean of the School for Library Economy at the University of Illinois, to recommend an individual who could manage the college library. Sharp recommended Charlotte Baker for the position who Saunders subsequently recruited. Although Baker's primary responsibilities were for the general library, she also taught English literature for the college. Baker's own description illustrates the range of duties at the college:

> As librarian I was supposed to manage the library and do anything else that seemed useful. I rang the bell for the change of classes, but forgot so often that that work was turned over to a student. Then I sold stationery for the community, ran a local mail distributing center, taught the English for the sub-freshmen, helped stage college entertainments, all for the munificent sum of fifty dollars a month. Gradually my salary was increased to seventy-five dollars.[31]

In 1906, Baker was recruited by another land-grant college, Colorado Agricultural College.

Some western land-grant colleges did not hire trained librarians until well into the twentieth century. Even when library collections grew to the point that a full-time librarian was needed to systematically monitor and develop the collections, the individual hired for the position usually had no experience managing library resources; alumni, local residents, or non-library staff were often hired instead of an educated professional. The first women librarians at these colleges often inherited small wharehouses of randomly collected materials, not libraries developed to support curricula. Like the institutions themselves, librarians were learning on the job, setting up services, managing acquisitions, and developing collections with few guidelines on which to base their decisions.

With few exceptions, most libraries reached a point after which a systematic approach to library management was required; the simple custodial abilities of passive library managers were no longer sufficient for growing curricula. A typical condition of the land-grant college library was given by New Mexico College President Saunders: "The library has been allowed to run down for years, until now it is in deplorable condition, and the amount of work required to set it right is so great, that it will require a good deal of time."[32] Such desperate situations were generally when individuals with library training and experience were hired. Recognition of this varied from college to college, usually depending on the vision of the college president, the degree and variety of collection growth, the competence of current library staff, and the demand for library services by faculty and students. Although unwilling or unable to offer adequate salaries, college administrators hoped to raise the level of professionalism of their library staff. Women librarians, either graduates of the various recently established library schools or experienced professionals, offered western land-grant administrators the necessary abilities at cost-effective salaries.

Library Expansion—Budget, Buildings, and Collections

As at all land-grant colleges, library expansion was erratic in the West. Inadequate collections, services and staffing are attributable to the inability of institutions to allocate a sufficient proportion of available funds for library operations.[33] Librarians at the land-grant colleges battled university administration, faculty, Boards of Trustees, and state legislatures for budget, space, and staff increases; although most college presidents had grandiose intentions of making the library a showplace of the college, few were willing to expend the funds necessary to make this dream a reality until well into the twentieth century. The ability to stretch resources was a necessary skill.

Rapport with college administrators was another important resource. Although few college adminstrators knew anything about library management, many retained control of policy and decision making responsibilities. As late as

1920, a large percentage of land-grant libraries reported to the college president, not to the librarian. Therefore, the ability to work well with adminstrators and faculty was a vital element in successful library management. Librarians utilized a variety of techniques to bring library issues of space and allocations to the attention of college governing bodies. At New Mexico College, Charlotte Baker relied on personal charisma and demonstration to persuade the college president to accede to her requests. One story adapted from correspondence between Baker and her successor, Lucy Lewis, illustrates Baker's relationship with the university president—and her success in accomplishing her goals:

> The physical plan of the Library did not allow for an opening so that one could go directly from behind the counter into the reading room. It was necessary to go outside into the hall through one door and then enter the reading room through another. Miss Baker had requested that President Luther Foster have a "hole" made for her to get out, but he refused, saying the counter was of such beautiful wood it should not be cut. However, the President entered the Library one day in time to see Miss Baker vault over the counter into the main part of the room. He expostulated with Miss Baker, saying her behavior was undignified, but she told him she was too busy to go through the hall. Each succeeding time the President entered the Library, he found the persistent Miss Baker flying over the counter. Subsequently, the hole was cut.[34]

Lewis was also successful. Despite initial reservations regarding her management inexperience,[35] college administrators supported Lucy Lewis, a 1906 graduate of the University of Illinois Library School. In a letter to Katharine Sharp, Lewis described the college's Library Committee which was responsible for budget and policies of the library: "I believe the three best men in the institution for the position, are on that Comm. At least as far as I can now judge. They give me full sway in most respects, but stand ready 'to back me up' if I need it."[36]

As late as the 1920s, complaints about poor resources were recorded at western land-grant colleges. Despite a study commissioned by state legislators which documented the poor conditions of the library in 1921, the University of Wyoming library faced budgetary *decreases*. Margery Bedinger,[37] hired by New Mexico College in 1926 to evaluate and reclassify all library holdings,[38] also found fiscal limitations. The only obstacle to Bedinger's complete overhaul of the library was lack of money:

> We are in sore need of a new library building and until we get this, the service the library gives can never be really satisfactory. We haven't proper means of shelving our periodicals or government documents. The arrangement of the library is necessarily confused because of our lack of space. We have no proper arrangement for the care of current magazines. Our work room is unheated in the winter, exceedingly hot in summer, and too far from the main desk and the catalog. There are no facilities for staff. The reading rooms are all together too small. One is so situated that it cannot be adequately supervised and the other is necessarily

somewhat noisy because it is so small and contains the delivery desk. When we get all of the magazines in the attic brought down and bound, I do not know where we can put them. Much of our equipment is inadequate and of the wrong kind. The staff is too small and there is no full time worker, and no trained worker except the Librarian. . . . Another crying need is for books. The library is fairly rich in sets of periodicals and government and state publications, but we are weak in books, especially modern up-to-date editions.

It is very unfortunate that there is so little money, because by spending a comparatively small sum now, not only time and effort, but also a larger sum of money would be saved in the future.[39]

As late as 1920, the total budget for the land-grant libraries averaged only $16,429, with colleges reporting as much as $40,000 and as little as $1,500 for their annual budget.[40] For most land-grant colleges, 1920 was a milestone after which few libraries reported no increases; library expenditures grew markedly during the 1920s, with a great increase in a relatively short amount of time (increases of double, triple, even five times the 1920 year are on record by 1930).[41]

Salaries at western land-grant colleges were equally inadequate and much lower than at other colleges. The proportion of monies allocated to libraries was small; the amount for salaries was even less. "In 1876 a Midwestern agricultural college [Iowa State College] fixed the librarian's salary at two hundred dollars per year. The previous rate of compensation had been increased from seven to nine cents per hour."[42] Women librarians were particularly vulnerable to the poor salaries. By 1900 salaries had increased, but still varied widely from college to college. Charlotte Baker was a newly hired librarian at New Mexico College for $600 a year. In 1903 seven-year veteran Sara Goodwin of Utah was making $900, only $100 less than her successor, Elizabeth Church Smith would earn. Estelle Lutrell was hired by the University of Arizona at the "high" salary of $1,000 in 1904. Despite satisfaction in her position as librarian at New Mexico College, Lucy Lewis was often frustrated by the administration's lack of financial commitment to the position of librarian. In a 1908 letter to Frances Simpson of the University of Illinois Library School, Lewis asks for "any statistics which will show the salaries paid librarians in similar positions" that she could present to the Board of Regents.[43] In 1912 William H. Powers, librarian of the South Dakota State College of Agriculture, considered a salary of $800 to $1,000 adequate to "secure a person altogether competent to manage a library in an agricultural college of 600 students."[44] As late as 1920, librarian salaries were still as low as $1,000 per year; few made a "high" salary of $3,500.[45]

Space restrictions were a chronic problem for librarians. Despite the paucity of library expenditures, collection growth and increased demand for services by faculty and students far outstripped the space allocated by the college. Many libraries grew by encroachment, slowly expanding into single rooms then whole buildings. Ultimately university administrators and state legislators were persuaded of the need for a new, separate library building; state legislators were often particularly hard to convince, and were "reluctant to grant funds for the construction of a building 'just for storing books.'"[46] By 1930 all land-grant colleges in the West had embarked on at least one library building project. The presence of a building expressly designed for library collections and services is a physcial representation of the success of the librarian in building collections, integrating the library into the campus curriculum, and establishing public services which increased use of the library. For land-grant colleges in particular, construction meant that the college was successful in promoting the college to state legislators who controlled the purse strings.

A successful library building project was the culmination of many librarians' careers at land-grant colleges. Beginning with a local resident's donation of 300 volumes in the 1880s, the University of Wyoming library relied on the growth of departmental libraries to avoid overcrowding. By 1904, the library, consisting of 17,000 "general use" books and government documents, occupied the main floor of the single building on campus. As early as 1911, despite the defeat for special appropriations funding for library construction, librarian Grace Raymond Hebard was planning requirements for a fireproof library to be submitted to the architect and lobbying university officials and influential friends to pressure state legislators. In 1921, space in the library was so limited that a proposed decrease in the University of Wyoming's share of oil revenues, a major source for the university's funding, aroused strong opposition. During a debate of the House floor, State Representative Richard C. May "told of the University's needs and of what he termed 'deplorable' conditions existing at the University. He said that in the library where students study, these students are forced to stand up while studying and must hold their hots [sic] and coats in their hands."[47] To voice their opposition, the students and university president hired a special train to take them to Cheyenne for a demonstration in the House Chambers; their effort so impressed legislators that appropriations included funds for a new library, which eventually opened in 1923.[48]

At the University of Arizona, Lutrell's first project upon arriving in the fall of 1904 was to prepare for the December move into the library's new location. In 1891 the library had begun as a single shelf of agricultural books in the office of the Dean of the School of Agriculture; by 1900 it had grown to 6,000 volumes. In 1901 the legislature appropriated $25,000 for construction of a multi-use building to house the library, the territorial museum, the president's office, and several classrooms.[49] Although the library increased its space by moving, conditions were still cramped. The need to store donations and federal depository materials aggravated the space problems.

After World War I, interest in college education increased. Between 1915 and 1920, registration at the University of Arizona doubled and library use increased to the point that one student suggested erecting posts in the aisles for readers to lean on when seats were unavailable.[50] In 1919 a legislative committee visited the campus and in 1922 recommended the addition of a new library:

The only building program desired or requested by the Board of Regents, was the construction of a new Library building, the need of which is very apparent to even the prejudiced observer. The University has a very good working library, housed in quarters inadequate to properly shelve the books and wholly inadequate to afford absolute requirements for study. It is submitted that the most important office a university may exercise, is the development in its students of independent initiative in reading and investigation, which under existing conditions, may be said to be almost impossible at the University of Arizona. For this program, the Board of Regents requested the sum of Eighty Thousand ($80,000).[51]

In the fall of 1922, the new College President, Cloyd Heck Marvin, considered the funding of a *new* library building a priority (instead of remodelling the existing location). Lutrell's optimism in the continued growth of the library is evident in the proposed library's specifications; at a time when the existing library contained slightly over 50,000 volumes, the new building was intended to have a projected stack capacity of 260,000 volumes, with an area of 500,000 cubic feet (63,230 gross square feet). Separate reading rooms were planned for reserved books, "special" reading, and seminars, including an additional "open air" reading room.[52] Lutrell's priority concerns for the new building were far-sighted and practical: fire-proof stacks, an enlarged reading room able to seat 20 percent of the student body, soundproofing, lighting, and corridor widths.[53] Determined to build one of the best library buildings in the country despite the fact that a local architect, inexperienced in library construction, was chosen for the project, Lutrell was recognized for her efforts, as the student yearbook documents:

> To Estelle Lutrell we dedicate the 1924 Desert. Her dream of a greater library for the State University has been realized, realized because she never forgot what she was striving for, never forgot the library of the future while she was working in the library of the present. The first spade full of earth has been turned for that new building, the foundation has been laid, and Arizona congratulates Miss Lutrell on the success that has come through her efforts.[54]

The new library was opened in September 1925, but was not completed until May 1927, when the furnishings arrived; the total cost was $450,000. Reaction to the new building was positive:

> It embodied many decorative and esthetic features which were prompted by the desire of making the library worthy of its importance in campus activities. . . . When expressing their appreciation of the [main reading] room in its entirety the students wrote, "We like this room because it inspires us to aim higher, to dream that all our surroundings may have charm, beauty, and loveliness . . . There has been little of this at our University."[55]

The new building was the physical expression of the importance of the library in land-grant education and Lutrell's farsighted planning; no additions to the library were necessary until 1951. Appropriations, collections, staffing, and salaries for library staff steadily increased after this date.

In contrast to its neighbor, New Mexico College was initially hampered by poor funding, and library construction was meager. In 1906, newly hired librarian Lucy Lewis thought the 25,000 volume collection "very good," but complained of space allocations: "I have the main library consisting of Loan Dept., Reference Dept., Reading room, work room stack room, and conversation room, *all in one room*—not more than half as large as the Library School room. . . . This room is on one Corner of the main building."[56] Lewis also lobbied for more space for the library, and in March 1910 the collection was relocated to larger quarters. A 1,500 volume reference collection was housed in one room, with additional rooms for a reading room, stack room, work room, and office. These quarters were spacious enough to allow some volumes in departmental libraries to become part of the general collection.[57]

By 1916, space was again a problem and technical books were removed from the general collection. In March 1927, the New Mexico legislature appropriated $75,000 for the construction of two buildings, including a library. The Board of Regents directed "That a two story building shall be constructed with classrooms and offices on the ground floor, and that the stack room shall be so built that it may be enlarged in the future without in any way affecting the main part of the library building."[58] In October 1928, the library was relocated to its new quarters.

At the Colorado Agricultural College, the library Charlotte Baker inherited from Joseph Daniels in 1910 was expanding, having tripled in size between 1901 and 1910 to 35,000 volumes. She also inherited three problems from her predecessor: poor funding, inadequate space, and poor location. During her 26 years as librarian, the library was relocated several times to accommodate its growth, at varying times being housed in a barn, a basement, and in classrooms before a library building finally was constructed.[59] Baker was involved in two library relocations and one complete planning and construction of a new building. That the library was popular with the students despite its poor physical condition is evident by its overcrowding: Although student enrollment for the academic year 1917–1918 decreased 25%, library attendance statistics, tallied during evening library use, increased 54%. Baker consistently lobbied for improved locations for the library, often using humor and sarcasm to support her position:

> Taking the health bulletin issued by the Kentucky Department of Education as a basis, the seating capacity of the periodical room should be seventeen. It is twenty-three. Often we have thirty students there. The hygienic capacity of the reference room is twenty-five. It seats thirty. We often have forty people there. There is a thermometer in each room, but when conditions are very bad, we are often too busy to notice until we feel limp from bad air.[60]

In 1927 a new library was built, the first designed solely for library purposes. After the move to the new building, library staff increased from two to eight. The new facilities increased the already heavy use of the library: In 1932–1933, over 93,000 books circulated (more than the total number of books contained in the library at the time), an average of 425 books per borrower. A use count of 1,710 was recorded for a single day in 1934.[61] By the time Charlotte Baker retired as librarian emerita in 1936, the library collection had more than doubled from 35,000 to 83,000 volumes.

Like New Mexico College, the Utah Agricultural College library began in a single room in a wing of the College Building in 1891, described as a "well equipped section of the college work [sic] and free to college students."[62] Available library resources included the book and document collections, a reading room with periodicals, and the libraries of several professors; the English professor's collection was large enough to warrant the designation departmental library. Despite appropriations to the library, accessions were considered insufficient to meet the requirements of the curriculum. In her annual report of 1899, librarian Sara Goodwin wrote a persuasive appeal for more funding and building space for the library, arguing the "library is a potent factor in the development of an institution of higher learning."[63] In 1901 the library and reading room moved to a new building that, while alleviating the space problem, was inadequate until the necessary shelving, furniture, and card catalog were installed. By early 1903 the library collection and activities had increased to the point that a full-time cataloger was hired; no cataloging had been done since November 1900. The cataloger, Elizabeth Church Smith, was a graduate of the University of Wisconsin Library School in 1896 and had worked in the library of the Wisconsin Historical Society.[64] Smith succeeded Goodwin as librarian in 1903 and continued the annual criticism of slow collection growth and inadequate appropriations.

The library relied on donations to assist in collection building. In 1926 the Brigham Young College[65] library was transferred to the college, adding 15,000 volumes to the collection. The Alumni Association initiated a library endowment fund drive of $100,000 in 1927, which, although well-intentioned, never realized its goal. Longer-lasting was a donation from the class of 1912 for the purchase of books and bound periodicals.[66] In 1929 the state legislature appropriated $175,000 for construction of a new library building. Librarian Hattie Smith was involved in the planning of the library, but was unable to oversee its immediate reorganization due to illness. In order to structure the best possible library in these new conditions, the president of the college invited Charles Harvey Brown of Iowa State College to survey the library collections, organization, and management and recommend improvements. The new library, constructed with Brown's recommendations in mind, was completed in 1930.

Most western land-grant colleges relied on donations and the availability of government documents to supplement appropriations for purchases. Many land-

Reprinted with permission from the Special Collections and Archives, Utah State University.

Sara Godwin Goodwin stands among the bookshelves at the Utah Agriculture College library.

grant college libraries purchased periodicals and technical literature that augmented coursework and received donations of humanistic literature;[67] funding limitations necessitated careful selection. Demand for library materials grew and the one-person, single room library of the late nineteenth century became inadequate–collections expanded and differentiated, students and faculty became more aware of library resources, library staff grew in experience, professionalism, and sheer numbers, and librarians became administrators and architects of programs and services.

Services to Campus and Community

In 1920, the services and collection of land-grant libraries were surveyed by Charlotte Baker and Lucy Lewis. As their *Survey of State Agricultural College and Experiment Station Libraries* documents, land-grant libraries attempted to do much with the few resources they were allocated. Most libraries operated with less than five staff, although over half were open in the evening, charged no fees, and provided reference service to citizens, in addition to students and faculty. At 21 of the 50 institutions responding, libraries also loaned material to rural readers, substituting for state libraries and boards of education.[68]

At Utah Agricultural College, Sara Goodwin was an early proponent of library public services. Despite her lack of professional training or prior experience in librarianship, Goodwin was very conscious of the qualities of good public service. As early as 1899, the "library and reading room [were] open to the students and to the general public every college day throughout the year." According to the library rules of this period, students were allowed to "retain" one book at a time for 14 days.[69]

As early as 1904, Wyoming's Grace Raymond Hebard instituted open stacks in the library, an innovation not available at most western land-grant colleges until the 1910s. Her justification for open stacks provides a good picture of the library in the early 1900s and Hebard's personal philosophy of public service:

> The Dewey Decimal System is used for the card catalogue. In addition to this, an author's catalogue has just been completed and a subject catalogue commenced. Each book, and each shelf, is open to the students. Since the inauguration of the open shelf system, by which the student may personally select books, a more extended use of the books has been noticed. If a student has only a few moments to 'browse' in the Library, he is much more inclined to go to the shelves and take a volume and enjoy himself than if he were obliged to have others wait upon him. Books will, however, mysteriously disappear and they as mysteriously return. One book, 'How to Get Strong,' was gone three years, when it suddenly appeared, no one knows when or how, but the presumption is that it accomplished its purpose without assistance.[70]

Charlotte Baker likewise instituted a policy of open stacks and circulation of non-reference materials to students while at New Mexico College.

Many colleges offered classes in bibliographic instruction. At Colorado Agricultural College, "classes in library handicraft as well as apprenticeship classes to train librarians" had been available since 1902.[71] Elizabeth Church Smith offered the Utah Agricultural College's first course in "Library Work" in 1904, "to familiarize the student with the library and to teach one how to obtain information quickly." The course was required of freshmen in the general science course and offered one hour per week for a year.[72] By 1914, library classes had expanded, with an individual class covering "General Reference" and a more advanced course in "Bibliography," offered alternating semesters. Elizabeth Smith and her assistant, Hattie Smith, taught the classes. By 1920 only six land-grant college libraries in the United States did not have at least one lecture in library education.[73]

Students responded to outreach service initiated by librarians with humor, support, and criticism. Charlotte Baker's rapport with students was evident when New Mexico College students exhibited her as a "trained librarian" on College Day: "If I only could have had a string tied to my belt and a hand organ to dance to, the illusion would have been complete."[74] By 1920, the library's first endowment fund was created by the Class of 1920, designated for book purchases. At Utah Agricultural College, articles about the library covering services, procedures, recent acquisitions, recommended reading, and humor began to appear in the student newspaper, *Student Life*, after 1905.[75] In 1913, students were demanding more services, particularly evening hours for the library (which were not effected until 1918), and applauding the efforts of the library to fill in gaps in the collection. Substantial gifts to the library were front page news.

Libraries also participated in extension services, augmenting the services the college provided to the surrounding rural communities. With the recognition of extension service in 1914 as part of the college mission, outreach services became increasingly important. In a 1904 publication of the Utah Farmer's Institute, Elizabeth Smith wrote an article on "Traveling Libraries" to promote their establishment as a state institution.[76] Charlotte Baker also wrote library promotion publications (*Books as Tools for Children, Books for the Farmer*, and *Books for the Farmer's Wife*), practical literature designed for citizens beyond the college campus. In addition to her travels and correspondence with librarians throughout Colorado, Baker loaned library materials to small schools and libraries, initiating a library service now commonplace in the state.

During World War I, many land-grant colleges served as training camps for soldiers, and library staff aided the war effort by sponsoring book drives and volunteering to assist at training and hospital camps throughout the country. The University of Arizona served as a training camp for soldiers; beginning in the summer of 1918, library hours were increased at most campuses to allow soldiers access to the library during off duty hours. Hattie Smith of Utah and Floy French of New Mexico organized book drives at their respective colleges to gather books to send to soldiers recuperating in hospitals. Estelle Lutrell was appointed by the American Library Association as State Agent for Arizona to collect books for soldiers at the temporary military stations in the state. At this same time, the Food Conservation Division appointed her Library Publicity Director for the state.

Several librarians were active in state library associations, serving as officers and coordinating public relations. Charlotte Baker was active in the American Library Association's Agricultural Libraries Section and collaborated with Lucy Lewis of Oregon Agricultural College to survey land-grant college libraries. Estelle Lutrell promoted librarianship at the local level as one of the organizers of the Arizona Library Association, serving as secretary from 1926 to 1930 and as president in 1931. Like Baker and Lutrell, Margery Bedinger's energy also extended beyond the campus. Five months after her arrival at Las Cruces in 1926, she was elected secretary of the newly formed New Mexico Library Association.[77] The N.M.L.A. began a publicity campaign to promote libraries in the state, which Bedinger felt would benefit the college as well.

Publicity for the library took many forms. Bedinger promoted the college library by inundating the campus and community with information: Articles about the library were sent to the state's newspapers, new books at the library were listed in a fortnightly publication by the Extension Service, a monthly book talk was given on the college radio station, and talks with county agents of the college Extension Service promoted the need for libraries throughout the state.[78] She also established cooperative relations with the librarians at the University of New Mexico in Albuquerque and at the nearby University of Texas at El Paso. Likewise, at the University of Arizona, Lutrell advertised library events. In 1928 the library began publishing the *Library Roadrunner*, which promoted new services and books available to students: the opening of a new scientific magazine room, reviews of titles received through the rental collection, a one-time "amnesty box" to encourage return of library materials, and various subject bibliographies of popular fiction.[79]

Unlike most of her peers in western land-grant colleges, Baker was particularly interested in promoting extension services to librarians in the region, not just the general community. Beginning in 1912 until World War I, the library participated in extension services by offering "package libraries," which circulated throughout Colorado as well as in neighboring states. Baker reorganized the Colorado Library Association, serving as its president 1912–1913 and initiating a library news bulletin, *The Occasional Leaflet* (later *Colorado Libraries*). In 1913 she received an honorary appointment to the State Library Commission on which she served as secretary 1913–1919. As a member of this commission she visited small libraries throughout the state and learned few of the librarians knew what their duties and responsibilities were.[80] To correct this deficiency, in 1918 she established the first summer training program in the region specifically designed for rural librarians (initially financed with her own funds). Although it was primarily intended for librarians working in small Colorado libraries, by 1920 students came from all over the country. The school was offered until 1932, at which time the University of Denver, financed with a Carnegie grant, established a library school. In 1940 she received the first "Distinguished Service Award" of the Colorado Library Association in recognition of her efforts in developing the profession in the state.

Like Charlotte Baker in Colorado, Dorothy Peters at New Mexico College (1924–1926) assisted rural school libraries in the surrounding county by organizing and arranging their materials. The library also began a policy of loaning sets of books to these rural libraries, extending the library into the immediate community.[81] Estelle Lutrell combined scholarly and social activities to extend library service. She chartered the university's Collegiate Club, which became the local chapter of the American Association of University Women. Like Grace Raymond Hebard, Lutrell's scholarly and cultural interests were wide-ranging; she published extensively on Arizona history and compiled bibliographies on numerous subjects. In the 1930s she directed the historical records survey in Arizona for the WPA and, just prior to her death in 1950, compiled a history of territorial newspapers.

Another important service was to develop collections appropriate for college and community needs. As early as 1908, Elizabeth Church Smith cited the need for current technical and scientific information as well as "other classes of books that the library must provide for the general reading and the preparation of the student for life and citizenship."[82] At Utah Agricultural College, the extension station library agreed to allow all students and faculty free access to its periodicals. The librarian also emphasized current events and subscribed to a large number of periodicals and newspapers from around the country. At Colorado Agricultural College, Baker continued the collection development initiated by her predecessor by acquiring scientific and technical publications and expanding access to the federal documents depository collection. Under her administration, book budget allocations were made to departments to ensure acquisition of primary teaching materials. Faculty were encouraged to assist in developing library collections. The University of Arizona library achieved recognition throughout the state for its collections of chemistry periodicals, Arizoniana, and Native American materials. Its collection of southwestern United States history, considered one of the most comprehensive in the country, dates from Lutrell's administration. Material collected during this early period of college library history formed the nucleus of collections which later became recognized strengths of the college.

Personal Motivation and Natural Ability

Despite the poor salary, ambiguous job descriptions, and hardship conditions, women librarians found western land-grant colleges places where personal ability, not gender, determined position and stature in the community. Many were required to build the a library from its foundations, while others had to step in and revitalize libraries which had suffered from years of mere custodial management. Whatever the specific situations required, they also provided tremendous opportunities. As Lucy Lewis learned at Las Cruces, where she had intended to stay only a short time, the "possibilities for great things" were irresistible; like other women given the opportunity for leadership, she relished the chance to participate in the land-grant experiment.

The successful women at land-grant colleges subscribed to land-grant college ideals and were able to communicate that idealism to their staff. Charlotte Baker represented the views of many women librarians in her belief in the importance of promoting libraries to agricultural students: "I believe in this work with the School of Agriculture boys, for a love of reading and the power of making books a working tool are both a personal pleasure and a business asset, but it takes the time and nervous energy of the librarian."[83] That the students recognized and responded to her interest is apparent in their giving her the title of "Ma" Baker. Perhaps the best testimonial to a woman librarian's accomplishments is that given Charlotte Baker by her successor, James G. Hodgson:

> I suppose a successor to as colorful a person as Miss Baker is about the only one who can sincerely judge the results of her work. For a person with but very little

technical training, she had a better knowledge of library science and a better spirit of librarianship than most of those who have had long formal training. The technical organization which she developed was excellent. The staff she gathered about her were not only particularly capable but were imbued with the idea that librarianship at its best is a service. She had a very broad conception of the part that a library must play in an educational institution, and did all she could to make it meet that need. The library which she helped to plan and build in 1927 was at that time an outstanding library building for the Rocky Mountain region. The only faults about it are those which the architect insisted on putting in over Miss Baker's strenuous objections.

I think we can say without any qualifications whatever that Miss Baker was the best college library administrator of her time in the Rocky Mountains. She did not, however, think only of her own library. But she gave much of her time and strength, limited though it was, for the advancement of other libraries of the State.[84]

IDA KIDDER: A REPRESENTATIVE WESTERN LAND-GRANT LIBRARIAN

There is probably no woman librarian from this early period of the western land-grant colleges who is better representative of her profession than Ida Angeline Kidder. A 51-year-old widow entering librarianship as a second career, she was hired as the first professional librarian at Oregon Agricultural College, Corvallis, where she was faced with the challenges common to land-grant college libraries: collection development, provision of services both on campus and to the extended community, and the design and construction of a new library building. Her success at responding to these challenges, her dedication to service, and her devotion to the students was of great importance and influence to the library, the college, and the community.

Kidder studied at the University of Illinois Library School under Katherine Sharp, where she earned her B.L.S. in 1906.[85] From there she went on to work at the Washington State Library in Olympia as organizer of state documents until 1907, and then as State Organizer for the Oregon State Library Commission in Salem from 1907 to 1908, where she participated in the travelling libraries programs and speaking at teachers' institutes. It was in 1908 that William J. Kerr, the new university president of the Oregon Agricultural College, hired her to manage the college's expanding, haphazardly collected library.

Although Kidder had worked in state libraries prior to coming to Corvallis, she was not familiar with the particular needs of land-grant institutions. In addition to serving the faculty and students on the campus, the library was required to support extension station research. The dilemma of meeting the sometimes contradictory needs of the agricultural researchers and educators was one of Kidder's first challenges:

It seems to me that the problem of administering the college and the experiment station library, whether separately or combined, must always present a number of almost insurmountable difficulties; men engaged in research demand all material for their work closely and immediately at hand, instructional work requires that all material on the campus shall be easily accessible to its use. To meet these so often conflicting demands without extravagant duplication requires of the librarian a broad-minded impartiality of judgement.[86]

Nevertheless, Kidder tried her best to serve researchers and students alike, enlisting the aid of Claribel Barnett, Librarian of the U.S. Department of Agriculture, and writing to her alma mater in Illinois for advice.

Kidder emphasized service, developing a philosophy of agricultural education that echoed the idealism of J. B. Turner of the 1850s. In 1909 she began a "Library Practice" course required of all freshmen. Kidder always taught the course since she "considered it one of the most important features of the work of the library."[87] Her commitment to cultural reading within the Library Practice course is evident in her essay, "Requisites of an Agricultural College Library":

In the classes for teaching the freshmen the use of the library, emphasis is put upon the value of that phase of education which embraces cultural study and an effort is made to interest the students in the news of the day, the progress of the world and in such occurrences [sic] of college life as will further their cultural education."[88]

She felt that the agriculture and industrial arts students needed to develop a habit of lifelong learning, what she called "culture reading," continuing beyond the four years they spent in college: "No librarian can be in a college where technical courses predominate without feeling deeply her responsibility toward the students in regard to their general culture."[89] For Kidder the library had the same teaching mission as the classroom.

Kidder fostered the already strong interest of the students in the library by involving herself with all aspects of student life. To promote lifelong learning, Kidder gave talks on literature, poetry, and ethics, and sponsored frequent literary discussions and poetry readings in the library and at her home in the women's dormitory on campus. As a part of the university's extension services, she initiated a lecture series on the library for farmers, library courses for advanced training of secretaries, and talks to farm groups. Kidder spoke throughout the Northwest on a variety of topics, including libraries and culture reading, and discussed subjects of interest to her listeners while promoting the agricultural college and the library; she considered it a privilege to talk to "real folks."[90]

That students responded to her warmth is evident by the appellation she soon earned: Mother Kidder. The student newspaper, *Barometer*, and student yearbooks, the *Orange* and the *Beaver*, contain numerous references to the library in general and Ida Kidder in particular. The 1919 Women's section of the

Reprinted with permission of the Oregon State University Archives.

Ida Kidder, seated behind her desk at Oregon Agricultural College, was considered one of the most beloved administrators on campus by students.

Beaver was dedicated to her: "We dedicate our section to the most universally loved woman on the campus, 'Mother' Kidder. An inspiring teacher and the best of friends."[91]

Student use of the library increased to the point that the *Barometer* protested the occasional closing of the library for the teaching of the Library Practice class.[92] In the fall of 1909, despite the initial lack of staff, Kidder increased library hours to include evenings and weekends, and additional reading rooms outside the administrative building currently housing the library were opened. Students, library staff, and university administrators agreed that a new library building was a priority funding issue, and finally, in 1917, the state legislature appropriated $158,000 for the construction of one designed according to Kidder's specifications. Despite the shortages and inflationary prices brought on by World War I, the 57,000 square foot building was constructed at projected budget cost and was ready for occupancy in November 1918.

During the construction of the library in the summer of 1918, Oregon Agricultural College, like many other land-grant institutions, became a temporary army installation. Ida Kidder participated in the war effort in two ways: She opened the library to soldiers stationed at the campus, and she volunteered her services during the summer of 1918 to the Army as part of the American Library Association's Library War Services program. The latter led to her position as Hospital Librarian at Camp Lewis, Washington. While at Camp Lewis, Kidder left Lucy Lewis, assistant librarian, responsible for the library with the instructions: "I should not have questioned your judgment for a moment. You know that I have this business principle, no one should be held responsible who is not given authority. 'It can't be did' [sic] successfully. Just do exactly as you would in your very own library for which you were absolutely responsible."[93]

Despite her unwillingness to follow the bureaucratic procedures prescribed by the camp supervisor, the military appreciated her work. As she confidentially related in a letter to Lucy Lewis in a rare letter of self-congratulation, the colonel in charge of the camp recognized her efforts in the hospital:

> Now, here is something, I would prefer you did not repeat. Yesterday he told me that he had been wathing [sic] my work and was greatly pleased, that it was best work being done for the hospital or ever had been done. I blushed scarlet I know and the tears rushed to my eyes, for quite a few people had acted as if my work was just tolerated because the authorities permitted me about.[94]

By the time she returned to Corvallis at the end of the summer, Ida Kidder had won the respect and affection of the soldiers at Camp Lewis. Like the students at the college, the soldiers recuperating at the camp addressed her as "Mother Kidder." One story characterizes her fame: "Some of them arranged a wager among themselves that she was so well known that a letter addressed to her only, 'Mother Kidder, Oregon'," would reach her. When she reached Corvallis, it was there waiting for her.[95]

Upon her return to Corvallis in September, Kidder had two immediate goals: to speak about her Camp Lewis experience, and to move the library collection into its new quarters. She was invited to speak at university meetings, P.T.A. meetings, library association meetings and religious gatherings throughout the Pacific Northwest. She was in the final preparatory stages of moving the library when she suffered a heart attack in November. Despite her illness, the library move proceeded, demonstrating how successful Kidder was in making the library a focus of the campus community. William H. Carlson, a recent director of the library, describes the participants in the move:

> In the wartime shortage of labor the faculty had stepped into the breach on a volunteer basis. From Deans on down they wheeled and carried the books over an improvised trestle from the second floor of Benton Hall to the second floor of the new building. Momentous and welcome events were shaping up on the war fronts as the last book truck made the trip to the new building on November 6, 1918.

Commenting to the *Barometer* on this faculty assistance with the moving, Mrs. Kidder said, "One of the beautiful things to cherish in our memory and tradition is the fact that our faculty helped to move our Library, and that the new home was built in this tremendous time in the world's history."[96]

Although frail in health, Kidder continued her activities with students, faculty, and surrounding community. After her heart attack she became increasingly immobile and moved about campus and city with an electric cart built by the engineering students. In January 1920 she requested a leave of absence without pay from President Kerr, who granted her request with the proviso that she take leave *with* pay. Kidder died February 29, 1920, of a massive brain hemorrhage. At the request of students, her body lay in state at the library. The following notice appeared in the *Barometer*:

> The body of "Mother" Kidder will lie in state in the corridor of the new Library building from 9 to 11 Tuesday morning.
> At 11 o'clock Rev. E. T. Simpson, rector of the Church of the Good Samaritan, will conduct a short service on the steps in front of the Library building.[97]

A church funeral was impossible because of the city health officials' ban on public meetings due to an influenza epidemic. The funeral was attended by students, faculty, and administrators; the honorary and active pallbearers included the president, deans of the college, the faculty, and several students.[98] The student newspaper, *Barometer*, gave her a fitting memorial:

> The life and influence of Mrs. Kidder, who died Sunday morning, have been an inspiration to all who knew her. She held a greater place in the hearts of the students than probably any other one person and this endearment gave her the name of "Mother" Kidder.
> Her greatest thought, after that of building up the Library was of inspiring ideals among the students. In her great mother heart she held a plan for all the students, and she had said that perhaps the thing in her life that she had best completed was that of touching the lives of the young people.[99]

The 1921 *Beaver*, the college yearbook, was dedicated to Kidder.

In many respects Ida Kidder was the quintessential land-grant librarian. During her tenure as librarian the library became identified with campus and regional community activities. She felt that the library could be the source of "education possibility"—if the librarian and library staff recognize their role and develop a rapport with the students. As a 1919 issue of *Public Libraries* noted: "Mrs. Ida A. Kidder, librarian of the Oregon Agricultural College, is known thruout [sic] the state as 'Mother Kidder,' because of her personal touch with every student who goes to the college."[100] Kidder was primarily concerned with patron access to the library collection and developed techniques to encourage use and inspire "culture reading" among industrial students:

To induce the reading of foreign modern languages, I have an illustrated magazine of those countries whose languages are studied in periodical covers and placed among the popular magazines. Near the door of the reading room I have a table with a placard marked "Interesting"; on this are beautiful art books and beautifully illustrated books of travel, the morning Oregonian, and a notice of specially interesting magazine articles and anything else of interest I can find, also a list of new words to be added to our vocabulary.[101]

Although best-known for her personal charisma, Kidder was an effective library administrator. Within a year after her arrival at the college, Kidder taught a library skills class as a required course, integrating the library directly into the academic curriculum. Library holdings increased tenfold during her administration, from slightly more than 4,000 volumes to well over 41,000 despite limited funds.[102] In Kidder's 12 years as librarian, the number of library staff grew steadily from one to nine.[103] Less than 10 years after her arrival on campus, she successfully lobbied for a new library building.

Kidder was a capable manager and valued her staff, considering them her peers, not subordinates. She encouraged her assistants' participation in library decision making. The best statement of her management style is expressed in the 1919 article "The Creative Impulse in the Library":

In our libraries, if we can arouse in our assistants the idea that they are working for a definite aim—to serve the public in obtaining knowledge and the use of books, then lead them to survey the tools which they have to use to accomplish this end, we may safely leave them to work out the problem of adaptation of means to an end.

We shall not only have secured better service for our public but we shall have aroused the creative impulse in these young women (most of our assistants are young women) and added to their joy in life; we shall not only have given them an interest in their work and principles to apply to it, but we shall have enlarged their vision of all life and equipped them better to meet its problems.

We owe it to our assistants, and to our public, to arouse all the power of our helpers; liberate for the world a force that, but for this larger view of our own duty, might lie forever dormant.[104]

This confidence in her staff is representative of her belief in the superiority of women in the library profession: "So far as I have come in contact with library workers of the country, the women have seemed to me much more alive, broadminded, and progressive. I have certainly received my inspiration from them rather than the men, with two or three exceptions."[105]

Kidder also interacted with fellow land-grant librarians, serving on ALA's Agricultural Libraries Section (and as chairperson in 1915). However, her outreach services were not limited to the library profession. Although she promoted library services throughout the Pacific Northwest by speaking to farmers, librarians, teachers, and students, Kidder intended to bring new *ideas* to her audiences, not just library services. Her interactions with members of her audience were based on her humanistic philosophy of the value and capabilities of all individuals.

Kidder was also active in the Pacific Northwest Library Association (P.N.L.A.) from its inception in 1909,[106] presenting several talks at annual conferences, among them "How to Increase the Culture Reading of College Students" (1910), "The Untrained Librarian" (1914), and "Libraries and Inspiration" (1917). She gave practical expression to the service ideal of librarianship. In developing the "Requisites of an Agricultural College Library," she based the requirements on the services practiced at Oregon Agricultural College. Her philosophies of service and management were based on her belief in the cumulative effect of individual actions; each staff member and activity of the library was a potential resource for enhancing the visibility of the library and the education of its patrons.

Like Charles Harvey Brown, Kidder believed that land-grant college students needed added encouragement and direction in their reading, and promoted the library collection through personal contact with students and by adding services addressing specific patron needs. However, she placed greater emphasis on the service ideal than Brown; for Kidder, collection building was subordinate and incidental to patron service. While recognizing the importance of providing technical information to faculty, students, and farmers, Kidder added humanistic education to the land-grant curriculum. Unlike other librarians who served their campuses for much longer time periods, Kidder was able to make a difference at Oregon Agriculture College in just 12 years; by mothering the agricultural students of Oregon, she communicated her concept of library service and of the role of the librarian in the university and in the local community.

CONCLUSION

The passage of the Morrill Act of 1862 signalled the beginning of a new era in higher education in which applied sciences, particularly agriculture and the mechanical arts, were recognized as components of the educational process. Despite rather fumbling beginnings with limited resources and an underqualified student body, land-grant colleges became recognized as central sites for research and experimentation in the United States. By the end of the first quarter of the twentieth century, these colleges began to receive increased state and federal financial support and attract qualified students.

Land-grant institutions were required to develop quickly, usually with limited faculty expertise, meager classroom space, and poor laboratory and library facilities. Like their institutions, land-grant college libraries developed sporadically, initially lacking a competent and trained staff, an adequate funding source, and a comprehensive collection development policy. Faculty and student assistants who did not consider the library a priority were often the ones responsible for the library in its earliest formative stages. Libraries rarely contained the scientific and technical publications necessary for experimentation and the development of a scientifically knowledgeable faculty and student body.

Once the college hired a trained librarian, the library expanded. Collections were organized and made accessible through public catalogs, library hours were extended, borrowing privileges were offered to students, faculty, and the general public, classes in library use were begun, and collections began to develop systematically. The library gradually emerged as an important component of land-grant education, and assisted its parent institution in offering extension service and practical education to a rural population.

Many of the individuals hired to develop the library at western land-grant colleges were women. Often among the few female administrators on campus, women librarians had an opportunity to prove their managerial abilities. Despite the lack of resources, these first librarians of the land-grant colleges set precedents for collection building and service that continued past their tenures. The degree to which they successfully associated the library with the progress of land-grant education is a measure of their achievements; in Charles Harvey Brown's words, "The functions of agricultural libraries cannot be considered apart from the functions of the universities and colleges which they serve."[108]

In the western United States, Brown's caveat was particularly true. In the late nineteenth century the colleges developed a commitment to serving the citizens of the state or territory through instruction, research and experimentation, and extension service. As reflections of their institutions, the libraries attempted to do likewise.

The success of the libraries varied by institution. Funding and resources were inadequate for the colleges as a whole, not just the library, since most state legislatures were unwilling to commit resources beyond the minimal requirements specified in the Morrill Act of 1862, generally providing only land and a single building. Like its parent, land-grant libraries lacked funding for salaries, resources, and buildings; initially, administrators did not want to expend scarce funding to establish a library, which they considered secondary to developing a college curriculum.

Prior to 1930, a great proportion of western land-grant college libraries were headed by women. With varying education, library training, and managerial skills, each of these women librarians responded differently to the challenge of developing a land-grant library. Although few achieved national recognition for their efforts even within their own profession, most of them demonstrably improved both the libraries and the colleges in which they worked. The library achieved campus visibility for its commitment to public services and to the advancement of student knowledge.

Ida Kidder and Charlotte Baker are the two best representatives of librarians at western land-grant institutions. These two women integrated library service with campus and community activities and successfully promoted and extended services to students, faculty, and citizens. Each was also instrumental in developing librarianship as a profession in her state. Baker offered library training courses to librarians of small rural libraries throughout the state of Colorado, attracting national attention, while Kidder participated in regional and national library organizations and corresponded with librarians throughout Oregon. However, their individual strengths were very different. Kidder's lasting influence on her campus and community was the high standard of library service and cultural education she considered primary. She applied her service idealism by participating in the college's extension service and making the library an integral part of the life of students and faculty. Baker's strength was her commitment to library education and her interest in small libraries throughout the Rocky Mountain states. Both Kidder and Baker entered the library profession as a second career; each was formerly a teacher. Their emphasis on education and their awareness of deficiencies in land-grant technical education may be attributable to their first careers.

By 1930, each land-grant college library had been involved in at least one major building project. After years of gradually expanding and relocating throughout the campus, the college library ultimately acquired its own structure. Generally, the building phase of library development occurred between 1918 and 1928. However, Utah's first designated library building was constructed in 1901, a testament to Sara Goodwin's abilities as a librarian and as an influential member of the campus; a second library building was completed in 1930. Buildings became more carefully designed as librarians became more cognizant of the unique requirements of libraries. They visited other libraries, corresponded with other librarians, and demanded their specifications be included in the building plans.

Although the most tangible, library building is only one type of accomplishment of these women librarians. The degree to which they participated in and initiated extension services is a better measure of success. The travelling libraries and interlibrary loan services offered by many libraries extended the campus to the regional community, and many land-grant libraries opened their collections for use by citizens. Baker's extension service to rural librarians provided otherwise unavailable services to the rural community. Ida Kidder's involvement in extension service and her determination to provide cultural and educational opportunities both on the campus and in the surrounding communities are yardsticks by which the other women librarians can be measured. Kidder and Baker are indeed "mother" figures, library professionals attuned to the needs of their institutions and constituents, and created a place for themselves, and their libraries, in the lives of students and citizens alike.

Professional involvement is another measure of the effectiveness of these land-grant librarians. Like their university administrators, who collaborated regularly through the Association of Land-Grant Colleges and Universities, librarians also met to discuss professional problems unique to land-grant institutions, such as the training of an undereducated student body and the provision of extension services throughout the community. What Klein discovered about faculty was also true of women librarians at land-grant colleges: "The unity of thought and purpose that unites the agricultural staffs of different institutions is more real and more vital than the ties of common institutional employment which bring teachers of agriculture into association with teachers of enginering, literature, and education."[109] A network of land-grant librarians developed throughout the country. Members of the American Library Association's Agricultural Libraries Section were land-grant librarians who maintained communication with the Department of Agriculture library. Land-grant librarians also participated in local, state, and regional library associations, often as charter members and as officers.

A network of land-grant librarians developed in the West, fostered in part by Katharine Sharp of the University of Illinois, who recommended her graduate students for positions in libraries. The Agricultural College of New Mexico appears to have been an early training ground for librarians of some of the most important land-grant librarians in the West: Charlotte Baker, Lucy Mae Lewis, and Margery Bedinger all started there and later became innovative and progressive librarians at other land-grant college libraries. Correspondence between these women land-grant librarians shows that they were not solely concerned with developments at their own institution; they looked to each other for consultation, inspiration, and guidance.

The women who were hired at these land-grant colleges were of varying abilities and education. Many were known college graduates, although few had had any training in librarianship. Grace Hebard was unique among the woman librarians in having a land-grant engineering education; her emphasis on open stacks and public service is undoubtedly a product of her own experience. At the Utah and Colorado institutions, several of the women librarians were students of the school, who were hired as librarian upon graduation. Although without library training, Estelle Lutrell had substantial practical library experience in addition to her undergraduate studies at the University of Chicago. The most successful librarians were those who combined innate ability with library training; Ida Kidder and Lucy Lewis were both graduates of the University of Illinois Library School, Elizabeth Church Smith of Utah was a graduate of the University of Wisconsin Library School, and Charlotte Baker had received training at the Denver Public Library. Trained librarians were also interested in educating their staff; at New Mexico College library, the library staff became more knowledgeable regarding the profession with each staff meeting, where one individual was responsible for presenting a talk on a topic of current library interest.[110]

Most of the women librarians of these states were single; Sara Goodwin, the first librarian of the Agricultural College of Utah, was the only one known to be married while working as a librarian. Like most women of this time period who worked, Ida Kidder entered the profession when she had to, after the death of her husband. It was the exceptional woman who continued to have a career after her marriage. Women who married while working at land-grant colleges usually resigned their position. Unfortunately, the abilities of women like Elizabeth Church Smith of Utah were lost to the profession.

The effects of the longevity of these women librarians at their institutions is inconclusive. The brief tenure of Margery Bedinger had a tremendous impact on the Agricultural College of New Mexico that influenced later practitioners at that institution. Ida Kidder's 12-year position as the first librarian at the Oregon Agricultural College set a precedent for effective library service and user education that became an expected service of the library for years to come. The 25-year appointment of Charlotte Baker allowed her to develop innovative projects and outreach services to students and community that later became commonplace library practices.

The importance of personality and personal ability cannot be underestimated—librarians with extroverted personalities like Baker and Kidder encouraged interaction with their audiences. The library service ideals espoused by both Kidder and Baker were the products of their humanistic beliefs in a well-rounded education and in the value of the individual. As Kidder postulated in her "Requisites of an Agricultural College Library," empathy and consideration for the library patron must characterize proper library service; the library staff must "realize what a wonderful thing it is to serve these boys and girls, unaccustomed to a library as most of them are, so pleasantly that they will have no feelings of diffidence or dread in coming to the library for help, and of helping them to form a beautiful life long habit of library use."[111] Women librarians developed the sentiment of this statement into a service-oriented philosophy that extended into the entire community as well as to their campus population.

The accomplishments of these women proved that the land-grant ideals originally proposed by Jonathan Turner in the 1850s could be practically implemented. These women librarians were important participants in the American educational experiment of the land-grant college movement and helped determine its success. Through their work in extension service and daily contact with a population unfamiliar with library collections and services, the land-grant college librarians helped prove that practical higher education at an academic level was possible. Education and research, allied with practical training, were valuable tools for farmers and miners as well as professionals and political leaders. As Brown discovered in the *Survey of Land-Grant Colleges and Universities*, despite poor resources, the libraries of land-grant institutions were characterized by high use of available materials. By promoting and extending library service on and off campus, the early women librarians at western land-grant colleges made significant contributions to the fulfillment of land-grant college ideals.

ENDNOTES

[1]"Proceedings of the Farmers' Convention, at Granville, Held November 18, 1851," in J. B. Turner, *Industrial Universities for the People* (Chicago: Robert Fergus, Printer, 1854), 15.

[2]Jonathan B. Turner, "Plan for an Industrial University for the State of Illinois." *Prairie Farmer*, 12 (February 1852): 69.

[3]Edward Danforth Eddy, Jr., "The Development of the Land-Grant Colleges: Their Program and Philosophy." Ph.D. Cornell University, 1956, p. 173.

[4]Quoted in George Works, *The Land-Grant Colleges*. U.S. Advisory Committee on Education, Staff Study Number 10 (Washington, D.C.: Government Printing Office, 1939), 9.

[5]Arthur Klein, *Survey of Land-Grant Colleges and Universities*. Department of Interior, Office of Education, Bulletin 1930 n. 9, v. 1, pt. 1, 22 (Washington, D.C.: GPO, 1930).

[6]Thomas Woody, *A History of Women's Education in the United States* (New York: Science Press, 1929), v. 2, 258.

[7]Ibid, p. 252.

[8]Ibid., p. 61.

[9]For example, educational efforts in New Mexico were hampered by the cultural diversity of the territory, which included Anglos, Mexicans, and Native Americans, and little was accomplished until an educated workforce arrived with the coming of the railroad in the 1880's. Utah was embroiled in a sectarian conflict between Mormons and non-Mormons (called Gentiles by the Mormons), which hampered statehood efforts as well as land-grant college development. However, Cache County residents temporarily united to secure the land-grant college in Logan. The Agricultural College of Utah was founded with the proviso that "no partiality or preference shall be shown by the trustees to one sect or religious denomination over another; nor shall anything sectarian be taught therein." *The Utah Agricultural College Announcement of Its Opening Year* (Logan: J.P. Smith, 1890–1891), 11.

[10]Klein, *Survey of Land-Grant Colleges and Universities*, v. 1, 21.

[11]Simon F. Kropp, *That All May Learn: New Mexico State University 1888–1964*, p. 29. Hadley further stated that the library had adopted the "most approved" methods of cataloging, and was open to community as well as students so that all could be in "communion with the greatest and best minds of all past ages." (Las Cruces, NM: New Mexico State University, 1972)

[12]Quoted in Cheryl Nancy Laslow Bandy, "The First Fifty Years of the New Mexico State University Library, 1889–1939," M.A. Thesis, University of Oklahoma, 1970, 10.

[13]"Agriculture College of Utah," *The Journal* 7 June 1890, 1. Typescript, Special Collections and Archives, Utah State University Library, Logan.

[14]"The College Library," *The Journal*, 19 March, 1890, and "The College Library Benefit," *The Journal*, 29 March, 1890. Typescript, Special Collections and Archives, Utah State University Library, Logan.

[15]John Hugh Reynolds and David Yancey Thomas, *History of the University of Arkansas* (Fayetteville: University of Arkansas, 1910), 313.

[16]William H. Carlson, *The Library of Oregon State University* (Corvallis, Oregon: 1966), 4–5.

[17]Willard Wallace Smith quoted in Carlson, 7.

[18]Turner, *Prairie Farmer*, 11 (February, 1852), 70.

[19]Charles Harvey Brown, "The Library," in *Survey of Land-Grant Colleges and Universities*, U.S. Department of Interior, Office of Education, Bulletin 1930 n. 9, v. I, 613.

[20]Walter Greenleaf, *Land-Grant Colleges Year Ended June 30, 1926*, U.S. Department of Interior, Office of Education, Bulletin 1927 n. 37, 26. Dormitories received one percent of a land-grant dollar; libraries received two percent.

[21]Ibid.

[22]Brown, 682–83. By 1927, few met the minimum qualifications required at the other institutions of a bachelor's degree, at least a year's training at a library school, and prior library experience.

[23]Janet M. Hooks, *Women's Occupations Through Seven Decades*. Women's Bureau Bulletin No. 218, U.S. Department of Labor, Women's Bureau, 169–170.

[24]Janell M. Wenzel, "Grace Raymond Hebard as Western Historian," M.A. Thesis, University of Wyoming, 2.

[25]Historical Card File, Kansas State University, University Archives, Manhattan.

[26]Richman is the first name listed in the annual reports of the college identified as librarian in 1892. An obituary notice for Goodwin in the student newspaper *Student Life*, identified Goodwin as succeeding Clare Kenyon in 1894. Joel Edwards Ricks, *The Utah Agricultural College: A History of Fifty Years*, cites Goodwin as Instructor in Music and

Librarian in his chronological list of faculty. The first pages of entries in the *Accessions to the Library of the Agricultural College of Utah*, beginning in September of 1890, appears to be in her handwriting, indicating that she was associated with the library at an early date.

[27]Although originally a Mormon, Goodwin became a Protestant after her father, Thomas D. Brown, converted. In 1877 she became principal of St. Mark's School in Salt Lake City.

[28]Estelle Lutrell, "History of the University of Arizona, 186?–1930," Typescript, Archives, University of Arizona, Tucson, 112.

[29]"She had been told that she could not survive tuberculosis, and both the year which she lived at Saranac [New York] and her trip to Colorado were supposedly on 'borrowed time.'" James G. Hodgson to Bess Harvey Smith, 22 October 1940, p. 4. Typescript, Special Collections, Colorado State University, Fort Collins.

[30]Charlotte A. Baker, "Life As It Comes" TMs [photocopy], p. 1, Special Collections, Colorado State University, Fort Collins.

[31]Hodgson to Smith, 22 October 1940, 2.

[32]"Letter Written to Miss Charlotte A. Baker by President F. W. Saunders Explaining the Necessity of Her Employment by the College Before July 1, 1900," in Bandy, 63.

[33]As late as 1930, Charles Harvey Brown criticizes college administrators for not funding libraries: "The customary excuse by college adminsitrators for such [poor] salaries [to librarians] is 'we ought to pay them more, the librarian is worth more, but we do not have the funds.' The facts do not justify this statement. The failure is not caused by the limited amount of funds available for the educational work of the institution; the deficiency is due to the proportion of educational funds used for library support. Amherst expends on its library (excluding expenses for care of building, light, head, etc.) more than 7 per cent of noncapital expenditures of the college; Bowdoin more than 8 per cent. The 4 land-grant institutions with salaries of librarians of less than $2,000 are spending, respectively, 1 per cent, 1.3 percent, 1.9 per cent, and 2.3 percent." Brown, in Klein, v. 1, 685–686.

[34]Bandy, pp. 17–18.

[35]Lucy Lewis to Miss Katharine Sharp, 3 July, 1906, Alumni Records, Archives, University of Illinois, Urbana. She tells Sharp that "Mr. Foster writes that he considers me well prepared for the position except for experience and that he is not yet prepared to reject my application because of that shortage."

[36]Lucy Lewis to Katharine Sharp, 4 November, 1906, p. 2. Alumni Records, University of Illinois, Urbana.

[37]Prior to her appointment in New Mexico, Bedinger had been the librarian at West Point.

[38]Bandy, 35. Her abilities were needed to put the library in order in preparation for the appearance of the North Central Association of Colleges and Secondary Schools accrediting committee.

[39]Ibid., pp. 69–70.

[40]Charlotte A. Baker et al. *Survey of State Agricultural College and Experiment Station Libraries, June 1920.* U.S. Department of Agriculture, 1922, 10.

[41]Brown, in Klein, v. 1, 703.

[42]Evangeline Thurber, "American Agricultural College Libraries, 1862–1900," *College and Research Libraries* 6 (1945), 351.

[43]Lucy M. Lewis to Miss Frances Simpson, 28 March 1908. Alumni Records, Archives, University of Illinois, Urbana. Lewis was making $800 a year in 1908 and hoped for a $100 salary increase.

[44]Powers' 1912 survey of fourteen land-grant colleges nationwide found that salaries for librarians ranged from a low of $700 to a high of $2,000 per year. William H. Powers, "Scope and Current Cost of Librarians in the Land Grant Agricultural Colleges," in *Papers and Proceedings of the Thirty-Sixth Annual Meeting of the American Library Association held at Washington, D.C. May 25–29, 1914* (Chicago: American Library Association, 1914), 195, 197.

[45]Charlotte A. Baker et al. *Survey*, 11.

[46]Emmett D. Chisum, "Development of the University of Wyoming Libraries and Special Collections," *Annals of Wyoming* 54(1982), 28.

[47]"Legislature Spends Morning Discussing Funds of University," *Laramie Boomerang*, January 22, 1921, 1.

[48]Chisum, 28. "Marching into the House chambers in which the Senate and the House gathered, the students then staged a demonstration such as has never before been seen in Cheyenne. Between college yells with the country-wide famous 'Ride 'em Cowboys' predominating and songs, representative students gave talks whenever the legislators would stop applauding long enough to give the students a chance to say something."

[49]"It was only by the utmost energy on the part of friends of the University, stressing repeatedly the many uses which such a building would serve that this appropriation was at last secured. It should be remembered also that this was the first appropriation of any considerable amount obtained from the Legislature since the initial one of $25,000 in 1885." Estelle Lutrell, "History," 111.

[50]Estelle Lutrell, "The Library, the Pivotal Point of the University," Building File, p. 2, Special Collections, University of Arizona, Tucson.

[51]Quoted in Lutrell, "History," p. 175.

[52]Estelle Lutrell, "Preliminary Sketch for a new Library Building," Building File, Special Collections, University of Arizona Library, Tucson.

[53]Building File, Special Collections, University of Arizona Library, Tucson. Surviving correspondence indicates that she consulted with numerous librarians and library suppliers to discover the "best" designs and products available for the library. Lutrell also wrote to the American Library Association and the Library Bureau for guidance.

[54]"Dedication," Photocopy, *Desert*, 1924, Special Collections, University of Arizona Library, Tucson.

[55]Lutrell, "History," p. 203.

[56]Lucy Lewis to Katharine Sharp, 4 November, 1906, p. 2. Alumni Records, University of Illinois, Urbana.

[57]Bandy, 22. In a letter to Francis Simpson, Lewsis indicates that the new library space was not all she had hoped: "Owing to lack of funds, they cut down the size of my rooms so much that I fear they will have to move the library again in a very few years." Lucy M. Lewis to Miss Francis Simpson, 21 August, 1908, p. 1. Alumni Records, Archives, University of Illinois, Urbana.

[58]Quoted in Bandy, p. 40.

[59]During one of its barn locations, the library was housed above the Veterinary department's experimental rabbits and guinea pigs. The odor from these animals was so pervasive that Charlotte Baker "wrote a note to Dr. Lory asking to have the bunnies and piggies sprinkled with cologne. This note brought results for the livestock was moved out soon afterwards." "College Library," from the Physical Plant Collection, p. 2, Special Collections, Colorado State University, Fort Collins.

[60]Laura Makepeace, "The History of the Library of Colorado State College [1879–1943]", p. 10–11. Special Collections, Colorado State University, Fort Collins.

[61]Ibid., p. 14.

[62]*Annual Catalogue of the Agricultural College of Utah, 1891–92*, 13. Special Collections and Archives, Utah State University Library, Logan.

[63]*Annual Catalogue of the Agricultural College of Utah for the Year 1899–1900*, 68. Special Collections and Archives, Utah State University Library, Logan.

[64]*Student Life* 2 (October 1903), 16. Special Collections and Archives, Utah State University Library, Logan. In her letter of application, Church details her library background: "My principal work has been catalogueing [sic], which is probably the most essential and technical part of library training. I mentioned I believe, the course in public documents which is being given here [Madison, Wisconsin] in public documents by Miss Hasse of the New York public, for the first time. She is the only authority in catalogueing public documents that I know about." USU Archives 3.1/4–2 Box 1, Applications for Faculty (Library), Special Collections and Archives, Utah State University Library, Logan.

[65]Brigham Young College was a Mormon college in Logan founded in 1877. It could not compete with the curriculum of the agricultural college and existed as a junior college before closing in the 1920s.

[66]USU Archives 7.2/2–3, Library Endowment Fund. Archives, Utah State University, Logan.

[67]New Mexico College was one exception to that tendency. In February, 1919, the library was designated a depository of the scientific research published by the Carnegie Institute of Washington. "The College had applied previously and was turned down because of inadequate facilities." Bandy, 28–29.

[68]Baker, *Survey*, pp. 3–16.

[69]*Annual Catalogue of the Agricultural College of Utah for the Year 1899–1900*, 68. Special Collections and Archives, Utah State University Library, Logan.

[70]Grace Raymond Hebard quoted in Chissum, 27. In 1904, the library contained 17,000 volumes.

[71]Baker, "A Brief History," 4. Special Collections, Colorado State University, Fort Collins.

[72]*Catalog of the Agricultural College of Utah for 1904–1905*. Special Collections and Archives, Utah State University Library, Logan.

[73]Baker, *Survey*, p. 15.

[74]Ibid., p. 18.

[75]Among the articles was "New Rules for Library as Drafted by Student Life" which is surprisingly modern in its ironic self-analysis of patron behavior. For example, "X. Make the Library your headquarters for gossip, horseplay, and general abandon. The books are only there to serve as ornaments and the people present are only pretending to read anyhow. Besides, too much study is not good for a person, and you 'don't owe nobody nothin' nohow.' In short use the table to sit on; rest your feet on the seat of the

chair, and if you see some particular article in one of the papers, or books that is of more than ordinary interest to you, cut it out and keep it. By doing this you will soon make the Library what it ought to be, viz: 'A place where a feller can have a good time.'" *Student Life*, 12 January, 1912. Archives, Utah State University, Logan.

[76]*Utah Farmer's Institute*, no. 7 (1904), pp. 166–170.

[77]"At the meeting of the New Mexico Educational Association at Santa Fe, last November, the Library Section met, seven people, one a teacher, one a representative of the Library Bureau, and five librarians. After the meeting the librarians organized the New Mexico Library Association. It had been organized before, but it was very young and struggling." Margery Bedinger, "New Mexico: A Great Library Opportunity," *Library Journal* 52 (April 1, 1927), 352.

[78]Ibid.

[79]*Library Roadrunner*, 1–2, 1928. Special Collections, University of Arizona Library, Tucson.

[80]Laura I. Makepeace, "Charlotte A. Baker," p. 4.

[81]Ibid., p. 35.

[82]*Annual Report to the Board of Trustees*, 1907–1908, pp. 87–89.

[83]Ibid., p. 5.

[84]Hodgson to Smith, 22 October 1940, p. 4.

[85]Ida A. Kidder, University of Illinois Library School Alumni Record, 23 July, 1917. Archives, University of Illinois, Urbana. Prior to attending library school, Kidder was a primary school teacher from 1878 to 1885. In 1885 she attended the New York State Normal School in Albany for two years before teaching natural sciences at the Medina High School in New York state (1887–1895).

[86]"Agricultural Libraries Section," *A.L.A. Bulletin* 6 (1912), p. 227.

[87]Mrs. Ida A. Kidder, "How to Increase the Culture Reading of College Students," *Public Libraries* 15 (1910), 420.

[88]Ida Kidder, "Requisites of an Agricultural College Library," RG9, Reel 1, Folder 28, Archives, Oregon State University Library, Corvallis.

[89]"Discussion on how to increase the culture reading of college students," Mrs. Ida A. Kidder to Miss Clara Barnett, 5 June 1912, RG 9, Reel 1, Folder 28, Archives, Oregon State University Library, Corvallis.

[90]Ida Kidder to Rev. Edgar H. Rogers, 10 September, 1918. RG 9, Reel 1, Folder 28, Archives, Oregon State University Library, Corvallis.

[91]Carlson, p. 22.

[92]Carlson, p. 24.

[93]"Mother-in-chief" to Lucy [Lewis], 20 June 1918, p. 2. RG 1 Reel 1 Folder 29, Archives, Oregon State University Library, Corvallis.

[94]Ida A. Kidder to Lucy Lewis, 22 June 1918, p. 2, RG 1 Reel 1 Folder 29, Archives, Oregon State University Library, Corvallis.

[95]Carlson, p. 25.

[96]Carlson, p. 26.

[97]"Mother Kidder O.A.C Librarian Called by Death," Alumni Records, Archives, University of Illinois, Urbana.

[98]Ibid.

[99]"Librarian's Life is an Inspiration," *Barometer* 2 March, 1920, Alumni Records, Archives, University of Illinois, Urbana.

[100]"Pacific Coast," *Public Libraries*, 24 (1919), 150.

[101]Ida A. Kidder to R.R. Bowker, 22 January, 1919, p. 1. RG9, Reel 1, Folder 28, Archives, Oregon State University Library, Corvallis.

[102]Statistics gathered from narrative throughout Carlson.

[103]Traditionally it has been easier for the librarian to acquire increases in staffing than increases in materials budgets which, Carlson believes, can be directly traced to Ida Kidder's administration and its promotion of library services and "non-book" emphasis on personal interactions between library staff and patrons. Carlson, 32.

[104]Mrs. Ida A. Kidder, "The Creative Impulse in the Library," *Public Libraries* 24 (1919), 156.

[105]Ida Kidder quoted in William H. Carlson, "Ida Angeline Kidder: Pioneer Western Land-Grant Librarian," *College and Research Libraries* 29 (May 1968), 220.

[106]Kidder, University of Illinois Library School Alumni Record, Archives, University of Illinois, Urbana.

[107]*Barometer*, 2 March 1920, 1.

[108]Charles H. Brown, "Some Objectives for Agricultural Libraries," *A.L.A. Bulletin* 20 (1926), 474.

[109]Arthur Klein, "Survey of Land-Grant Colleges," *Journal of Higher Education* 2 (April, 1931), 171.

[110]Bandy, pp. 44–47.

[111]Ida Angeline Kidder, "Requisites of an Agricultural College Library," RG 9, Reel 1, Folder 28, Archives, Oregon State University Library, Corvallis.

appendix A

Land-grant Institutions Established in the Western United States*

Arizona	University of Arizona at Tucson, established 1891, designated land-grant college October 1891.
Arkansas	Arkansas Industrial University at Fayetteville, established as land-grant college January 1872.
California	College of California at Berkeley designated land-grant University of California at Berkeley in 1868.
Colorado	Colorado Agricultural College, established 1877, designated as land-grant college 1879.
Idaho	University of Idaho, established 1889, designated land-grant college 1892.
Iowa	Iowa Agricultural College at Ames, chartered 1956, designated land-grant college 1862.
Kansas	Bluemont Central College (Methodist) designated land-grant college in 1863, became Kansas State Agricultural College.
Louisiana	Old Louisiana State University at Baton Rouge and the Agricultural & Mechanical College of New Orleans united at Baton Rouge in 1877 as the land-grant Louisiana State University.
Minnesota	University of Minnesota, established 1851, designated land-grant college in 1868.
Missouri	Agricultural & Mechanical College at Columbia and Missouri School of Mines at Rolla both designated as land-grant colleges in 1870.

Montana	Montana College of Agriculture & Mechanic Arts at Bozeman established 1893.
Nebraska	University of Nebraska at Lincoln established in 1869 as land-grant college.
Nevada	Preparatory Department opened at Elko in 1874, School of Mines in 1882 (moved to Reno in 1886) as land-grant colleges.
New Mexico	New Mexico College of Agricultural & Mechanic Arts in Mesilla Park founded 1889 as Territorial land-grant college.
North Dakota	Agricultural College established at Fargo in 1891.
Oklahoma	Oklahoma Agricultural & Mechanic Arts College established at Stillwater in 1891 as land-grant college.
South Dakota	Agricultural College established as territorial college in 1881, designated land-grant college in 1889 as South Dakota State College of Agriculture & Mechanic Arts.
Texas	Agricultural & Mechanic College of Texas established at Brazos County (College Station) in 1862 as land-grant college.
Utah	Agricultural College of Utah at Logan established 1888 as land-grant college.
Washington	Agricultural College, Experimental Station, and School of Science of the State of Washington established in 1890 as land-grant colleges.
Wyoming	University of Wyoming established in 1886 at Laramie as territorial land-grant college.

---

*Adapted from: Benjamin Andrews, *The Land Grant of 1862 and the Land-Grant Colleges*. Bulletin 1918 (Washington, D.C.: Department of the Interior, Bureau of Education,) n.13.

Women Librarians at Western Land-Grant Institutions Prior To 1930

Institution	Librarian
University of Arizona at Tuscon	Estelle Lutrell
Arkansas Industrial University	Julie A. Garside
	Susie H. Spencer
	Ida Pace
	Mrs. Neil Carothers
	Mrs. Stella Lawrence
	Martha Brownfield
	Mrs. Mary Austin
Colorado Agricultural College	Lillian Stroud
	Lerah G. Stratton
	Cecilia May Southworth
	Marguerite E. Stratton
	Charlotte Baker
Iowa Agricultural College	Fanny Thomas
Kansas State Agricultural College	Julia Pearce
	Helen J. Wescott
	Josephine T. Berry
	Henrietta Calvin
	Margery J. Minis
	Ann M. Boyd
	Gertrude A. Barnes

University of Minnesota	Ina Ten Eyck Firkins
Montana College of Agriculture and Mechanic Arts	Mabel Ruth Owens Mary K. Winter Elizabeth Forrest Elizabeth T. Stout
University of Nebraska	Mary L. Jones
New Mexico College of Agricultural and Mechanic Arts	Charlotte Baker Lucy Mae Lewis Mrs. Floy French Dorothy Peters Margery Bedinger
Oregon Agricultural College	Ida Kidder Lucy Mae Lewis
Oklahoma Agricultural and Mechanics Arts College	Cora A. Miltmore Lois Davidson Jane Leslie Stone Elsie D. Hand
Agricultural and Mechanic Arts College of Texas	Willie Davis Mrs. Ira Cain
Agricultural College of Utah	Sara Godwin Goodwin Lettie Richman Clare Kenyon Elizabeth C. Smith Hattie Smith
State College of Washington	Nancy Van Doren Miran Tannatt Gertrude Saxton Stella A. Wilson
University of Wyoming	Grace Raymond Hebard Reba Davis

chapter 4

Adelaide Hasse:
The New Woman as Librarian

Clare Beck

Adelaide Hasse was born in 1868, a year of peculiar significance for American women, the year in which ratification of the Fourteenth Amendment to the Constitution for the first time limited a constitutional right to male citizens. In so explicitly denying women the vote, Congress and the states shocked American women with the recognition that civil equality would not be granted by a beneficent male power structure.

This discovery was a contributing factor to the era of the New Woman, which lasted until women finally won the vote with ratification of the Nineteenth Amendment in 1921. The New Woman sought independence and equality in many ways, and the period was marked by expanding education for women, their growing participation in the workforce, and their increasing involvement in civic affairs. Much of this involved institutions for women: women's colleges, women's clubs, and the so-called women's professions. In them, American women could achieve some degree of education, economic independence, and political influence, while remaining apart from the male spheres of power in business, the professions, and electoral politics.

The rise and fall of Adelaide Hasse's career in libraries from 1890 to 1918 coincides with the era of the New Woman. In many respects, Hasse illustrates the opportunities and the perils library work offered to an ambitious and independent New Woman. She encountered now familiar issues for working women: the influence of mentors, sexual harrassment, single motherhood, stereotyped expectations, glass ceilings, and complicated relations with male peers. Her experience demonstrated the dangers to a woman librarian who passionately sought to be part of the great world—to be involved in the issues and movements of her time as a librarian—rather than accepting the gender-typed roles of library service to women and children or behind the scenes cataloging and order work. Hasse was controversial, self-confident, and an open feminist. As an ambivalent observer, Richard Bowker commented, "Her virile personality has made her both friends and foes."[1] "Virile" of course means masculine or manly, and it was sometimes applied to the New Woman as an indication that she was unnatural.[2] According to Carroll Smith-Rosenberg:

> The New Woman constituted a revolutionary demographic and political phenomenon. . . . For half a century, American women and men bitterly debated the social and sexual legitimacy of the New Woman. Through her, they argued about the 'naturalness' of gender and the legitimacy of the bourgeois social order. They agreed on only one point: The New Woman challenged existing gender relations and the distribution of power."[3]

Hasse's name is known to librarians, but the gender issues raised by her career have not been discussed. Indeed, she has barely been acknowledged by library historians since her abrupt dismissal from New York Public Library in 1918. Only in recent years has her firing been mentioned in several brief biographical articles by Laurel Grotzinger.[4] When the influential Dee Garrison concluded that the public library was stunted "because the first generation of library women did not question their sex-typed roles," she did not discuss what happened to New Women like Hasse and her first mentor, Tessa Kelso, or consider whether the rejection of such women sent a message to the mass of women library workers.[5] That Hasse's dismissal came in 1918, at the peak of tumultuous change in the status of American women, was a sign of the backlash that would bring an end to the era of the New Woman.

EARLY LIFE

Hasse's early years were spent in two communities, Milwaukee and Los Angeles, that were uniquely likely to encourage a bright, energetic girl to seek a role different from that of her mother's generation.

Milwaukee was the center of German-American culture, sometimes called the German Athens of America, with a vibrant public life of music, theater, lectures, beer gardens, a German-language press and schools, and a public library established in 1878 when the city took it over from a private association. The original staid German element of Milwaukee had been enlivened by the arrival of the idealistic and high-spirited "Forty-Eighters," the refugees from the revolutionary movements of the 1840s in Central Europe. The Forty-Eighters, many of them upper class and well-educated, became something of an elite, often active in political reform movements, and their children would be among the leaders of American Progressivism, including Oswald Garrison Villard, the Dreier sisters, Louis Brandeis, Walter Weyl, and Josephine Goldmark. Hasse proudly identified her paternal grandfather with the Forty-Eighters: "My father's father collected his belongings after the revolution of 1848, and collecting himself, he obeyed his government's orders to leave Germany, and came to the United States. Here he soon collected sufficient support to secure for himself a seat in the Wisconsin State Legislature."[6]

Hasse's father was a doctor educated in American and German universities. As an Army surgeon who had served through the four years of the Civil War in the Army of the Cumberland, he must have seemed a particularly heroic figure to his first-born, Adelaide. Hermann Hasse also pursued botanical research, publishing studies of lichens.[7] Hasse seems to have been educated mostly or entirely at home under the direction of a father with high standards.

In the late 1880s, the family moved to Los Angeles, then booming with the completion of the Santa Fe Railroad, but still a small, remote city with an idyllic climate and dramatic setting at the endpoint of westward movement. As Hasse described it: "The Los Angeles of those days was an unusual community. Vastly more isolated than at present, its population was largely composed of families accustomed to an environment of culture and attainment."[8] The upper class migrants from the East and Midwest often came hoping to improve their health, but for many there was also the sense of California as a place to seek a new way of life.

The atmosphere of the 1880s already offered new models for young American women. Ida Tarbell recalled "the out-of-door girl of the eighties, the girl who had rebelled against lacing, high heels, long skirts, and substituted for them an admirable uniform of independence—tailor-made coat and skirt, high-neck shirtwaist with four-in-hand tie, flat heels."[9] More practical clothing enabled women to be more physically active, particularly to take part in that "great giver of freedom to women's bodies," the bicycling craze of the 1880s and '90s.[10] Hasse's energetic involvement won her the title "Champion Fast Lady Bicycle Rider" of Los Angeles at a time when not only was the bicycle frame heavy but each wheel weighed more than sixty pounds.[11]

During her Los Angeles years, Hasse was exposed to constant discussion about women's suffrage and the idea of the New Woman. The local newspapers, the *Times* and the *Herald*, frequently featured debate about the "New Woman" versus the "Traditional Woman" or the "Feminine Woman." Sexist stereotypes in the press would bring quick responses in letters from local feminists. In 1894, the many women's organizations of Southern California held a "women's parliament," where there was much discussion of such gender issues as women's opportunities in the workplace and how child-rearing practices shaped sex roles. Though women could not vote in California, there was no law against their holding office, which inspired Kate Galpin to run unsuccessfully for Los Angeles County Superintendent of Schools in 1894. Charlotte Perkins Gilman, who had come to Pasadena to recover from the breakdown described in *The Yellow Wallpaper*, began her career as a feminist lecturer in Los Angeles in the years 1891–1894 when the young Adelaide Hasse was beginning her career as a librarian.

TESSA KELSO

In this atmosphere of lively feminism, Hasse fatefully entered the workplace as an assistant in the Los Angeles Public Library and encountered an extraordinary woman librarian, her first mentor, Tessa Kelso.[12] Only 5 years older than Hasse, Kelso had already led an adventurous life as a journalist in the Midwest and California. A library user since childhood, she became interested in the professionalization of library work while covering the 1886 conference of the American Library Association, and three years later she convinced the trustees of the Los Angeles library to hire her as head librarian despite her lack of experience. She quickly transformed the library, substantially increasing and improving its collection, staff, and use. Just as quickly, she became a visible and articulate part of the library profession, active in ALA, quoted in *Library Journal*, even writing a provocative article on libraries for the progressive journal, *The Arena*.[13]

Hasse soon was given wide responsibilities as Kelso's first assistant. The two became close friends, and Kelso's influence would reverberate throughout Hasse's career. It was Kelso who encouraged her to organize the library's government publications, which became the focus of Hasse's career as a specialist in government information. Kelso had many ideas, sometimes controversial and always vigorously asserted, that would be carried on by Hasse, especially since the two would remain close and live in the same city for 20 years. Kelso's journalistic flair for publicity and her belief that libraries should operate like business, actively seeking to expand services and attract customers, her determination that women not be consigned to a separate sphere as either librarians or library users, and her willingness to engage in conflict with powerful men, all would continue in the more prominent career of her protégé.

Although Kelso's service as head of the library was by most measures successful, it lasted barely 6 years. Los Angeles politics was a ruthless rough-and-tumble in which the librarian was vulnerable to factions wanting the job for patronage, looking for an official to attack, or seeking control of the independent library board. What makes Kelso's experience distinctive in library history was the flair and combativeness with which she fought back with that classic American weapon, litigation. In 1893–94, she generated considerable controversy by bringing two lawsuits against prominent men who had attacked her professional reputation. First, she sued the city auditor, who had refused to reimburse her for expenses in attending the meetings of ALA and the World Congress of Librarians on the grounds that: "The benefits to be derived by the taxpayers and patrons of the library from what might be learned by a delegate to a congress of librarians are too remote, too speculative, too chimerical to make the expenses of such a delegate a legal charge upon the public funds."[14] Kelso's position was upheld by the Los Angeles Superior Court and the California Supreme Court, which ruled that the city charter gave the library board the authority to approve such expenditures, so the auditor had no legal basis for refusing to follow the procedure for payment of an authorized appropriation. A year later, in a case that won national attention, Kelso brought suit for slander against a prominent Methodist minister who had publicly prayed for her when the *Los Angeles Herald* accused the library of harboring an indecent French novel. Kelso had been under attack by the *Herald* throughout the year and apparently decided that offense was the best defense. Though the judge's initial rulings were in her favor, establishing that the minister could not claim immunity for his public prayers, the case was unresolved when Kelso resigned in 1895 in the face of a hostile new board. Hasse resigned with her, and the two women left for the East. There Kelso established a long career with the book distributor Baker and Taylor and she continued to be a vocal participant in ALA, always arguing that libraries should be more active and businesslike in promoting their services. Though conceding that "libraries have much to learn in this direction," Kelso's proposals "savor too much of commercialism" sniffed *Library Journal* in 1912.[15]

Many years later, Kelso's feistiness would echo in Hasse's battle over her dismissal from New York Public Library. Kelso never played the role of the helpless, hapless female, and neither would Hasse. Shortly before they left Los Angeles, the *Herald* published a comment on the New Woman by Jessie Bartlett Davis that expressed how the two young librarians would live their lives and shape their careers: "I believe in the new woman most fully. I believe in her capacity, her ambition and her success . . . no matter what may be her doctrines I respect and admire the woman who is not afraid to express her opinions, who is not afraid to strike out for herself no matter what difficulties are before her."[16]

WASHINGTON, 1895–1897

Helped by the networking Kelso had encouraged and the attention given the checklist of U.S. Dept. of Agriculture publications she had compiled in Los Angeles, Hasse quickly landed a job in the newly created library of the Superintendent of Documents in the Government Printing Office. This was another situation that reinforced her sense of being on the cutting edge of an exciting profession, doing work that women had not done before. The Printing Act of 1895 had established the position of Superintendent of Documents with responsibility to collect and catalog both past and future publications of the federal government, and Hasse plunged into these tasks with her usual energy.[17]

In six weeks, she had gathered 300,000 documents from the attics and cel-
lars of government buildings, where they had been moldering so long that
Hasse wore a surgical mask for protection from the dust and molds. In her vivid
account of her adventures, she emphasized what an exotic sight she was leading a crew of African-American porters around the city. Washington was in
many respects a provincial Southern city, and a statuesque young white woman
working with a half-dozen black men was a strikingly unconventional image of
the New Woman.

More important to her development was the intellectual atmosphere in Washington, which was becoming a lively center of research in the Smithsonian, the
Dept. of Agriculture, the Dept. of Labor, and other government agencies.
Hasse's family background had given her an initial interest in research, for her
father, uncle, and German cousin all were involved in scientific or statistical research. Her two years in Washington reinforced her belief in the importance of
government publications to researchers, and the newly formed District of Columbia Library Association provided a meeting ground for librarians from the
agencies and the Library of Congress who shared her interests.[18]

Although Hasse later insisted that her time at GPO was "without at any time
. . . any friction with any fellow worker," she apparently was not pleased with
her coworkers, Supt. of Documents Francis Crandall and a staff of Albany-
trained catalogers, to whom she referred scornfully as "a few catalogers and a
journalist."[19] Faced with the task of organizing a library of government publications from many agencies, there was some conflict about what would be a peren-
nial library issue, how best to classify public documents. Although her agency-
based system ultimately prevailed over the Dewey Decimal System, the
dissatisfied Hasse soon sought a position at New York Public Library, where
John Shaw Billings had been hired to create an American equivalent of the great
European research libraries. Here again, Hasse showed her confidence and assertiveness in seeking a desirable position and a good salary. Though she gave
the impression that Billings saw her work on a visit to GPO and called her to
New York, Billings' letters show that she approached him about a job in 1896
and initially was told he had no openings. She persisted, and in 1897 Billings
wrote that he could not hire her at what she was asking and would not offer
more than $75 per month. A few months later, however, he did hire her to cat-
alog documents for $100 a month, and the next year she was raised to $125.[20]

NEW YORK, 1897–1913

Billings was ideally suited to be Hasse's next mentor. They were tempermen-
tally alike, remarkably energetic and hard-working, obsessed with building and
cataloging great collections, impatient with bureaucratic structures and financial
restraints, and determined to improve access to government publications. With

his strong personality and heroic career, Billings was a revered father figure to his staff. Like Hasse's own father, he was a doctor and had been an Army surgeon in the Civil War, followed by years of achievement as a researcher, administrator, and librarian. According to his biographer, he was unusual for a man of his time in that he was not impressed by female beauty or charm but instead related to women as "a sincere friend or a kindly mentor."[21] Hasse's recollection was of a special relationship with Billings, a collegial and communicative leader who appreciated her workaholic nature. Hasse's zealous temperament responded to Billings' brusque military manner, and she fondly recalled his "reprimand of a soldier" response to her explanation of the difficulties of an assignment: "Miss Hasse, if it had been easy I would not have asked you to do it."[22]

Hasse's career flourished at NYPL under Billings. As head of the Public Documents Division, she built the collection from 10,000 to 300,000 volumes in a decade and developed an elaborate system of cataloging. She was active professionally, speaking, writing, and serving in ALA as a longtime member of the Public Documents Committee and an elected member of the ALA Council. In 1908, she was one of the elite elected as a fellow of Melvil Dewey's American Library Institute. With Billings' support, she pursued her ambition to become a distinguished bibliographer of government publications, issuing her multivolume *Index to Economic Materials in the Documents of the States*, her book on the cataloging of documents, bibliographies in periodicals, and her edition of the supposedly lost "Bradford's Journal," the first book published in New York, which she tracked down in the British Public Record Office in 1902.[23]

Her position in the Astor Library (before the move to the new central research library in 1911), a collection well known to researchers, gave her opportunities to establish connections with leading scholar-activists of the Progressive era, a time when "research often served as an engine of reform."[24] In her memoirs, Ida Tarbell paid tribute to Hasse's help in locating the rare copies of public documents needed for her influential, muckraking history of Standard Oil.[25] Florence Kelley of the National Consumers League, perhaps the greatest reformer of that age of reform, consulted her about data to support the fight for Oregon's protective ten-hour labor law; Hasse guided Josephine Goldmark and other NCL staff to the government reports that formed the basis of Louis Brandeis' historic brief to the Supreme Court in *Muller v. Oregon*.[26] A young economist named John R. Commons came often to the library to work on a pioneering effort to develop statistical indicators and continued to consult Hasse from his subsequent position at the University of Wisconsin. There he became a key figure in transforming Wisconsin into a model of progressive, activist government under Governor Robert LaFollette; an essential part of the state's government was Charles McCarthy's legislative reference library, as Commons described it "an entirely new kind of library," a visionary concept of library activism that inspired Hasse's idea of what she might do.[27] Other major figures who consulted Hasse included W.E.B. Dubois, Charles Beard, Walter Weyl, and Ernst Freund.

New York in those years was the nation's intellectual and financial capital, the city that offered refuge from provincialism for intellectuals, artists, and reformers. Like many New Women, Hasse lived in Greenwich Village, in an atmosphere of "brilliant young people, full of vitality, ardent about saving the world."[28] Her friendship with Tessa Kelso also gave her connections among reformers and in the press, for Kelso kept a hand in journalism with a weekly column on women's organizations for the *New York Evening Post*, the leading Progressive newspaper of the era, and also wrote a study of prostitution for the Women's Municipal League.[29] From her arrival in New York in 1897, Kelso's contacts and her own courting of the press made Hasse the subject of newspaper feature stories in which she was portrayed as a new breed of career woman and described as the nation's leading authority on government publications, one of the New Women who were becoming professional experts in an era that expected the expert to transform society.

Among librarians, Hasse and Kelso's liveliness stood out to an extent that they were chosen as two of the three women members of the Bibliosmiles, a mildly rowdy organization founded by their old friend from Los Angeles, the flamboyant Charles Lummis, as a refuge from the solemnity of ALA meetings.[30] The Bibliosmiles, "Librarians who are Nevertheless Human" dedicated to "keeping the dust off our top shelves," specialized in comic songs and speeches, but the group was also a meeting place for some of the iconoclasts of the library world, men like Lummis and John Cotton Dana, who thought highly of Hasse and reinforced her belief that libraries could be a vital and innovative part of progressive change.

Another man who valued Hasse both personally and professionally was the aging lion of American libraries, Melvil Dewey. Correspondence suggests that Hasse was one of the women who found Dewey's behavior offensive in the years 1905–06 when Dewey's alleged sexual improprieties caused a behind-the-scenes storm in the American Library Association.[31] Dewey was in a position of power on the ALA Publications Board when Hasse sought his support for her index to state economic documents; while exploring her idea, he seemed interested in a personal relationship and behaved in a way that Hasse found "obnoxious."[32] When Richard Bowker and Edwin Anderson, Dewey's successor at the New York State Library, wanted ALA to censure Dewey, Hasse objected that it was a private matter, not appropriate for ALA involvement. In demanding that her name be kept out of it, she argued for the principle that, even if chivalrously motivated, ALA should not take action against private behavior, but she probably also feared that any connection with scandal would damage her career and the prospects of women librarians generally. Ironically, a decade later, she would make ALA a battleground in her own bitter struggle with the same Edwin Anderson.

NEW YORK, 1913–1918

As Hasse followed Billings' flag-draped caisson to Arlington National Cemetery in 1913, she was "aware that I had lost a friend" and vaguely sensed problems ahead. In fact, she had lost her protector, and the coming years, when she seemed to be at the peak of her career, would be a time of turmoil and loss, as "a vast change came over the library." On Easter, 1919, she again visited Arlington and felt, "It was difficult to realize that in the short period of six years since Dr. Billings' death, the work of sixteen years of unremitting effort under Dr. Billings direction, had been effectively scrapped."[33]

If Billings was Hasse's ideal leader, his successor, Edwin Anderson, was a man whose temperament and values were likely to clash with Hasse's. Anderson was reserved, genteel, and a cautious, bureaucratic manager. To Hasse, he was hopelessly uncommunicative, never emerging from his office, never giving her "a single positive direction," and overly concerned with budgetary limitations.[34] Anderson regarded her as an egocentric attention-seeker, an annoyance as he struggled with chronic budget problems in a particularly difficult organizational, political, and financial situation.

Anderson had tried a number of careers—law, journalism, mining—but found success only as a library director. His skills included a knack for cultivating wealthy library supporters, from Andrew Carnegie in Pittsburgh to the aristocrats and plutocrats of NYPL's Board of Trustees, and a subtlety in undermining those he wished to be rid of that would baffle the direct and outspoken Hasse. Anderson wrote little and seldom participated in public discussion at ALA, but he was known for his fervent interest in bringing more men into librarianship.[35] If there were complaints about women's low pay at NYPL, his answer was that more men in the profession would raise salaries.[36] The logical problem with this was, of course, that, given the low pay, men would enter the field only with the assurance of well-paid administrative jobs, so it was unclear how their presence would raise the pay of the women stuck below the glass ceiling. As Hasse became ever more prominent as both a division chief in NYPL's research library and a feminist who publicly criticized women's low pay in libraries, she was a threat both to Anderson's strategy and to what was essentially a male oligarchy in which the directorship of NYPL passed internally to Anderson, then to Harry Lydenberg, and then to Franklin Hopper. Women might supervise the many small branch libraries, but the prestigious research library was a largely male domain where the young men favored by Anderson, such as Charles Williamson, Keyes Metcalf, and Rollin Sawyer, moved quickly into leadership positions.

All three had sometimes tense relations with Hasse. Williamson, hired by Anderson to head the Economics Division in the new building, complained that Hasse was hostile to him because she had wanted his job. If so, she had some reason for resentment, for Williamson had a Ph.D. but no experience as a librarian when he became a division chief, and he had been found unsatisfactory in his previous employment on the faculty of Bryn Mawr College by its feminist president, Martha Carey Thomas. In 1914 Williamson transferred to the Municipal Reference Library, and Hasse became head of the Economics Division, into which her Documents Division was merged. By 1918 however, Williamson had left the Municipal Reference Library and, unable to find a position in an academic library, was in need of a job just when Hasse's dismissal conveniently enabled Anderson to put him back in charge of the Economics Division.[37]

Anderson, Lydenberg, and Williamson all were reserved, conservative, and unbending personalities, likely to be discomfited both by a woman of Hasse's temperament and by the whole atmosphere of turmoil and change in the century's second decade. After Madeleine Day, head of the periodical room, left in 1912 to marry Lydenberg, the head of the research library, Hasse was the only woman head of a division, and the archival evidence suggests that she was increasingly isolated in an atmosphere in which her ideas were rejected, her actions were criticized and undermined, and she was classified in the negative stereotypes used against active women: hysterical female, shrew, harridan, definitely not a team player. Though the archival records show no more than the normal level of conflict in a large organization, there seemed to be a determination to project blame on to the allegedly difficult Hasse. Some of the problems arose from the not uncommon library conflict over how best to handle government documents; for Hasse, this became a crisis when Anderson removed the cataloging of documents from her control. Although Hasse made it clear she disagreed with the decision, about which she was not consulted, and felt profoundly wounded by it, she continued to work hard and make constructive suggestions. Her emotional distress was building, however, with sleepless nights and "bitterness and utter loneliness in my heart."[38] The tensions in the library were compounded by external factors in Hasse's life and in the larger society, making a spiral to disaster of what should have been the prime years of her forties.

At about the same time as the move to the new library, Hasse made a major change in her life by adopting a three-year-old boy. A few years later, she adopted a second child. In an example of the publicity she attracted, this became the subject of a feature that appeared in the *Evening Mail* under the headline "Being adopted mother to red-headed boy her relief from her highbrow job. Though she's chief of dept. of Economics in daytime Miss Hasse is more interested in kiddie's shoe and stocking problems."[39] In lively tabloid style, the article informed New Yorkers that the unmarried woman division head at NYPL was a happy single mother who recommended adoption to "all business women who have been too busy hitting the bulls-eye of success to marry and have sonnies of their own." Though most of the article was about Hasse's professional expertise ("certainly the highest authority in the world on public documents and technical reports") and the services her division provided to a wide range of researchers, the reporter's emphasis on Hasse's single motherhood may well have sent a shudder through the proper men of the research library and its board. Frank Hill, director of Brooklyn Public Library and a friend of Anderson's, linked her motherhood to a negative perception of Hasse when he wrote to Charles Lummis: "I don't believe you missed much if Adelaide did not see you [on a visit to California]. Of course you knew her in Los Angeles and probably still have a very high opinion of her. I wonder if her children were with her."[40]

Becoming a middle-aged, single mother of two did not slow Hasse's pace. If anything, her whirl of activity become more frenetic. She was now a mother with a suburban home to maintain and a cook, housekeeper, and governess to pay, while continuing to work long hours in the library, write, speak, teach, work on bibliographic projects, and participate in civic affairs. She became increasingly outspoken on fundamental issues of library service and the condition of women library workers in ways that stirred controversy and angered her coworkers, especially as her comments sometimes were critical of NYPL and of the profession generally for its "dead level of mediocrity."[41] Hasse's forceful advocacy of change brought her enthusiastic letters from John Cotton Dana and others, but she could hardly have expected to avoid making enemies when she wrote of libraries as a land of the living dead:

> But it is difficult to see how an occupation, sought by the great majority of those engaged in it as a refuge rather than as a career, could be other than the grave it is.

> But the library death rate is tragically high. With your eyes wide open for once, see the sad exhibition of library corpses strewing this country! Dead! Killed by neglect! Died, from lack of exercise! Succumbed, because of too little fresh air! Drowned in a sea of petty jealousies! Smothered to death under their own cloud of dust![42]

Up until the move to the new building on Fifth Avenue in 1911, Hasse had worked with researchers in the Astor Library and devoted herself to building the collection and to improving the bibliography of government publications. When she moved into the magnificent new home of the flagship of American research libraries, the cumulative influence of Kelso, Billings, McCarthy's concept of legislative reference, Dana and the special libraries movement, and the Progressive movement's faith in expertise and research, all led to Hasse's determination to develop and promote reference service that would be more active in finding information for "the men and women in the world of affairs."[43] Pursuing her goals with her usual energy while feeling increasingly isolated in the library, she put more and more effort into promoting her division's library service, writing and speaking about what libraries could do and directly contacting businesses, journalists, and social scientists with offers of reference services that would find any information, including writing reports of data and preparing bibliographies. As she told *American Magazine,* "I had something to sell, and I sold it."[44] Repeatedly, she described the library in business terms as a utility, a service plant, an unused asset that should be seen as something more active than a building with a collection. "One of these days there is going to be a Library Revolution," she warned. "A library is a utility, not a monument."[45]

The more visible and active she was, the greater the resentment in the other divisions, where there was concern that she was promoting more service than the library could deliver when the staff already felt overwhelmed by mass use of the new building. She also was suspected of having an egotistical need to work on important projects with important people. One example of this negative attitude toward Hasse involved Julius Henry Cohen, a prominent, well-connected attorney, who was representing the state of New York and the Chamber of Commerce in seeking to establish the interstate Port of New York Authority. Establishment of such intergovernmental authorities was considered a key reform by Progressives. Cohen wrote to both Anderson and Hasse of his appreciation for the help he received from Hasse and her staff.[46] When Hasse later cited his letter as evidence of her good work, the administration replied that she had done too much for Cohen and had shown her usual grandiose need to work with important people.[47] If Hasse enjoyed working with important people, that is hardly an uncommon trait. Library administrators may be concerned about whether the status of patrons influences the quality of service, but the reality is that library directors would expect reference librarians to make an extra effort for an influential attorney representing the state government and the Chamber of Commerce on a case important to the local economy. That Hasse was criticized even under these circumstances suggests sexism or personal animosity as factors in her worsening situation.

Sexism was an issue in Hasse's mind as she became increasingly involved in issues of the status and pay of women library workers. She wrote several articles for women college graduates in which she portrayed library work as a potentially exciting occupation for women but one constrained by excessive technical detail in library education, the limited vision of library administrators, and the inequities in salaries. In a 1916 article, she complained, "The men in the library profession . . . command the big salaries. . . . Equal pay for equal work is absolutely essential in this profession as in any other."[48] The following year, she referred to "higher salaries being secured as often through favoritism as through any inherent ability."[49] As chair of the Economics Committee of the NYPL Staff Association in 1917, she recommended establishment of a personnel board of at least five library staff to mediate between staff and administration over the issues of pay and promotion that were causing employee unrest.[50] To Anderson, such a proposal was interference with administrative prerogatives, and he apparently suspected Hasse of conspiring against him with the feminist New York Library Employees Union (LEU). Hasse privately supported the union and was close to its president, Tilloah Squires, and Anderson may have blamed her for the union's attacks on his administration in the press, which appeared shortly before he fired her.[51] Hasse was not alone in her concern about the situation of women in libraries, however. At the 1917 meeting of ALA, Anne Carroll

Moore, head of NYPL's children's services, commented frankly about library work's lack of appeal for young women, but her remarks were limited to a discussion among librarians, while Hasse addressed a wider audience outside the profession in print and acted on her concerns through the Economics Committee and the union.[52]

Hasse's views were hardly radical in New York at the time, but, as the era of the New Woman reached its peak, she may have seemed the essence of social trends profoundly disturbing to the personally and politically conservative men of NYPL. The long-term movement of women into the workforce had increased dramatically, especially when young men went into the military in 1917–18 and women took many traditionally male jobs. These working women increasingly were involved in activist unions that worked together for reform through the Women's Trade Union League and were allied with the women's suffrage movement. Their spirit was expressed by Margaret Dreier Robins when she told the 1917 conference of the National Women's Trade Union League, "This is the woman's age! At last after centuries of disabilities and discriminations, women are coming into the labor and festival of life on equal terms with men."[53]

Even women's appearance was changing, with shorter hair and skirts and more practical, tailored clothing that seemed unfeminine to traditionalists. Women's movements were interfering with male pleasures, achieving national Prohibition and shutting down brothels in many cities. Margaret Sanger's indictment for disseminating birth control information in her alarmingly titled magazine, *The Woman Rebel*, raised the fundamental issue of women's control of their bodies.

Above all, women were pressing for the right to vote with a determination that, after titanic struggle, finally succeeded in passing women's suffrage in New York in 1917 and in Congress in 1919. To Hasse, the landmark suffrage campaign in New York was thrilling evidence of the organizational ability that women could put to use in libraries.[54] It was not such a happy sign to Elihu Root, leader of the Eastern establishment and chairman of the executive committee of the NYPL Board of Trustees. Root had led the fight against women's suffrage in New York from 1894 to 1917. Soon he would have an opportunity to show Adelaide Hasse that men were still in control.

DISMISSAL, 1918–19

After the United States entered the war against Germany in 1917, Anderson saw a chance to get rid of Hasse indirectly. During the years of debate over U.S. neutrality, it had taken an intense campaign of anti-German propaganda to win public support for war. After the U.S. declared war on Germany, the country was swept by a hatred of all things German and hysterical suspicion of German-Americans. Not only was Hasse of German ancestry, she had advocated

American neutrality (as had millions of other German-Americans and many Progressives). She was even suspect because she had been in Germany, representing ALA at the Leipzig book exposition, when war broke out in 1914.

To discourage the considerable opposition to the war, the government encouraged a witch-hunting atmosphere with the sedition and espionage laws of 1917 and President Wilson's call for Americans to report any information about possible disloyalty. One of those who did so was Edwin Anderson, who in January of 1918 went to the Secret Service to report that he suspected Adelaide Hasse of disloyalty and to suggest that her house might be searched during her trip to California to teach in a library school.[55] While she was away, government agents searched her home four times. On her return, Hasse indignantly reported to Lydenberg that the agents' conversation had indicated to her housekeeper that someone in the library had reported her; she suspected Rollin Sawyer.[56] Though the government brought no charges against Hasse, the library was soon awash in rumors that she was being investigated, greatly adding to the tensions surrounding her in the frenzied atmosphere of 1918.

As the year went on with no government action against her, Hasse was busy planning a new bibliographic project. During the summer, the LEU published several attacks on NYPL that went beyond complaints about pay and promotion to criticize the whole atmosphere of Anderson's administration. Though Hasse had no visible connection with them, they probably were perceived as linked to her in what seemed to be a chorus of public criticism from women.

Meanwhile, the campaign for the woman's suffrage amendment to the Constitution was reaching fever pitch. On Sept. 30, President Wilson went before the Senate to urge support for the amendment; the following day, the Senate rejected it by two votes. With the fall elections approaching, women able to vote in many states, and senators now elected by popular vote, the suffrage amendment was within striking distance of passage in Congress.

On October 7, Hasse received a two-sentence message from Anderson informing her that the executive committee of the trustees had decided that her services were no longer wanted and that she was being "given an opportunity to tender your resignation at once." Pressuring her to go quietly, he told her, "In view of your long connection with the library, I am authorized to deal with you in the matter of salary after today as generously as your attitude may warrant."[57]

Hasse did not go quietly. She immediately requested an explanation. Anderson refused to see her and sent her another brusque note telling her he was not authorized to tell her the reasons for the committee's action, "but you know those reasons better than anyone else, and they are sufficient." Hasse persisted in writing to both Anderson and Elihu Root, asking that she be informed of the charges against her and be given a hearing to reply. Anderson replied mysteriously that there were no charges against her but the executive committee had observed her performance and concluded the "best interests of the library required them to dispense with your further services." She was therefore terminated with two months pay in severance (and no pension).[58]

In the face of this stunning blow, Hasse fought back with her usual vigor. It is unlikely she really hoped to get her job back, but dismissal had liberated her to vent the indignation that had built up over years of what she believed was harassment by Anderson. Her professional reputation was to be defended, of course, but she seems also to have sought to expose the conditions at NYPL and show the need for civil service procedural protections for library employees. Although Hasse soon had a new job with the War Labor Policies Board in Washington, she persisted in seeking an explanation and a hearing from the NYPL Board of Trustees. A leading trial lawyer, George Gordon Battle, contacted the trustees on her behalf, urging them to reconsider. Governor Al Smith wrote to his friend among the trustees, Judge Morgan O'Brien, who was the only member of the board to meet with Hasse.[59] Though she never received any official statement, individual board members explained they had been led to believe she did not work cooperatively with the rest of the staff. Hasse never saw it, but the board had been given a statement against her from other library staff. When Elihu Root reported to the board on the executive committee's action, his presentation was that of an experienced lawyer making a case against Hasse, who was not present or represented.[60] The authority of Root, a former U. S. senator, Secretary of War, Secretary of State, Nobel Peace Prize winner, and leader of every sort of civic endeavor, was unlikely to be challenged by other board members, especially since to do so could only lead to an awkward situation among gentlemen.

The statement against Hasse that carried so much weight with the trustees was signed by 20 staff members, most of them the male division chiefs, but also including four women.[61] The first part of it shows that the main complaint against Hasse was her published criticism of libraries and librarians and her efforts on behalf of the staff. Hasse, it said, "has been conducting through newspapers and periodicals a campaign which is injuring the library, misrepresenting the library profession, and is definitely calculated to bring discredit upon us as librarians. . . . she is systematically working to undermine your administration, and to cause discord and dissatisfaction among the staff." The second part of the letter accused Hasse of "habitual rudeness" and "frequent disregard for the interests of other divisions and of the rights of her colleagues." No specifics were given, and the weight of the accusation was somewhat undermined by a letter to Anderson from William Gamble of the Technology Division, who wrote that he had not personally experienced Hasse's rudeness but felt strongly about her "disloyalty to the library" in seeking "her own aggrandizement . . . in the public prints."[62] A letter from another division chief informed Anderson that he had refrained from signing the statement to avoid "making a 'public martyr' out of a person whose motives are or may be purely political or antipatriotic" and urged that Hasse be dealt with in secret.[63]

The statement against Hasse was initiated by Keyes Metcalf, who was certain that Hasse was responsible for the LEU's public attacks on the NYPL administration. Whether it confirms Anderson's portrayal of Hasse as an impossible woman or Hasse's account of a poisonous atmosphere created by Anderson is a matter of judgement. The other evidence assembled in the case against Hasse is equally ambiguous and can as well be interpreted as proof of Anderson's harassment as of Hasse's uncooperativeness. One of the few specific examples of Hasse's problematic behavior was her own typically frank reply to Harry Lydenberg, when he had reproved her for the "carping" tone of her comments about errors in the catalog: "I know I am disagreeable, but I don't mean to be carping. The trouble is when I am friendly or kindly or diplomatic, I am ineffectual."[64] She went on to comment on the level of conflict in the library and unfair treatment of her department, ending with the remark that she had had nothing to eat since 8 a.m. and it was now 8 p.m. Besides being tired and hungry, Hasse clearly had a morale problem typical of middle-aged people who have spent many years in large organizations and find their patience wearing thin. Quite possibly, she also was describing the common double bind in which the "kindly or diplomatic" woman is invisible, while any display of anger by women is labelled monstrous.

What makes the rest of Hasse's fight over her dismissal so fascinating in terms of women's history is the rarity of the anger she openly expressed. By the summer of 1919, she had given up on polite, reasonable appeals to the trustees and instead sent them a letter denouncing Anderson and the conditions he had created in the library and, in a pointed dig at Root, suggesting that the board never would have taken such action under its previous leader, the distinguished attorney John Cadwalader.[65]

A month later, the American Library Association conference was shaken by a resolution against sex discrimination offered by the New York Library Employees Union. Though Hasse's name was not mentioned, the LEU clearly was referring to her dismissal when it proclaimed that women were discriminated against in libraries in general and particularly at NYPL:

"Women may get as far as branch librarianships. Beyond that they cannot go. With one exception, and that an unimportant department, all the heads of departments in the New York Public Library are men, the director is a man, all the members of the boards of trustees are men. Selection of these upper officers is not made on the basis of superiority of intellegence or ability: it is simply made on the basis of sex."

The union declared itself determined to change this situation: "Be it resolved: We are against the system of removing women without cause and are in favor of throwing open of positions in library work, from Librarian of Congress down to that of page, to men and women equally, and for equal pay."[66]

This may be the strongest feminist resolution ever presented to ALA. It was defeated by a vote of 121 to 1 in a group that was four-fifths women. Since women said little in a discussion dominated by Richard Bowker, Arthur Bostwick, and George Bowerman, the reasons for their opposition are uncertain. Garrison suggested the women librarians were alarmed by the LEU's eloquent Maud Malone, who attacked professional status as a caste system and argued "librarians are sweated labor." The focus of discussion seems to have been unions, not the broader of issue of sex discrimination, and Bostwick's linking of unions to radicalism may have stirred fears at a time of revolution in Europe and the "Red Scare" in the U.S.

After the LEU's defeat at ALA, Hasse issued a public attack on NYPL in a widely distributed pamphlet, *The Compensations of Librarianship*. She frankly described her years of growing bitterness towards Anderson for his "total lack of inspiration, the sordid discrimination, the vicious clique system."[67] Since Anderson never made any public reply, Hasse's denunciation tended to confirm stereotypes of the hysterical female, the shrill feminist, the utter unreasonableness of the angry woman. It so alarmed Richard Bowker that he in turn attacked Hasse in an editorial in *Library Journal*, arguing she deserved to be fired because she was a woman who always had to have her own way.[68] The only reply came in a letter from Tilloah Squires of the LEU, who disputed Bowker's version of the facts and argued that the treatment of Hasse showed the need for "civil service as a solution to the impossibility of obtaining a hearing for library employees before an unbiased board."[69] After that, the whole distressing subject of conflict and anger, especially women's anger, vanished from library literature. Hasse, however, had long since moved beyond worrying what people thought or fearing to show her feelings. When George W. Lee, librarian of an engineering firm, responded to her pamphlet with the fatuous advice that she should love her enemies and the suggestion that perhaps the federal government had only hired her to keep her under observation, she replied, "I feel justified in calling you a contemptible ass." Lee was shocked and sent a copy to Edwin Anderson with the note, "What is the matter with her anyway?. . . . Perhaps, after all, her biggest trouble is that she has no sense of humor."[70]

AFTERWORD

The remainder of Hasse's long career was spent in Washington, continuing to work with government information in various federal agencies and the Brookings Institution and teaching library science. She was active in the DC Library Association and the Special Libraries Association. She never again worked in a major research library, and eventually she identified herself as a bibliographer rather than a librarian in *Who's Who in America*.

Hasse is remembered now for her bibliographies and her classification system, still used by the Superintendent of Documents and hundreds of depository libraries. The provocative ideas she put forth, her involvement in the Progressive movement and the stormy controversy surrounding her departure from NYPL all have been ignored by library historians, as though they were an irrelevant aberration. If Hasse was indeed an anomaly among librarians, she was far from unusual among the reforming New Women of the Progressive era, of whom Jill Ker Conway has written, "Their language was pungent, their schedules were enough to daunt a professional athlete, and, for those who worked with them, their force of character something of primal dimensions." Yet most of them were careful to present a conventionally feminine public image, Conway concludes, because "in American society, a woman who does not fit the romantic stereotype of the female has difficulty mustering public support."[71] Conway writes of her own discomfort as a biographer with evidence of egotism and selfishness in Jane Addams, and perhaps there has been similar uneasiness with Adelaide Hasse's driving energy and ambition, her sharp criticisms, her public fight with her director and board. Ultimately though, Hasse cannot be ignored, for, in the words of her ambivalent critic Richard Bowker, "No one has won a more distinctive position or made more stir in the library profession than Miss Adelaide R. Hasse."[72] The issues raised by her writings and by her career are important to a full understanding of the history of American librarianship and the experience of women librarians.

ENDNOTES

Adelaide Hasse's papers in the Archives of New York Public Library, hereafter cited as "Hasse papers," are in five boxes in Record Group 7, Economics Division. Most of them are her office files that were kept when she left in 1918, while the box labelled "Adelaide R. Hasse Case" includes the NYPL administration's papers related to her dismissal.

[1]Richard Bowker, "Women in the Library Profession," *Library Journal* 45 (August 1920), 640.

[2]Carroll Smith-Rosenberg, "The New Woman as Androgyne: Social Disorder and Gender Crisis, 1870–1936" in her *Disorderly Conduct; Visions of Gender in Victorian America* (New York: Oxford University Press, 1986), p. 280.

[3]Ibid., p. 245.

[4]*Dictionary of American Library Biography*, s.v. Adelaide Rosalie Hasse; *ALA World Encyclopedia of Library and Information Services,* s.v. Adelaide Hasse.

[5]Dee Garrison, *Apostles of Culture: The Public Librarian and American Society, 1876–1920* (New York: Free Press, 1979), p. 241.

[6]Adelaide Hasse, *The Compensations of Librarianship.* (n.p., 1919).

[7]*National Cyclopaedia of American Biography,* s.v. Hermann Hasse.

[8]"Tessa Kelso, Librarian, 1889–1895," Los Angeles Public Library, *Annual Report for the Year Ending June 30, 1936*, p. 44.

[9]Ida Tarbell, *All in a Day's Work* (New York: Macmillan, 1939), p. 54.

[10]Andrew Sinclair, *The Emancipation of the American Woman* (reprint, New York: Harper and Row, 1966), 107. Originally published as *The Better Half.*

[11]"Miss Adelaide R. Hasse," *New York Times Illustrated Magazine* (June 27,1897), p. 15.

[12]Hasse, *Compensations*, 3–4; Gail K. Nelson and John V. Richardson, "Adelaide Hasse and the Early History of the U.S. Superintendent of Documents Classification Scheme," *Government Publications Review* 13 (Jan.–Feb.1986), pp. 79–88.

[13]Tessa Kelso, "Some Economical Features of Public Libraries," *Library Journal 18* (Nov. 1893), p. 473 (reprinted from *The Arena* 7 (May 1893) pp. 709–713). *Library Journal* contains numerous references to Kelso beginning with her attendance at the 1886 ALA conference.

[14]*Kelso v. Teale, City Auditor*, 106 Cal. 477 (1895)

[15]Editorial, *Library Journal* 37 (Aug. 1912) p. 417.

[16]*Los Angeles Herald*, March 8, 1895.

[17]Hasse, *Compensations*, p. 4–9; Nelson and Richardson, "Adelaide Hasse and the Early History," pp. 89–94.

[18]John Y. Cole, *Capital Libraries and Librarians: A Brief History of the District of Columbia Library Association* (Washington: Library of Congress, 1994).

[19]Hasse, *Compensations*, p. 9; Richard Bowker to AH, Feb. 2, 1898, Hasse papers.

[20]John Shaw Billings to AH, March 14, 1896, March 31, 1897, June 1, 1897, July 1, 1898, Hasse papers.

[21]Fielding Garrison, *John Shaw Billings: a Memoir* (New York: G.P. Putnam's Sons, 1915), p. 387.

[22]Hasse, *Compensations*, p. 12.

[23]Adelaide Hasse, *Index to Economic Material in Documents of the States of the United States* (Washington: Carnegie Institution, 1907–22), 13 vols. in 16; Adelaide Hasse, *United States Government Publications; a Handbook for the Cataloger*, (Boston: Library Bureau, 1902–03), 2 vols; New York General Assembly, 1695, *A Journal of the House of Representatives for His Majestie's Province of New York in America*, repro-

duced in facsimilie from the first edition printed by William Bradford, 1695, with an introductory note by Adelaide Hasse (New York: Dodd, Mead, 1903).

[24]Ellen Fitzpatrick, *Endless Crusade: Women Social Scientists and Progressive Reform* (New York: Oxford University Press, 1990), p. xiii.

[25]Tarbell, *All in a Day's Work*, p. 209.

[26]Florence Kelley to AH, Nov. 21, 1907, Dec. 30, 1907, Hasse papers; Phillipa Strum, *Louis D. Brandeis, Justice for the People* (Cambridge: Harvard University Press, 1984), pp. 114–124.

[27]John R. Commons, *Myself* (New York: Macmillan, 1934), 65, 108; Marion Casey, *Charles McCarthy: Librarianship and Reform* (Chicago: American Library Association, 1981).

[28]Judith Schwarz, *Radical Feminists of Heterodoxy: Greenwich Village, 1912–1940* (Norwich, Vt: New Victoria Publishers, 1986), p. 14.

[29]Marian Manley, "Tessa L. Kelso, August 13, 1933," *Library Journal* 58 (Oct. 1, 1933) p. 800; Tessa Kelso, *Clause 79h; report to Committee of Woman's Municipal League of the City of New York* (New York; n.p., 1911).

[30]Dudley Gordon, "Charles F. Lummis, Litt.D., Librarian Extraordinary, and Founder of the Bibliosmiles," *California Librarian* 22 (Jan. 1961), pp. 17–22.

[31]Garrison, *Apostles*, pp. 153–156.

[32]Melvil Dewey to AH, April 13, 1905, May 13, 1905, Hasse papers; AH to Isobel Lord, Richard Bowker, and Edwin Anderson, June 2, 1906, Richard Bowker papers, Manuscripts and Special Collections, New York Public Library.

[33]Hasse, *Compensations*, p. 13.

[34]Ibid.

[35]*Dictionary of American Library Biography*, s.v. Edwin Hatfield Anderson; "American Library Association; 34th Annual Meeting," *Library Journal* 6 (Aug. 1912), p. 440. Phyllis Dain, *The New York Public Library: a History of its Founding and Early Years* (New York: New York Public Library, 1972) provides the fullest account of Anderson's administration, though it does not discuss his conflict with Hasse.

[36]Peter Hernon, "Keyes DeWitt Metcalf" in *Leaders in American Academic Librarianship, 1925–1975* (Pittsburgh: Beta Phi Mu, distributed by the American Library Association, 1983), p. 221.

[37]Paul Winkler, *The Greatest of Greatness: the Life and Work of Charles C. Williamson* (Metuchen, NJ: Scarecrow Press, 1992).

[38]Hasse, *Compensations*, pp. 15–16.

[39]*New York Evening Mail*, Sept. 17, 1915, (clipping in AH folder, Staff Biographical box, Record Group 9, Archives of New York Public Library).

[40]Frank Hill to Charles Lummis, March 20, 1918, Lummis papers, Southwest Museum, Los Angeles.

[41]Adelaide Hasse, "Women in Libraries," *Journal of the Association of Collegiate Alumnae* 11 (Oct. 1917) p. 74.

[42]John Cotton Dana to AH, Sept. 15, 1916, Feb. 8, 1918, Hasse papers; Hasse, "Women in Libraries," p. 74; Adelaide Hasse, "Making a Market in Libraries," *Library Journal* 42 (April 1917), p. 272.

[43]Adelaide Hasse, "Library Preparedness in the Fields of Economics and Sociology," *Library Journal* 41 (August 1916), p. 559.

[44]Alfred Grunberg, "How to Make Your Public Library a Business Asset," *American Magazine* 87 (May 1919), p. 61.

[45]Hasse, "Making a Market," pp. 271–272. Similar comments are in: Adelaide Hasse, "Why Not?" *New Republic* (Jan. 19, 1918), p. 341; Interview with AH, *New York Evening Sun*, March 18, 1918, clipping in Hasse papers.

[46]Julius Henry Cohen to AH, Cohen to Edwin Anderson, both Feb. 26, 1917, Hasse papers.

[47]"Comments of the Director on Miss Hasse's Statement sent to the trustees by Mr Battle," undated typescript, Hasse papers. This nine page statement expresses Anderson's detestation of Hasse.

[48]Adelaide Hasse, "Library Work as a Profession for Women," typescript of article for *Hunter College Bulletin* (March 24, 1916), Hasse papers.

[49]Hasse, "Women in Libraries," p. 74.

[50]Economics Committee, AH, Chair, to Edwin Anderson and Executive Board, Staff Association, Jan. 18, 1918, Hasse papers.

[51]Clippings in the Hasse papers: T. Squires' letter, *New York Evening Post*, July 26, 1918; T. Squires' articles in *Civil Service Chronicle*, Aug. 23, Sept. 6, 1918.

[52]"Is Camp Library Work Worth While? [discussion]," *ALA Bulletin* 43 (1918), pp. 285–286.

[53]J. Stanley Lemons, *The Woman Citizen: Social Feminism in the 1920s* (Urbana: University of Illinois Press, 1973), p. 20.

[54]Hasse, "Women in Libraries," p. 45.

[55]Frank Burke, U.S. Secret Service, to Edwin Anderson, Jan. 19, 1918, Hasse papers.

[56]Harry Lydenberg memo, March 23, 1918, Hasse papers.

[57]Hasse, *Compensations*, p. 17.

[58]Ibid., pp. 18–19.

[59]Ibid., 20; George Gordon Battle to Elihu Root, Dec. 12, 1918; Henry Fairfield Osborn to Battle, Dec. 27, 1918, Hasse papers.

[60]NYPL Board of Trustees, Minutes, Jan. 8, 1919, Hasse papers.

[61]Letter to Edwin Anderson signed by twenty NYPL staff, Sept. 21, 1918, Hasse papers; Keyes Dewitt Metcalf, *Random Recollections of an Anachronism or Seventy-five Years of Library Work* (New York: Readex Books, 1980), pp. 184–187.

[62]William Gamble to Edwin Anderson, Sept. 20, 1918, Hasse papers.

[63]Heryk Arctowski to Edwin Anderson, Sept. 23, 1918, Hasse papers.

[64]Harry Lydenberg to AH, AH to Lydenberg, both Feb. 16, 1916, Hasse papers.

[65]Hasse, *Compensations*, pp. 20–21.

[66]"Asbury Park Conference," *ALA Bulletin* 13 (1919) pp. 358–59, 376–86; Garrison, *Apostles*, pp. 229–30; James Milden, "Women, Public Libraries, and Library Unions: The Formative Years," *Journal of Library History* 12 (1977) pp. 150–58.

[67]Hasse, *Compensations*, p. 13.

[68]Editorial, *Library Journal* 44 (August 1919), p. 488.

[69]T. Squires, Letter, *Library Journal* 44 (Oct. 1919), p. 672.

[70]George W. Lee to AH, July 16, 1919; AH to Lee, July 19, 1919; Lee to Edwin Anderson, July 22, 1919, Hasse papers.

[71]Jill Ker Conway, *True North* (New York: Knopf, 1994), pp. 149, 160–61.

[72]Richard Bowker, "Women in the Library Profession," p. 639.

of her favorite authors. As a young girl, she participated in local literary societies, a practice that she would continue throughout her life.[1]

Julia attended Lake Forest College in Illinois from 1891 to 1893, transferring to Tarkio College in Missouri when the family moved there. She graduated in 1895, honored as the class salutatorian. She considered a career in light opera because of her love of music, but she felt that her father would object to a profession then regarded as somewhat scandalous. Instead, she decided to become a teacher, and for the next four years, she taught in schools in Iowa and Missouri. She later said that one of her concerns while teaching was finding books for her students to read. In 1899, she left teaching to attend the Drexel Institute in Philadelphia to be trained as a librarian. She graduated in 1901, and was asked to remain at Drexel as a teacher. She taught cataloging and acquisitions until 1903.[2]

Wishing to be closer to her family, who had moved to Phoenix, Arizona, Julia accepted a position at the University of New Mexico as a librarian and history instructor.[3] New Mexico was still a territory, and the university was just over a decade old. The library was in one room and had been looked after by a math instructor with failing eyesight.[4] Julia was the first trained librarian at the university and probably the first in the entire territory. She organized the library, cataloging the books, creating a card catalog, and issuing library cards.[5] While doing all this, she also sponsored the girls' basketball team, taught history and served on university committees for athletics and music.[6]

While at the University of New Mexico, she met Rupert Asplund, a Professor of Latin and Greek, who had come to the university in 1902. Their daughter has described Rupert as a man of "uncorruptible integrity" [sic] who was easy to get along with but "rock-like on all matters of principle."[7] Rupert and Julia were married on August 3, 1905, in Mexico City, in a service performed by her father. Julia resigned from the university and became active in Albuquerque social affairs. She was a member of the Tuesday Literary Club, a charter member of the Albuquerque chapter of the Daughters of the American Revolution, and a member of the Albuquerque Public Library Commission. On June 22, 1906, their daughter, Carolyn Elizabeth, was born.[8]

In 1909, the Asplunds moved to the capital of the Territory, Santa Fe, where Rupert became the chief clerk for the Department of Education, a position he held until 1916. After a year as secretary of the New Mexico Tax Commission, he became director of the New Mexico Taxpayers' Association in 1918. He remained interested in education, editing the *New Mexico Journal of Education*.[9]

CIVIC ACTIVITIES

Julia joined several Santa Fe cultural organizations, including the Santa Fe chapter of the Daughters of the American Revolution; the Fifteen Club, a literary group; and two very influential organizations, the Santa Fe Woman's Club

chapter 5

Julia Brown Asplund and New Mexico Library Service 1875–1958

Linda K. Lewis

The issues in Julia Brown Asplund's professional career included servi[ng] rural areas, ethnic minorities, the poor, and children; literacy; increas[ing] nancial and political support for libraries; cooperation among libraries; inade[quate] funding; and resource sharing. She served as an academic librarian, a teac[her,] university regent, a public library board member and director of a state li[brary] agency. She worked closely with the legislature, lobbying for the rights of w[omen] and children. She joined in social and cultural organizations actively worki[ng to] improve conditions in the community. The description may sound familiar[; the] surprise comes in realizing that Julia began her career as a librarian in 190[1.]

EARLY LIFE

Julia Brown was born in Missouri on October 6, 1875. Her mother tat[ght] piano; her father was a minister and educator. The family moved freque[ntly] during Julia's childhood because her father was president of several diffe[rent] schools in Kansas and Missouri. Julia grew up surrounded by books at h[ome] and read widely in the libraries of the schools where her father worked. At [age] 12, she read Louisa May Alcott and Sir Walter Scott; Charles Dickens was [one]

1

and the Santa Fe Woman's Board of Trade and Library Association. The Santa Fe Woman's Club and the Santa Fe Woman's Board of Trade, which eventually merged, were very active advocates of the rights of women and children, combining philanthropic, political and social interests.[10]

Julia had been interested in politics as a young girl, and she became very active in political affairs in Santa Fe. While a member of the Legislative Committee and president of the State Federation of Women's Clubs, she lobbied the New Mexico legislature for a number of bills related to women and children. Among these were bills on women's property rights, on women's suffrage, on requiring that there be women on all state boards, on the treatment of delinquent girls, and on the involvement of local governments in charity. Although many of these proposals were defeated initially, the efforts to revise laws on women's property rights and on public charities were successful in 1915. As Julia said in reviewing that legislative session, "We have made a beginning ... from now on every session of the legislature will see the enactment of some laws which have as their object the welfare of women and children."[11] She was persistent—and correct. Eventually, most of the legislation defeated in 1915 did become law.

In 1919, a Girls' Welfare Board was created to determine appropriate treatment for each delinquent girl. The legislation was supported by the State Federation of Women's Clubs, and Julia was among the women appointed to the board in recognition of her leadership in creating the program.[12] Although earlier efforts to get laws requiring that women be appointed to state boards had failed, the desired result was being achieved by persuasion, and Julia was among the first women to serve on a state board.

Julia was active in the Republican party, serving as a member of its executive committee, and she was the first woman in the state to address a state political convention, speaking at the Republican convention in 1920.[13]

In 1921, Julia was appointed by the Governor to the Board of Regents of the University of New Mexico, the first woman on the board.[14] She was concerned about the university library, even 16 years after her resignation from the faculty. She was so persuasive about the needs of the library that her fellow regents agreed to postpone their favored project, a proposed engineering building, in favor of a new building for the library that Julia advocated.[15]

Julia was a strong supporter of women's suffrage. When she was 15, she had written, "I am very strong for woman's rights, you know. I think I shall become a second Susan B. Anthony."[16] She lobbied the legislature continually until New Mexico approved suffrage in 1920. She helped organize the New Mexico Woman's Suffrage League.[17] In October 1915, she was one of the leaders of the state's first suffrage parade when over 150 women held an automobile parade through Santa Fe to meet with U.S. Senator Catron to urge him to support suffrage. Julia spoke on the merits of the Susan B. Anthony amendment and on the logic of granting the right to vote to women, because many of them owned property and paid taxes already. Senator Catron was polite, but not persuaded to

Reprinted with permission.

Julia Brown Asplund in 1950.

change his opposition.[18] According to their daughter, Rupert was also a strong supporter of equal rights for women and always supported Julia in her efforts.[19]

In the November 16, 1927, issue, *The Outlook* magazine asked its readers to respond to questions about the past and future of women's rights. It asked "Do women believe their old leaders really knew what they wanted when they fought for suffrage? . . . What do they want now?"[20] Julia's response, which was not printed, said that women wanted to participate in government, partly because any exclusion based only on sex was "a self-evident absurdity," and partly to address issues relating to children and women that "had not appealed to men as being of vital importance." Her determination shows clearly in her statement: "Yes, thank you—we knew exactly what we wanted and we got it. More than that, we are using it and we expect to go on using it."[21]

ESTABLISHING LIBRARIES

Julia's work for women's and children's rights did not mean that she abandoned her interest in libraries. In Santa Fe, as in many places in the West, there were very few libraries, and most of the public libraries had been established by local women's organizations. The Santa Fe Woman's Board of Trade had established the Santa Fe Public Library—initially created as a public reading room in 1896—and ran it until 1962. Julia was on its library committee from 1910 until her death, except for four years when she was head of the Library Extension Service. She was actively involved in interviewing employees, working for better facilities, and raising funds for the library. Although the city and county contributed some funds, the Santa Fe Woman's Board of Trade raised much of the money needed through appeals and fund raisers. Julia helped organize these efforts, doing everything from helping write press releases to singing in musical events.[22]

In 1909, the Superintendent of Public Instruction asked Julia to survey the school libraries of New Mexico. She found conditions to be very poor; only 6 counties out of 26 had more than 500 volumes in their schools. Julia felt that the only possibility for improving these poor conditions was funding from the legislature.[23] Working with the Santa Fe Woman's Board of Trade and the State Federation of Women's Clubs, Julia attempted to get legislative funding to set up free traveling libraries. The bill creating these was first introduced in 1912, but was defeated then and again in 1913. Much of the opposition was due to the cost; with many competing needs and few funds, libraries were not a high priority. Some additional opposition came from people who believed that books could become contaminated by germs and infect other readers. This fear, which may seem unreasonable today, was widespread in a time when knowledge of germs and public health was still limited. One newspaper ridiculed the idea, saying that its logical development would be for everyone to live in isolated bubbles.[24]

Regardless of the opposition, Julia persisted, and in 1917, the first traveling library collections were begun. The State Federation of Women's Clubs supplied 4 collections of 50 books each, and the University of New Mexico coordinated the work of shipping them out to libraries and groups across the state. Unfortunately, the legislature refused to fund any staff to run the program, and the university was not able to continue it.[25]

STATE LIBRARY EXTENSION SERVICE

In 1925, legislation allowing counties to set up library departments was approved, but most of the counties were too poor and too sparsely populated to support libraries.[26] Julia believed that a strong state system was the best way to bring good library service to the people of New Mexico. Working with the State Federation of Women's Clubs and the librarians, she concentrated on legislation that would begin such a system.[27] In 1929, a bill creating the Library Extension Service was approved with an initial budget of $2,000 for salaries and equipment and a charge to help state libraries, to create a traveling library collection, to compile statistics about state libraries and to serve as the librarian for the state museums.[28] The Santa Fe *New Mexican* called the job of creating the service "herculean" but felt that Julia was well equipped for the tremendous task.[29] Julia used part of her salary to pay for an assistant and additional expenses.[30] Because there was no money allocated for books, Julia built the collection from donations, especially from the state women's clubs, and had 2,000 books by June 1930.[31] The first shipments went out by November 1929; the first one sent to a public library went to the district of State Senator Louise Coe who led the fight for the service in the legislature.[32] Collections of about 40 books went to schools, libraries or groups, which could keep them for three months. In the first year, the service loaned nearly 800 books to 13 libraries and over 150 books to individuals.[33]

Julia traveled throughout the state, talking with librarians, teachers and clubs to promote the new service and to advise librarians in need of help. In 1932, the service began publishing the *New Mexico Library Bulletin*, which she created to promote the service and to inform librarians of issues that concerned them.[34]

During this time, when Julia was setting up a library service without a collection or book budget, a visitor saw her surrounded by piles of books and asked her how one could organize a library under those conditions. Her response was that you took one book at a time, did it, and then did the next, until the work was done. Her advice of "one book at a time," reflecting her determination and perseverance, was remembered by librarians in New Mexico for many years.[35]

While creating and running the Library Extension Service, Julia also organized the collections of the Museum of New Mexico and oversaw their move into a new building. At the dedication services for the new building in January 1931, Julia was acknowledged as the "moving spirit" behind the creation and organization of the library.[36] In 1932, after four years of hard work, Julia resigned as Director of the Library Extension Service.[37]

STATE LIBRARY COMMISSION

There was a growing feeling among librarians in New Mexico that if there were to be adequate library service in the state, it would take a strong centralized organization. The State Extension Service was a beginning, but under its existing structure, it could not provide the additional support and leadership necessary. The efforts to create a state library agency began formally in 1932, when the New Mexico Educational Association, the New Mexico Library Association and the New Mexico State Federation of Women's Clubs adopted resolutions urging the creation of a state library commission.[38] Efforts to create a commission continued during the rest of the 1930s, with various committees working on the proposed legislation. Julia was deeply involved in these efforts, as an advisor or member of the different committees. In 1936, a State Planning Board was created to plan for a state agency and to provide advice to the Library Extension Service, with Julia as chairman of the Board.[39]

In 1941, the efforts of the committees were finally successful and the State Library Commission was created by the legislature. The charge of the commission was to administer the State Library Extension Service, to encourage professional training for librarians, to raise standards of library service, to advise and help libraries, to administer grants-in-aid to libraries and to cooperate with other education agencies.[40] Julia was appointed chairman, a position she would hold until 1954.[41]

Before Julia could address the official duties or any other concerns of the commission in any depth, the United States entered World War II. During the commission's first years, it coordinated a project of training volunteers for library service to replace those library employees serving in the military, surveyed the valuable collections of the state in order to create a record, and supplied books to military camps in the state.[42]

In addition to its wartime activities, the commission began organizing library courses for those teachers who were also librarians in the schools, and worked with libraries to support local library funding.[43]

Julia continued to lobby for increased library support, both on local and state levels, throughout her career. Her annual reports regularly gave figures on the per capita funding for libraries in New Mexico, as compared with the recommended levels from the American Library Association. She was always pleased at the gradual increases, while deploring the large gap still remaining. In 1944, Julia reported that 57% of the people in the state were still without any library service, and that the state was spending only 10¢ per capita on library service as compared to the recommendation of the American Library Association of $1.00 per capita for good library service.[44] She persuaded the legislature to fund a program of grants to help the public libraries. Under her administration, grants were made to libraries across the state, with the available funds increasing steadily. Many libraries were able to acquire desperately needed materials, ranging from basic reference sources to children's materials, which were always needed.

The commission was successful in raising standards for librarians. In 1948, legislation was passed that set up a state certification test for librarians. The commission administered the test, using it as one way to improve the levels of librarians and of library service.[45] Julia was an active member of the New Mexico Library Association, the American Library Trustees Association and the American Library Association, and encouraged librarians to continue to raise their standards and improve their libraries by participating in these professional organizations.[46]

ASPLUND HERITAGE

Rupert Asplund died on December 7, 1952.[47] Julia never fully recovered from her husband's death and resigned from the State Library Commission in 1954, after 50 years of service to libraries in New Mexico.[48] She died on July 26, 1958, but her legacy survives.[49]

Julia believed that everyone should have excellent library service, regardless of age, social class, ethnic background or place of residence. She wanted the researcher to be able to use the archival records and the child to be able to read about Peter Rabbit; their needs were equally important.[50] During World War II, she frequently spoke in favor of continuing or even increasing funding, in spite of the other financial demands, because an informed citizenry was vital to the survival of the open system of government.[51] In 1930, the *New Mexican* carried an appeal to voters by the Library Committee of the Woman's Board of Trade to support funding for the public library. Julia was a member of the committee, and the statement shows her strong influence. It tells of the use of the library by those people too poor to buy books and by those seeking to improve their way of life; of the children seeking free, safe recreation; and of those seeking books in Spanish. It describes the library as promoting "racial sympathy and understanding" and as a place where children, "particularly the under-privileged children," might find wider opportunities.[52]

New Mexico presented special challenges to Julia's goal of providing library service to everyone. The state resources were very limited, with little money available to create a library system. Much of the population was Hispanic and read Spanish, not English, so materials in both languages were needed. The illiteracy rate was high. The population was scattered over a large area, isolated by long distances and poor roads.

There appeared to be two different ways in which library service could develop in New Mexico. In one case, libraries in the larger towns could be encouraged to develop, creating a few excellent, independent libraries in the major centers of population. On the other hand, there could be a centralized state system, with an organization that could help all libraries in the state and provide service to those areas that could not afford their own libraries. Arizona chose the first pattern and did achieve excellent libraries in its larger cities, but much weaker service to rural areas. New Mexico, under Julia's leadership, chose the second pattern, and created a system where the smaller libraries received support—grants, advice, and loans of material—from the State Library.[53]

In discussing the work of the State Library Commission, Julia called supplying the rural areas with materials work of the "very first importance."[54] In the annual reports of the Library Extension Service and the State Library Commission, Julia continually stressed the need to serve the rural population and to report the successes of the traveling library collections and of the state grants given to the smaller libraries.

It was Julia's goal to "provide all the people of New Mexico with the best library service" that the combined efforts of the state and local libraries could achieve.[55] She felt it was obvious that the smaller communities must have state help to achieve such high levels of service, and she used all her political skills to persuade the reluctant legislatures to help.

Beyond the problems created by serving a widely scattered rural population, New Mexico presented other challenges. The state was officially bilingual, but very few people were fluent in both Spanish and English; many other people were illiterate. Throughout her career, Julia worked for better service to the Spanish-speaking community. The law creating the Library Extension Service, which Julia helped draft, included the requirement that there be traveling library collections in English and Spanish.[56] One of her first appeals as director was a request for donations of Spanish texts to meet the many requests received by the Library Extension Service.[57] The *New Mexico Library Bulletin* published lists of books available for lending from the Library Extension Service, and its list of Spanish books grew steadily. In 1933, the *New Mexico Library Bulletin* cover reflected Julia's beliefs: "In all communities where there are Spanish-speaking residents there should be books available in the Spanish language. . . . It is the aim of the director of the New Mexico Extension Service to build up a collection of the best and most interesting titles, both fiction and non-fiction, that are available, for the use of the Spanish-Americans in the state." The issue included excerpts from a speech she had given at a New Mexico Library Association conference advising librarians on the need for Spanish language materials, and the best ways to obtain these books.[58] Although Julia had officially resigned before this issue appeared, it was a goal she believed in deeply and had shared with her successors.

Four years later, when Julia was the Chairman of the State Library Planning Board, board members discussed "at great length" the need for more Spanish language materials, and agreed to work at locating additional sources especially of children's literature, which was very hard for smaller libraries to acquire.[59] The State Library Commission often compiled bibliographies of recommended sources for librarians and teachers. Among these were bibliographies on the history of New Mexico and the traditions and culture of the Hispanic community created to help others learn about the Spanish-speaking population of the state.[60]

Julia never forgot that New Mexico was a multicultural state, and she always worked to provide materials in Spanish and English, in spite of the problems in acquiring such materials on a severely limited budget. Her commitment to serving all the people of the state was strong, and that meant materials in both languages for all levels of readers.

As a child, Julia had been an avid reader. As a teacher of young children, she had tried to find books for her students to read. Her reports of the Library Extension Service and the State Library Commission stressed the need for more books for children and told of the delight with which new books were received by the children. The largest part of the book funds spent during the first years of the Extension Service was spent for children's books.[61]

The State Library Commission promoted children's books and literature, sponsoring exhibits and workshops. The loan of an exhibit of illustrations from children's literature prompted Julia to state her belief that such exhibits could promote reading, encourage children to read at home and, therefore, reduce the state's rate of illiteracy.[62] At the end of her career, Julia summed up her conviction at a conference on libraries in the Southwest by stating that working with children is "the most important work that the majority of us as librarians do or ever can do."[63]

CONCLUSION

The terms used to describe Julia's career in New Mexico seem extravagant; she is described as a legend who was responsible for the creation of state-wide library service and for many of the laws concerning the rights of women and children.[64] In 1949, the American Library Association honored her with their Citation of Merit in recognition of her leadership in providing library service to the people of New Mexico.[65] The language and the amount of praise might have embarrassed Julia, but in fact, they are not exaggerations. Her work with the State Federation of Women's Clubs and other women's organizations did indeed result in major legislation concerning women's and children's rights. Her role in the libraries of New Mexico is inestimable. She created the organization that would become the State Library, organized the libraries of the University of New Mexico and the Museum of New Mexico, and helped organize and expand the Santa Fe Public Library. Because of her decades of work, library service was made available throughout the state. In a time when many libraries served only the middle and upper classes of the larger towns, Julia was committed to serving everyone, regardless of residence, class, race, ethnic background, age or language ability. Her inclusion in a 1976 exhibit organized by the American Association of University Women as one of 13 women honored for their outstanding contributions to New Mexico was an appropriate acknowledgment of her accomplishments, but Julia might be more pleased to know that the organization she began is still actively serving all the people of the state.[66]

ENDNOTES

[1]Ann Burleson Honea, "Julia Brown Asplund; New Mexico Librarian 1875–1958." (M.L.S. Thesis, University of Texas, Austin, 1967), 3–4.

[2]Honea, pp. 7–9.

[3]Honea, p. 9.

[4]Dorothy Hughes, *Pueblo on the Mesa.* (Albuquerque: University of New Mexico Press, 1939), 88.

[5]Erna Fergusson, "A Writer's View of Southwest Libraries," in *Libraries in the Southwest; Their Growth—Strength—Needs.* ed. Lawrence Clark Powell. (Los Angeles: University of California, Los Angeles, 1955), 7–8.

[6]Terry Gugliotta, University of New Mexico Archivist, letter, October 11, 1990.

[7]Carolyn A. Ruch, letter, March 8, 1980.

[8]Honea, pp. 10, 12.

[9]Honea, p. 11.

[10]Honea, pp. 13–15.

[11]"State Women's Federation is Well-pleased with Beginning Made in Getting Legislation; Actual Results Not Imposing." *New Mexican*, 15 March 1915.

[12]"Girls' Welfare Board." *New Mexican*, 19 February 1919. "Welfare Board Personnel Named by the Governor." *New Mexican*, 24 March 1919.

[13]"Services Here Tuesday for Mrs. Julia Asplund." *New Mexican*, 28 July 1958.

[14]Gugliotta.

[15]"Mrs Julia Brown Asplund Wins Trustees Award," *New Mexico Library Bulletin* 19 (July 1950): 2.

[16]Honea, p. 16.

[17]"A Local Branch of the Woman Suffrage Union is Organized." *New Mexican*, 19 October 1915.

[18]"150 Santa Fe Suffragists in Demonstration at Home of U S Senator Catron." *New Mexican*, 21 October 1915. "Deputation to Senator Catron of New Mexico," *Suffragist* (November 1915): 7.

[19]Ruch.

[20]"From Publisher—To You," *The Outlook* 147 (November 16, 1927): 321.

[21]Honea, pp. 25–26.

[22]Honea, pp. 12, 17.

[23]Julia Brown Asplund, "School Libraries in New Mexico," *New Mexico Journal of Education* 6 (September 15, 1909): 15–16.

[24]"Cultivating the Book Germ." *New Mexican*, 19 April 1912.

[25]Mildred A. Barrett, *Development of Library Extension Service in New Mexico*. (Rochester, NY: University of Rochester Press and the Association of College and Research Libraries, 1958. ACRL Microcard Series No. 97). pp. 16–24.

[26]Barrett, pp. 26, 32.

[27]Julia Brown Asplund, "A Discussion," in *Libraries in the Southwest; Their Growth—Strength—Needs*. ed. Lawrence Clark Powell. (Los Angeles: University of California, Los Angeles, 1955), p. 56.

[28]"Laws Creating New Mexico State Library Extension Service," *New Mexico Library Bulletin* 1 (January 1932): 3–4.

[29]Editorial. *New Mexican*, 5 August 1929.

[30]"New Mexico State Library Extension Service First Annual Report," *El Palacio* 29 (October 10, 1930): 214.

[31]"New Mexico State Library Extension Service First Annual Report," p. 218.

[32]"Outlying Communities Eager for Library Extension Books," *New Mexican* 27 November 1929.

[33]"New Mexico State Library Extension Service First Annual Report," p. 218.

[34]"In Issuing the First Number . . . ," *New Mexico Library Bulletin*, 1 (January 1932): 1.

[35]Barrett, p. 40.

[36]"Museum Library Dedicated," *El Palacio* 30 (January 21, 1931): 70

[37]Julia Brown Asplund, "A Farewell," *New Mexico Library Bulletin*, 1 (September 1932): 1.

[38]"Recent Resolutions Concerning the New Mexico State Extension Service," *New Mexico Library Bulletin*, 1 November 1932): 3–4.

[39]"New Mexico State Library Planning Board," *New Mexico Library Bulletin*, 5 (October 1936): 2–3.

[40]"New Mexico State Library Commission," *New Mexico Library Bulletin*, 5 (August 1941): 5.

[41]"State Library Commission," *New Mexico Library Bulletin*, 23 (July 1954): 2.

[42]"New Mexico Libraries and the War," *New Mexico Library Bulletin* 11 (November 1941): 2.

[43]"Training for Teacher–Librarians," *New Mexico Library Bulletin* 11 (March 1942): 2.

[44]"Why Aid for Rural Libraries?" *New Mexico Library Bulletin* 13 (October 1944): 42.

[45]"Annual Report of the State Library Commission," *New Mexico Library Bulletin* 17 (July 1948): 2.

[46]"State Library Conference," *New Mexico Library Bulletin 10 (January 1942): 2–3.*

[47]"Rupert F. Asplund," *New Mexico Library Bulletin* 22 (January 1953): 13.

[48]"State Library Commission," *New Mexico Library Bulletin* 23 (July 1954): 2.

[49]"Services Here Tuesday for Mrs. Julia Asplund." *New Mexican* 28 July 1958.

[50]Asplund, "A Farewell".

[51]Julia Brown Asplund, "Post-War Planning for Library Service," *New Mexico Library Bulletin* 13 (April 1944): 1.

[52]"No More Library Drives." *New Mexican* 24 March 1930.

[53]Asplund, "A Discussion," pp. 56–57.

[54]Asplund, "A Discussion," p. 58.

[55]"Annual Report of the State Library Commission," *New Mexico Library Bulletin* 15 (July 1946): 5.

[56]"Laws Creating New Mexico State Library Extension Service," *New Mexico Library Bulletin* 1 (January 1932): 3.

[57]"New Mexico State Library Extension Service," *El Palacio* 29 (October 10 1930): 254.

[58]"Spanish Books for Spanish Americans," *New Mexico Library Bulletin* 2 (January 1933):1, 3–4; 2 (February 1933): 4–5.

[59]"State Library Planning Board," *New Mexico Library Bulletin* 6 (April 1937): 2.

[60]"State Library Commission," *New Mexico Library Bulletin* 21 (July 1952): 3.

[61]"Third Annual Report of the New Mexico State Library Extension Service, Museum of New Mexico, Santa Fe, New Mexico," *New Mexico Library Bulletin* 1 (September 1932): 2.

[62]"Annual Report of the State Library Commission," *New Mexico Library Bulletin* 13 (July 1944): 27.

[63]Asplund, "A Discussion," p. 58.

[64]"Services Here Tuesday for Mrs. Julia Asplund," *New Mexican*, 28 July 1958. Patricia Paylore, "The Effects of Climate and Distance on Libraries in the Arid Regions,"

in *Libraries in the Southwest: Their Growth—Strength—Needs.* ed. Lawrence Clark Powell. (Los Angeles: University of California, Los Angeles, 1955), p. 48.

[65]"Mrs. Julia Brown Asplund wins Trustees Award," *New Mexico Library Bulletin* 19 (January 1950): 3.

[66]*Women in New Mexico.* (Albuquerque, N.M.: Museum of Albuquerque and American Association of University Women, Albuquerque Branch, 1976).

chapter 6

Fannie Elizabeth Ratchford— Librarian, Literary Detective and Scholar

Clara L. Sitter

Fannie Elizabeth Ratchford (1887–1974), the first librarian of the Rare Books Library at The University of Texas at Austin, acquired fame in not one but three areas: as a librarian, a literary detective and a scholar. During her 38-year tenure (1919–1957) she was the force in the growth of the University of Texas Rare Books Collections to over 50,000 volumes including the best 17th, 18th and 19th century English literature.

The term "literary detective" was given to Ratchford for her work in two areas: her discoveries of some early manuscript writings of Charlotte Brontë and her research on the Brontës (Charlotte, Anne, Emily and Branwell); and her study of literary forgeries and the linking of Thomas J. Wise and Henry Buxton Forman to forgeries found in The University of Texas Wrenn and Aitken Rare Books Collections.

The scholarly interests of Fannie Ratchford were broad and her works were of many types and on numerous subjects. English literature was her great love and much of her research was related to 19th century English authors. She began her writing career with local and regional histories and throughout her life dabbled in historical writing, particularly on Texas and Southern history. Other areas of work included education, libraries and library collections, exhibitions and biographical publications. She edited several collections of letters and unpublished works of other authors, and contributed to about 100 publications during her life.

This essay will briefly trace Ratchford's childhood and then discuss each of the areas for which she is known: as a librarian, as a literary detective and as a scholar–writer. It will describe how each contributed to the career of this "rare librarian." Much of the information is based on interviews with Ratchford and research done during the spring and summer of 1965 in connection with the author's master's thesis on the history of the Rare Books Library of The University of Texas.[1]

BACKGROUND AND CHILDHOOD

Fannie Elizabeth Ratchford was born on June 5, 1887, to James Wylie (1840–1910) and Malinda Rose (1852–1934) Ratchford in the little Texas town of Paint Rock. Her family was committed to the South, Texas, the Presbyterian Church and education. These commitments shaped her values throughout her life.

The Ratchford family is among the oldest Anglo-Saxon families in America, first settling in the Jamestown–Williamsburg area of Virginia before 1620. As the family grew they spread beyond Virginia. Fannie Ratchford's father, James Wylie Ratchford, was born in South Carolina. He grew up in the Carolinas and was educated at Davidson College and the North Carolina Military Institute. His graduation from the Military Institute coincided with the outbreak of the Civil War. During the next four years he took part in more major battles than any other man on either side and by the end of the war he had attained the rank of Major in the Confederate Army.

After the war he went to Texas and in 1872 married Malinda Rose, daughter of one of the early plantation owners of Victoria County, in south Texas. A few years later he bought the Rose plantation, Buena Vista, but the prevalence of malaria in the area forced him to sell the plantation and move his family to a more healthful area.

In September of 1879 Major Ratchford, with his wife and three children and several other families of relatives and close friends headed west in a train of cattle, wagons and carriages. In November they pitched their tents in the unorganized county of Concho, in west central Texas. The following spring they moved to the northern edge of the county to the town of Paint Rock, selected as the county seat when the county was organized in 1879. The town overlooked the Concho River east of the painted rocks on which were found outstanding pictographs of early Indians.[2] The families were strong Presbyterians, and Major Ratchford set about to organize a church as soon as possible. The church was organized in 1881 and was an important part of their lives. The Ratchford family continued to grow and almost eight years after they settled in Paint Rock, Fannie Elizabeth Ratchford was born on June 5, 1887, the seventh of nine children.

Reprinted with permission

Fannie Elizabeth Ratchford as a girl in Texas.

At her baptism, when the Presbyterian minister asked the child's name, her father said "Frances Elizabeth Ratchford." He was immediately corrected by his wife, Malinda, who said, "Fannie Ratchford." And it was "Fannie" that she was baptized and was known by all of her life.

Ratchford described her childhood as happy, carefree, wild and "harum-scarum." She read nearly everything she could get her hands on, but was especially interested in history. While reading Julius Caesar at the age of 10 or 12 years old, she discovered the story of a hardy tribe that rode without saddles and did not sleep under a roof for 14 years. Impressed with Caesar and being something of a tomboy who loved the outdoors, she immediately began riding bareback and started sleeping outdoors. Her mother objected, but her father supported her wishes and she was allowed to "camp" outside for some time.

Teaching Career

Major Ratchford taught his children at home but they also attended the two-teacher school in Paint Rock. At that time most children left school when they were 14 or 15 years old, but Fannie and three other students stayed longer and made up the first class to graduate from the tenth grade in 1904. The principal encouraged Fannie to take the examination to qualify for a first-grade teaching certificate—the highest of three levels of teacher certification. She qualified for the certificate and began teaching officially at about age 17, though she had been helping with the younger students in her school for some time before her graduation.

The following story is told about one of Fannie Ratchford's first teaching jobs in Hamilton, Texas:

> Alighting from the train, she went straight to the depot master and informed him that she was the new school teacher. 'I need a place to live. Any recommendations?'
>
> The gentleman thought he knew his town. He replied, 'No, there are no vacancies in any lodging in Hamilton.'
>
> 'Well, then, I suppose I have to convince someone the school teacher needs a room,' was her instant comment. 'May I leave my valise here for a while?'
>
> Fannie went out, sized up the small town in a few seconds, and headed straight up the hill toward the largest, finest house in sight. A few minutes later, Mrs. Carl Hobde answered her door to see a small, slim and very determined girl dressed in white. 'I've come to live with you while I teach school,' was Fannie's first announcement. 'They tell me there are no rooms in town, but no decent town would expect the school teacher to live in a tent. It appears you have plenty of room.' Overwhelmed and speechless, Mrs. Hobde accepted her roomer; and thus began a lifelong friendship.[3]

Ratchford taught in the rural schools of west Texas and later in the school systems of Brownwood and Fort Worth. She taught most subjects including mathematics, English and history. At this time in Texas, teaching was one of the few careers acceptable for women. Many teachers were forbidden to marry, so the choice of a lifetime of teaching was often accompanied by an acceptance of spinsterhood.[4]

In 1905, at the age of 18, she entered The University of Texas. She completed one year before withdrawing and returning to teaching full time. For a few years she taught during the academic year and attended summer school at various universities. After teaching the 1917–1918 school year she returned to The University of Texas for the summer session of 1918 and enrolled again in 1919 to complete the requirements for her bachelor's degree. There were few teachers at that time who held a first-grade certificate and fewer still who had earned a college degree.

Fannie Ratchford was a teacher for 15 years before she began her career as a rare books librarian. Though her official duties at The University of Texas did not include formal teaching, she served as teacher–mentor to many bright university students and young instructors. She was very devoted to the students who worked for her during their studies at the university and to the circle of rare book patrons. She took a great interest in research that was being done with materials in the Rare Books Collections, and she never lost her early identification as a teacher.

THE UNIVERSITY OF TEXAS

The University of Texas was graduating its first class of seniors at about the same time that Fannie Ratchford was born. During its first 30-odd years the university continued to grow, and by 1917 there was an enrollment of nearly 2,000 students and approximately 120 faculty members. During the next 40 years, to 1957, the year of Ratchford's retirement, both figures multiplied by 10, resulting in a student enrollment of nearly 20,000 and a faculty of over 1,200.

In recalling the university setting as it was when she began to work, Ratchford said "Anyone so bold as to think of research had to go to the Eastern seaboard or to England. The University was located in the midst of a desert, barren of research materials." But by 1957, the university had developed outstanding collections in English and American literature, Texas history, and Latin American history and literature. It had become a center for research and had claimed its place as the outstanding university of the Southwest.

Ratchford held five titles during the 38 years of her tenure: Wrenn Library Assistant (1919–1927), Wrenn Librarian (1927–1948), Rare Book Librarian (1948–1951), Curator of Rare Books and Lecturer in Bibliography (1951–1952), Curator of Rare Books and Director of Research in Rare Book Bibliography (1952–1957). She was never awarded faculty rank, but librarians at The University of Texas did not have faculty rank during this period.

In 1917 the university library was made up of the general library and a single departmental library in the law school. The combined holdings, including all bound volumes and pamphlets, totaled less than 200,000 items. In 1957 the library system had 14 departmental libraries and contained well over a million items. The university library was made up of a number of gift collections in addition to the books purchased with general library funds.

The first notable gift to the library was made in 1897 when Sir Swante Palm (1815–1899), long-time Swedish consul at Austin, presented his library of 10,200 volumes, plus several thousand pamphlets and a large newspaper collection, to the library. Some items from the Palm collection were later transferred to the Rare Books Library. While The University of Texas was in its infancy, books that would later find their way into the Rare Books Library were being gathered by collectors in the United States and England. Fannie Ratchford played an important role in the acquisition of those collections by the university.

LIBRARY CAREER—EARLY YEARS 1919–1937

The Wrenn Collection (1917)

The cornerstone of the Rare Books Library was the Wrenn collection developed by John H. Wrenn (1841–1911), who was born in Ohio not long after Texas Independence. He began collecting books in the 1880s but most of his library was acquired after 1902 when he met Thomas J. Wise (1859–1937), an English bibliographer and book dealer, who helped him build his collection. When John H. Wrenn died in 1911, he left his library of 5,300 items, mainly first editions of 16th-to-18th century literature, to his son Harold and his daughter Alice Wrenn Norcross.

The Wrenn heirs wanted the collection to be kept intact, but neither could afford to purchase the other's interest. In 1917, the Wrenn Library had not been sold and still remained in the old family home in Chicago. Harold Wrenn was persuaded by Thomas Wise, his father's friend, to prepare a catalog of the collection. Wrenn devoted several years of his life to preparing a detailed catalog that was later published in five volumes.

Dr. Reginald Harvey Griffith (1873–1957), a faculty member in the English department at The University of Texas, arranged to visit the Wrenn Library during the Christmas holidays of 1917, on his way to attend a meeting of the Modern Language Association in Wisconsin. Dr. Griffith was an Alexander Pope scholar and was searching for material for his Pope bibliography. He was impressed with the Pope materials as well as other literature he found in the collection and visited it again after his return from the meeting. He expressed his desire to have it at The University of Texas, and when he returned to Austin he aroused the interest of the university president, Robert Ernest Vinson (1876–1945). Together they approached Major George Washington Littlefield (1842–1920), benefactor of the university and a member of its board of regents.

Major George Washington Littlefield was a Texas Ranger and fought in the Civil War, where he earned the rank of Major. His LFD and LIT ranches in the Texas Panhandle and on the Pecos River in New Mexico spread his fame throughout the West. In 1890, he organized the American National Bank of Austin and served as its president until his death in 1920. He was a member of the board of regents of the university and during his lifetime gave nearly $3,000,000 in gifts to the university.

In February of 1918, Mr. William Henry Burges (1867–1946), former regent of the university and member of the law firm of Gregory, Burges and McNab in Chicago, was appointed to negotiate for the acquisition. President Vinson and Dr. Eugene Campbell Barker (1874–1956) were involved in the agreement. Dr. Barker was a professor of history at the university and a good friend of Major Littlefield. It is believed that he was a strong influence in Major Littlefield's decision to buy the Wrenn Library.

Harold B. Wrenn, son of John H. Wrenn, and his brother-in-law, Frederick F. Norcross, who, following the death of his wife in 1914, had been acting as trustee for his daughters, agreed to accept half of the estimated value of the book collection on certain conditions. The conditions were that the library be kept intact; that it be known as the Wrenn Library and that it be suitably housed. Agreement for the purchase was reached in 1918.

Major Littlefield's gift of $225,000 in 1918 for the purchase of the Wrenn Library established the Rare Books Collections. He put up an additional sum for the construction of proper quarters for the library. Thomas Eddy Tallmadge (1876–1940), Chicago architect, designed and decorated the Wrenn Room which was completed in June of 1919. The dedication of the Wrenn Library was in March of 1920, with an address given by Dr. Griffith entitled the "Torch Bearers."

The Wrenn Room had just been finished when Ratchford returned to the university campus for another summer to complete the requirements for her undergraduate degree. Lena McGhee, her friend and employee at the university library loan desk, had just returned from Europe and was temporarily helping Dr. Griffith in the Wrenn Room before she returned to her position in the main library. The Wrenn books had not been unpacked, so it happened that the first book in the Rare Books Collections was not a Wrenn title but a gift from an English professor—a rare Arabic book.

Dr. Griffith, the professor who had first brought the Wrenn Collection to the attention of the university administration, envisioned the position of Wrenn Library Assistant as a fellowship to be held by a graduate student for one or two years. He knew Ratchford as a student, and he described the position to her as simply caring for the books and seeing that the library was open during designated hours. Although she had not applied for the job, he offered it to her and she accepted with the intention of keeping it for a year or two while she did graduate work. Fannie's mother, Malinda, had relocated to Austin, and her mother's ill health contributed to Fannie's decision to stay in Austin to help care for her. Fannie Ratchford was 32 years old when she began working in the Rare Books Library in 1919.

Ratchford completed the course work and wrote her master's thesis during the next two years while working in the Wrenn Library. She received a Master of Arts degree in British colonial history in 1921. After receiving her master's degree, Fannie Ratchford continued to take courses for credit and sat in on many other classes to further her education. She read widely and began writing.

The period from the official dedication of the Wrenn Library to 1937, the date of the move into the new quarters in the main building, was marked by growth for the Rare Books Library. The two largest additions, the Aitken Library and the Stark Library, were acquired by the university, as were a number of other collections. Ratchford modestly credited Dr. Griffith with securing the Wrenn, Aitken and other notable collections for the university, although she herself played a major role in the acquisition of all except the Wrenn, which had been negotiated for before her arrival. Dr. Griffith was never officially connected with the Rare Books Collections except for a short time when he held the honorary title "Curator of the Wrenn Library."

The Aitken Library (1921)

George Atherton Aitken (1860–1917), an Englishman who served in various capacities with the British government during his lifetime, was a scholar. He was best known for his two-volume biography of Richard Steele[5], published in 1889. Aitken died in November 1917, leaving his library of more than 3,000 volumes. Harold Wrenn purchased the Aitken library from George Aitken's widow with the idea of selling it to The University of Texas. Upon learning of the possibility, Ratchford enlisted the help of State Senator Louis H. Darwin who introduced a bill in the Texas Legislature to appropriate $10,000 toward the purchase. After much lobbying by Ratchford and others, the bill was passed. The University Board of Regents matched the money and the Aitken Library was purchased from Harold Wrenn in 1921 for the $20,000 he paid for it—a bargain for a collection valued at ten times that amount.

The Stark Library (1925)

Mrs. Miriam Lutcher Stark (1859–1936) of Orange, Texas, had for many years collected books and antiques for her own enjoyment. Mrs. Stark's husband had served on The University's Board of Regents (1911–1915) and her son, Lutcher, was serving as chairman of the Board in the early 1920s. One day in 1923, Lutcher Stark visited the Wrenn Room to see the Byron materials in the collections and casually mentioned that his mother had the manuscript of Byron's *Don Juan*. Ratchford was astounded when he began telling her of his mother's collection and she could not rest until she had seen the books. "I just couldn't believe my eyes when I saw them," she said. In 1924, Ratchford asked Mrs. Stark if some of the materials could be exhibited on campus during the Byron Centennial that year. She recalled the trip she made to Orange to get the books for the exhibit, bringing back $10,000 to $20,000 worth of books in her suitcase. It was during Prohibition, and she later said that she fully expected to be arrested for refusing to let anyone touch her suitcase.

In December of 1925, it was announced that Mrs. Stark's collection of books, as well as her fine art objects, would be given to the university. The fine arts collection included antique furniture, oriental rugs, statuary, 150 oil paintings, porcelains, glass, tapestries, laces, inlaid and carved boxes, carved ivories and jades and many other items collected for their beauty or uniqueness.[6] Mrs. Stark offered $150,000 for the construction of a building or the remodeling of quarters within a building to house the museum materials. The agreement that she required was: (a) that she be permitted during her lifetime to remove temporarily for private exhibits certain articles in the collection; (b) that the collection be properly housed, protected and preserved, and; (c) that the collection and building be known as the Miriam Lutcher Stark Museum.

Selected books were moved back and forth between Orange and Austin for several years before adequate housing on campus was available. The complete library was transferred to the university in 1937, when the new area for the Rare Books Library was completed in the new main building. By 1953 the university had still not provided the remainder of the funds for the proper housing of the museum pieces so part of the gift was withdrawn by H. J. Lutcher Stark and his wife. The book collection remained in the Rare Books Library.

Housing for the Rare Books Library

The first housing for the Rare Books Library was the Wrenn Room, which had been designed by Thomas Tallmadge and was located in the old library building. The Rare Books Collections soon outgrew the space. Plans were drawn for a new Main Building and tower that included quarters for the Rare Books Collections on the east side of the third floor. The plans did not provide adequate office or work space nor did they allow for expansion. Ratchford persuaded the administration to revise the plans for the front part of the main building to include housing for the rare books on the fourth floor. The front part of the main building was completed in 1937 and the books were moved to the new quarters soon after that. The Stark Library was moved directly to the new rooms in 1939 from the home of Mrs. Stark in Orange, Texas, nearly 14 years after the announcement of her gift to the university. The Wrenn Room was taken apart and replaced exactly as it had been constructed in the old library building.

LIBRARY CAREER—THE PERIOD OF FURTHER DEVELOPMENT 1937–1957

During the years from the move into the new facility in the main building until Ratchford's retirement, the Rare Books Library continued to grow. The availability of the John A. Spoor Library in the spring of 1939 aroused the interest and support of Austin bankers and citizens. The gift of the library of Everette L. DeGolyer (1886–1956) in 1946 was an important addition to the collection. The 1947 acquisition of a number of Byron letters through the subscription of Austin and Dallas residents showed support by individuals in the state.

The John A. Spoor Library (1939)

The John A. Spoor Library was put on the auction schedule at Parke-Bernet Galleries in New York in the spring of 1939. Ratchford said that the collection as a whole did not hold much interest for the Rare Books Library—except for two books of great importance: *The Necessity of Atheism* by Percy Bysshe Shelley and *Fugitive Pieces* by Lord Byron. "Nobody had any idea what they would cost." The money was not available from university funds so Ratchford approached Malcolm H. Reed (1876–1945), an Austin businessman who was a loyal university supporter. He arranged a $25,000 interest-free loan backed by 12 Austin citizens. Dr. Griffith made the trip to New York to purchase the two books and several others, which supplemented the University's collections.

DeGolyer Collection (1946)

Mr. Everette L. DeGolyer, a geologist by profession but a book collector by nature and practice, had been collecting books on geology, particularly of the Southwest, when Ratchford first met him. He was especially drawn to beautiful maps and beautiful books. A secondary interest was American literature, and many contemporary writers were among his friends. Ratchford became acquainted with him in the early 1940s. They were contemporaries, as he was just one year older than she, and they shared an appreciation for books. In speaking of his collection Ratchford said, "His library of Americana was very rich where we had nothing. I did a lot of missionary work on him . . . finally he gave them to us." His collection totaled more than 12,000 volumes and his gifts to the university continued until his death in 1956.

Byron Letters (1947)

In the early 1940s, a collection of 36 letters of Lord Byron was discovered in a New York shop by Dr. Clarence L. Cline (1905–   ), professor of English at The University of Texas. The $11,000 price was more than the university could pay for them at the time. But seven years later, in 1947, after the death of the owner, Gabriel Wells, the collection became available for $4,500. Ratchford enlisted the support of a number of Austin and Dallas residents and the Rare Books Collections again gained a major addition.

Other Issues

The collection development plan for the rare books was only generally defined. The focus was on English and American literature; the emphasis was on 16th, 17th and 18th century materials, although a number of 19th and 20th century items were included. There were, however, some incunabula and some materials in the related areas of philosophy, religion, history, biography and science. Items were added because of rarity, monetary worth or value in completing areas in existing collections.

By 1957, the Rare Books Collections contained a number of periodical holdings representing some of the earliest newsbooks through the 18th century. The 17th and 18th century English and American periodical holdings were supplemented by the 19th and 20th century holdings in the main library. The Rare Books Library had also acquired a number of manuscripts, including a few illuminated manuscripts from the 13th and 14th centuries. Probably more significant were the collections of correspondence relating to important individuals and the beginning of a collection of manuscripts of literary works. The foundation was laid for the ambitious manuscript acquisitions that followed Ratchford's retirement.

Part of the justification for the development of the collections was to provide source material for faculty research as well as a laboratory where students could learn the methods and techniques of literary research and bibliography. The collections were visited by many scholars who came to use the materials. Another important function was to share the collection with proud Texans and university visitors through exhibits and publications. By 1957, the Rare Books Library had become a showplace of the campus where first editions and original manuscripts were displayed. Ratchford made a special effort to encourage Texans (especially influential Texans) to feel that the collections belonged to the State of Texas. Each visitor was treated as an important guest and Ratchford was always a willing speaker on campus and throughout the state. Her circle of "Friends of the Library" was unparalleled.

Publications were an important part of the public relations work for the library and were often financed by revenues from two special publication funds: the Walter Marion Manly Fund and the John Lang Sinclair Fund. Ratchford played a part in the development of both funds.

Walter Marion Manly III, a brilliant student who had worked as a library assistant in the Rare Books Library, was killed in action with General George Patton's Army in Germany in November 1944. The fund was established by Ratchford in 1946 with money from the sale of her book, *Between the Lines*. It was said that she expected him to return to work in the library and perhaps follow her as curator. His death was a great personal loss to her.

The John Lang Sinclair Publication Fund was established by Ratchford and Dr. Griffith in 1948 for the Rare Books Library. The fund honored another former student, John Lang Sinclair (1880–1947), who developed a means of burning the thorns off the prickly pear to make it edible by cattle. He organized a company and sold shares to many people on campus, including Dr. Griffith. It was a complete failure and the stockholders lost all of their money. Sinclair spent the next 40 years struggling to repay to the last penny the money lost by the stockholders. When Dr. Griffith received a check from Sinclair he established the fund, and the next year the Ex-Students Association made the fund a major project. John Lang Sinclair is also remembered for writing the song, "The Eyes of Texas."

From the beginning Ratchford knew every item in the collection—its location, its reason for being in the collection, where it came from and how much the university paid for it. One of the things she enjoyed most was helping students and faculty in their research. She felt that only serious students or scholars should be allowed to use the materials and was inclined to reserve important items for research by The University of Texas faculty. She was firm in her policy that no materials ever left the library. There were many fights with faculty on that policy. Ratchford was willing to stay after hours in order to accommodate people who needed to work longer. She was very proud of the fact that not one item in the collection was lost during the time she was in charge of the collections.

Full cataloging was insisted upon and it was only after 15 years of effort that she was able to have the books cataloged the way she wanted them done. In 1934, during the Depression, when the federal government was trying to find work for everyone, she discovered William H. McCarthy, who had been a cataloger and bibliographer in the rare books library at Yale. He was employed as the cataloger and proved to be excellent, but support for the job was cut off after three months. When Ratchford was unable to get him hired by the University Library, she went directly to the Board of Regents, which agreed to employ him to finish cataloging the collection. During the next five years the Aitken Library was cataloged.

One of the traditions Ratchford established early was the serving of tea. She preferred that the library staff members not leave the library for breaks, so tea was served morning and afternoon for library staff and anyone else who happened to be around. Students, faculty and visitors were included in the tea times, which prompted much lively, literary discussion and created a very warm, family feeling with patrons.

She was very close to the students and many of the patrons of the Rare Books Library. She was generous in her financial aid to and other encouragement of a number of students over the years. She had many nieces and nephews who attended the university and some lived with her while in school. Fannie Elizabeth Ratchford was her legal name, but she was affectionately called "Miss Fannie" by those who knew her best. Many students, as well as her many nieces and nephews, called her "Aunt Fan." She never married but she had a large extended family and she was a mentor to many young faculty members as well as students.

One of the brightest young faculty members to come to The University of Texas during Fannie Ratchford's tenure was Harry Huntt Ransom (1908–1976), who arrived as a 27-year-old English Department instructor in 1935. He was 21 years younger than Ratchford, but they had a common appreciation for English literature and the development of the Rare Books Collections at the university. He advanced quickly through the academic ranks, and became full professor by 1947. He then began a rise through administrative ranks serving as Assistant Dean of the Graduate School, Associate Dean, and Dean of Arts and Sciences. In 1957 he became Vice President and Provost and later held the titles of President, Chancellor, and Chancellor Emeritus before his death in 1976 at age 68.

Harry Huntt Ransom has been described as brilliant, charismatic and ambitious. He was the brightest rising star in the power structure of the university system during the last 20 years of Fannie Ratchford's association with the university. Fannie Ratchford and Harry Ransom worked together for a number of years on a common goal—the development of the Rare Books Library. He was advisor and scholar and she was administrator and scholar. His strong interest in the Rare Books Library continued to increase over the years, and as he became more powerful his influence became stronger.

Perhaps the saddest chapter in the life story of Fannie Ratchford is the one related to the clash with Harry Ransom at the end of her association with the university. The result was a permanent split between these two brilliant people who cared deeply about the Rare Books Library. The whole story will probably never be known since the individuals are no longer living and correspondence that would explain the situation was destroyed or has not been made public.

The facts we know are that when Fannie Ratchford was 70 years old, in 1957, after 38 years as librarian of the Rare Books Library, she was subject to mandatory retirement. She accepted a third Guggenheim Fellowship for the academic year 1957–58, expecting to return to her office in the Rare Books Library the following year on part-time status in an emeritus position. Fannie Ratchford's family and friends assume that something happened during that year between Fannie and Harry Ransom because she returned in the fall of 1958 to find that all of her things had been removed from the Rare Books Library and moved to an office in the library tower. What prompted the actions remains a mystery. Ratchford was so angry and hurt that she never set foot in the new office and never again spoke to Harry Ransom. Consequently her contributions to the university were never officially recognized, she was never awarded emeritus status with the university, and the special friendship between Harry Ransom and Fannie Ratchford was ended.

After Fannie Ratchford's retirement in 1957, Harry Huntt Ransom controlled the development of the Rare Books Collections from his various positions, and during the next 15 or so years he raised millions of dollars for the acquisition of countless collections of rare books and manuscripts. His interest was in copyright and his plan was to have copies of every variant edition of a work. In 1971, a multi-story building named the Harry Huntt Ransom Humanities Research Center was dedicated to house the Rare Books Collections. His accomplishments were remarkable.

LITERARY DETECTIVE

Serving as chief administrator of the Rare Books Library was a very important part of Fannie Ratchford's life but it was not her only interest. The term "literary detective" was attributed to her for her work in two areas: her discovery and study of manuscripts of the Brontës written while they were children and her discovery and study of the Wise forgeries—a real-life case of literary crime.

Brontë Mystery

Not long after she became associated with the Rare Books Library, Fannie Ratchford discovered a number of booklets written in microscopic hand by Charlotte Brontë. The miniature booklets, some as small as a postage stamp, proved to be a part of a long serial story written during the childhood of the Brontë siblings.[7] The manuscripts were a part of the Wrenn Library when it came to the university. The pieces had been sold to John Wrenn by his friend, Thomas Wise, who was unaware of the significance of the booklets and had sold them to collectors in England and the United States.

During 1929–30 Ratchford was awarded a traveling research fellowship from the John Simon Guggenheim Memorial Foundation, which enabled her to spend the year in England tracing the booklets that were scattered throughout the world. For the next 20 years she searched for the booklets and was able to locate over a hundred separate manuscripts, nearly all of which were written in the same tiny handwriting. She explained the booklets in an article before an exhibit of Brontë materials in the Rare Books Library in 1947:

> The first chapter is told in tiny booklets of almost microscopic handprinting, revealing a play world centering around a set of 12 wooden soldiers brought by the Rev. Patrick [Brontë] to his son Branwell on the night of June 5, 1826.
>
> These wooden soldiers were not only the heroes of countless adventures played out by the four little Brontës through two years and longer, they were also writers and artists who celebrated the great deeds of their group—'The Young Men' or 'The Twelves,' as the children variously called them—in histories, poems, and dramas, 'published' by Capt. Tree, one of their number, in tiny 'volumes' proportional in size to their toy authors. . . . The literary aspect of the game is further emphasized by Charlotte's 'catalog' of the 'books' she had 'published' through her 16th year, containing 22 entries.
>
> A second chapter is told in booklets of larger size, but in even smaller handprinting, carrying all the old concepts of setting, characters and adventures into romances highly colored by the reading of Scott and Byron. . . . In this period the four children, who had originally played together and written of the same imaginary people and incidents, broke into pairs—Charlotte and Branwell, continuing the old story of Angria; Emily and Anne writing of a new world of imagination, dubbed Gondal.
>
> A third chapter or stage of development shows Charlotte, continuing her familiar themes with greater and greater power, until realizing the absurdity of the play as a vehicle for her vivid conceptions, her burning emotions, and her lyrical prose, she bade a moving farewell to Angria, and began to naturalize her Angrians into Yorkshire English folk. The end of this process of naturalization, that is,

the adaptation of purely imaginary but vividly realized characters and incidents to realistic settings, was the immortal *Jane Eyre*, *Shirley* and *Villette*. . . .

Unfortunately Emily and Anne destroyed . . . their histories and novels of Gondal, saving only its poetry. Anne's manuscripts in ordinary careful script are commonplace enough, though written in persons of her favorite Gondal characters. Emily's by contrast, all but indecipherable, in crabbed microscopic handprinting, breathe the vigorous originality of her unique genius.[8]

In 1933 Ratchford published a volume titled *Legends of Angria*, which contained transcripts of some of Charlotte's stories written before she was 16, and over the years transcriptions of different booklets were published by other Brontë scholars. In 1941 Ratchford published *The Brontës' Web of Childhood*, revealing to the literary world her theory of the story behind the booklets. This book was a major contribution to Brontë research and established her as a world authority on the Brontë family. She is cited in countless studies on the Brontës and her work is still considered a landmark in literary scholarship. After her retirement, she was asked by Oxford University Press to serve as editor for the publication of the complete works of the Brontës. She published more than 20 works on the subject of the Brontës, and her scholarship was recognized by fiction writers. In *The Poison Cross Mystery*, written by Inez Haynes Irwin and published in 1936, references are made throughout to Ratchford's connection with the Brontës. The Wise story inspired another mystery writer.

The Literary Crime of Thomas J. Wise

Thomas J. Wise was the highly respected bibliographer and book dealer who had helped John Wrenn develop his collection. He was one of England's greatest authorities in the rare book market and had sold a number of Brontë items to John Wrenn, including some of the tiny manuscript booklets as well as some pamphlets. Wise was an English oil merchant and had a passion for collecting books for his library, which he named the Ashley Library. He was not a wealthy man but was able to indulge his hobby by careful dealings in essential oils and in books. He received an honorary degree from Oxford University and was an active member of the Bibliographical Society. Catalogues were issued for parts of his collections, a number of bibliographies were compiled, and some 250 privately-printed reprints of small rare pieces were produced. For 30 years before the scandal broke he was widely known and highly respected for his expertise in bibliography and rare books and for his generosity in making his books available to students and scholars. In addition to assisting John Wrenn in the development of his collection, Wise also sold many items to George Aitken and to the British Museum.

The events leading to Ratchford's interest in the Thomas J. Wise scandal began in 1934 when John (Waynflete) Carter (1905–1975) and (Henry) Graham

Pollard (1903–1976), two young English booksellers, published their *Enquiry into the Nature of Certain Nineteenth Century Pamphlets*. This book shocked the world by proving that between 40 and 50 pieces of forgery could be traced to Wise. The suspected forgeries included titles found in the Wrenn Collection and titles related to the Brontës. This number was later revised to include about 100 items of proven or suspected forgeries.[9]

Thomas Wise was 74 years old and in ill health when *Enquiry* was published. He made an ineffective attempt to defend himself with two weak letters of denial in the *Times Literary Supplement* immediately after the exposé, but the scandal would not die. As the controversy raged into the next year, Wise became silent about the accusations when the evidence against him was conclusive. He died three years later, but many articles were published about him during the interval and have continued to be published.

The incident prompted a surge of bibliographical study involving proof sets, minute examination of printing types, chemical analysis of paper, study of sales records and other tests of authenticity.[10] The Wrenn Library was involved because it contained the only complete collection of the forgeries and had been partially built by Wise. The Aitken Library also contained a number of the fakes. The other two libraries directly involved were the Rare Books Library at the British Museum and Wise's personal library, the Ashley Library, which was presented to the British Museum after his death.

Ratchford had the exclusive access to the correspondence between Wise and John Henry Wrenn, and these letters plus other materials in the possession of Carl H. Pforzheimer (1879–1957), a book collector and investment banker from New York City, led her to believe that Wise was not alone in his guilt but that he had been assisted by Henry Buxton Forman (1842–1917) and perhaps even Edmund Gosse (1849–1928). Forman was a highly respected editor and bibliographer and Gosse was a critic and essayist and a knighted Englishman. Forman and Gosse were both dead when the Enquiry was published. Wise, Forman and Gosse were all highly respected in the field of literary scholarship and bibliography. Wise gave Ratchford permission to publish the letters after his death. Following his death, she received a Guggenheim Fellowship for the academic year 1939–40, which gave her an opportunity to follow her hunch.

In 1942 Ratchford completed "Thomas J. Wise to John Henry Wrenn on Nineteenth Century Bibliography," that was published in the *Papers of the Bibliographical Society of America*. Two years later her research resulted in *Letters of Thomas J. Wise to John Henry Wrenn; a Further Inquiry into the Guilt of Certain Nineteenth Century Forgers*, which was published by Alfred A. Knopf, and was a large and well-documented record of Wise's marketing methods. Ratchford implicated Harry Buxton Forman but could not produce the proof because Mr. Pforzheimer withheld his documents from publication. In interviews with Ratchford during her later years, she said, "My, the row that raised! They said I didn't know what I was talking about and was a wicked woman to scandalize a great and good man like Forman." Her accusations of Forman and Gosse so angered the British authorities that she was unwelcome in England for a number of years.

Finally Mr. Pforzheimer was persuaded to consent to the publication of the evidence in his possession, and in 1945, the year after Fannie Ratchford's *Further Inquiry* was published, the Pforzheimer documents were released in *Between the Lines: Letters and Memoranda Interchanged by H. Buxton Forman and Thomas J. Wise*, with a foreword by Carl H. Pforzheimer and an introductory essay and notes by Fannie E. Ratchford. Forman would write to Wise on a desk pad with a big blunt pencil in widely spaced lines; Wise would then answer between the lines in red ink. One sentence plainly showed that they both worked on the forgery of *Last Tournament*. She presented a very good case against Forman and held her ground in articles which followed, such as "A Review of Reviews; Part I" and "A Review of Reviews, Part II" published in 1945 and 1946. Ratchford continued to believe that Gosse was also involved but she was not able to convince many others of her suspicions. Her theory was based on a handwritten note which Ratchford believed to have been written by Gosse, but the sample was too small to produce positive identification. The contest was not over in 1946 when the Rare Books Collections prepared an exhibit of Wise's forgeries, accompanied by a catalogue.

At age 70 Ratchford received a third Guggenheim Fellowship for the academic year 1957–58, which she spent in England doing additional work on the Wise forgeries. By this time she had been forgiven by the British for her accusations of Forman, since she had proven him to be involved. While in London she was invited to speak before the National Book League on Thomas J. Wise. She said, " I accepted, knowing that Carter had instigated the invitation as a dare to me and that he and Pollard would be there with their knives sharpened." During that year she was also invited by the British Broadcasting Company (BBC) to speak for two separate hours. One program was regarding the Wise scandal and the other one was on the subject of the Brontë studies.

In the 60-plus years since the exposé there has been much written on the subject of the literary crime of Thomas J. Wise. Bibliographical research at the University of Texas has been continued by William Burton Todd (1919–), who was director of bibliographical research from 1958 until 1982. In 1983 a second edition of *An Enquiry into the Nature of Certain Nineteenth Century Pamphlets* and a companion volume, *A Sequel to "An Enquiry." The Forgeries of Buxton Forman and Wise Re-examined* were released. Richard D. Altick devotes a 27-page chapter, "The Case of the Curious Bibliographer," to the Wise story in his book, *The Scholar Adventurers*. (He gives Ratchford additional coverage in the chapter, "Discoveries," in which he discusses her discoveries of the Brontës' childhood fantasies.)

The story of the Wise forgeries is one of those "stranger than fiction" incidents. The subject appeared in a mystery novel, *Murder Stalks the Circle*, by

Lee Thayer, published in 1947, and the references to the forgeries played a major role in the story line.

WRITING AND RESEARCH

It was only natural that Ratchford would do her own research. She is credited with nearly a hundred publications that she wrote, edited or introduced, including articles of a literary, historical, biographical or bibliographical nature. Her publications appeared in newspapers, magazines, journals, society publications and encyclopedias. Some of the works she authored related to the Rare Books Collections but many of them were the result of her own research interests.

Ratchford was especially fascinated with history and said that while growing up she read every history book she could find. Her first serious writing began at the age of 15 in a project with her father to record his experiences in the Civil War. James Wylie Ratchford did not like to talk about his battle experiences, but he did have an important story to tell. He was apparently the first Confederate wounded in a land battle. It was believed that he fought in more battles than any other soldier in the war on either side, and he knew intimately all of the great men of the Confederacy. He was persuaded by his daughter, Fannie, to write about some of his memories and to allow her to write other stories of his war experiences. The collection was privately published in 1909 in Richmond, Virginia, just one year before the death of Major Ratchford, under the title *Some Reminiscences of Persons and Incidents of the Civil War*. Fannie Ratchford's name does not appear on the book. She gave all of the credit to her father although, according to family members, it was just as much her work as his. Writing the stories and seeing that they were published was a labor of love for her father.

Ratchford loved recording the legends of west Texas and published a number of them in the Texas Folklore Society publications, *Legends of Texas* and *Coyote Wisdom*. J. Frank Dobie (1888–1964), the popular Texas author, and his wife, Bertha, were good friends of Fannie Ratchford and they shared a love of Texas folklore.

During the 1920s Fannie Ratchford began her research on the history and development of private libraries in Texas. The Texas Library Association's *News Notes* published a number of these findings. This project put her in touch with many people in the state who were interested in collecting books and who had the money to indulge their hobby.

Ratchford received a Rockefeller grant in 1934 to study early Texas homes constructed before the Civil War. She was on leave of absence from the university for parts of the academic years 1934–35 and 1935–36 to pursue that research. The results of the project became a part of the *Measured Drawings for Texas* (1938), which includes positive blueprints with scale drawings of the houses.

Reprinted with permission.

Fannie Elizabeth Ratchford as scholar-librarian.

Although many historical writings are credited to her, Ratchford always maintained that history was an area in which she "had no business playing around." Publications were an important part of the public relations work for the library. She often wrote about special collections housed in the Rare Books Library and frequently prepared bibliographies or exhibit catalogs to accompany special exhibits. Literature was the area of her greatest expertise and her personal research interests often related to British authors.

Fannie Ratchford is best known for her literary writing on 19th century English literature. Her works on the Brontës and on the Wise forgeries brought her world-wide recognition and many of her literary works relate to them. Other subjects of her literary study included A.C. Swinburne, Samuel Taylor Coleridge, Alexander Pope, O. Henry, Sir Walter Scott, Alfred Lord Tennyson and Sidney Lanier.

MEMBERSHIPS

Ratchford was never a joiner but she did hold memberships in historical, literary, religious and social organizations as well as library-related organizations. She never considered herself a professional librarian since she did not attend library school. She was never a member of the American Library Association but she maintained her membership in the Texas Library Association. She served on committees for the association and spoke at its meetings on a number of occasions. For many years she was a member of the Austin Library Club and belonged to The University of Texas Library Staff Association, occasionally serving on its committees.

Fannie Ratchford also belonged to the American History Club of Austin, the National Society of Colonial Dames of America, and the Texas State Historical Association, for which she served as Secretary–Treasurer for a number of years and as an occasional speaker on the annual program. She contributed to the publications of the Texas Folklore Society.

The most active memberships held by Ratchford were those in literary organizations. She read a number of papers before the Modern Language Association of America, most of them dealing with her work on the Brontës or on her discoveries relating to the Wise forgeries. She also read papers at meetings of the Bibliographical Society of America, and while in England she attended meetings of the Bibliographical Society of London.

Ratchford grew up in a family active in the Presbyterian Church and she continued to be an active member of the church throughout the years. Other memberships included the Texas Ex-Students Association, the American Association of University Women, the Anglo-Texan Society, and the Philosophical Society of Texas.

CONCLUSION

Fannie Ratchford was loyal and committed to certain ideals and people. Her determination and persistence, sources of strength in most instances, were perceived by some as stubbornness. Though some disagreed with her, no one doubted her commitment to the development of the Rare Books Library, her belief in her research, and her dedication to scholarship. She never married, and her work was probably the most important thing in her life. She was respected by those who knew her—as a librarian, as a scholar and as a person. As librarian of the Rare Books Collections at The University of Texas for nearly 40 years, she was undoubtedly the most important factor in their growth and development during the early years. Her work on the Brontës was a landmark, and to this day she is cited in major works on the Brontës. Her role in the Wise forgery saga was unparalleled. Her contributions to Texas history and folklore, English literature research, and librarianship in Texas are significant.

Ratchford's many honors included the Rockefeller Research Fellowship for 1934–36; Guggenheim Traveling Research Fellowships for the years 1929–30, 1939–40 and 1957–58; the 1936 Centennial Lecture Award of the Texas Ex-Students Association; and an honorary degree of Doctor of Letters from Western College for Women in Oxford, Ohio, awarded in 1954.

Several years after the return to Austin from her last Guggenheim fellowship, she was interviewed by this author during the spring and summer of 1965. The following winter she fell and broke a hip and spent the next eight years in hospitals and nursing homes. She died in Austin on February 9, 1974, at the age of 87. After her death Harry Ransom wrote a brief article for the *Library Chronicle* in which he referred to her as "constantly informed by imagination and ingenuity as well as rigorous study. . . . A voluminous and cordial correspondent, she was a friend of many leading scholars in the United States and England. . . . Her influence upon library development in Texas is permanent. So is her example as a gracious, disciplined, and devoted lover of books."[11]

Any single aspect of Fannie Ratchford's accomplishments would be important, but the fact that she achieved so much in multiple areas is remarkable. Even more remarkable is the fact that her achievements came at a time in American history when most women her age rarely even finished high school. She was indeed unique for her time and she was a special library pioneer who played a major role in the development of a foundation for research in the Southwest.

ENDNOTES

[1]Sitter, Clara Marie Loewen. *History of the Rare Books Library of The University of Texas Based on Recollections of Miss Fannie Ratchford*. M.L.S. thesis. Austin: The University of Texas, 1966.

[2]The Paint Rock Indian Pictograph Site is a registered historic place. Located 1 mile NW off US 83 it is a Pre-Columbian site and the most extensive pictograph area in central Texas.

[3]Hestir, Bluford B. "Fannie Elizabeth Ratchford" in *This is Texas*. Austin: Furura Press, 1927. 184–185.

[4]Manning, Diane. *Hill Country Teacher; Oral Histories from the One-Room School and Beyond*. Boston: Twayne Publishers, 1990. xvii–xv.

[5]Sir Richard Steele (1672–1729), an Irish-born writer who published the popular journalistic essays, *The Tatler*. He later worked with Joseph Addison in writing the essays published as *The Spectator*.

[6]Ratchford, Fannie. "University's Greatest Woman Benefactor Dies." *Alcalde*, XXV (December, 1936): 53–54.

[7]In 1846 the sisters, Charlotte (1816–1855), Emily (1818–1848) and Anne (1820–1849), published a joint venture of poems under the masculine pen names of Currier, Ellis and Acton Bell. The following year, 1947, they each had a novel published: *Jane Eyre* by Charlotte, *Wuthering Heights* by Emily and *Agnes Grey* by Anne. Branwell (1817–1855) did not continue to write.

[8]Ratchford, Fannie. "The Brontës on Exhibit at Texas U." *The Daily Times Herald, Dallas*. November 22, 1947. 5–6.

[9]Barker, Nicholas and John Collins. *A Sequel to "An Enquiry:" The Forgeries of Buxton Forman and Wise Re-examined.* London: Scolar Press, 1983. 368–375.

[10]Carter, John and Graham Pollard. *An Enquiry into the Nature of Certain Nineteenth Century Pamphlets.* Second Edition. London: Scolar Press, 1983. "Preface" 8–9.

[11]Ransom, Harry Huntt, "Fannie Ratchford," Library Chronicle of The University of Texas, 1974 (9): 11–12.

BIBLIOGRAPHY

Altick, Richard D., *The Scholar Adventurers.* New York: Macmillan, 1950. Reprinted Columbus: Ohio University Press, 1987. pp. 37–64, 312–317.

Barker, Nicholas and John Collins. *A Sequel to "An Enquiry:" The Forgeries of Buxton Forman and Wise Re-examined.* London: Scolar Press, 1983.

Carter, John and Graham Pollard. *An Enquiry into the Nature of Certain Nineteenth Century Pamphlets.* London: Constable and Company Limited, 1934.

Carter, John and Graham Pollard. *An Enquiry into the Nature of Certain Nineteenth Century Pamphlets.* 2nd Edition. London: Scolar Press, 1983.

Craig, Wilma Ratchford (compiler), *The Ratchfords ... I Reckon.* Baltimore: Gateway Press, 1971. pp. 344–351.

Handbook of Texas; a supplement vol. III. Austin: Texas State Historical Association, 1976. pp. 779–780.

Hestir, Bluford B. "Fannie Elizabeth Ratchford" in *This is Texas.* Austin: Furura Press, 1927. pp. 183–189.

Irwin, Inez Haynes. *The Poison Cross Mystery.* New York: Harrison Smith and Robert Hass, 1936.

Manning, Diane. *Hill Country Teacher; Oral Histories from the One-Room School and Beyond.* Boston: Twayne Publishers, 1990.

McAdams, Ina Mary Ogletree, *Texas Women of Distinction; A Biographical History.* Austin: McAdams Publishers, 1962.

Ransom, Harry Huntt, "Fannie Ratchford," *Library Chronicle of The University of Texas,* 1974(9): pp. 11–12.

Ratchford, Fannie. "The Brontës on Exhibit at Texas U." *The Daily Times Herald, Dallas.* November 22, 1947. pp. 5–6.

Ratchford, Fannie. "University's Greatest Woman Benefactor Dies," *Alcalde,* XXV (December, 1936): pp. 53–54.

Sitter, Clara Marie Loewen. *History of the Rare Books Library of The University of Texas Based on Recollections of Miss Fannie Ratchford.* M.L.S. thesis. Austin: University of Texas, 1966.

Thayer, Lee. *Murder Stalks the Circle.* New York: Dodd, Mead & Company, 1947.

Wiley, Audrey Nell "Our Frontispiece, Fannie Elizabeth Ratchford" in *Bulletin of Bibliography* 20, May–August, 1950, pp. 29–31 and reprinted in Texas *Library Journal,* vol. 27, 1951, pp. 15–19.

Selected Works
by Fannie Ratchford:

This is a partial list of the works of Fannie Elizabeth Ratchford. Among her credits are literary, historical, biographical and bibliographical titles. The list includes works which she authored, edited, compiled, introduced, provided notes for or contributed to in some other significant way.

1909 *Some Reminiscences of Persons and Incidents of the Civil War.* (Richmond, Virginia: Whittet and Shapperson, 1909.) Told to Fannie Ratchford by her father, James Wylie Ratchford. Fannie Ratchford's name is not on the work.

1921 *Anglo-Indian Trade of the First Half of the Seventeenth Century.* Unpublished master's thesis, The University of Texas, 1921.

1923 "B. Harvey Carroll, '94; Gonfalonier of San Marco," *Alcalde*, XI (April, 1923): 1–11.

"Passing of the Waggoner Home," *Alcalde*, XI (December, 1923): 429–32.

"Swinburne at Work," *Sewanee Review*, XXXI (July, 1923): 353–62.

"Summer School South of the Rio Grande," *Survey*, X (July 15, 1923): 450–51.

1924 "First Draft of Swinburne's Hertha," *Modern Language Notes*, XXXIX (January, 1924): 22–26.

"A Library Census," Texas Library Association, *News Notes* I no. 1 (November, 1924): 2

"Moro's Gold," in *Legends of Texas*. 2nd ed. Publications of the Texas Folk-Lore.

"Notes on Byron," in *Texas University Studies in English No. 4.* (Austin: The University of Texas, 1924): 88–96.

"Native Treasure Talk up the Frio," in *Legends of Texas*, 2nd ed. Publications of the Texas Folk-Lore Society No. 3. (Austin: Texas Folk-Lore Society, 1924): 57–59.

1925   "Census of Private Libraries in Texas," Texas Library Association, *News Notes*, I no. 2 (March, 1925): 5–8.

"Census of Private Libraries in Texas," Texas Library Association, *News Notes*, I no. 3 (June, 1925): 6.

"S.T. Coleridge and the London Philosophical Society," *Modern Language Review*, XX (January, 1925): 76–80.

1926   "A $700,000 gift to The University," Texas Library Association, *News Notes*, II no. 1 (January, 1926)

"Details of the Stark Gift," *Alcalde*, XIV (March, 1926): 340–45.

1927   "Pope and the Patriot King," in *Studies in English, No. 6.* (Austin: The University of Texas, 1927).

1928   "Charlotte Bronte's Angrian Cycle of Stories," *Publications of the Modern Language Association*, XLIII (June, 1928): 494–501.

1929   "A Need for Texasana," *Alcalde*, XVII (May, 1929): 380.

1930   "The Gondal Poems," *Times Literary Supplement* (London, December 4, 1930): 1041–42.

1931   "Brontë's Web of Dreams," *Yale Review* (new series), XXI (September, 1931): 139–57.

"The Stark Library–A Survey of This Rare Collection of Books," *Alcalde*, XIX (January, 1931): 129–30.

1933   *From Texas to Mexico and the Court of Maximilian, 1865.* By A.W. Terrell. (Dallas: The Book Club of Texas, 1933) Edited by Fannie Ratchford.

"Introduction; The History of Angria," in *Legends of Angria; Compiled From the Early Writings of Charlotte Brontë.* (New Haven: Yale University Press; London: H. Milford, Oxford University Press, 1933) pp. 19–45. With the Collaboration of William Clyde DeVane.

"Some New Notes on the Brontë-Heger Letters," *Bookman* (London), LXXXV (December, 1933): 180–82.

1934   "The Rolling Stone . . . The Life History of an O Henry Rarity," *Colophon*, XVII (June, 1934): 1–4.

"Gondal: The Background of the Poems." in *Two Poems: "Love's Rebuke," "Remembrance."* by Emily Brontë (Austin: Early Martin Press, 1934): 6–30.

1936 "University's Greatest Woman Benefactor Dies," *Alcalde*, XXV (December, 1936): 53–54.

1937 *The Correspondence of Sir Walter Scott and Charles Robert Maturin with a Few Other Allied Letters.* (Austin: The University of Texas Press, 1937) Edited by Fannie Ratchford.

Sir Walter Scott as a Patron of Literature. (Austin: The University of Texas Press, 1937) Edited by Fannie Ratchford and W.H. McCarthy.

The Story of Champ d'Asile as Told by Two of the Colonists. Translated from the French by Donald Joseph (Dallas: The Book Club of Texas, 1937). Edited with an introduction by Fannie E. Ratchford.

1938 "Legend Making on the Concho," in *Coyote Wisdom* Publications of the Texas Folk-Lore Society, No. 3. (Austin: Texas Folk-Lore Society, 1938): 174–84.

Historical American Buildings Survey. *Measured Drawings for Texas; positive blueprints of originals located in the Library of Congress at Washington D.C. and listed in the catalog of the measured drawings . . . January 1, 1938.* (Washington, D.C: Department of Interior, National Park Service, Branch of Plans and Designs, 1938).

1940 "The Wise Forgeries," *Southwest Review*, XXV (July, 1940): 363–377.

1941 "Idylls of the Hearth," *Southwest Review*, XXVI (Spring, 1941): 317–25.

Brontës' Web of Childhood. (New York: Columbia University Press; London: Oxford University Press, 1941).

"The Gondal Story" and "Emily Brontë's Poems Arranged as an Epic of Gondal." in *Complete Poems of Emily Jane Brontë* edited by C. W. Hatfield. (New York: Columbia University Press, 1941) pp. 14–21.

1942 *Alfred Lord Tennyson, 1809–1892. An Exhibition of Manuscripts and Printed Books at The University of Texas, October 1–30, 1942* by Fannie E. Ratchford. An exhibit catalog.

The Carl H. Pforzheimer Catalogue. (Austin: The University of Texas Press, 1942).

The Rare Books Collections of The University of Texas. (Austin: The University of Texas Press, 1942).

Sidney Lanier's Letters to Col. John G. James. (Austin: The Mirium Lutcher Stark Library, 1942) Printed for private distribution.

"T.J. Wise to John H. Wrenn on Nineteenth Century *Bibliography*" in *Bibliography Society of America Papers* XXVI (1942): 215–228.

1943 "Pauline Comes to Texas," *Southwest Review*, XXVII (Spring, 1943): 429–32.

1944   *Letters of Thomas J. Wise to John Henry Wrenn, A Further Inquiry into the Guilt of Certain Nineteenth-Century Forgers.* (New York: Alfred A. Knopf, 1944) Edited by Fannie Ratchford.

"The Pope Bicentennial Exhibition," *Library Chronicle of The University of Texas*, I Summer, 1944): 3–9.

"Recent Gifts from Mr. H. J. Lutcher Stark," *Library Chronicle of The University of Texas*, I (Fall, 1944): 7–17.

1945   *Between the Lines; Letters and Memoranda Interchanged by H. Buxton Forman and Thomas J. Wise.* (Austin: The University of Texas Press, 1945) Introductory essay and notes by Fannie Ratchford.

"A Review of Reviews; Part I, An Enquiry," *Library Chronicle of The University of Texas*, I no. 4, (Fall, 1945): 3–32.

1946   *An Exhibition of Certain Nineteenth Century Forgeries.* (Austin: The University of Texas Press, 1946)

"The Proof that Forman Knew," *Library Chronicle of The University of Texas*, II (Fall, 1946): 136–55.

"A Review of Reviews; Part II, Wise's Letters," *Library Chronicle of The University of Texas*, II (Spring, 1946): 21–55.

"Texas Adopts the Brontës," *Brontë Society Publications* XI, Pt. 56 (1946): 33–34.

1947   "An American Postscript," *Brontë Society Publications* XI, Pt. 57 (1947): 87–88.

"An American Postscript," in *The Brontës Then and Now: A Symposium of Articles Reprinted from Various Issues of the Brontë Society Transactions, and Now Published as a `Jane Eyre' and `Wuthering Heights' Centenary Tribute.* (Shipley, England: Outhwaite Brothers, Caxton Press, 1947): 41–42. A reprint of the article in the *Brontë Society Publications* 1947.

"The Brontës on Exhibit at Texas U.," *Dallas Times-Herald Daily*, (November 23, 1947).

"John Kingston, Baltimore Publisher," *Library Chronicle of The University of Texas*, III (Fall, 1947): 10–26.

"War in Gondal; Emily Brontë's Last Poem," *The Trollopian*, II no.3 (December, 1947): 137–155.

1948   "The Brontës'," Times Literary Supplement (London), (December 11, 1948): 697.

Five Essays, Written in French by Emily Jane Brontë Now Translated by Lorine White Negel (Austin: The University of Texas Press, 1948) Introduction and Notes by Fannie E. Ratchford.

"Review: The Brontës by Phyllis Bentley," *The Trollopian* III no. 1 (June, 1948): 73–78.

"Thomas J. Wise and the Wrenn Catalogue," *Modern Language Notes*, LXIII (February, 1948): 138–39.

1949   "Remember that The Eyes of Texas are Upon You," *Alcalde*, XXXXII (January, 1949): 85–86.

1951   "The Significance of the Diary Paper," *Brontë Society Transactions* XII, Pt. 61 (1951): 16–17.

1952   "Brontë Cousins in America," *Library Chronicle of The University of Texas*, IV (Fall, 1952): 176–88.

"The Rare Books Collection of The University of Texas," *Texas Library Journal*, XXVII (March 1952): 28–29. Summary of an address given at the Texas Library Association Meeting.

"Rare Book Collections" in *Handbook of Texas* 2 (1952): 441

1953   "Family of Scribblers," *Saturday Review*, XXXVI (January 20, 1953): 21.

1955   *Gondal's Queen; a Novel in Verse.* By Emily Brontë. (Austin: The University of Texas Press, 1955) Introduction and notes by Fannie Ratchford.

1964   *Brontës Web of Childhood* (New York: Russell & Russell, 1964).

1965   "Biography" in Emily Brontë's *Wuthering Heights*. (New York: Harper & Row, 1965).

chapter 7

Dorothy Porter Wesley: A Bibliographer, Curator, and Scholar

Helen H. Britton

The uniqueness of the professional work of Dorothy Louise Burnett Porter Wesley (1905–   ) ensures her a place not only in the history of American women in librarianship but also a place in the history of notable American librarians, male and female. A study of her professional contributions reveals that she has an affinity with bibliomania, an exceptional aptitude for and skills in the practice of librarianship, and an ability to enlighten her peers through lectures and through publications. Dr. Wesley's accomplishments as librarian, administrator, curator, scholar, author, consultant, and now curator emerita give her peers a reason to confer upon her special appellations. They refer to her as "Dean of ethnic-collections librarians,"[1] "Dean of Black Research Bibliographers,"[2] and the "doyenne of black bibliography."[3] They also address her as Dr. Porter or Dr. Wesley in recognition of her honorary doctorates from three universities: Susquehanna University in Selinsgrove, Pennsylvania, June 1971; Syracuse University, May 1989; and Radcliffe College, February 1990.

From 1930 to 1973, Dr. Dorothy Porter Wesley dedicated her professional life at Howard University to the organization and development of a research center for materials by and about African-Americans and others of the African diaspora. Beginning with several modest collections of materials, she pioneered in developing a premier resource, one of the largest ethnic research libraries in

America. As the library reached new plateaus in its development, its name changed. In 1932, Dr. Wesley began to promote use of the name, "Moorland Foundation: A Library of Negro Life," in reference to the ethnic collections she assembled in the Trustee's Room of the Carnegie Library at Howard University. The Board of Trustees of Howard University established that name, Moorland Foundation: A Library of Negro Life, in 1915 as a tribute to Jesse E. Moorland (1863–1940) who donated a voluminous collection to the university in 1914. It was and still is not uncommon to hear the name "Moorland Library" or "Negro Library" used in reference to this special library. When the library moved to the Founders Library in 1939, it still officially bore the name, "The Moorland Foundation: A Library of Negro Life." In 1958, in recognition of the prominence of the Negro Authors Collection and of the Negro Musicians Collection acquired from Arthur Barnett Spingarn (1878–1971), in 1946 and in 1958 respectively, the name of the university's ethnic materials became the Moorland–Spingarn Collection. During the 1960s and the early 1970s, the name commonly used for the Moorland–Spingarn Collection was the Moorland–Spingarn Research Library. The current name, Moorland–Spingarn Research Center, became official in 1973.[4] Each of the appellations of this special collection at Howard University will be historically associated with its long-term curator, Dorothy Porter Wesley.

HOWARD UNIVERSITY AND THE GENESIS
OF THE MOORLAND FOUNDATION:
A LIBRARY OF NEGRO LIFE

Dorothy Porter Wesley's appointment to the library staff of Howard University in 1930 came during the beginning of a "glorious period" in the history of the university. It came during the tenure of the late Dr. Mordecai W. Johnson (1890–1976), the first African-American president of the university. From September 1, 1926, through June 30, 1960, Mordecai Johnson guided the development of the institution into a university of distinction.[5] The late President John F. Kennedy's praise of Dr. Johnson, "You have truly been one of the outstanding leaders in American education in this century,"[6] was not an uncommon testimony to this man of accomplishments, who set a yet unsurpassed record of serving as president of Howard University for the longest span of years. Howard University, with its "dual mission of educating Negroes and other youths without distinction as to race, sex, religion, or national origin," has historically produced the majority of the successful African-American lawyers, dentists, physicians, pharmacists, social workers, and engineers. This university with a predominantly African-American student population, staff, and faculty has also trained innumerable, distinguished African-Americans with specialities in the ministry, teaching, business, and government.[7]

In a dynamic academic setting, Dorothy Porter Wesley in 1930 commenced her work at Howard University with the formidable task of bringing together materials from several locations within the general library. She brought together in one reading room and in an adjacent book stack area of the university library the scattered collections of donated materials on Africa and people of African descent, including a large quantity of documentation on the abolitionist movement and the Civil War. General Oliver Otis Howard (1830–1909), a Caucasian, a founder for whom the university is named and its third president, donated material on Africa and people of African descent in his efforts to begin a library at the new school. Joining General Howard in donating the first-acquired material to Howard University on the abolitionist movement and Civil War material were trustees and faculty of Howard University and other individuals interested in creating a library shortly after the chartering of the university in 1867. In 1873, Lewis Tappan (1788–1873), a noted, wealthy New York abolitionist and one of the organizers of the American and Foreign Anti-Slavery Society, gave the university its basic Anti-Slavery Collection. Tappan's collection

Reprinted with permission of the Moorland–Spingarn Research Center, Howard University.

Dorothy Wesley Porter at the Moorland–Spingarn Research Center at Howard University.

accounts for more than 1,600 books, pamphlets, newspapers, letters, pictures, clippings, and periodicals in the library. To these materials, Dr. Wesley added the extensive and previously private collection of "some 3,000 books, pamphlets, and other historical items" donated to the university in 1914 by Jesse E. Moorland, referred to earlier in this study. Moorland was a minister, an alumnus, and a trustee of Howard University from 1907 to 1940.[8]

The materials so far identified formed the foundation of a bellwether repository and working laboratory that Dr. Wesley developed at Howard University. This repository, which has claim to being the "first research library in an American university devoted exclusively to materials on the Negro,"[9] became a magnet to persons seeking historical, political, social, educational, cultural, and economic information by and about people of African descent in North America, in Latin America, in the West Indies, and in Africa. The Moorland Foundation attracted such scholars as Benjamin Brawley (1882–1939), Alain Leroy Locke (1886–1954), Edmund Franklin Frazier (1894–1962), Horace M. Bond (1904–1972), Charles H. Wesley (1891–1987), Howard W. Thurman (1900–1981), John Hope Franklin (1915–   ), Rayford W. Logan (1897–1982), Lerone Bennett (1928–   ), Maya Angelou (1928–   ), John W. Blassingame (1941–   ), and Mary Francis Berry (1939–   ).

FROM THE MOORLAND FOUNDATION
TO THE MOORLAND–SPINGARN RESEARCH LIBRARY

A quantum leap in the resources of the Moorland Foundation came in 1946 when Howard University, acting upon the advice of Dr. Wesley, purchased approximately 5,000 volumes in the Negro Authors Collection from Arthur Barnett Spingarn, an insatiable bibliophile. The name of this collection obscures its inclusiveness, for it includes African, African-American, African-Brazilian, and Caribbean writers. Spingarn, who had a "mania for completeness," continued to collect books by Negro authors after parting with his massive collection in 1946. He later donated the books by Negro authors as additions to the basic Spingarn Collection the university previously purchased. The works in the Spingarn Collection are in many languages, more than 60 according to Elizabeth Steven's report in the December 25, 1965, issue of the *Washington Post*. In addition to the books in English, French, Spanish, Dutch, Russian, Arabic, and Latin, some works are in African languages, such as Swahili, Kikuyu, Zula, Yoruba, Vai, Lunganda, Ga, Sotho, Amharic, Hausa, and Xhosa. Several of the rare items in the Spingarn Collection are from the 16th, 17th, and 18th centuries. Among these rare items is *Ad Catholicum Pariter et Invicitissimum Philippum dei Gratia Hispaniarum Reguem*, a volume published in 1573 by the former black slave, Juan Latino, an outstanding Latinist and professor at the University of Grenada, Spain. Another is Jacobus Elisa John Capitein's *Disser-*

tation on Slavery, a defense of the practice, published 1742 in Latin and in Dutch in Leyden. Capitein's *Sermons* published in Dutch the same year is also a rarity in the Spingarn Collection. Other items, perhaps the rarest pieces of early Americana, are two works by Phillis Wheatley: "An Elegiac Poem on the Death of the Celebrated Divine ... George Whitefield," a 1770 broadside, and *Poems on Various Subjects, Religious and Moral*, 1773.[10]

In 1958, the Moorland–Spingarn Research Library acquired Arthur B. Spingarn's Negro Music Collection. This collection had the distinction then of being the largest in the world, encompassing the gamut of American composers and including many foreign composers, such as Brazil's Antonio Carlos Gomes, Haiti's Justin Elie, France's Joseph Boulogne, and Cuba's Amadeo Rolden.[11] After Spingarn's death in 1971 and in accord with his will, Spingarn's Lincoln Collection was added to the resources bearing his name.[12]

Within four decades and with very modest funding, Dr. Wesley successfully fostered the expansion of the Moorland Foundation in depth, breadth, and quality. Quantitatively, the number of cataloged books, pamphlets, and bound periodicals rose from 5,788 in 1932[13] to 70,098 in 1973.[14] This growth in numbers may appear impressive, but these figures of cataloged material are not complete indicators of the quantity of materials in the library in 1932 or in 1973. With the aggressiveness of Dr. Wesley in acquiring materials and with a limited budget and a limited staff, the library amassed a substantial amount of materials that for many years remained uncataloged. In 1943, Dr. Wesley estimated that less than one-third of the material in the library was cataloged. This was especially true of the expanding manuscript collection.[15]

"Whether cataloged or uncataloged, the resources in the library were accessible to researchers," states Dr. Wesley. Availability of resources and personal library service was as important to her as collecting. She was always accessible to assist the users of the library with their research. In June 1973, on the occasion of the dedication of the Dorothy Porter Reading Room in Founders Library, historian Benjamin Quarles was quoted as saying, "Without exaggeration, there hasn't been a major Black history book in the last 30 years in which the author hasn't acknowledged Mrs. Porter's help."[16] John Hope Franklin, history professor emeritus of Duke University, has related his assistance from Dr. Wesley with his 1985 publication of *George Washington Williams: A Biography*, a book that he researched for 30 or 40 years and that became a finalist for the Pulitzer Prize in 1986. When some 40 years ago Franklin was in a quandary over how to begin the biography, he told Curator Wesley about his problem with research on the subject. In her role as a knowledgeable curator of the collection and with her sensitivity to assisting researchers in using the collection, she searched, found, and gave to Franklin an autobiographical letter from among materials on Williams in the Moorland–Spingarn Collection. He says, "It got me going. I don't know where I would have been without that letter."[17]

Along with the tremendous, quantitative expansion of the historic manuscript and archival collections between the mid-thirties and early seventies came growth in the breadth and quality of primary resource materials in the Moorland–Spingarn Research Library. Among the primary sources that came from individuals, agencies, and organizations are the Jesse Edward Moorland Papers, the Joel Elias Spingarn Papers, the Alain Leroy Locke Papers, the Marion Anderson Papers, the Louis T. Wright Collections of Papers by Negro Physicians, the Works Progress Administration Records, the Collection of Patents by Negroes assembled by Henry E. Baker, the Rose McClendon Memorial Collection of Photographs by Carl Van Vechten, and the Black Press Archives.[18]

AN ENDING AND A BEGINNING: FROM THE MOORLAND–SPINGARN RESEARCH LIBRARY TO THE MOORLAND–SPINGARN RESEARCH CENTER

In 1973, the year in which Dr. Wesley retired, the university administration and the Board of Trustees recognized that this prestigious research library, developed within the administrative structure of the university library under the capable supervision of this indomitable librarian and scholar, had come of age. The actions following this recognition resulted in an independent status for the Moorland–Spingarn Research Library, an increased budget, and an official change of name to the "Moorland–Spingarn Research Center," hereafter referred to as the Center. The appointment of a new director to succeed retiring Dorothy Porter Wesley also came in 1973. The new director, Michael R. Winston (1941–   ), with additional staff, enlarged facilities, and a revised mission for the Center, restructured the organizational pattern into a tripartition: the Library Division, the Manuscript Division, and the Support Units. The abundant resources in the Library Division, the most frequently used unit, and the countless items in the Manuscript Division, the fastest-growing unit and the "most diverse repository of primary research materials documenting the black experience in America," are complemented by the innumerable resources in the Howard University Archives, the Black Press Archives, the Ralph J. Bunche Oral History Collection, and the Howard University Museum.[19]

The Center, though changed administratively and organizationally in 1973, continues to include among its goals the essence of six objectives set forth by Dr. Wesley as far back as 1932 in a Moorland Foundation report. The following three of these objectives give an insight into what she then envisioned as the mission of the research library:

- To accumulate, record and preserve material by and about Negroes
- To circulate, publish and discuss historical information concerning the Negro and thus contribute in a positive way to the enlargement of universal knowledge

- To make the Moorland Foundation the basis for scholarly reconstructive excursions into Negro history and literature

These objectives promulgated decades ago by Dr. Wesley are traceable in statements on the redefined mission of the Center:

- To "produce research in addition to carrying out traditional curatorial and library functions"
- To "pursue the programmatic analytical collecting of documentary sources that would enable scholars to probe more deeply beneath the deceptively simple surfaces of Black history and culture"[20]

CONGRUENCY OF PERSONAL AND PROFESSIONAL LIVES

In the background of Dr. Wesley's professional accomplishments lies the story of her personal life, including years of formal and informal educational preparation for a career. An Episcopalian, she was born May 25, 1905, in Warrenton, Virginia, to Hayes Joseph Burnett, M. D. (1877–1922), a graduate of Howard University and Bertha Ball Burnett (1887–1961) a professional tennis player.[21] Early in her life, both parents taught her, the oldest of four children (three daughters and a son), to be proud of her heritage and nurtured her interest in the books in their home by and about African-Americans. Dorothy Porter Wesley grew from childhood into early womanhood in Montclair, New Jersey, where she attended elementary and secondary schools. In 1925 she received a diploma from Miner Normal School, Washington, D. C., and in 1928 a bachelor of arts degree with honors from Howard University, entitling her to election to Phi Beta Kappa some years after graduation. She continued her formal training at Columbia University, earning a bachelor's degree in library service in 1931 and a master's degree in the same field in 1932. She became one of the first two African-American women to receive a master's degree in library service from Columbia University. Dr. Wesley says it was never verified whether it was she or Mollie Dunlap, former librarian at Wilberforce University, who was the first in-hand recipient of the degree in 1932.[22] In 1957 she earned a Preservation and Administration of Archives Certificate from American University. Since then she has completed several graduate courses at Howard University and at American University.

Dr. Wesley's experiences as a part-time library assistant in the Division of Negro Literature, History, and Prints of the 135th Street Branch Library of the New York Public Library added practical experience to her academic preparations for her career. Working in this division during the summers of 1930–32 while she attended Columbia University, Dr. Wesley became more intensely interested in the study of African-American writers and their works. As she worked in the branch, she acquired more than a cursory knowledge of African-

American writers from Edward Christopher Williams (1871–1929), a brilliant, renaissance-like man, who is reported to be the first professionally trained African-American librarian.[23] Williams, who was the chief librarian and a romance language instructor at Howard University, also worked during the summers in the Division of Negro Literature, History, and Prints of the 135th Street Branch Library of the New York Public Library. Dr. Wesley assisted Williams with his special project, the organization of the Alphonso Schomburg Collection in the Division and learned from him much that she found useful in subsequent years. The Division evolved into what is today the Schomburg Center for Research in Black Culture.

In speaking of Edward Christopher Williams, Dr. Wesley recalls that Williams met on Wednesday evenings in the library at Howard University with a few students and faculty to discuss Negro literature as well as the classic literature produced by authors throughout the world. Through Dr. Wesley's association with him, Williams became her mentor and model. She compliments him not only for introducing her to study critically Negro authors but also for introducing her to the study and appreciation of world-wide authors. Dr. Wesley expresses her esteem of Williams when she comments that he was "the most scholarly librarian I have ever known."[24]

This tireless bibliographer, collector, and organizer of information, who set benchmarks in providing access to resources related to African and African-American history and culture, has enjoyed and continues to enjoy family support and empathy. First these affirmations came from her parents and later from her spouses and her daughter. Her first husband, Dr. James Amos Porter, (1905–1970), was her professional and cultural companion, sounding board, and patron. He, a former chairman of the Fine Arts Department, Howard University, was an authority on African, African-American, and European art; a book collector; a distinguished artist; an art historian; and an educator, whose *Modern Negro Art* became a standard reference work on African-American art.[25] He was also father of her only child, Constance Porter Uzelac (1939–), a librarian and business woman, who in 1960 became a third generation graduate of Howard University.

On November 30, 1979, Dorothy Porter ended her nine years of widowhood when she wedded another man of national prominence, Dr. Charles Harris Wesley, (1891–1987). He left contributions to society as a historian, a minister, an educator, and an administrator, having served as head of the History Department and dean of the Graduate School, Howard University. He also served as president of Wilberforce University and as president of Central State University, both located in Wilberforce, Ohio. At the time of his death, he was President Emeritus of the Association for the Study of Afro-American Life and History. Charles H. Wesley's prolific authorship began in the 1920s and continued through the 1980s. Among his works are *The History of Alpha Phi Alpha: A Development in College Life* (1929); *The Collapse of the Confederacy* (1937);

Negro Labor in the United States, 1850–1925 (1937 and reprinted in 1968); *The Quest for Equality* (1968); *Henry Arthur Callis: Life and Legacy* (1977); and *The History of the National Association of Colored Women's Clubs; A Legacy of Service* (1984).[26]

RECOUNTING SELECTED, SUCCESSFUL ACTIVITIES

The focus now turns from the general and personal aspects of Dr. Wesley's life to other highlights of her professional career. As Dr. Wesley went about many routine duties in the Moorland–Spingarn Research Library, she accepted professional responsibility for providing personal assistance to library users and for preparing bibliographical guides and aids that would be used advantageously by local, state, national, or international students, professors, and researchers of every level in identifying and using materials in the ethnic library at Howard University. She became a living encyclopedia. When she discovered that the existing library classification and cataloging schemes lacked what she considered adequate, schematic divisions and subdivisions for classifying and describing the types of special items in the Moorland–Spingarn Collection, Dorothy Porter Wesley developed a classification scheme for the collection.[27] She consulted with the Dewey Decimal staff at the Library of Congress as she worked on this project.

Simultaneously with all these activities, Dr. Wesley energetically engaged in "hunts" for unique collections that she judged could be acquired by purchase or by donation. She compiled "wish lists" from the bibliographies in the Moorland–Spingarn Research Library and from other sources, such as catalogs of other libraries and catalogs from book publishers and dealers. She kept alert to the availability of rare and valuable material through her professional and personal contacts with other bibliophiles, antiquarian book dealers, and scholars. Although Dr. Wesley sought to attract donors, she also attracted those who required monetary compensation for their collections or for items from their collections. In either case, collectors looked favorably upon a repository, such as the Moorland–Spingarn Research Library, in which their former treasures would be carefully organized, studied for effective consultation service, and preserved for posterity. Her reputation as a bibliographic detective for locating and procuring unique and valuable material became widespread. Using these and similar approaches, Dr. Wesley managed successfully to identify and collect more primary and secondary resources for the study of interdisciplinary and cross-cultural aspects of the African diaspora than did most of her counterparts in other institutions.

Book dealers frequently initiated communication with Dorothy Porter Wesley when they procured items likely to be of interest to her. In her "Fifty Years of Collecting," an autobiographical essay, she recalls the special relationship she developed with Charles Egbert Tuttle (1915–   ), bookseller and publisher in Rutland, Vermont. Through him she was able to purchase an extensive collection of fugitive materials on slavery and black history for the library at nominal cost. Dr. Wesley pleasantly remembers that on many occasions she received packages of books, pamphlets, manuscripts, prints, and documents with enclosed notes from Charles Tuttle that read "no charge."[28]

The circle of bibliophiles with whom she had personal acquaintance and who supported her with her work included Arthur Alphonso Schomburg (1874–1938), a celebrated collector of works by Negro authors, whose memory lives in the name Schomburg Center for Research in Black Culture. Dorothy Porter Wesley met Schomburg in New York in 1931 shortly after he accepted an appointment as curator of what was then the Negro Department of the New York Public Library. She maintained communications with him until his death in 1938. Another was Henry Proctor Slaughter (1871–1958), the godfather of her daughter, Constance, and a "natural-born" collector, formerly of Louisville, Kentucky, and later of Washington, D. C. He sold his famous slavery collection to Atlanta University in the spring of 1946. Before the collection moved to Atlanta University, Dr. Wesley inventoried the manuscripts, broadsides, and prints in the collection. She accepted an invitation from Dr. Rufus Clement (1900–1967), then president of Atlanta University, to assist in establishing the Slaughter Collection in its new location. She spent the month of June 1946 at Atlanta University organizing and describing the slightly fewer than 9,000 items in the collection. A third bibliophile in this circle was Arthur Barnett Spingarn, referred to earlier. Of these three, it was Spingarn with whom Dr. Wesley worked most closely for the longest period of time, beginning in the early thirties when she was a student at Columbia University and continuing through the next four decades as she spearheaded the growth of the ethnic resources in the library at Howard University.[29] A bit more information about Spingarn will reflect his interest in the development of the research library at Howard University and his work with Dr. Wesley.

Spingarn, a Caucasian attorney, possessed extensive knowledge of history and literature by and about people of African descent and by and about Africans. He studied the books he so zealously collected for his Negro Authors Collection, lectured about them, and permitted "bona fide scholars" to use the collection for research if the scholars had exhausted the resources in public institutions to which they had access. The genesis of his building this special collection came about in his efforts to present to some of his "doubting friends" evidence of the intellectual capacity of the African-American, an ethnic group to which he became sensitive and which he defended as far back as his military days during World War I. In 1944, Arna Bontemps (1902–1973) provided a vivid description of how Spingarn's initial objective developed into a lifelong goal and obsession to collect everything everywhere for his Negro Authors Collection and of how he methodically set about the task of collecting.[30] Spingarn's sensitivity to the plight of the African-American not only increased with his avid collecting but also with his involvement in the National Association for the Advancement of Colored People (NAACP), for which he served as chairman of the legal committee and as vice president from 1911 to 1939 and later as president from January 2, 1940, to January 2, 1966.[31] He was elected NAACP president to succeed his brother, Joel Elias Spingarn (1895–1939), president from December 8, 1930, until his death on July 26, 1939.[32] To Arthur Spingarn, a special calibre of a man and book collector, Dr. Wesley gives a personal tribute, calling him her "most helpful mentor" from 1932 until his death on December 1, 1971.[33]

Dr. Wesley will readily discuss the fulfillment of one of her objectives, "to acquire rarities, preserve and exhibit them, and make them available to scholars and students," but she awaits questions for discussion of her fulfillment of another objective, "to study and analyze" the materials in the Moorland–Spingarn Research Library. Acknowledgments of her success in fulfilling this first objective already abound in this study; now comes time to address her fulfillment of the latter objective. A typical acknowledgment of her fulfillment of the second objective comes from Werner Sollors, who while acting director of the W. E. B. DuBois Institute, commented on her scholarly accomplishments in the October 14, 1988, issue of the *Harvard University Gazette*. He says she "has contributed as much as any living individual to the critical analysis . . . of Afro-American source material."[34]

SHARING BIBLIOGRAPHICAL RESEARCH AND EXPERTISE

Attesting to her study and analysis of the materials in the research library at Howard University are Dr. Wesley's countless book reviews, many of which appeared in local newspapers and bulletins and in such publications as the *Journal of Negro Education* and the *American Archivist*; her informal speeches; her lectures; her published biographical sketches of historical persons; and her published bibliographies and anthologies.

It was inevitable that Dr. Wesley, who possesses "impeccable intellectual standards and . . . passion to preserve the record of the Afro-American past,"[35] would compile such bibliographies as *A Catalogue of the African Collection in the Moorland Foundation, Howard University* (1958) and *Afro-Braziliana: A Working Bibliography* (1978), and such an anthology as *Early Negro Writings, 1760–1837* (1971). These are three of her major reference works. Her publication record of biographical sketches includes those appearing in the *Dictionary of American Negro Biography* (1982), edited by Rayford W. Logan (1897–1984) and Michael R. Winston (1941–   ). Dr. Wesley wrote the brief biographies of Maria Louise Baldwin (1856–1922), Pauline Elizabeth Hopkins (1856–1930), Mary Edmonia Lewis (1845–??), Patrick Henry Reason (1816–1898), Charles Lenox Remond (1810–1873), Sarah Parker Remond 1826–1894), David Ruggles (1810–1849), Henry Proctor Slaughter

(1871–1958), Joshua Bowen Smith (1813–1879), Edward Christopher Williams (1871–1929), and Monroe Nathan Work (1866–1945). The 1971 edition of *Notable American Women, 1607–1950*, contains biographical notes she wrote on Maria Louise Baldwin (1856–1922), Mary Edmonia Lewis (1845–??), and Sarah Parker Remond (1826–1894). The *Dictionary of American Biography* (1936) contains biographical sketches that Dr. Wesley wrote on Daniel Joshua Sanders (1847–1907) and on Harriet Tubman (1821–1913).

Dr. Wesley's list of papers, among which is a paper read in October 1951 at the International Colloquium on Luso-Brazilian Studies at the Library of Congress, gives insight into her multifaceted research. Others of her papers are "The Remonds of Salem: A Forgotten Nineteenth Century Family," Howard University, March 30, 1973; "The Religious Activities of Black Women in Antebellum America," Princeton Theological Seminary, February 16, 1979; "Non-Federal Records in the Study of the History of the District of Columbia," Mid-Atlantic Regional Archives Conference, May 16, 1980; and "Collecting Afro-American Historical Materials," Philobiblio Club, Philadelphia, November 1980.

Among her countless lectures are the critiques she gave at the Conference Evaluating Black Research Studies, Jackson, Mississippi, June 18–24, 1971; "Paths and Subtleties in Pursuit of Black Heritage," a lecture given at Cornell University, January 29, 1972; and the "Sojourner Truth Lecture 1987–1988: In Honor of American Black Women," given at Claremont Colleges, California, March 24, 1988. During her residency in 1988–89 as a Senior Visiting Scholar at the W. E. B. DuBois Institute of Afro-American Research, Harvard University, she presented several lectures on the Remond Family. On September 28, 1989, Dr. Wesley was one of three speakers on a program that she initiated in commemoration of William Cooper Nell (1816–1874), an African-American abolitionist and a pioneer historian. This program held at the African Meeting House, Boston, Massachusetts, paid tribute to "one of Boston's most illustrious figures," says Dr. Wesley.

Other sources of insight into Dr. Wesley's quest to be professionally, culturally, and socially involved are her records of frequent travels to attend conferences, seminars and committee meetings within the United States and in foreign places, as well as her records of affiliations with a variety of organizations. A few of the conferences that she attended abroad are the First International Congress of Africanists in Accra, Ghana, 1962; the First World Festival of African Arts in Dakar, Senegal, 1966; and the Luso-Brazilian Congress in Bahia, Brazil, 1971. Other places to which she traveled abroad include the islands of Trinidad, Tobago, and St. Thomas; the cities of Quebec, Montreal, Havana, Mexico City, London, Paris, Rome, and Florence; and the countries of Scotland, Ireland, Chile, Uruguay, Argentina, Nigeria, Ivory Coast, Senegal, Dahomey (now named Benin), Guinea, and Togo.

Dr. Wesley's curriculum vitae contains the names of at least 20 organizations and societies in which she has or has had membership and the names of

**Reproduced with permission from Moorland–
Spingarn Research Center, Howard University.**

Dorothy Wesley Porter receives an honorary degree from Susquehanna University. She is standing next to former governor of Pennsylvania
William Scranton.

committees and commissions to which she received appointments. Among
these are the Bibliographical Society of America, Society of American
Archivists, Boston Public Library Associates, Black Academy of Arts and Letters, Library Company of Philadelphia, Association of Afro-American Museums, Association for the Study of Afro-American Life and History, American
Antiquarian Society, Phi Beta Kappa, and Delta Sigma Theta Sorority. Two of
her historic appointments were to the President's Committee on Employment
of the Handicapped and to the National Trust for the Preservation of Historic
Sites.

Within the past few years, this librarian and curator served as a consultant for the Black Women's Oral History Project, Radcliffe College; the
Women's History Sources Survey, University of Minnesota; the National
Gallery of Art Exhibition: Black Presence in the American Revolution; and
the *Dictionary of Notable Women*. She also served on the Frederick Douglass
Papers Advisory Board, Yale University; the D. C. Historical Records Advisory Board for the Historical Publications and Records Commission; and on
boards for the Black Abolitionists Papers and the Booker T. Washington Papers. The prestigious Boston publisher of voluminous and authoritative bib-

liographies, G. K. Hall, selected Dr. Wesley as one of the editors of its Black Studies Series. Now she engages in research to complete two manuscripts for publication between 1995 and 1996. One manuscript is on the life of William Cooper Nell, 1816–1874, an African-American abolitionist and pioneer historian, referred to earlier; the other manuscript is on the life of Sarah Parker, 1826–1887, an African-American abolitionist who became a practicing physician in Rome.

BEFITING HONORS FOR "THE DEAN"

For her accomplishments, Dr. Wesley has garnered scholarships and grants, numerous awards, honors, and testimonials of appreciation. She received a Julius Rosenwald Scholarship for study toward the master's degree in library service at Columbia University, 1931–32; a Julius Rosenwald Fellowship for research in Latin American Literature, 1944–45; a Ford Foundation Grant for research on the Remond family in England, Scotland, Ireland, and Italy, 1973; and a Charitable Foundation Grant from the Prince Hall Masons for research on the Remond family, 1977.

When the Ford Foundation provided assistance to establish a national library in Lagos, Nigeria, it underwrote the expenses for the services of Dr. Wesley as the on-site librarian responsible for the acquisition of appropriate materials for this library for over a 12-month period in 1962 and 1963. Her capabilities and record of performance made her a match for this formidable task.

In 1988–89, Dr. Wesley was in residence at Harvard University as a Senior Visiting Scholar in the W. E. B. DuBois Institute of Afro-American Research, a coveted honor. Her project was additional, in-depth research on the Remonds, a 19th century black family of Salem, Massachusetts. Werner Sollors, spoke in complimentary fashion of her residency in the October 14, 1988, issue of the *Harvard University Gazette*: "We" [referring to the staff of the W. E. B. DuBois Institute of Afro-American Research] "are honored to have so distinguished a scholar at the institute this year."[36]

To date, the number of Dr. Wesley's awards and public honors totals over 35. Among the recognitions of her contributions to society are the three honorary doctorates referred to earlier; a distinguished achievement plaque presented by the D. C. Chapter of the National Barristers Wives, August 2, 1968, for outstanding service in the area of Human Relations; the dedication of the Dorothy B. Porter Room in Founders Library, Howard University, as a tribute to her "outstanding contributions to the University and the world of scholarship" upon her retirement, June 8, 1973; an alumni award for distinguished achievements presented during Howard University's annual Charter Day program on March 1, 1974; a bicentennial award presented by Delta Sigma Theta Sorority, August 11, 1976; a cultural achievement award in recognition of significant contributions to the preservation of America's cultural resources given by the U. S. Department of Interior, Heritage Conservation and Recreation Service, November 19, 1976; and a set of resolutions for achievements presented by the Pennsylvania Historical and Museum Commission, April 3, 1985.

The list of recognitions that Dr. Wesley has received continues with an inclusion of her photograph in a presentation of "fifteen great Afro-Americans of the Century" in the Schomburg Center's 1986 exhibition, "O, Write My Name," which was a collection of photogravures made from original negatives by Carl Van Vechten; a silver plaque presented by the Library Company of Philadelphia on April 15, 1989, at the Symposium "Turning the World Upside Down," in commemoration of the 150th anniversary of the Anti-Slavery Conventions of American Women, 1837–1839; and the establishment of the Annual Dorothy Porter Wesley Lecture at Howard University, the first of which was held April 13, 1989.

As recently as October 27, 1989, Ethnic Studies, University of Utah, awarded Dr. Wesley the "Olaudah Equiano Award of Excellence for Pioneering Achievements in African-American Culture." Even more recently, The Black Caucus of the American Library Association (ALA) honored her on June 24, 1990, with a Trailblazer Award during the celebration of its 20th anniversary at the 1990 ALA Conference in Chicago, Illinois.

With the abundance of evidence presented in this essay on the accomplishments and recognitions of Dorothy Porter Wesley, along with the following selected list of her publications, the author trusts that any inadvertent omissions discovered in this account will not detract from aptly referring to this information specialist as "The First Lady of Ethnic Bibliography," a title worthy of her multitudinous contributions.[37]

ENDNOTES

The primary and basic resources for this bibliographic profile are letters from Dr. Dorothy Porter Wesley to the author, a personal interview with Dr. Wesley by the author, several telephone interviews with Dr. Wesley by the author, and Dr. Wesley's curriculum vitae. Only in a few instances does the author make specific citations to these sources. Citations of the secondary sources are in the notes that follow.

Appendix A lists primary and secondary references used in this study, including several secondary sources to which the author did not make specific citations but read for a general overview of and sensitivity to the subject of this profile.

[1]E. J. Josey and Marva L. DeLoach, dedication, *Ethnic Collections in Libraries*, ed. E. J. Josey and Marva L. DeLoach (New York: Neal Schuman, 1983) p. iii.

[2]"Porter, Dorothy Louise Burnett," *In Black and White*, 3d ed., vol. 2, by Mary Mace Spradling (Detroit: Gale Research Co., 1980) p. 775.

[3]Thomas C. Battle, introduction, *Black Bibliophiles and Collectors: Preservers of Black History*, ed. Elinor Des Verney Sinnette, W. Paul Coates, and Thomas C. Battle (Washington, DC: Howard University Press, 1990) p. xv.

[4]Thomas C. Battle, "Moorland–Spingarn Research Center, Howard University," Library Quarterly 58 (Apr. 1988): 144, 148; Betty M. Culpepper, "Moorland–Spingarn Research Center: A Legacy of Bibliophiles," in *Black Bibliophiles and Collectors: Preservers of Black History*, pp. 106, 108–109.

[5]Rayford W. Logan, *Howard University: The First Hundred Years, 1867–1967* (New York: New York University Press, 1969) pp. [245]–449.

[6]Logan, p. 449.

[7]Logan, p. 579.

[8]Dorothy Porter Wesley, personal interview with author. Washington, DC, 10 July 1990; Logan 171, pp. 308–309; Culpepper p. 104; Battle, "Moorland–Spingarn Research Center" 143–145. Culpepper's account of 6,000 items donated by Moorland to Howard University differs from Battle's account of "some 3,000 books, pamphlets, and other historical items." Further research into the primary sources at Howard University is a future task to be undertaken to resolve the wide-spread diference in the number of items donated. Perhaps Culpepper's account is more inclusive of historical items, such as portraits and artifacts.

[9]Culpepper. p. 107.

[10]Arna Bontemps, "Special Collections of Negroana," *Library Quarterly* 14 (July 1944): 193–196; Battle, "Moorland–Spingarn Research Center, Howard University" pp. 146–147; Culpepper, p. 107; "Howard University Acquires the Most Comprehensive Collection of Works by Negro Authors in the World," *Howard University Bulletin* 28 (Dec. 1948–Feb. 1949): 3–5.

[11]Battle, "Moorland–Spingarn Research Center" pp. 147–148.

[12]Dorothy B. Porter, "Fifty Years of Collecting," introd., *Black Access: A Bibliography of Afro-American Bibliographies*, comp. Richard Newman (West Port, CT: Greenwood Press, 1984) p. xxiv. This introductory essay is Dr. Dorothy Porter Wesley's most important autobiographical statement to date.

[13]Moorland Foundation, Howard University Report, Oct. 1932 (Washington, DC, photocopy of typescript) n. pag.

[14]Moorland–Spingarn Research Center, Howard University, Annual Report, 1973–74 (Washington, DC, photocopy copy of typescript) p. 106.

[15]Bontemps, p. 200; Battle, "Moorland–Spingarn Research Center" p. 149.

[16]Harriet Jackson Scarupa, "The Energy-Charged Life of Dorothy Porter Wesley," *New Directions* 17 (Jan. 1990): 11.

[17]Phil McCombs, "Touching History at Howard; University's Library of Black Cultures Celebrates 75 Years of Growth," *Washington Post* 16 Dec. 1989, city ed., Arts/Television/Leisure: D1+.

[18]Josey and DeLoach, p. 134; Battle, "Moorland–Spingarn Research Center" p. 147.

[19]Battle, "Moorland–Spingarn Research Center" pp. 148–149; Culpepper, pp. 109–110.

[20]Battle, "Moorland–Spingarn Research Center" pp. 148–149.

[21]Dorothy Porter Wesley, telephone interview with author, 27 July 1989. Information from this telephone interview confirmed that Washington, D. C. was not the place of birth of Dorothy Burnett Porter Wesley as stated in *Living Black American Authors: A Biographical and Bibliographical Survey*, by Ann Allen Shockley and Sue P. Chandler (New York: R. R. Bowker, 1973) p. 128; and as stated in *Black American Writers Past and Present*, by Theresa Gunnels Rush, Carol Fairbanks, and Esther Arata Spring, 2 vols. (Metuchen, NJ: Scarecrow Press, 1975) 2: 598.

[22]Porter, "Fifty Years of Collecting" p. xxi.

[23]Culpepper, p. 107; Dorothy B. Porter, "Phylon Profile, XIV: Edward Christopher Williams," *Phylon* 8 (Fourth Quarter 1947): 315–316, 320; Porter, "Fifty Years of Collecting" pp. xix–xx.

[24]Porter, "Fifty Years of Collecting" p. xix.

[25]"James A. Porter: Art Historian, Painter," *Negro Almanac: A Reference Work on the Afro-American*, comp. and ed. Harry A Ploski and James Williams (New York: Wiley, 1983) p. 1029; "Porter, Dr. James Amos," Spradling p. 776.

[26]"Wesley, Charles H., *"Who's Who among Black Americans*, 4th ed., 1985; "Charles Wesley; Historian," *Negro Almanac* pp. 1000–1001; "Dr. Charles Harris Wesley," Spradling p. 1023.

[27]Karen L. Jefferson, "Moorland–Spingarn Research Center," *American Visions* 4 (Aug. 1989): 46; Battle, "Moorland–Spingarn Research Center" p. 145; Wesley, personal interview with author.

[28]Porter, "Fifty Years of Collecting" p. xxv.

[29]Porter, "Fifty Years of Collectin" pp. xxi–xxiv.

[30]Bontemps, pp. 193–196; Batttle, "Moorland–Spingarn Research Center" p. 146; Howard University Acquires the Most Comprehensive Collection" p. 5.

[31]Minnie Finch, *The NAACP: Its Fight for Justice* (Metuchen, NJ: Scarecrow, 1981) pp. 103–104; "Spingarn, Arthur B.," *Who Was Who in America with World Notables*, 1969–1973; "Spingarn's Work Hailed at Rites," *New York Times* 6 Dec. 1971, late ed.: p. 42; "Heads Welfare Group; A. B. Spingarn Named by Association Aiding Negroes," *New York Times 3* Jan. 1940, late ed.: p. 19. Finch gives Oct. 30, 1939, as the date on which Arthur B.Spingarn was appointed president of the NAACP to succeed his brother, Joel E. Spingarn; the *New York Times* gives Jan. 2, 1940, as the date of his election to the presidency.

[32]Finch, pp. 76–77, 103; " Spingarn, Joel Elias," *Who Was Who in America*, 1897–1942, Library ed., 1943; Marshall Van Deusen, J. E. Spingarn (New York: Twayne Publishers, 1971) 73. Finch gives date of Joel E. Spingarn's death as Sept. 11, 1939; *Who Was Who* gives date of death as July 26, 1939, and so does Van Deusen give the date of death as July 26, 1939 in the biography, *J. E. Spingarn* (New York: Twayne Publishers, 1971) p. 73.

[33]Porter, "Fifty Years of Collecting" p. xxiii.

[34]"Curator at Howard University Is Visiting Scholar," *Harvard University Gazette.* 14 October 1988: p. 5.

[35]Richard Newman, preface, *Black Access: A Bibliography of Afro-American Bibliographies*, comp. Richard Newman (West Port, CT: Greenwood Press, 1984) pp. xi–xii.

[36]*Harvard University Gazette*, p. 5.

[37]Dorothy Porter Wesley died on December 17, 1995, in Fort Lauderdale, Florida, where she had moved one month earlier to live with her daughter, Constance Burnett Porter Uzelac.

Selected Publications
of Dorothy Porter Wesley*

A ll entries in this list appear in publications under the surname "Porter," except the third entry in the section, "Parts of Books." This entry appears under the surname "Wesley," as printed in the chapter heading.

Books

Afro-Braziliana: A Working Bibliography. Boston: G. K. Hall, 1978.

A Catalogue of Books in the Moorland Foundation. Comp. workers on projects 271 and 318 of the Works Progress Administration. Margaret R. Hunton and Ethel Williams, supervisors. Dorothy B. Porter, director. Washington, DC: Howard University Library, 1939.

A Catalogue of the African Collection at Howard University. Comp. students in the Program of African Studies. Ed. Dorothy B. Porter. Washington, DC: Howard University Press, 1958.

Early Negro Writing, 1760–1837. Selected and introd. Dorothy Porter. Boston: Beacon Press, 1971.

Howard University Masters' Theses, 1918–1945. Washington, DC: Howard University, Graduate School, 1946.

Journal of Negro Education: Index to Volumes 1–31, 1932–1962. Comp. Dorothy B. Porter and Ethel M. Ellis. Washington, DC: Howard University Press, 1963.

The Negro in American Cities: A Selected and Annotated Bibliography. Prepared by Dorothy B. Porter for for the National Advisory Commission on Civil Disorders. Washington, DC: Howard University Library, 1967.

---

*First compiled by Helen H. Britton for a chapter, "Dorothy Porter Wesley: A Bibliographic Profile," in *American Black Women in the Arts and Social Sciences: A Bibliographical Survey,* by Ora Williams, 3rd ed., rev. and enl. (Metchuen, NJ: Scarecrow, 1994) 20–23.

The Negro in the United States : A Selected Bibliography. Washington, DC: Library of Congress, 1970.

Negro Protest Pamphlets: A Compendium. Selected and ed. with the preface by Dorothy Porter. New York: Arno Press, 1969.

North American Negro Poets: A Bibliographical Checklist of Their Writings, 1760–1944. Hattiesburg, MS: The Book Farm, 1945.

A Working Bibliography on the Negro in the United States. Ann Arbor, MI: Xerox, University Microfilms, 1969.

Parts of Books

"Africana at Howard University." In *Handbook of American Resources for African Studies.* Ed. Peter Duignon. Stanford, CA: Stanford University, Hoover Institution on War, Revolution and Peace, 1967. pp. 33–39.

"A Bibliographical Checklist of American Negro Writers about Africa." In Africa *Seen by American Negroes.* Pref. by Alioune Diop. Introd. by John Aubrey Davis. Paris: Présence Africaine, 1958. pp. 79–99.

"Black Antiquarians and Bibliophiles Revisited, with a Glance at Today's Lovers of Books and Memorabilia." By Dorothy Porter Wesley. In *Black Bibliophiles and Collectors: Preservers of Black History.* Ed. Elinor Des Verney Sinnette, W. Paul Coates, and Thomas C. Battle. Washington, DC: Howard University Press, 1990. pp. 3–20.

"Fifty Years of Collecting." Introduction. By Dorothy B. Porter. In *Black Access: A Bibliography of Afro-American Bibliographies.* Comp. Richard Newman. Westport, CT: Greenwood Press, 1984. pp. [xvii]–xxviii.

"The Librarian and the Scholar: A Working Partnership." In *Proceedings of the Institute on Materials by and about the American Negro.* Atlanta: Atlanta University, School of Librarianship, 1967. pp. 71–80.

"The Water Cure—David Ruggles." In *The Northampton Book.* Northampton, MA: Northampton, Massachusetts Tercentenary History Committee, 1954? pp. 121–26.

Articles

"African and Caribbean Creative Writing: A Bibliographical Survey." *African Forum* (Spring 1966): 107–11.

"The African Collection at Howard University." *African Studies Bulletin* 1 (Jan. 1959): 3–5.

"Bibliography and Research in Afro-American Scholarship." *Journal of Academic Librarianship* 2 (May 1976): 77–81.

"The Black Role during the Era of the Revolution." *Smithsonian* 4 (Aug. 1973): 52–58.

"David Ruggles, 1810–1849: Hydropathic Practitioner." *Journal of the National Medical Association* 49 (Jan. 1957): 67–72; 49 (Mar. 1957): 130–34.

"Documentation on the Afro-American: Familiar and Less Familiar Sources." *African Studies Bulletin* 12 (Dec. 1969): 293–303.

"Early American Negro Writings: A Bibliographical Study." *Papers of the Bibliographical Society of America* 39 (Third Quarter 1942): 192–268.

"Early Manuscript Letters Written by Negroes." *Journal of Negro History* 24 (Apr. 1939): 199–210.

"Family Records: A Major Resource for Documenting the Black Experience in New England." *Old-Time New England* 63 (Winter 1973): 69–72.

"Fiction by African Authors: A Preliminary Checklist." *African Studies Bulletin* 5 (May 1962): 54–66.

"A Library on the Negro." *American Scholar* 7 (Winter 1938): 115–17.

"The Negro in the Brazilian Abolition Movement." *Journal of Negro History* 37 (Jan. 1952): 54–80.

"Negro Women in Our Wars." *Negro History Bulletin* 7 (June 1944) 195–96+.

"Organized Educational Activities of Negro Literary Societies, 1828–1840." *Journal of Negro Education* 5 (Oct. 1936): 555–76.

"Padre Domingos Caldas Barbosa, Afro-Brazilian Poet." *Phylon* 12 (Third Quarter 1951): 264–71.

"Phylon Profile XIV: Edward Christopher Williams." *Phylon* 8 (Fourth Quarter 1947): 315–21.

"Preservation of University Documents: With Special References to Negro Colleges and Universities." *Journal of Negro Education* 11 (Oct. 1942): 527–28.

"The Remonds of Salem, Massachusetts: A Nineteenth-Century Family Revisited." *Proceedings of the American Antiquarian Society* 95 (Apr. 17–Oct. 16, 1985): 259–94.

"Research Centers and Sources for the Study of African History." *Journal of Human Relations* 8 (1960): 854–63.

"Sarah Parker Remond: Abolitionist and Physician. *Journal of Negro History* 20 (July 1935): 287–93.

Selected References

Battle, Thomas C. "Moorland–Spingarn Research Center, Howard University." *Library Quarterly* 58 (Apr. 1988): 143–51.

Black Bibliophiles and Collectors: Preservers of Black History. Ed. Elinor Des Verney Sinnette, W. Paul Coates, and Thomas Battle. Washington, DC: Howard University Press, 1990.

Bontemps, Arna. "Special Collections of Negroana." *Library Quarterly* 14 (July 1944): 187–206.

Britton, Helen H. "Dorothy Porter Wesley: A Bio-Bibliographic Profile." In *American Black Women in the Arts and Social Sciences: A Bibliographical Survey.* By Ora Williams. 3rd ed., rev. and enl. Metchuen, NJ: Scarecrow Press, 1994. 3–23.

"Charles H. Wesley: Historian." *Negro Almanac: A Reference Work on the Afro-American.* Comp. and ed. Harry A. Ploski and James Williams. 4th ed. New York: Wiley, 1983. pp. 1000–01.

Culpepper, Betty M. "Moorland–Spingarn Research Center: A Legacy of Bibliophiles." In *Black Bibliophiles and Collectors: Preservers of Black History.* Ed. Elinor Des Verney Sinnette, W. Paul Coates, and Thomas C. Battle. Washington, DC: Howard University Press, 1990. pp. 106–14.

"Curator at Howard University Is Visiting Scholar." *Harvard University Gazette* 14 Oct. 1988: 5.

Dictionary of American Biography. Vols. 9, 16, 18. New York: Scribner, 1928–58. 23 vols.

Dictionary of American Negro Biography. Ed. Rayford W. Logan and Michael R. Winston. New York: W. W. Norton, 1982.

Encyclopedia of Black America. Ed. W. Augustus Low and Virgil A. Clift. New York: McGraw-Hill, 1981.

Finch, Minnie. *The NAACP: Its Fight for Justice.* Metuchen, NJ: Scarecrow Press, 1981.

"Heads Welfare Group; A. B. Spingarn Named by Association Aiding Negroes." *New York Times* 3 Jan. 1940, late ed.: 19.

"Howard University Acquires the Most Comprehensive Collection of Works by Negro Authors in the World." *Howard University Bulletin* 28 (Dec. 1948–Feb. 1949): 3–5.

"James A. Porter: Art Historian, Painter." *Negro Almanac: A Reference Work on the Afro-American.* Comp and ed. Harry A. Ploski and James Williams. 4th ed. New York: Wiley, 1983. p. 1029.

Jefferson, Karen L. Moorland–Spingarn Research Center. *American Visions* 4 (Aug. 1989): 46–47.

Josey, E. J., and Marva L. DeLoach, eds. *Ethnic Collections in Libraries.* New York: Neal Schuman, 1983.

Logan, Rayford W. *Howard University: The First Hundred Years, 1867–1967.* New York: New York University Press, 1969.

Lubin, Maurice A. "An Important Figure in Black Studies: Dr. Dorothy B. Porter." *CLA Journal* 16 (June 1973): 514–18.

McCombs, Phil. "Touching History at Howard; University's Library of Black Culture Celebrates 75 Years of Growth." *Washington Post* 16 Dec. 1989, city ed.: Arts/Television/Leisure, p. D1+.

Moorland Foundation, Howard University. Report, Oct. 1932. Washington, DC. Photocopy of typescript.

Moorland–Spingarn Research Center, Howard University. Annual Report, 1973–74. Washington, DC. Photocopy of typescript.

Negro Almanac: A Reference Work on the Afro-American. Comp. and ed. Harry A. Ploski and James Williams. 4th ed. New York: Wiley, 1983.

Newman, Richard, comp. *Black Access: A Bibliography of Afro-American Bibliographies.* Westport, CT: Greenwood Press, 1984.

"Porter, Dorothy." *Black American Writers Past and Present: A Biographical and Bibliographical Survey.* By Theresa Gunnels Rush, Carol Fairbanks, and Esther Arata Spring. Vol 2. Metuchen, NJ: Scarecrow Press, 1975. 2 vols.

Porter, Dorothy B. Curriculum Vitae. Washington, DC, 1988.

"Fifty Years of Collecting." Introd. *Black Access: A Bibliography of Afro-American Bibliographies.* Comp. Richard Newman. Westport, CT: Greenwood Press, 1984. pp. [xvii]–xxviii.

"Phylon Profile, XIV: Edward Christopher Williams." *Phylon* 8 (Fourth Quarter 1947): 315–21.

"Porter, Dorothy Burnett: Librarian." *Living Black American Authors: A Bibliographical Directory.* By Ann Allen Shockley and Sue P. Chandler. New York: R. R. Bowker, 1973.

"Porter, Dorothy Louise Burnett." *In Black and White.* By Mary Mace Spradling. Vol. 2. 3rd ed. Detroit: Gale Research Co., 1980. 2 vols.

"Porter, Dr. James Amos." *In Black and White.* By Mary Mace Spradling. Vol. 2. 3rd ed. Detroit: Gale Research Co., 1980. 2 vols.

Rhodes, Lelia G., comp. A Biographical Profile of Distinguished Black Pioneer Female Librarians (Selected). Jackson, MS: Jackson State University, 1963. Photocopy of typescript.

Roses, Lorraine Elena, and Ruth Elizabeth Randolph. *Harlem Renaissance and Beyond: Literary Biographies of 100 Black Women Writers, 1900–1945.* Boston: G. K. Hall, 1990.

Rush, Theresa Gunnels, Carol Fairbanks, and Esther Arata Spring. *Black American Writers Past and Present: A Biographical and Bibliographical Survey.* Vol. 2. Metuchen, NJ: Scarecrow Press, 1975. 2 vols.

Scarupa, Harriet Jackson. "The Energy-Charged Life of Dorothy Porter Wesley." *New Directions* 17 (Jan. 1990): 6–17.

Shockley, Ann Allen, and Sue P. Chandler. *Living Black Authors: A Bibliographical Directory.* New York: R. R. Bowker, 1973.

Sims, Janet L., comp. *Progress of Afro-American Women: A Selected Bibliography and Resource Guide.* Westport, CT: Greenwood Press, 1980.

Spingarn, Arthur B. "Collecting a Library of Negro Literature." *Journal of Negro Education* 7 (Jan. 1938): 12–18.

"Spingarn, Arthur B." *Who Was Who in America with World Notables.* 1967–73.

"Spingarn's Work Hailed at Rites." *New York Times* 6 Dec. 1971, late ed.: 42.

"Spingarn, Joel Elias." *Who Was Who in America.* 1897–1942. Library ed. 1943.

Spradling, Mary Mace. *In Black and White.* Vol. 2. 3rd ed. Detroit: Gale Research Co., 1980. 2 vols.

Van Deusen. *J. E. Spingarn.* New York: Twayne Publishers, 1971.

"Wesley, Charles H." *Who's Who Among Black Americans.* 4th ed. 1985.

"Wesley, Dr. Charles Harris." *In Black and White.* By Mary Mace Spradling. Vol. 2. 3rd ed. Detroit: Gale Research Co., 1980. 2 vols.

Wesley, Dorothy Porter. Letters to the author. 1 Sept. 1989; 22 Nov. 1989.

Personal interview with author. Washington, DC. 10 July 1990.

Telephone interviews with author. 28 Mar. 1988; 26 Feb. 1989; 27 July 1989; 7 Sept. 1989; 13 Sept. 1989; 15 Sept. 1989; 22 Sept.1989; 7 Aug.1990; 20 April 1995.

Williams, Ora. *American Black Women in the Arts and Social Sciences: A Bibliographical Survey.* 3rd ed., rev. and enl. Metchuen, NJ: Scarecrow Press, 1994.

chapter 8

Anne Carroll Moore (1871–1961): "I Have Spun Out a Long Thread"

Anne Lundin

Annie Dillard speaks of the books of her childhood: "Books swept me away, one after the other, this way and that; I made endless vows according to their lights, for I believed them."[1] Graham Greene reflects on his early reading, "Perhaps it is only in childhood that books have any deep influence on our lives ... But in childhood all books are books of divination, telling us about the future, and like the fortune teller who sees a long journey in the cards or death by water, they influence the future."[2] Eudora Welty recalls the beginnings of her full, rich literacy as a "sweet devouring," in which she learned the bare bones of language from a love of the alphabet.[3] If distinguished writers raise the books of their childhood to the status of prophet or muse, how does the profession itself charged with the education and cultivation of children's librarians regard this very activity and those most distinguished in the history of this service?

The development of children's services in American public libraries is a story that still needs to be told, much less extolled. Despite rhetorical flourishes about "the classic success of the public library" or "an American innovation," children's services as a speciality has been marginalized, along with its history, as the most feminized speciality in a female-intensive field.[4] Margo Sassé in a seminal article written over 20 years ago, calls for a reordering of priorities, whereby, "If the service is significant, then the significance of its practitioners must be recognized."[5] I am suggesting that we do just that: re-vision our priorities in American library history to view the female pioneers of children's services as more problematic than "tender technicians" or "social homemakers." While it is commonplace to relegate children's services within the female domain of cultural custodianship, this canonical view tends to deflect their contributions as mere societal reflection, rather than construction, as if it were a gendered expectation in the late nineteenth century to establish library services to children. As Joanna Russ's work illustrates, there are many ways to suppress women's writing—or their works.[6]

Anne Carroll Moore provides a revealing example of the agency of women as maternal creators and constructors of the profession, or, in the words of Gerda Lerner, "institution builders." The maternal metaphor draws on the provocative work of Sara Ruddick, who presents creation as a continuous process of nurturing and helping the creation develop to maturity. Maternal creation starts before birth and works toward an equal and self-sufficient creation, through collaborative and interactive relations. In Ruddick's words, "Mothering is a sustained response to the promise embedded in that creation."[7] This is a feminist endeavor, as defined by Nancy Miller, "to articulate a self-consciousness about women's identity both as inherited cultural fact and as process of social construction" and "to protest against the available fiction of female becoming."[8] Anne Carroll Moore's career subverts "common expectations of domesticity," as described by Barbara Melosh, and suggests instead a dynamic image of *powerful* women working to construct a maternal paradigm of service.[9] *Power* is a word often denied to women's history, but it is a force defined by Carolyn Heilbrun as "the ability to take one's place in whatever discourse is essential to action and the right to have one's part matter."[10] The discourse aligned toward action and the assumption of personal value recalls for me the description by Henry James in *The Portrait of A Lady* of women "who insist on mattering." Anne Carroll Moore's powerful position in women's library history indeed matters.

The origins of children's librarianship coincided with a changing societal posture toward women and their roles along with a new emphasis on the condition of children, particularly in urban settings. The prevalence of women on the staff of public libraries was conducive to the growth of children's services. Professional women tended to diversify into other specialities other than those already subsumed by men, such as schools, settlement houses, hospitals, and library service to children. Sheila Rothman's *Woman's Proper Place* shows the connection between changing ideas of women's proper roles and changing principles of American social policy toward women.[11] Barbara Brand's research on female-intensive professions notes the connections between children's services and kindergarten work—both areas considered to be in the female domain.[12] The autonomy granted to women in the child care field enabled them to develop their own philosophy of service and heightened leadership roles. As Dee Garrison writes, "Here, as in no other area, library women were free to express, unchallenged, their self-image."[13] Women were entrusted with educating children and caring for the poor, more and more of whom flocked to public libraries for literacy, social programs, and access to books. At the same time, children's rooms were being recognized as a necessary accompaniment to regular adult services, even if just to lessen the chaos of children underfoot. As Sara Fenwick points out, the origins of children's services within a library setting was shaped by the changing status of children in the family and in community relationships that emphasized education.[14] The 19th century witnessed an ever-expanding awareness of childhood as a separate state, one which warranted special treatment: the provision of books for juveniles as well as institutions to house and maintain these burgeoning collections. Children's librarianship became woven into the Progressive reform movement, part of a political context that Suzanne Hildenbrand has explored in her writing.[15]

Anne Carroll Moore is one of a few women pioneers of children's librarianship who has received historical coverage in the literature of the field. In Margo Sassé's study of the inclusion of children's librarians in standard biographical dictionaries in the field, Moore is included as an entry in *Dictionary of American Library Biography* (1978) and *Notable American Women* (1971), but absent from the 1957 edition and from the *National Encyclopedia of American Biography* (University Microfilms, 1893–1968), which aspires to include people "who are doing work and molding the thought of the present time."[16] Moore is mentioned in seminal historical surveys of children's services by Harriet Long and Sara Fenwick, is the subject of a biography by her New York Public Library protégé, Frances Clarke Sayers, and is substantively covered in two dissertations by Fannette Thomas and Sybille Jagusch.[17] Tributes to Moore's influence are included in the biographies of Bertha Mahony Miller and Margaret Wise Brown, as well as in Phyllis Dain's history of the New York Public Library.[18] Moore herself has chronicled much of her childhood in essays included in her collected reviews, *Roads to Childhood* (1920) and *Cross-Roads to Childhood* (1926), many of which are reprinted in *My Roads to Childhood* (1961).[19] The most extensive bibliography of writings by and about her— which, appropriately, is subtitled "A Contribution toward a Bibliography"—is that by Elizabeth Harriet Weeks and Frances Lander Spain.[20] Moore is accorded due attention in Margaret McElderry's recent article in *School Library Journal* and in the latest professional history, the subject-oriented *Encyclopedia of Library History*, in the entry by Christine Jenkins on "Children's Services."[21]

While Moore's life and influence have been honored in library history, less attention has focused on her powerful agency in a number of discourses that have shaped the field of children's literature as well as children's services, and, that I speculate, have influenced the service paradigm—the construct of library public service in the United States.

Library educator Margaret Monroe has conceptualized the paradigms of public library service. Drawing on earlier work by Samuel Rothstein (1955), Monroe in her extensive writing identified four specific functions that exist and interact in service to the public: information, instruction, guidance, and stimulation. *Information* consists of the reference tasks of supplying needed information to users; *instruction* consists of the educational mission of interaction with curricular and user needs; *guidance* consists of advisory services for readers; and *stimulation* consists of public relations and creating a climate for use.[22]

Anne Carroll Moore's agency in the field exemplifies these functions at play at an early period in library history, one in which her bold entry into a variety of discourses shaped the literature as well as the profession. This is my focus here: to illuminate her instrumental role in constructing the service paradigm in children's services, which I suggest is a foundation to the whole field of public librarianship. After "writing a woman's life," in the words of Carolyn Heilbrun, I will highlight Anne Carroll Moore's paradigmatic construction of the field of children's literature and librarianship.

BIOGRAPHY

Although Anne Carroll Moore's career is associated with Pratt Institute and New York Public Library—large urban public library institutions—she grew up in rural Maine. Annie, as she was christened, was the only daughter of Luther Sanborn and Sarah Barker Moore. She later changed her name in 1923 to Anne to avoid confusion with another New Yorker colleague named Annie Moore. The middle name, "Carroll," was chosen not for any family associations but for its melodic resonance. She and her seven older brothers lived on a farm named Alderwood in southwestern Maine, in sight of Mt. Washington. Moore recalled a happy childhood where, "I cannot remember ever feeling bored or at a loss for things to do, places to go, or interesting people to know."[23] She also credits her small town with introducing to her the realities of life in microcosm, the human drama at play in its many expressions.

Moore's parents were clearly influential in developing her strong personality. Luther Moore was a farmer, lawyer, and politician who served as president of the Maine Senate and trustee of the State Agicultural College, which later became the University of Maine. Anne drew literary interests from her father, who often brought her along as company in visits and read to her. Anne absorbed her cultured mother's love of beauty, particularly in the form of flowers and gardens. Her educational experiences were particularly positive: Limerick Academy, a preparatory school in Maine, and the Bradford Academy in Massachusetts, a two-year college with which she sustained a long association. After her formal education, she returned home to study law under her father's tutelage, despite the unpromising prospects for women in the field.

All her plans drastically shifted when her parents died suddenly in 1892 from a severe bout of influenza, followed by the death of a sister-in-law in that same year. She helped her brother raise his two children for several years, her only child-rearing experience. Career options seemed unappealing to her—either missionary work or teaching. A brother, recognizing her kinship with books, suggested the new field of librarianship. She applied to the state library school in Albany, New York, for which she lacked the requisite college degree, and then applied to Pratt Institute Library School in Brooklyn, New York, where she began her professional studies and career.

At Pratt, Moore began a tutelage under Mary Wright Plummer, director of the library at Pratt. Plummer came to Pratt in 1890 and was made director in 1894, after which she helped design an expanded facility which included a children's room, the first of its kind to be built. The one-year training course did not include the subject of children's librarianship, which was not offered until 1899–1900. Moore's intention was to return after graduation in June 1896 to Maine in the new area of county library service. In her words, "Traveling libraries and traveling librarians! The idea of it fascinated my imagination and gave the first touch of reality to an experimental study of library science."[24] However, the state librarian discouraged that prospect as impractical. The state superintendent of schools invited her to give a course of summer lectures in Saco, Maine, to elementary school teachers. On her way that summer to the American Library Association convention in Cleveland, she met Caroline Hewins, the director of the Hartford Public Library, who pioneered the profession's interest in library service to children. Hewins, who frequently addressed ALA meetings and is considered to be the first woman to do so, spoke at the Cleveland conference on "Old and New Books—What to Buy," arguing for the value of older books as well as the latest literature.[25] After returning from the conference, Moore received a job offer from Mary Wright Plummer to assume responsibilities for the new children's room at Pratt.

These two women—Mary Wright Plummer and Caroline Hewins—became Moore's mentors in the field. Both women assumed high positions in the American Library Association. Plummer founded the library school at Pratt and was elected president of ALA. Moore saw in Plummer a highly cultured woman, a writer and poet as well as a skilled administrator, with national and international stature. In 1897, in an address before the Friends' Library Association of Philadelphia and the New York Library Club, which was reprinted in *Library Journal*, Plummer characterized the requisites for the ideal children's library as "suitable books, plenty of room, plenty of assistance, and thoughtful administration," and defined the ideal children's librarian as "well read and well educated, broadminded, tactful, with common sense and judgment, attractive to children in manner and person, possessed, in short, of all desirable qualities.

. . ."[26] Plummer attended organizational meetings of the new Children's Librarian section of ALA and addressed the need for high standards in the selection of children's books.[27]

Like Mary Wright Plummer, Caroline Hewins was a library director, not a children's librarian, but another woman ardently committed to the cause of children and their literature. She began children's work while director of the Hartford Public Library, where she separated children's books into a special collection and campaigned within the profession for greater attention to children's reading. "What are you doing to encourage a love of good reading in boys and girls?" she asked 25 librarians in her own survey, the results of which she announced at the Cincinnati Conference of ALA in 1882, and followed up with a series of yearly reports on "Reading for the young."[28] In 1882 she also wrote a pamphlet for *Publishers' Weekly* the first guidebook to children's books, *Books for the Young, a guide for parents and children*, which recommended specific titles and gave suggestions for teaching "the Right Use of Books," such as "Give childen something that they are growing up to, not away from." The next year she began to contribute a monthly column in *Library Journal*, "Literature for the Young," in which she listed new books with excerpts from reviews and a section, "Notes and Suggestions," a miscellany of comments on children's reading materials and how to select and organize them. Later, in 1926, Hewins wrote her autobiography, *A Mid-Century Child and Her Books*, in which she dwelled on her early experiences with books. Hewins became a close friend of Moore's shortly after their first meeting. They collaborated on a project to encourage librarians across the country to collect annotations by children on their own reading, with the intention to compare children's responses and to capture "the spontaneous comment of the child."[29] One letter from Hewins to Moore, dated 1898, ends fondly with the words, "How hungry one grows for one's own kind, and how worn the paths are from some stations to some libraries!"[30] Moore regularly included Hewins as a speaker at the annual holiday exhibition of books and dedicated her first book to her, *Roads to Childhood*, with the inscription: "To Caroline M. Hewins, who has passed on to children of many races the rare gift of a companionship with books based on friendship rather than on desire for knowledge."[31]

Moore spent 10 years at Pratt, from 1896 to 1906, under the visionary mentoring of Plummer. Plummer was a cultured, literary woman, a linguist, a poet, and a librarian with an international reputation. Her professional writing was read widely abroad in the 1890s and early 1900s. She was chosen as the United States delegate to the International Congress of Librarians held in Paris in 1900, where she planned a graphics exhibit and delivered two papers in French: one on bibliography and the other on library and school cooperation. International educators often visited Pratt to see the work inspired by Plummer. She, like Caroline Hewins before her, advocated for an active role of libraries with children's reading. The opening of a separate children's room inspired Plummer to

Anne Carroll Moore selects children's books.

reflect in her annual report that this new department "has led us into channels of knowledge and usefulness of which we had not heretofore dreamed."[32] In a letter to a friend in 1932, after receiving a special award Diploma of Honor from Pratt, Moore expressed her regret that Mary Wright Plummer was not there to see work with children be especially recognized, since Plummer was the first to elevate the children's department to equal status with other units of the library, rather than be a mere appendage to the circulation department. Moore recalled that Plummer challenged her to be imaginative in her conception of the children's room, urging her to do with it whatever she had it in her to do.

At Pratt, Moore developed the professional practices that shaped her subsequent career: managing the children's room, participating in professional activities, and writing. In her first year report, Moore wrote about the challenges of opening a new department for children, which "presented daily new questions of government, logic, and ethics, and opened our eyes to the sociological value of all dealings with children."[33] In this report, she expressed her interest in "the kindergarten spirit," with the reservation that the library be unique in its own character and intellectual potential for child growth.

The kindergarten movement in the late 19th century was inspired by the writings of the German educator, Friedrich Wilhelm August Froebel (1782–1852). Influenced by the Swiss educator Johann Pestalozzi, Froebel's educational philosophy, outlined in *The Education of Man* (1826), was based on his belief in the unity of the universe, which led him to advocate cooperation rather than competition in education, manual training to unite hand and brain, a thorough study of nature, and the practice of play as an aid to the harmonious expression of all human faculties. Froebel's work inspired the child-centered Progressive movement in education and was heralded by Kate Douglas Wiggin in the United States. Wiggin, the author of *Rebecca of Sunnybrook Farm* (1903), organized the first free kindergarten in the Far West in 1878 and wrote extensively about books and children in the periodical press.[34] Moore was clearly influenced by Wiggin. Many of Moore's review essays in *Roads to Childhood* recommend titles by Wiggin, who was also invited by Moore to be the speaker at the first Children's Book Week celebration in 1919.

Moore's intention at Pratt, which included kindergarten methods, was to open access to books for children, to organize a system of circulation, to create thematic exhibits of pictures and book displays, and accompanying reading lists, and to extend the influence of the library beyond its walls. In 1898 she introduced her well-known register pledge, which pledged the child to take good care of all books, to pay all fines, and to obey all rules. She also began work with schools: making contacts, giving talks, and providing special library services, such as storytelling.

Moore had first been exposed to the call of stories when she heard Marie Shedlock speak at Pratt in 1902, under the invitation of Marie Plummer. Shedlock awed Moore with "the music in her voice, the quality of her diction, her inimitable gesture, the sheer magic of her presentation of a complete drama in miniature."[35] After hearing the noted storyteller speak, Moore became increasingly more active in organizing evening storytelling sessions, which often followed literary or holiday themes. Moore wrote about her storytelling activities in *Library Journal* in 1905, describing each month's special festivities and her own distinctive management approach: "Like every other form of work it requires clear definition of purpose and plan and careful organization of method."[36]

It was during the Pratt years that Moore became a leader in the profession in the new practice of children's services. At the 1899 ALA Montreal Conference, Moore was chosen as the chair of the Club of Children's Librarians, which later became the Children's Services Division of ALA.[37] She presented a landmark paper at the 1898 conference, "Special Training for Children's Librarians," in which she stated for the first time what was needed in this new field, including attributes of personal fitness, general library training in relation to special training for children's work, and special training in library work for children. For the latter, certain specific requirement are noteworthy, particularly in terms of the development of the picture book, still in its infancy: "knowledge of children; of their books; of good pictures; and the recognition of their interrelationship, or a sense of the fitness of things."[38] Her leadership role in ALA was instrumental in forming an organizational identity of children's librarians and in raising concerns of critical importance to the field, such as her 1907 paper on "Library Membership as a Civic Force" and her 1933 paper on "The Creation and Criticism of Children's Books: A Retrospective and Forecast." Her most pronounced professional role continued to be her own writing and criticism to enhance the stature of children's literature.

Anne Carroll Moore was recruited for the position of Superintendent of Work with Children at New York Public Library in 1906, where she served for 35 years, until her retirement in 1941. Moore's annual reports during these years showed the extension of her previous activities at Pratt into the wider arena of 35 branches of the New York Public Library. In each branch she opened a children's reading room, which included picture books, historical books, and other noncirculating materials, to enable young readers to appreciate the art of the book as well as to build a sense of place. A library could be more than just a place to take out books to bring home; a library could be an inviting environment in its own right, conducive to the selection and reading of books and artwork. She expanded the nonfiction collection, liberalized circulation policies, and added story hours, exhibits, and a school program. After the opening of the New York Public Library's new building at Fifth Avenue and 42nd Street in 1911, Moore developed the Children's Room into a cosmopolitan site of international interest, where foreign visitors often toured, and immigrant populations felt connected to their own native culture. It was here that the expanding children's book community was centered as Moore became a leader in the publishing as well as the provision of books for children. Moore's sense of place—the notion that the children's room has a distinctive character and aesthetic appeal— inspired Bertha Mahony, founder and first editor of *Hornbook* in 1924, in the creation in 1916 of her own Bookshop in Boston for children's books.[39]

After her first decade at New York Public Library, Moore's interest began to shift from professional issues to the literature of childhood. Her interest in communities now encompassed the publishing industry, just beginning to diversify into the children's book market. These interests emanated from her high standards of selection for branch libraries and her heightened sense of the quality desirable in the content and production of children's books. Her choices for books to appear in the annual holiday exhibition—which were published in pamphlet form and exhibited with much fanfare—were an economic impetus for publishers to be attentive to her standards and heed her counsel. With her proximity to the major publishing houses situated in New York City, Moore built relationships with numerous editors, writers, and illustrators, who often sought her favorable responses to their stories or art for children. In 1918 Moore was invited to review children's books for the literary magazine *The Bookman,* the first ongoing critical column on children's books, which she continued until the demise of the journal in 1926. In 1924 she also began writing a regular column in the *New York Herald Tribune,* under the heading, "The Three Owls," emphasizing the role of author, illustrator, and critic—all artists in the art of the book. After she ceased writing the newspaper column in 1930, she used the title for her own column in the newly founded *Horn Book* magazine.

Moore was prolific in her writing—not only the regular book columns, but also professional lists of recommended titles. Her first was a pamphlet she prepared for the Iowa Library Commission as an instructor of the Iowa Summer School in 1902: "A List of Books Recommended for a Children's Library." It was here that she stated her well-worn dictum "to give each child the right book at the right time" and began to create her annotations, which were often considered masterful prose.[40] Other booklists emerged out of special library exhibits, such as "Heroism" (1914), or "Children's Books of Yesterday" (1933). The annual "Christmas Books Suggested as Holiday Gifts," which appeared from 1918–1941, were a desiderata in appearance for authors and illustrators. Her "Seven Stories High," written in conjunction with a *Compton's Encyclopedia* article, appeared in 1932 and was frequently revised and reprinted, was well circulated throughout the country for many years.

Anne Carroll Moore also expanded into the discourse of children's book authorship with the publication of two novels for children, *Nicholas: A Manhattan Christmas Story* (1924), centered in New York City, and *Nicholas and the Golden Goose* (1932), set in France and England. The first Nicholas novel heralds the history and old landmarks of New York City, weaving in fairy-tale conversation and information about the city's historical figures. Nicholas, a little boy from Holland, arrives one day at the Children's Room of the Public Library and is met by a troll named Brownie, who can turn into a brown bear whenever desirable, and by Ann Caraway, a girl who directs his New York expedition. After a Christmas party in the library rotunda, visited by many famous book characters, from Sinbad the Sailor to Rip Van Winkle, Nicholas and friends tour landmark sites from the Battery to Van Cortlandt Park. The second Nicholas novel travels to France where he visits the Children's Library at Soissons and Vicsur-Aisne, Paris, the French countryside, and the war-devastated parts of France and Belgium. Nicholas also goes to England, to the home of Beatrix Potter and visits Walter de la Mare, Alice Meynell, and Leslie Brooks. The character of Nicholas originated from an eight-inch wooden doll that Moore adopted as a kind of alter ego or talisman of children's libraries, which became famous—and infamous—enough to receive his own correspondence at the New York Public Library directed to "Nicholas."[41] Appearing first on a Christmas Eve as a gift from staff, Nicholas embodied Moore's sense of tradition and festivity, which she expressed in her work with children. However, to those who did not share in the Nicholas fantasy, Moore's use of the doll was often intrusive and irritating.

In 1941 Moore retired after nearly a half-century of leadership in library service for children. She taught at the School of Librarianship at the University of California–Berkeley, presented lectures at Pratt and at library conferences, continued the "Three Owls" column in *Hornbook,* and wrote introductions to books on Kate Greenaway and Beatrix Potter. In 1955 Pratt Institute awarded her an honorary doctorate, and in 1960, the Catholic Library Association honored her with the Regina Medal. She died on January 20, 1961.

PARADIGM OF SERVICE

Anne Carroll Moore's work in the field shaped the critical concerns of children's librarianship and the service paradigm of public librarianship: information, instruction, guidance, and stimulation. She also contributed another dimension to the service imperative: a commitment to *advocacy.* By connecting her work and writings to these basic service constructs, I hope to show Anne Carroll Moore as a powerful figure in the discourse of both children's literature and the institutionalization of children's services, with implications for the larger provenance of public librarianship and women's library history.

Information

Information refers to the service function of providing personal, one-on-one attention to the reference needs of each user. When Anne Carroll Moore assumed responsibilities as Superintendent of Work with Children at New York Public Library, one of her first efforts was to examine the existing collection and upgrade the quality and currency of the materials. She also focused on the nonfiction collection. Moore's interests went beyond building a collection to the necessity of training the sensibilities of librarians who worked with children to enhance their own knowledge of the literature. In her benchmark paper on training children's librarians, Moore emphasized the need for librarians to know the *contents* as well as the reputation of books. If children's histories or science books are inaccurate, "we need to know just where to find the good points and the weak points."[42] She also emphasized knowledge of the public school curriculum so that librarians could work effectively with children and teachers.[43] Moore's reviews in *Bookman, Herald Tribune,* and *Horn Book* often covered nonfiction titles and urged greater readability and aesthetics in text and illustration, in the entire art of the book. In an early article in *Bookman,* Moore denounced "the dead wood on the shelves" and insisted that informational books must not be dull, inaccurate, or didactic in propaganda. In Moore's words, "We are asking for a more spacious order of book than a textbook can ever be."[44] In a later *Bookman* article, Moore distinguished two classes of literature: "*creative:* belonging to the very essence of literature, timeless and ageless in its appeal, and *informative:* belonging to the social period for which the books are written."[45]

Instruction

Instruction refers to the function of user education and the instructional role of the librarian. Despite Anne Carroll Moore's initial resistance to enter teaching as a career, she spent much of her life training children's librarians to be able to work with children and to instruct them in the literature. Her first experience was with elementary school teachers in Saco, Maine, which was followed by several summers teaching at the library school of the State University of Iowa. At the New York Public Library, she initiated a special personnel grade for children's librarians, with accompanying tests, supervision, and written work. She trained her staff with regular meetings at the various branches, at which she urged them to stay informed: "Keep up with children's work all over the country!"[46] Moore was also active in a broader instructional mission toward the public. Her reviews, columns, and lectures were designed to educate the profession as well as parents, teachers, publishers, authors and illustrators about the requisite qualities of juvenile books. Her attention to illustration and the book as a physical object enlarged understandings of a neglected area in book arts and publishing. The artist James Daugherty noted appreciatively in a letter to Moore that her newspaper columns were the first critical notice given to book illustration, despite the distinguished tradition of Pyle, Frost, and other American artists.[47]

Guidance

Anne Carroll Moore drew upon the inspiration of Caroline Hewins in the writing of recommended lists and reviews. Not only was Hewins the first to write a selection guide to children's books, but she also exhorted librarians to go beyond annotations and library lists toward the development of critical judgment and a more substantive knowledge of books.[48] Moore's concerns were clearly in these two areas: guiding the public in the selection "of the right book for the right child" and educating the profession to know the books themselves through a constant interchange of criticism and experience with children and their books. Moore's reviews have been rightfully celebrated as the first sustained criticism in the field.[49] Her reviews do not constitute the first coverage of children's books, which had been prominent, as notice if not criticism, in mainstream American literary periodicals since the post-Civil War period.[50]

Moore's criticism is distinctive in the history of children's book reviewing for its substance. She wrote lengthy articles which examined a wide range of literature for the youngest readers as well as middle readers and young adults. Moore was the first one to advise on selection—the principles which may govern which books to choose. She presented various tests: reading the books aloud and insisting on books well produced as major criteria.[51]

Stimulation

Stimulation entails the creation of a climate for use, outreach, and public relations. This is another area in which Anne Carroll Moore was particularly sensitive. She understood intuitively the need to create in a children's room an environment receptive to children and adults from diverse backgrounds. New York City, particularly around the turn-of-the-century, was indeed a challenge. Despite a rural background in Maine, Moore quickly became absorbed into the multicultural life of the city at a time of expanding immigrant populations. She was sensitive to the various cultures of the city and made an effort to celebrate other holidays, customs, languages and their literature. Moore also worked at finding assistants from various cultural groups who could work in the library branches. At a time when international children's books were sparsely known, she took a particular interest in foreign authors and illustrators and in the translation of their works. Several of her book columns dealt with British, French, Italian, or Swedish children's books.

Anne Carroll Moore had a distinctive sense of place. She knew that the children's room—an innovation—must be aesthetically pleasing and attractive for children and adults. She recognized early the visual impact of pictures and recommended their use, even in her first piece on requisite qualities for children's librarians, specifying "personal appreciation of pictures" as a prominent point of "personal fitness."[52] Moore's aesthetics—which naturally led to her interest in picture books—were particularly distinctive in her appreciation of children's literature and characterized her criticism as well as her training of librarians. Moore was active in moving library service beyond library walls. She pioneered in her work with schools, even in her first professional month at Pratt, where she saw the need for "active human relations between the children's librarian and the teacher, the children of the library, and the children of the school room."[53] Her senses of play, of festivity, and of a library celebrating holidays and authors and illustrators' birthdays were dramatic.

Advocacy

Anne Carroll Moore introduced another function into the paradigm of public library service that Margaret Monroe envisioned, one that is distinctive to children's and youth services. Moore saw the role of the children's librarian as not only providing information, presenting instruction to a dual audience of children and adults, guiding the publishing and selection of children's books, and stimulating the environment of a children's room to inspire interest and use; she also saw the need to advocate for children and their literature, to be an interpreter between the world of the child and the larger world of the public.

What was extraordinary about Anne Carroll Moore was her vigorous delving into various discourses to advocate for children and their literature. Her writing, speaking, and leadership roles were distinctive in this pursuit. She was an impassioned and articulate critic who was charged with a sense of possibilities in reaching an audience that extended well beyond the profession. At a time when few books were available for children, when many would argue for more rather than better, she insisted on quality. Hear her words:

> We are tired of substitutes for realities in writing for children. The trail of the serpent has been growing more and more clearly defined in the flow of children's books from publisher to bookshop, library, home, and school—a trail strewn with patronage and propaganda, moralizing self-sufficiency and sham efficiency, mock heroics and cheap optimism—above all, with the commonplace in theme, treatment, and language—the proverbial stone in place of bread, in the name of education.[54]

In a letter of 1897 to classmates of Bradford Academy, Anne Carroll Moore recounted her activities and added, "I have spun out a long thread."[55] Throughout her long career—nearly half-a-century—Moore wove the thread of *literature*: its quality, its access, its livelihood in diverse domains of home, school, library, and the public.

ENDNOTES

[1]Annie Dillard, *An American Childhood* (New York: Harper & Row, 1987), p. 85.

[2]Graham Greene, *The Lost Childhood and Other Essays* (London: Eyre & Spottiswoode, 1951), p. 13.

[3]Eudora Welty, *One Writer's Beginnings* (Cambridge: Harvard UP, 1983), p. 9.

[4]Robert D. Leigh, *The Public Library in the United States* (New York: Columbia UP, 1950), p. 100; Paul Hazard, *Books, Children and Men* (Boston: Horn Book, 1944), p. 88.

[5]Margo Sassé "The Children's Librarian in America." *Library Journal* (January 15, 1973): 217.

[6]Joanna Russ, *How to Suppress Women's Writing* (Austin: U of Texas P, 1983).

[7]Sara Ruddick, *Maternal Thinking: Toward a Politics of Peace*. (Boston: Beacon, 1989), p. 49.

[8]Nancy Miller, *Subject to Change: Reading Feminist Writing* (New York: Columbia UP, 1988), p. 7.

[9]Barbara Melosh, *The Physician's Hand: Work, Culture, and Conflict in American Nursing* (Philadelphia: Temple UP, 1982).

[10]Carolyn Heilbrun, *Writing a Woman's Life* (New York: Ballantine, 1988), p. 18.

[11]Sheila Rothman, *Woman's Proper Place: A History of Changing Ideals and Practices, 1870 to the Present* (New York: Basic, 1978).

[12]Barbara Brand, "Librarianship and Other Female-Intensive Professions," *Journal of Library History* 18:4 (Fall 1983): 391–406.

[13]Dee Garrison, *Apostles of Culture: The Public Librarian and American Society, 1876–1920* (New York, Free Press, 1979), p. 180.

[14]Sara Fenwick, "Library Service to Children and Young People," *Library Trends* 25:1 (July 1976): 329–360.

[15]Suzanne Hildenbrand, "Ambiguous Authority and Aborted Ambition: Gender, Professionalism, and the Rise and Fall of the Welfare State, *Library Trends* 34:1 (Summer 1985): 185–198.

[16]Margo Sassé, "Invisible Women: The Children's Librarian in America," *Library Journal* (January 15, 1973): 215–16.

[17]Harriet G. Long, *Public Library Service to Children: Foundations and Development* (Metuchen, NJ: Scarecrow, 1969); Sara Innis Fenwick, "Library Service to Children and Young People," *Library Trends* 25:1 (July 1976): 329–60); Frances Clarke Sayers, *Anne Carroll Moore* (New York: Atheneum, 1972); Fannette Thomas, "The Genesis of Children's Services in the American Public Library: 1875–1906, Ph.D. diss., University of Wisconsin–Madison, 1982; Sybille Jagusch, "First Among Equals: Caroline M. Hewins and Anne C. Moore. Foundations of Library Work with Children," Ph.D. diss., University of Maryland–College Park, 1990.

[18]Eulalie Steinmetz Ross, *The Spirited Life: Bertha Mahony Miller and Children's Books* (Boston: Horn Book, 1973); Leonard S. Marcus, *Margaret Wise Brown: Awakened by the Moon* (Boston: Beacon, 1992); Phyllis Dain, *The New York Public Library: A History of Its Founding and Early Years* (The New York Public Library, 1972).

[19]Annie Carroll Moore, *Roads to Childhood: Views and Reviews of Children's Books* (New York: George H. Doran, 1920); Anne Carroll Moore, *New Roads to Childhood* (New York: George H. Doran, 1923); Anne Carroll Moore, *Cross-Roads to Childhood* (New York: George H. Doran, 1926); Anne Carroll Moore, *My Roads to Childhood* (Boston: Horn Book, 1961).

[20]Elizabeth Harriet Weeks and Frances Lander Spain, "Anne Carroll Moore: A Contribution Toward a Bibliography," *Reading Without Boundaries: Essays presented to Anne Carroll Moore on the occasion of the Fiftieth Anniversary of the Inauguration of Library Service to Children at The New York Public Library*, edited by Frances Lander Spain (The New York Public Library, 1956), p. 629–36.

[21]Christine Jenkins, "Children's Services, Public," *Encyclopedia of Library History*, ed. by Wayne Wiegand and Donald Davis (New York, Garland, 1994), p. 127–31.

[22]Gail E. Schlacter, ed., *The Service Imperative for Libraries: Essays in Honor of Margaret E. Monroe* (Littleton, CO: Libraries Unlimited, 1982).

[23]Anne Carroll Moore, *The Junior Book of Authors*, 2nd ed., ed. by Stanley J. Junitz and Howard Haycraft (New York: H.W. Wilson, 1951), p. 226.

[24]Anne Carroll Moore, "Touchstones for Children's Literature." *Bookman* (July 1926): 580.

[25]"Cleveland Conference: Third Day," *Library Journal* 21 (September 1896): 415.

[26]Mary Wright Plummer, "Work with Children in Free Libraries," *Library Journal* 22 (November 1897): 686.

[27]"Section for Children's Literature," *Library Journal* 26 (August 1901): 166.

[28]C. M. Hewins, "Yearly Report on Boys' and Girls' Reading," *Library Journal* 7:7–8 (July-August 1882): 182–90.

[29]"A List of Children's Books with Children's Annotations," *Library Journal* 24 (October 1899): 575.

[30]Caroline Hewins to Anne Carroll Moore, January 7, 1898.

[31]Annie Carroll Moore, *Roads to Childhood: Views and Reviews of Children's Books* (New York: George H. Doran, 1920).

[32]Mary Plummer, *Report of the Free Library for the Year ending June 30, 1897*, p. 3.

[33]Anne Carroll Moore, "Children's Room," in *Report of the Free Library for the year ending June 30, 1897* (Brooklyn, NY: Pratt Institute): 11.

[34]For example, see Kate D. Wiggin, "The Kindergarten–Frobel Society," in *Current Literature* 3:1 (June, 1889), p. 16–19.

[35]Anne Carroll Moore, "Foreword," in *The Art of the Story-teller* by Marie L. Shedlock, 3rd ed. (New York: Dover, 1951), vii.

[36]Anne Carroll Moore, "The Story Hour at Pratt Institute Free Library," *Library Journal* 30 (April, 1905): 209.

[37]"Section for Children's Librarians," *Library Journal* 26 (August 1901): 163–70.

[38]Anne Carroll Moore, "Special Training for Children's Librarians," *Library Journal* 23 (August 1898): 81.

[39]Eulalie Steinmetz Ross, *The Spirited Life: Bertha Mahony Miller and Children's Books* (Boston: Horn Book, 1973), p. 53.

[40]Frances Clarke Sayers, *Anne Carroll Moore* (New York: Atheneum, 1972), p. 86.

[41]The Special Collections department of New York Public Library holds many letters addressed to "Nicholas" or "Ann Caraway" from authors as well as child readers.

[42]Anne Carroll Moore, "Special Training for Children's Librarians," *Library Journal* 23 (August 1898): 81.

[43]Anne Carroll Moore, "Library Visits to Public Schools," *Library Journal* 27 (April 1902): 181–86.

[44]Anne Carroll Moore, "Viewing and Reviewing Books for Children," *Bookman* (September 1919): 32–34.

[45]Anne Carroll Moore, "The Reviewing of Children's Books, *Bookman* (May 1925): 325.

[46]"Notes of Meetings of Assistants in charge of Children's Rooms," *Notebook*, October 1909 to February 1914, Office of Work with Children, New York Public Library.

[47]James Daugherty to Anne Carroll Moore, November 4, 1930, Arendts Collection New York Public Library.

[48]"Section for Children's Librarians," *Library Journal* 26 (August 1901): 164.

[49]Cornelia Meigs, *A Critical History of Children's Literature: A Survey of Children's Books in English from Earliest Times to the Present* (New York: Macmillan, 1953), p. 421.

[50]Richard L. Darling, *The Rise of Children's Book Reviewing in America, 1865–1881* (New York: Bowker, 1968); Anne H. Lundin, "Victorian Horizons: The Reception of

Children's Books in England and America, 1880–1900," *Library Quarterly* 64:1 (Winter 1994): 30–59.

[51]Anne Carroll Moore, "Tests for Children's Books," *The Three Owls* (New York: Macmillan, 1925), p. 245–46.

[52]Anne Carroll Moore, "Special Training for Children's Librarians," *Library Journal* 23 (August 1898): 80.

[53]Anne Carroll Moore, "Library Visits to Public Schools," *Library Journal* 27 (April 1902): 181.

[54]Anne Carroll Moore, "Writing for Children," *Roads to Childhood* (New York: George H. Doran, 1920), p. 26.

[55]Frances Clarke Sayers, *Anne Carroll Moore* (New York: Atheneum, 1972), p. 61.

part two

Professional Issues

chapter 9

"You Do Not Have to Pay Librarians:" Women, Salaries, and Status in the Early 20th Century

Joanne Passet

"The salaries of trained librarians are not tempting" wrote Gratia A. Countryman in 1913; however, "No one enters any kind of educational work for the sake of financial reward, but for something better."[1] Decades have passed and librarianship is still being promoted as an exciting and a satisfying profession that provides innate rewards in lieu of impressive salaries.[2] While a number of historians have focused on the negative impact of feminization on the professions, few have explored women's attitudes about their employment and the compensation they receive. As a result, the general impression is that, historically, women have passively allowed themselves to be channeled into service professions and willingly accepted inadequate wages. Using the case of librarianship, this essay looks at one female-intensive service profession and establishes that early women librarians did express dissatisfaction with their salaries. It also explores the strategies that women developed to improve their prospects, and considers the efforts of library school directors to improve salaries nationwide.

BACKGROUND

A longer period of formal training, higher credentials for entrance, and the formation of a professional association are among the characteristics that Magali S. Larson identifies as characteristic of a modern profession.[3] The nation's first library school had opened in 1887, 11 years after the formation of the American Library Association. Unlike some professions that require a license or sanction to practice (e.g., physicians must have a license to practice medicine, attorneys must pass the bar), librarianship has never followed suit.[4] While this may be indicative of the library profession's more tentative status and lower political clout, it also may stem from the fact that early practitioners of librarianship believed that "service, not goods, is the informing idea."[5]

Because salaries serve as one index of a profession's success, one would expect remuneration to increase commensurately with educational requirements and credentials. Frank Stricker's study of college teachers suggests, however, that a weak profession can remain an attractive occupational choice without offering competitive salaries.[6] Even though the economic gap between the middle and working classes decreased during the early 20th century, people continued to seek careers in higher education because they valued such non-pecuniary benefits as autonomy, community, status, and a sense of cultural elitism.

Librarianship represented one "dignified and congenial profession" open to cultured, educated women. Moreover, leaders in the profession promoted it as a more refined level of educational service than the alternative of teaching. Before the advent of library education, women typically entered library work through apprenticeships or by virtue of their feminine traits, local availability, and cultured backgrounds. In many instances, communities appointed impoverished widows or the daughters of prominent residents. In her 1891 article promoting library work as an occupation for women, Connecticut librarian Caroline Hewins observed that there were "many inefficient middle-aged women in libraries, who were put there because they had no means of support."[7] Even 15 years later a librarian in Washington observed that the professional librarian seemed to be an innovation in the Pacific Northwest. She lamented the result, which was that the "trained librarian, working in competition with the local, untrained product, has her salary lowered thereby."[8] Thus, while the number of women in library work increased dramatically at the turn of the century (over 3,000 women librarians by 1900, over 8,500 by 1910), only a small percentage actually had entered librarianship via professional training.

To prepare for a career as a professional librarian, the turn-of-the-century woman needed one or more years of college, one or two years of library training, knowledge of foreign languages, and familiarity with literature, history, and current events. If she began work in 1899, she could expect to earn an average annual salary of $686 in a position that required her to work approximately 42.5

hours per week, 48 weeks of the year. By 1913, the outlook had improved somewhat: her salary had risen approximately 36% (to $1081), she worked a 40-hour week, and she received, on the average, six weeks of vacation.[9]

Although work conditions and salaries showed some improvement during the early 20th century, professionally trained librarians were among the growing numbers of women who encountered obstacles as they attempted to obtain full-time appointments. Many who sought positions in such "feminine" areas as nursing, teaching, and librarianship discovered that it was necessary to first displace a corps of untrained practitioners. As Susan Reverby's study of nursing has shown, a schism developed during the late 19th century between professionally trained American nurses and scores of apprentices.[10] The situation worsened as hospitals failed to employ graduates of their own training programs (the first hospital school of nursing opened in 1873).

Meanwhile, women who wanted to enter "masculine" fields, for example, those who sought positions in science, discovered that segregation, both topical (working in such feminine areas as home economics and hygiene) and hierarchical (working as lab assistants under male supervision) was the key to employment.[11] Ultimately, this strategy also was employed in feminized fields. Women became elementary school teachers instead of high school teachers or school administrators, nurses worked under the supervision of male doctors, and librarians obtained positions in small public or school libraries while men became directors of prestigious urban and research libraries.

Library boards in small communities displayed an initial aversion to the permanent appointment of "foreign" professionals but gradually began to employ them on a temporary basis when necessary. Katharine L. Sharp (1865–1914), director of the Illinois State Library School, observed in 1897 that "positions at first upon leaving the Library School are apt to be temporary."[12] Indeed, many library school graduates began their careers as itinerant library organizers, spending a few weeks to several months cataloging collections according to the Dewey Decimal System, providing advice about library buildings, and training local women to continue the work. Although temporary catalogers helped modernize many American libraries, they inadvertently perpetuated the employment of amateur librarians and further reinforced the precedent for low salaries.

GROWING DISSATISFACTION

At a time when garbage men, wall paper hangers, and milk wagon drivers struck for $10 a day, women librarians could expect to earn $40 to $75 a month.[13] It is not surprising that early 20th century librarians, who obtained professional positions after an extended period of study sometimes followed by an unpaid probationary period of several months, increasingly became dissatisfied with their salaries. While an ideology of service inhibited the promotion of self-interest, it became less satisfying as Americans enthusiastically entered the consumer age.[14]

Standards of living continued to rise, and librarians became painfully aware that they were losing ground. At the same time, librarianship became a less attractive option for ambitious modern women. An article in the March 1920 issue of *The Independent Woman*, the official bulletin of the National Federation of Business and Professional Women's Clubs, commented that "Those whose tastes incline them toward the literary [refrain] from adopting library work as a career.[15]

Comparable, systematically collected salary data for early professionals are difficult to obtain, but Table 9.1 includes the salaries for women in three feminized occupations—public health nursing, teaching, and librarianship. For comparison, one should note that the minimum subsistence wage for women living apart from their families, circa 1908–1914, ranged from $416 to $520 per year.[16] A precise comparison of teachers with librarians is difficult because many public school teachers boarded with families and worked only a portion of the year.

Although Table 9.1 indicates that librarians fared substantially better than did teachers in terms of compensation, many professionally trained librarians remained convinced that teachers earned better salaries and benefits. One normal school librarian observed in 1906 that "teachers are paid better," concluding that librarians needed to "educate the people to believe they must pay for good library service in proportion, at least, as they pay for school service."[17] An article appearing in the April 1913 issue of *Bostonia* reported that library work provided a greater degree of interest and variety than teaching, but "the work of the average library affords fewer holidays and vacations than does teaching."[18] Yet in 1915 a librarian who wanted to hire an assistant discovered that "any one who can get a 3rd grade [teaching] certificate can go out and teach for $60.00 a month," whereas the library assistant's position offered a mere $35 to $45 per month.[19] Clearly, the additional education required for library positions did not appear to yield economic rewards.

Prominent librarians recognized that women earned lower salaries than did their male counterparts and, on occasion, used this fact to promote their presence in libraries. Librarian, editor, and historian Justin Winsor (1831–1897) observed that they were "infinitely better than equivalent salaries will produce of the other sex."[20] In an address before the 1892 ALA Woman's Meetings Mary Salome Cutler (later Fairchild, 1855–1921), Vice Director of the New York State Library, attributed lower salaries to the political nature of many appointments (and the resulting uncertain tenure in office), the fact that library work was regarded as genteel and without the strain of teaching, library trustees lack of exposure to the concept of modern librarianship, and women's willingness to work for less.[21]

Articles in popular journals also reinforced the belief that service and monetary rewards usually did not coexist and stressed that the former were more

Table 9.1   Average Annual Earnings in Real Dollars of Workers in Three Feminized Professions 1892–1913

Year	Trained Public Health Nurses	Public School Teachers	Trained Librarians (women only)
1892	—	$270	$570
			subordinates: $300–$500
			catalogers: $699–$900
			head librarians: $1,000
1899	—	$318	$686*
1913	staff: $600–$1,020 supervisors: $960–$1,020	$547	$1,081*

*Further breakdown unavailable.

Sources: Mary S. Cutler, "What a Woman Librarian Earns," *Library Journal*, 17 (1892): 90; Paul H. Douglas, *Real Wages in the United States, 1890–1926* (Boston: Houghton Mifflin Co., 1930); Josephine Adams Rathbone, "Salaries of Library School Graduates," *Library Journal*, 39 (1914): 190; Susan M. Reverby, *Ordered to Care: The Dilemma of American Nursing, 1850–1945* (New York: Cambridge University Press, 1987), p. 108; and U.S. Bureau of the Census, *Historical Statistics of the Unites States: Colonial Times to 1970, Part I* (Washington: Government Printing Office), p. 168.

important. A piece in a 1903 issue of *World's Work* described the power of the school and the library "to transform crude and frequently poisonous material," while a piece in *The Dial* emphasized the "missionary work of pushing out the library frontiers."[22]

The first women to enter librarianship via library school justified their entrance into the work place by emphasizing the contributions they could make to society: Letters of reference describe young women who desired to lead busy and useful lives and who were "not content to sit down in idleness" nor to spend their time "entirely in the dissipations of society."[23] As time passed, however, Victorianism gave way to a society that focused on leisure and consumption, and growing numbers of women desired to become independent and self-sufficient.

While some women craved autonomy, others began working out of economic necessity. Colorado's Charlotte A. Baker enrolled in the Denver Public Library Training Class in 1895, a time when many people regarded librarianship as genteel work for girls who lived at home and wanted pin money, but she had turned to library work in order to support herself. Concerned about looking professional, she resorted to laundering shirtwaists in her room because library salaries did not allow her to take them to a laundry.[24] Other librarians supported parents or siblings. A librarian whose sister was a student at Teachers College stressed that she would "need to help her a good deal."[25] Thus, need to work increasingly became a primary motivation for entering library work.

Some prospective library school students, however, voiced concern that the extra year or two of library school would not reward them with higher salaries nor would it guarantee positions upon graduation. One observed: "There is only one thing that makes me hesitate [to enroll in library school] and that is the question of practicability financially. I can command a *good* salary teaching, but I enjoy the library work very much."[26] Another wondered if there was a "less expensive and equally good way of getting into the work."[27] And a librarian at the University of Idaho, asked by a library school director to recruit qualified college women, replied: "Most of the Idaho students feel that they can not devote six years to preparation for work before they begin to earn."[28]

Emphasis on service continued to erode as women librarians, like other members of society, became consumer-oriented and desirous of personal as well as professional advancement. A public librarian in Seattle regretted that her salary would not allow her to purchase an electric toaster and a percolator.[29] Some expressed dissatisfaction with the clerical aspects of their work, and desired responsibilities in accord with their training: "One may type cards and file for eight hours a day and receive a salary of $100 . . . but it does not quite satisfy when one has had a good deal of experience and feels herself fit for a little more work."[30]

Women also began to value status and titles. The practice in many turn-of-the-century colleges was for college professors to retain the nominal title of librarian while a student or recent graduate, often a woman, would perform the librarian's duties. One library school director informed a university president that the graduate in question "would not care to accept a place like the one under consideration and have a professor in some other department carry the title 'librarian'."[31]

Correspondence between graduates and library school directors during the early 20th century reflects both a growing sense of individual worth and resulting discontent with their salaries. One woman, representative of many, wrote that she had received the same small salary for two years and wished to "make such efforts as are in my power to secure a position more in accordance with my training and experience."[32] Some began to decline offers of positions, informing employers that they could not meet all their responsibilities "with that small salary."[33] Evidence of increasing assertiveness appears in another woman's declaration that she expected "to be worth it, or worth nothing for your work," and in a librarian's threat that there would have to be an advance if she were to remain.[34] Because many worked "of economic necessity," they could not remain indefinitely "as an assistant with no advance in salary."[35] They were disappointed to observe that education and experience did not seem to be a significant factor in determining salaries.

Librarians also became increasingly aware that other groups of professional women received better salaries and benefits. Although she found the work of building up the library to be interesting and rewarding, one academic stressed that her "professional pride" rebelled at "a salary less than assistants in other departments."[36] Mabel Reynolds, a teacher turned librarian, was quite distressed to learn that she received a lower salary than any other woman on the faculty, save one, a person of very limited training and experience. She informed the normal school principal that it lowered her position and the work she did "in the eyes of all" and that she was "ashamed" to find herself "working longer hours than the others on the faculty." He did not think her inefficient or subordinate, however, but informed her that "you do not have to pay librarians" because "whether trained or not, they did the work."[37] The precedent for low salaries established by amateur librarians had persisted.

STRATEGIES FOR IMPROVEMENT

Women librarians recognized but seldom contested the fact that the few men who graduated from library schools received higher salaries. Library school directors struggled to recruit men into their programs, believing that the placement of more men would raise salaries for all. They had difficulty, however, convincing young men and their families that the profession would be rewarding in terms of remuneration or status. One young man "gave up the idea because his mother thought library work too shabby a trade."[38] Nonetheless, those who became librarians soon discovered that it was easier to "gain recognition for a man . . . than for a woman."[39]

Many librarians believed that unions, strikes, picketings, and similar devices, while used by various trades to improve salaries, were inappropriate for librarians. According to the director of the University of Washington Library School, professional ethics inhibited the use of such tactics, which ultimately would result in a "loss of the spirit, and the dignity."[40] As a group, librarians took few steps to improve their collective condition. The Library Employees' Union did take credit for taking action to standardize the entrance wages at the New York Public Library to $66 per month in 1920, a sum they considered to be "far from adequate."[41]

Over time, women librarians began to recognize that the most effective way to improve their salaries was by changing positions. Loyalty to employers and institutions did not seem to inhibit them: "They knew that they couldn't hope to keep me long at my present salary."[42] This led library schools to maintain lists of current graduates, as well as of those in the field, who needed to be placed or who desired a change. Library school directors encouraged women to refrain from changing positions too often, suggesting that they remain in the same place for a minimum of two years. Librarians who did not try this technique later concluded that "It would have been better for me had I moved more often."[43]

Some librarians accepted new positions at the same rate of pay, believing that such moves ultimately would create new opportunities for professional advancement. One woman admitted that in doing so she was putting herself and "everyone else to the inconvenience of a change," but she was convinced that the move represented an advancement.[44] Often, these moves would be from a one-person rural library to a larger urban system. Librarians also moved with abandon between different types of library work (from public to academic libraries and vice versa), believing that other areas were more lucrative.

Library school directors recognized that this practice—of changing positions—merely reinforced low salaries in many institutions. Katharine Sharp reminded one student that once she had left her post, "the President would doubtless fill the position with some young graduate who would be glad for $65 or $75."[45] They also cautioned women that this strategy had its limitations: "When a librarian reaches a certain salary, a change of position to a larger salary is not easily made." While many changes were possible among the ranks of graduates "going from the first to the second salary," changes from the second to third, and third to fourth positions became progressively slower because positions were fewer and competition intensified.[46]

THE LIBRARY SCHOOL DIRECTOR'S ROLE

Library school directors wanted to place their graduates in the field—for the sake of the graduate, the school's reputation and the state of the library profession. Typically, employers contacted library school directors for the names of candidates, and the directors used this process as an opportunity to give advice about salaries. In 1902 Sharp responded curtly to a potential employer who had asked her to recommend a $600 per year librarian: "Those who are worth only $600 could not be recommended for such a position as competent ones receive more."[47] Three years later Charles Lummis, Librarian of the Los Angeles Public Library, gave a similar reply to another employer, indicating that he could not "find one person [in the Los Angeles Public Library Training Class] . . . who would take the position at $40.00 a month." He continued: "If we have any one that we would like to get rid of we wouldn't like to palm them off on another library . . . you will economize much better in some other direction than salary of your librarian."[48]

Library school directors also informed boards of trustees that it would be difficult to retain employees if they offered salaries that were too low. On the occasions when directors advised students to accept poorly paid positions, they stressed to employers that these women were being public-spirited, and that they should be rewarded with increases as soon as possible. Directors encouraged graduates to accept modest salaries in exchange for "invaluable" experience: "I know this is not as much as you are getting now, but for the sake of change and the larger opening, I would advise you to take it."[49] They expressed hope that positions ultimately would lead to advances: "You will be having actual administrative experience, and a promotion to a better position will come naturally in due time."[50]

Finally, a few library educators believed that inexperienced librarians needed to prove themselves before making demands for higher salaries. Alice S. Tyler (1859–1944), director of the Library School of Western Reserve University, informed graduates in 1916 that they should accept salaries of $60 per month "and be thankful of the opportunity to show what they can really do."[51]

Library school directors could do little with the women library school graduates who, because they wished to live in particular regions of the country or to be near their families, chose to work for less. The West's geographic beauty and healthful climate, for example, appealed to many and led them "to make sacrifices in salary since the locality and spirit of the people will be sufficient recompense."[52]

Others accepted reduced salaries for the opportunity to work under the direction of librarians whom they admired: "She is such a splendid woman . . . to work with her has been worth all the sacrifice I made in salary to come here."[53] And a few hoped that changes, even for lower salaries, would provide new opportunities for professional growth: "Even though the salary is less than I am now getting the opportunity for a wider experience appealed to me."[54] Such cases, however, gave employers the impression that women librarians, as a group, were content with lower salaries than men requested.[55]

Thus, both librarians and library school directors gave employers conflicting messages. In 1919 Frances Simpson, on the faculty of the University of Illinois Library School, concluded that librarians, by their conscientiousness and willingness to defer financial rewards, had done themselves a disservice by "making library boards conservative in regard to salaries." The trouble with the profession, she concluded, was that "we are *too* good."[56]

CONCLUSION

The femininization of librarianship is not the sole factor contributing to depressed salaries for librarians. Although it appears that early library school graduates and their directors were in a position to request higher salaries in recognition of the professional librarian's unique knowledge and skills, many employers did not distinguish between the amateur librarian and the library school graduate. Early library school graduates left school with high expectations but quickly discovered that local amateurs not only held many positions in libraries but also they had established a precedent for low salaries. And because professionally trained librarians believed that their education entitled them to certain advantages, they felt demeaned when they learned that colleagues in other occupations—especially those requiring less education—received better salaries and benefits.

Initially motivated by a philosophy of service, early librarians often tolerated minimal remuneration because they viewed the work as a contribution to society. As the missionary phase of librarianship passed and librarianship became more routinized and bureaucratic, librarians derived less satisfaction from the work. Librarians, along with many others in society, began to value consumer goods and individual advancement. Moreover, growing numbers of women became self-sufficient living apart from families but continuing to support parents or siblings. Library salaries seemed increasingly inadequate in the face of new responsibilities to self and family.

Although well-intentioned library school directors made attempts to set salaries, their familiarity with local economic conditions and the realities of the job market led them to encourage graduates to accept low salaries in order to gain a footing in the profession. They suggested that advances would follow, but it quickly became evident that this was the exception rather than the rule. And while librarians increasingly voiced their dissatisfaction, very few indicated that they would leave the profession because of its low salaries. Instead of taking a collective stand in an attempt to raise salaries, early professional librarians opted for the security of positions, even those with low wages, and tended to seek personal advancement by moving from position to position. While this tactic succeeded on an individual basis, the majority of librarians continued to earn inadequate wages. As William E. Henry, founder of the University of Washington Library School observed in 1919, low salaries would be impossible to overcome as long as library school graduates continued to accept "less than decent pay."[57]

ENDNOTES

[1]Gratia A. Countryman, "Librarianship," in *Vocations Open to College Women* (Minneapolis: University of Minnesota, 1913) p. 18.

[2]Articles promoting librarianship even appear in such popular periodicals as *Cosmopolitan*. See Lisa Cushine, "Shh! There are Great Jobs in the Library," *Cosmopolitan* vol. II (July 1990): 86–88.

[3]Magali S. Larson, *The Rise of Professionalism: A Sociological Analysis* (Berkeley: University of California Press, 1977).

[4]For a discussion of education versus certification and licensing, see Christopher Jencks and David Riesman, *The Academic Revolution* (New York: Doubleday & Company, Inc., 1968).

[5]William E. Henry, "Attention-Learners and Earners," *The Independent Woman I* (April 1920): 8.

[6]Frank Stricker, "Economic Success and Academic Professionalization Questions from Two Decades of U.S. History (1908–1929). *Social Science History*, 12 (Summer 1988): 144–170.

[7]Caroline M. Hewins, "Library Work for Women," *Library Journal* 16 (September 1891): 274.

[8]Mabel M. Reynolds to Frances Simpson, 18 April 1906, Reynolds Library School Alumni File, University of Illinois Archives, Urbana.

[9]Josephine Adams Rathbone, "Salaries of Library School Graduates," *Library Journal*, 39 (1914): 188–190.

[10]Susan M. Reverby, *Ordered to Care: The Dilemma of American Nursing: 1850–1945* (New York: Cambridge University Press, 1987).

[11]Margaret W. Rossiter, *Women Scientists in America: Struggles and Strategies to 1940* (Baltimore, MD: The Johns Hopkins University Press, 1982).

[12]Katharine L. Sharp to Louise Clarks, 12 November 1897, Library School Director's Letterpress, University of Illinois Archives, Urbana.

[13]"Lo, the Poor Librarian," *The Independent Woman* (January 1920): 4.

[14]For a discussion of a related profession, college professors, see Frank Stricker, "American Professors in the Progressive Era: Incomes, Aspirations, and Professionalism," *Journal of Interdisciplinary History*, 19 (Autumn 1988): 231–257.

[15]"Why Not Try This," *The Independent Woman* (March 1920): 4.

[16]Leslie Woodcock Tentler, *Wage-Earning Women: Industrial Work and Family Life in the United States, 1900–1930* (New York: Oxford University Press, 1979) pp. 191, 194.

[17]Mabel M. Reynolds to Frances Simpson, 18 April 1906, Reynolds Library School Alumni File, University of Illinois Archives, Urbana.

[18]"Opportunities for College Women in the Library Profession," *Bostonia* 14 (April 1913): 2.

[19]Mary Belle Sweet to Edna Goss, 9 April 1915, Sweet Letterpress, Department of Special Collections, University of Idaho, Moscow.

[20]Justin Winsor, "The Executive of a Library," *Library Journal* 11 (November–December 1877): 280.

[21]Mary S. Cutler, "The Woman's Meeting," *Library Journal* 17 (Conference Number 1892): 90.

[22]"The Day's Work of a Librarian," *World's Work*, 6 (1903): 3686; and Ernest C. Richardson, "Modern Library Work: Its Aims and Its Achievements," *The Dial*, 38 (1905): 75.

[23]Albert Hardy to Katharine L. Sharp, 15 January 1896, Sharp Papers, Box 2, University of Illinois Archives, Urbana.

[24]John Edwards Van Male, "A History of Library Extension in Colorado, 1890–1930" (M.A. Thesis, University of Denver, 1940), p. 21.

[25]Lucy M. Lewis to Ida A. Kidder, 25 April 1911, Library Correspondence, RG 9, Microfilm Reel 31, Oregon State University Archives, Corvallis.

[26]Della Northey to Katharine L. Sharp, October 1906, Northey Library School Alumni File, University of Illinois Archives, Urbana.

[27][Mary] Elizabeth Allen to Joseph F. Daniels, 22 November 1914, Allen Library Service School Student Record, Riverside County and Public Library, Riverside, California.

[28]Mary Belle Sweet to Phineas L. Windsor, 20 February 1917, Sweet Library School Alumni File, University of Illinois Archives, Urbana.

[29]Maud Osborne to Frances Simpson, 23 September 1911, Osborne Library School Alumni File, University of Illinois Archives, Urbana.

[30]Margaret Eastman to Joseph F. Daniels, 11 February 1920, Eastman Library Service School Student Record, Riverside County and Public Library, Riverside, California.

[31]Phineas L. Windsor to C. A. Duniway, 16 April 1913, Flora M. Case Library School Alumni File, University of Illinois Archives, Urbana.

[32]Pauline Gunthorp to Katharine L. Sharp, Gunthorp Library School Alumni File, University of Illinois Archives, Urbana.

[33]Ellen Garfield Smith to J. M. Hitt, 20 June [1907], Washington State Library General Correspondence, 1900–1919, Out-Of-State, RG 078, Box 19, Washington State Archives, Olympia.

[34]Mabel Prentiss to J. L. Gillis, 11 November 1905, Library Organizer's Files, F3616: Folder 761, California State Archives, Sacramento.

[35]Olive Pratt Young to Mary Frances Isom, 23 January 1908, Oregon State Library Correspondence, RGL8, 61-8/1, Box 2, Oregon State Archives, Salem.

[36]Mary Royce Crawford to Joseph F. Daniels, 18 May 1920, Crawford Library Service School Student Record, Riverside County and Public Library, Riverside, California.

[37]Mabel Reynolds to Katharine L. Sharp, 26 May 1907, Reynolds Library School Alumni File, University of Illinois Archives, Urbana.

[38]Duncan Burnett to Phineas L. Windsor, 19 July 1913, Charles H. Stone Library School Alumni File, University of Illinois Archives, Urbana.

[39]William E. Henry to Phineas L. Windsor, 16 May 1918, Robinson Spencer Library School Alumni File, University of Illinois Archives, Urbana.

[40]"Attention—Learners and Earners," *The Independent Woman* (April 1920): 8.

[41]"About Librarians and Salaries," *The Independent Woman*, 1 (February 1920): 5–6.

[42]Mayme Batterson to Anna Price, 9 January 1910, Batterson Library School Alumni File, University of Illinois Archives, Urbana.

[43]Mary Belle Sweet to Edna Goss, 9 April 1915, Sweet Letterpress, Department of Special Collections, University of Idaho, Moscow.

[44]Doris Greene to Mary E. Hazeltine, 20 June 1913, Greene Library School Student Record, University of Wisconsin–Madison Archives.

[45]Frances Simpson to Mabel M. Reynolds, 2 April 1907, Reynolds Library School Alumni File, University of Illinois Archives, Urbana.

[46]Mary E. Hazeltine to Mary Egan, 17 July 1918, Egan Library School Student Record, University of Wisconsin–Madison Archives.

[47]Katharine L. Sharp to William E. Henry, 11 June 1902, Indiana State Library Correspondence, L971, Indiana State Archives, Indianapolis.

[48]Charles F. Lummis to M. T. Owens, 7 November 1905, Loomis Papers, M1 PL5, Southwest Museum, Los Angeles, California.

[49]Mary E. Hazeltine to Mary McIntyre, 22 May 1907, Wisconsin Library School Placement Files, University of Wisconsin–Madison Archives.

[50]Mary E. Hazeltine to Harriet Bixby, 7 February 1910, Bixby Library School Student Record, University of Wisconsin–Madison Archives.

[51]Alice S. Tyler to Cornelia Marvin, 16 June 1916, Oregon State Library Correspondence, RGL8, 61-8/2, Box 4, Oregon State Archives, Salem.

[52]Helen V. Calhoun to J. M. Hitt, 9 August 1907, Washington State Library General Correspondence, 1900–1919, Out-of-state, Box 19, RG 078, Washington State Archives, Olympia.

[53]Lotta Fleek to Mary E. Hazeltine, 11 April 1915, Fleek Library School Student Record, University of Wisconsin–Madison Archives.

[54]Margaret Winning to Frances Simpson, 24 February 1917, Winning Library School Alumni File, University of Illinois Archives, Urbana.

[55]Salome Cutler Fairchild, "Women in American Libraries," *Library Journal*, 29 (December 1904): 157–162.

[56]Frances Simpson to Margaret Winning, 30 October 1919, Winning Library School Alumni File, University of Illinois Archives, Urbana.

[57]William E. Henry to Mary E. Hazeltine, 28 April 1919, Wisconsin Library School Placement Files, University of Wisconsin–Madison Archives.

chapter 10

"Since So Many Of Today's Librarians Are Women . . ." Women And Intellectual Freedom In U.S. Librarianship, 1890–1990*

Christine Jenkins

Since so many of today's librarians are women, the question arises: Does the great hassle in libraries over censorship result primarily from the too-shrill and puritanical dominant voice of the woman librarian? . . . Few women are involved with library censorship cases—again a head count is yet to be made, but a cursory examination of the literature indicates few women ever make the headlines for defending this or that title from the censor. It may well be that the basic fact of the librarian's sex is an enormously important factor in the formation of a selection policy.[1]

Since the late 1800s, the preponderance of women in American librarianship has been noted again and again, and the various real and imagined effects of this phenomenon have been discussed and debated at length. The quotation above on the role of women in censorship cases was made by Bill Katz, library

*The author would like to thank Suzanne Hildenbrand, Dianne Hopkins, Louise Robbins, Susan Searing, and Kathleen Weibel for their thoughtful responses and helpful suggestions to earlier versions of this chapter.

221

educator and editor, in a speech delivered at the 1971 American Library Association (ALA) conference. In these three sentences, Katz expressed several stereotypes regarding women and censorship. First, women are too strident regarding censorship; second, women are too reticent regarding censorship; third, women are "natural" censors. These sentiments are not unique, having been voiced by numerous speakers and writers ever since American librarianship first became concerned about intellectual freedom in the late 19th and early 20th centuries.

Librarianship has had an evolving relationship with intellectual freedom issues, with its initial role of gatekeeper or censor on the public's behalf eventually metamorphosing into that of intellectual freedom advocate, as marked by ALA's adoption of the Library Bill of Rights in 1939 and the establishment of ALA's Intellectual Freedom Committee in 1940.[2] Myths about the role of female librarians on these issues have likewise evolved, from early complaints about women's "natural" tendency to censor to later complaints about women's "natural" reticence in the struggle against censorship. It is time to look at the reality behind the myths.

The following is an exploratory investigation into the nature of women's participation in the evolving relationship of American librarianship to censorship and intellectual freedom. The history of this issue falls into two chronological periods spanning the years from roughly 1890 to 1990. The first time period begins in the final decades of the 19th century with the founding of ALA, the entrance of large numbers of women into the profession, and the beginning of the elitist versus populist debate regarding library collections that ended with ALA's adoption of the Library Bill of Rights in 1939. The second period begins in 1940 and continues to 1990, marking 50 years of ALA activity on behalf of intellectual freedom in libraries.

The specific role of women librarians within this history can likewise be divided into two corresponding parts framed by the two assumptions voiced by Katz. First, during the time when the issue of intellectual freedom and libraries was being actively debated, women were perceived as arguing (in their "characteristically shrill and puritanical" manner) in favor of censorship. Then, once the profession became officially involved in advocating intellectual freedom, women were perceived as absenting themselves from the defense of their collections.

As stated earlier, the questions under investigation are ones of myth versus reality. The myth blames women for library censorship. What, then, is the reality? If one gives more than Katz's "cursory examination" of library literature and other historic sources, what can be seen about the nature of women's relationship to intellectual freedom issues within American librarianship? First, in looking at the available data in library literature from before 1940, what was being written about the relationship between women, librarianship, and censorship, and what were women librarians saying about these issues in relationship to themselves? Second, once ALA's Intellectual Freedom Committee was formed and additional data from committee rosters and activities became available, what was the extent and nature of women's involvement with the committee and other ALA intellectual freedom advocacy activities? Finally, Katz's suggestion that "the librarian's sex is an enormously important factor" in his or her attitudes toward censorship will be investigated through an examination of the existing survey research that has looked at the librarian's gender as a variable in attitudes and activities regarding censorship and intellectual freedom. What patterns, if any, may be detected in women librarian's involvement in intellectual freedom advocacy, and what factors may have been significant to that involvement?

"THE TOO-SHRILL AND PURITANICAL DOMINANT VOICE:" WOMEN LIBRARIANS AND INTELLECTUAL FREEDOM, 1890–1940

The mission articulated for the American public library in the earliest years of the profession—to uplift, educate, and improve native and immigrant working-class citizens—has been viewed by historians as both progressive and an effort at social control.[3] During those final decades of the 19th century, library professionals were expected to make only literature "of the highest quality" available to patrons; dime novels, newspapers, and books representing non-mainstream viewpoints were systematically excluded from both adult and children's library collections.[4] There was general agreement within the profession on the role of the librarian as protector of public morals in print, a role that also fit conveniently into the perceived social role of the educated middle-class women who were entering the profession in increasing numbers.

The movement of white middle-class women into librarianship, and particularly into library service to children, was supported by the prevailing middle-class Victorian notion of what Barbara Welter and other historians have called the Cult of True Womanhood. According to this view, the world was "naturally" divided into public and private spheres, with men ruling the former and women the latter. In ruling her home sphere, the ideal middle-class woman embodied the qualities of piety, purity, submissiveness, domesticity, and nurturance.[5] By the late 19th century, however, alongside the Cult of True Womanhood's enshrinement of women inside the home, was the growing reality of waged work for women outside the home. Not surprisingly, the movement of educated middle-class white women into the workforce was accompanied by idealistic rhetoric about the particular fitness of their work such that they could perform waged work in the public sphere and still remain True Women. Librarianship was promoted as ideal because in it the True Woman could use her qualities of piety and purity (in selecting and distributing books that would be a good influence on readers), submissiveness (in serving the public), domesticity (in maintaining a home-like environment in the library), and nurturance (particularly in library service to children). While the evidence of prescriptive literature does not reveal how thoroughly the audience took such messages to heart, due to a number of factors—including the growth of higher education for women, the increased social acceptance of middle-class women's waged work, the Progressive Era promotion of service professions, and individual library leaders' interest in training and hiring women—large numbers of middle-class women moved into librarianship during this time,[6] and the profession grew from 20% to 75% female between 1870 and 1900 (see Appendix A).[7]

By the turn of the century, however, the debate among librarians between elitist and populist views of library collections became increasingly lively. Very slowly, librarians' practice shifted toward creating and defending diverse collections representing the reading preferences and information needs of many groups of library users, and ALA's attitude toward censorship began its slow evolution toward intellectual freedom advocacy. The first published arguments in library literature against the profession's role as protector of public morals in print appeared in 1897, when author and editor Lindsay Swift delivered a speech to a meeting of the Massachusetts Library Club that railed against the choices and exclusions of library selection committees, which were "a group mostly of one sex, let us admit, and of a rather narrow social range" that rejected realistic modern literature as unsuitable for public library collections.[8] It is telling that this opening volley of the anti-censorship forces was not only against restrictive selection policies, but also against women, who were perceived to be the ones doing the restricting. Arthur Bostwick's 1908 inaugural speech as ALA president lauded women librarians for their instinctive feminine notions of beauty and fitness, but criticized women's "intuitive equation" of ugliness with sinfulness.[9] In the years following, librarians defending inclusive collections often assumed that it was women's special propensity to censor and restrict. For example, in 1926 an editor of *Library Journal* lamented the absence of Flaubert, Joyce, Huxley and other current and controversial writers from public library shelves, asking, "Will our libraries now mainly reflect the taste and patronage of a feminine public or, perhaps more accurate, the prejudices of their female staffs?"[10]

Not surprisingly, the conflict between the librarian's role as gatekeeper and right-to-read defender was particularly evident in professional literature touching on the most female-intensive specialty, library service to young people.[11] Here the duty to protect the young was considered paramount, and even librarians who spoke up for non-restrictive adult collections bridled at the thought of giving children free access to the collection. For example, in one of the first censorship studies, conducted in 1922 at the behest of *Library Journal*, Louis Fiepel surveyed "representative public librarians and state library commissioners" on their policies and procedures concerning "questionable books." He did not tabulate the results, but instead quoted representative portions of most of the 33 responses, which came from both male and female librarians. All of the librarians reported some sort of restrictions in the acquisition or circulation (or both) of "questionable books." Many emphasized the library's duty to stock potentially controversial books, but this view was concurrent with the belief that young people constituted a special population requiring special restrictions, as in the District of Columbia Public Library's policy of being "very strict in their choice of books for children, but . . . as liberal as possible in their choice of books for adults." The Portland (Oregon) Public Library had a typical policy: "If a book has sufficient literary merit to receive good reviews in creditable columns, it should be on the library shelves . . . [but] a label reading, 'This book is not issued to minors' is pasted in every objectionable book".[12] Within librarianship, and more widely in American society, the concept of a variable right to read based on age was evident in the expressed views of both men and women. However, it was women, as primary providers of child care inside and outside the home, who were made the de facto enforcers of purity in library materials for children.

During the 1920s, both female and male librarians began writing about the desirability of acquiring the works of contemporary (and controversial) authors such as Theodore Dreiser, Sinclair Lewis, and H.G. Wells for adult collections, but it was not until 1928 that an article appeared in the library press that addressed the intellectual freedom needs of young people. Margery Bedinger, then a public librarian in Seattle, vividly described the conflicts that child protection mandates created for women librarians in their roles as both information providers and guardians of the young. These conflicts were particularly difficult for middle-class women because, as girls raised to become True Women, they had been insulated from "unsuitable" realities and had found such insulation to be a liability. Although Bedinger felt that librarians should be responsive to all of the information needs of contemporary young people (including information about sex), she feared that children's librarians censored young people's materials based on the limitations of their own upbringings.

> O, my sisters, we have thought that upon us lay the heavy burden of guarding the morals of the youth, 90 per cent of whom could tell us many things. . . . and the way we tried to help our young people was to weigh them down with the same narrowing shackles of ignorance and limited experience that we ourselves were struggling with. . . . It is our duty to let them have all we can give them, provided it is true knowledge, sincerely expressed. I maintain that it is dangerous for us to try to limit their knowledge of life.[13]

Three favorable letters in response to Bedinger's article appeared in the following issue of the journal, with one expressing the hope that it would be read by "the genteel but timorous ladies who tighten the purse strings".[14]

The association of female censorship with the Cult of True Womanhood conditioning described by Bedinger and the financial considerations mentioned by the above response were echoed several years later as part of a lengthy series of letters regarding censorship that appeared in *Wilson Library Bulletin* (*WLB*). At that time, *WLB* editor Stanley J. Kunitz's column, "The Roving Eye," served as a forum for professional debate regarding social concerns, and in his column of September 1935, Kunitz proposed that a "Liberal League of Librarians" (LLL) be formed to "keep on the watch for invasions of our civil liberties, with special reference to the issue of the free press".[15]

In the November 1935 issue, a retired librarian from Cleveland asked to join Kunitz's LLL, citing the need for librarians to defend "the freedom to write and freedom to find reading . . . [because] the time has come when all liberal thinkers must band together or be lost in the flood of red-baiting mediocrity," and signed herself "Old Stormy Petrel".[16] (The petrel, a sea bird, is an age-old symbol of impending rough weather.) In the December 1935 issue, Jesse Shera, who signed himself "Young Petrel," asked to join the LLL. In the following months about 20 other librarians (10 women, 6 men, and several others not identified by gender) wrote asking that they be enrolled in the LLL, the only membership requirement of which was a professional commitment "to present all sides of controversial questions." Some signed their names, while others used pseudonyms. One of the most interesting letters was written by a woman who signed herself "Long-Winded Petrel":

> You score heavily when you attack the passivity of most librarians, but don't you realize that this is the natural outgrowth of years of having it drummed into us that "we must be ladies"? Much of the blame for the craven conservatism of thought and action of librarians might be laid at the door of their boorish, autocratic board members, who control the purse-strings. Fear of losing her job shackles the thought-processes of many an otherwise assertive librarian. The truth is terribly important, and any librarian worth her salt knows it. . . Ideally, libraries should contain all knowledge, and they are manned (womanned, really!) by expert delvers. The truth, whether palatable or not, should be easily accessible.[17]

"Long-Winded Petrel" described low wages, oppressive governance, and traditional feminine conditioning as strong forces in the lives of female librarians. As intellectual freedom advocates, women were forced to deal with the particular difficulties associated with their position in society in addition to the censorship problems they shared with their male colleagues. The rhetoric of the Cult of True Womanhood, which was originally used to argue for the desirability of women librarians, continued to be used both to justify the poor conditions for women librarians within the workforce and to reinforce the stereotype of the censorious female librarian. Nonetheless, it was the effects of institutionalized sexism in the form of low wages and lack of access to power, rather than the truth of the feminine stereotype, that "Long-Winded Petrel" blamed for hindering women librarians from better withstanding censorship pressures.

In the years before ALA's adoption of the Library Bill of Rights, both the earlier role of gatekeeper of public morals and the later role as defender of First Amendment rights had champions and detractors of both sexes. Qualities such as soft-spokenness, deference to authority, protectiveness toward the young, and willingness to please were (and continue to be) labelled as feminine, ascribed specifically to women, and then attacked as attributes that played into the hands of censors. Such assumptions were made by various librarians, many of whom were women who were strong intellectual freedom advocates. In addition, the literature reveals an awareness on the part of some women of the burden that sexism placed on female librarians who wished to acquire and maintain diverse collections. As Geller concluded from her exhaustive reading of library literature from 1876 to 1939, "Though women were not more prudish than men, they were blamed for its [the public library's] restrictiveness—by both women and men—as they were blamed for other faults of the profession".[18] Given the initial role of the American librarian as preserver of public morality, the preponderance of women in the profession, the ascendency of the middle-class ideal of True Womanhood, and the special duty of the (female) children's librarian to protect the child reader, it is not surprising that the image of the censorious female librarian emerged during the early years of American librarianship.

"FEW WOMEN EVER MAKE THE HEADLINES": WOMEN LIBRARIANS AND INTELLECTUAL FREEDOM, 1940–1990

Katz identified two oppositional images of women librarians' relationship to intellectual freedom issues within the profession. The first, that of the shrill library censor, was replaced by a second image, that of the quiet avoider of controversy. It is this demure stereotype that has received more emphasis in recent decades and is exemplified in the near-absence of women in most histories of ALA intellectual freedom activity.

The story of American libraries' and librarians' involvement in First Amendment advocacy since ALA's adoption of the Library Bill of Rights has been told in accounts by Berninghausen, Boll, Castagna, Dix, and the authors of ALA's *Intellectual Freedom Manual*.[19] Edwin Castagna's account is the most comprehensive and is an example of both the standard version of this history and the limitations that this view poses in obtaining a full picture of intellectual freedom history within the profession. Castagna was a public library director, ALA president 1964–65, and IFC member 1968–74. His 1971 essay begins by tracing a brief chronology of Western thought regarding intellectual freedom, then focuses primarily on the history of American librarianship and ALA's role in the development of intellectual freedom advocacy. Castagna then describes the debate within librarianship over the inclusion or exclusion of controversial books throughout the late 19th and early 20th centuries, the adoption of the Library Bill of Rights in 1939, and the subsequent establishment of ALA's Intellectual Freedom Committee (1940), *Newsletter on Intellectual Freedom* (1952), Office for Intellectual Freedom (1967), and Freedom to Read Foundation (1969).

In Castagna's factually accurate history of libraries and intellectual freedom, some telling patterns emerge with respect to gender. The author names 27 individual librarians in the course of his narrative: 7 women and 20 men. Four (57%) of the women named are described as supportive of intellectual freedom, 2 are in opposition, and 1 is ambivalent. Seventeen (85%) of the men named are described as supportive, 3 are in opposition, and none are ambivalent. Castagna's representation of these individuals' views differs not only in numbers but in presentation as well. Five women are quoted directly, three of which are from the early years of librarianship. One spoke out against "exotic, erotic, and tommy-rotic literature" and the "daring sensualism" of a *Cosmopolitan* magazine story, one recommended that young people should be offered "good and attractive books" to counter "books that would be bad for them," and one voiced concern that realistic writing "drags us through the mire for no purpose." Two are from more recent years: one brief quote from Marjorie Fiske's benchmark 1959 study of library censorship and one longer passage from a speech by IFC chair Martha Boaz in which she quoted the words of John Stuart Mill.[20]

The words of most of the 20 men are also quoted directly, but their quotes are generally longer, and frequently serve to illustrate major landmarks in ALA's advocacy of intellectual freedom. Several of the men are further described as being "a fine example for the librarians of the country in those fear-ridden [McCarthy] years," "one of the most persuasive and articulate antagonists of censors," or "one of librarianship's staunchest and most effective fighters against censorship." According to this account, it was primarily these Great Men who crystalized ALA's official stand against censorship, directed ALA's Intellectual Freedom Committee, issued statements, edited the *Newsletter*, established the Office of Intellectual Freedom, testified before Congress, and "honored as freedom fighters".[21] Meanwhile, the appointment of Judith Krug as director of the Office for Intellectual Freedom is simply stated, and her report to the IFC is briefly summarized, followed by "Mrs. Krug went to work getting this program underway".[22]

In writing his history of librarians' involvement with intellectual freedom, it is unlikely that Castagna set out intentionally to omit women or valorize men. But his Great Men approach to library history, in focusing almost entirely on spokesmen and public figures, omits the teamwork involved in any effort of this duration. Archetypal tales of humanity's journey from ignorance to enlightenment have always held a strong appeal—particularly to librarians—but it seems unlikely that the story of American librarianship's gradual commitment to the First Amendment rights of library users is simply a John Bunyanesque tale of singular great men leading the predominantly female library profession out of the Slough of Censorship and into the Celestial City of Intellectual Freedom. Given the profession's relative lack of authority in American society and thus the necessity of grassroots coalition-building to successfully defend a library collection against censorship, plus its consistent 80–90 percent female composition at that time, it stands to reason that a historical account that is 74 percent male may well be flawed.

The establishment of ALA's Intellectual Freedom Committee in 1940 created another source of information in the records of IFC membership and activities. These quantitative data may be used to examine the patterns of gender representation within the IFC over time and may help the reader gain an understanding of not just those who were considered authoritative writers and speakers, but those who worked within ALA toward intellectual freedom advocacy. The following is an introductory look at these membership patterns over time and an exploration of some of the factors that may have affected female participation in the IFC during its first 50 years.

In order to speculate meaningfully about the gender ratios in the IFC, it is first necessary to be aware of gender ratios in American librarianship and in ALA over time. The U.S. census figures for librarians give the percentage of females in the profession (see Appendix A). However, ALA itself does not keep records on the gender ratio of its membership, so there is little information available to indicate the percentage of ALA members who are women. The single exception was in 1915, when the ALA *Handbook* reported that 1,897 (74.5 percent) of its 2,546 personal members were women,[23] a figure that may be viewed with reference to the 1910 and 1920 census figures for librarianship as 80.4% and 88.3% female respectively. The only other available figures about the gender ratio of ALA members during the time period under consideration are in the findings of two ALA salary surveys conducted in 1970 and 1980. Data drawn from the 1970 survey, based on a small questionnaire sent to every ALA personal member, indicated that ALA membership was 72.8% female,[24] a figure that may be compared to the 81.9% figure for female librarians reported in the census of that year. Data from the 1980 survey, which was a random sample of that year's ALA membership, indicated that ALA membership was 78.3% female,[25] a figure closer to but still somewhat lower than the 1980 census figures of librarianship as 82.6% female. Further research is clearly needed to create a full picture of female membership and involvement in ALA, but the data gathered thus far suggest that during the years under consideration, an estimated 70 to 80% of ALA membership has been female, and that census figures may be used to predict female ALA membership, keeping in mind that the ratio to women to men is somewhat lower in ALA than in the profession as a whole (see Graph 10.1 for this and IFC membership data).[26]

The Library Bill of Rights, adopted by ALA in May of 1939, was an adaptation of a bill of rights for libraries written by Forrest Spaulding, director of the Des Moines Public Library. The first Committee on Intellectual Freedom to

Safeguard the Rights of Library Users to Freedom of Inquiry (shortened to "Intellectual Freedom Committee" in 1947) was created by ALA Council in May of 1940 and appointed by ALA's president-elect. The first committee had three members, but the membership was gradually expanded in the 1940s and finally become a standing committee of 11 in the early 1950s. As noted earlier, the IFC served as focal point for intellectual freedom work within ALA. Over the years, the committee created revisions and interpretations of the Library Bill of Rights, sponsored preconferences and programming at ALA's annual conferences, made recommendations to ALA Council regarding intellectual freedom issues, and provided guidance to ALA's Office of Intellectual Freedom, which was established in 1967.

The first IFC was chaired by Forrest Spaulding and was comprised of three men, but Marian Manley joined the following year, and Emily Miller Danton, who served for eight years, was appointed in 1942. From 1945 to 1948 women made up more than half the committee's membership, with Alice Higgins, a faculty member of the New Jersey College for Women's Library School, becoming the committee's first female chair in 1945.[27] Female IFC membership dropped markedly in the 1950s, with women comprising only one quarter of the IFC's membership throughout that decade. The percentage of women then rose to an average of 32.7% for the decade, and in 1964 Martha Boaz became the second woman appointed to IFC chair.[28] Female IFC membership for the 1970s reached an average of 43% female, though it did not reflect the more than 70% female ALA membership for that same time. However, women held the post of IFC chair in seven years of that decade. In the 1980s, women chaired the IFC during only three of the decade's 10 years, but the proportion of female membership averaged 63% overall (See Graph 10.1).

While an ALA committee assignment is frequently a reflection of an individual's interest in the committee's particular task, a variety of other factors also play a part in committee membership. An examination of possible significant factors in IFC gender ratios must begin with an acknowledgement that the IFC is an appointed committee, and so is affected by the same ALA appointment policies and practices as other, comparable ALA committees. Historical events and trends within ALA itself also affect the formation and composition of ALA committees.

In viewing ALA committee appointments, a span of several years in ALA history must first be noted. In 1969, the Activities Committee on New Directions for ALA (ACONDA) was formed in response to criticisms from ALA membership regarding the unresponsiveness of the organization's bureaucracy. ACONDA had a series of meetings and in 1970 made its recommendations, some of which were finally passed in 1971. ACONDA was appointed with the charge of making recommendations regarding the restructuring of ALA to address specific problems. One such problem was the perceived lack of democracy caused in part by the ingrown and closed nature of ALA committee membership. Individual ALA members were officially limited to three positions on committees or boards, but this rule was not always followed, which resulted in a smaller number of administrators of large public and academic libraries—members who were considered part of an old guard elite—dominating committee and board appointments.[29] A recommendation was made to enforce the existing but unenforced three-appointment limit, in hopes that the dispersal of appointments would increase committee involvement by younger and newer ALA members and by more members than those of a constantly recycled elite.[30]

This span of years also includes the founding of the Task Force on the Status of Women, the first women's group within ALA, in 1970.[31] The creation of the task force was the beginning of a flowering of consciousness-raising and feminist activism within the profession, with ALA's standing committee on the Status of Women in Librarianship forming in 1976. The changes that began in 1970 with the passage of the ACONDA resolutions and the formation of the task force make the first years of the 1970s significant ones to keep in mind when examining ALA committee statistics.

In looking at the fluctuations in Graph 10.1, it is intriguing to speculate as to the patterns of female representation in the IFC. For example, it is interesting to note that the three highest "spikes" are all in years (1946, 1966, and 1984) in which a female ALA president made the appointments. Thus far, there has been little research regarding any aspect of ALA committee appointments. In looking at women's participation in ALA activities, however, one must be aware of gender-related patterns within the profession throughout most of its history. Studies of professional rank and salaries have documented women's lower pay and status and men's domination of administrative positions in all types of libraries.[32] Historically, men have also been represented disproportionately in positions of power and prestige within ALA.[33] Rosenberg and Suvak's 1973 study of ALA committees from 1968–1971 revealed a gender ratio close to 1:1, but this did not reflect the more than 70% proportion of female ALA members.[34] The following is a brief and primarily demographic examination of IFC membership that seeks to remedy women's relative invisibility in the standard histories of intellectual freedom activism within ALA.

To investigate the IFC as a reflection of appointment practices, it is first necessary to examine the committee in the context of comparable ALA committees. There have been, and continue to be, many ALA committees, but few with the longevity of the Intellectual Freedom Committee. The 1989–1990 ALA Handbook listed 27 standing committees, but only five of which existed in 1940, the year the IFC was formed: Awards, Constitution and Bylaws, International Relations, Library Legislation, and Research committees.

Tables 10.1A and 10.1B represent a comparative spot-check of committee gender ratios for every fifth year from 1940 to 1990 in order to give a general picture of the gender composition of the IFC and the five other ALA committees of similar longevity and status. The figures have been further divided into 1940–1970 and 1975–1990 so that possible changes in appointments may be

Graph 10.1.   Proportion Of Female Membership On ALA's Intellectual Freedom Committee By Year Of Committee

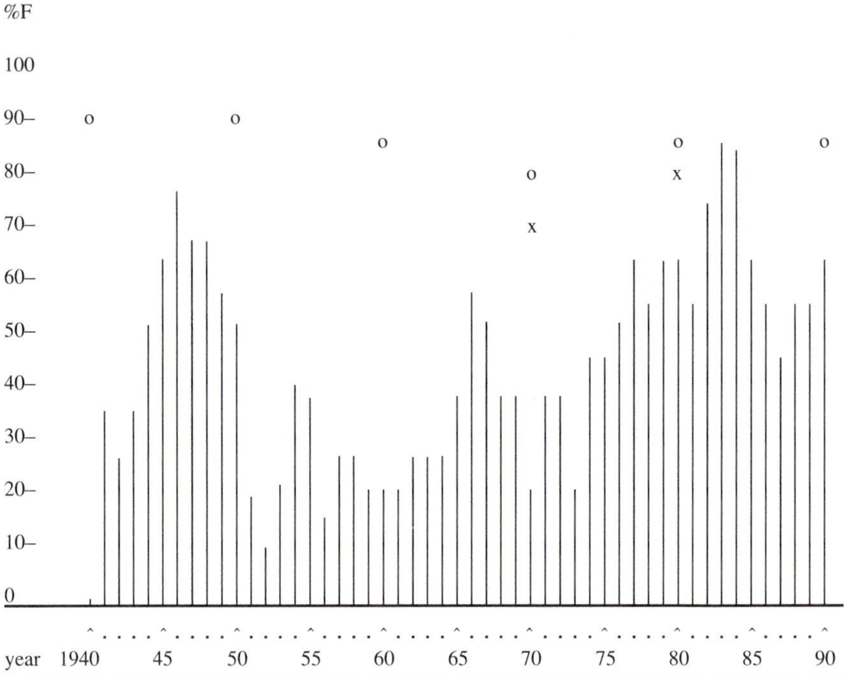

%F

100

90–   o   o

                          o   o   o
80–   o   x

70–   x

60–

50–

40–

30–

20–

10–

0

year   1940   45   50   55   60   65   70   75   80   85   90

o = percentage of female librarians according to U.S. Census
1940   89.5%
1950   88.8%
1960   85.8%
1970   81.9%
1980   82.6%
1990   81.3%
x = percentage of female ALA membership
1970   72.8%   (Manchak 1971)
1980   78.3%   (Heim & Estabrook 1983)

seen following the passage of ACONDA's resolutions in 1971, and the formation of the SRRT Task Force on the Status of Women in 1970.

The average proportion of female members in these committees was quite
low in comparison to the proportion of female librarians from 1940–1970, but
there was a marked increase in the years after 1970, and the IFC's pattern was
quite similar to that of the other committees. It must also be noted that the
Awards Committee, the only one not showing an increase, was the single committee in which membership showed a high proportion of female membership
from the start. The mean increase in the proportion of female committee members from 39% to 55% between the first span of years and the second suggests

Table 10.1A. Comparison Of Six ALA Committee F/M Gender Ratios 1940–1990

Year	1940	1945	1950	1955	1960	1965	1970	Subtotal
Awards[a]	6/2	—	5/1	3/2	5/0	4/3	3/3	26/11
%f	75%		16%	60%	100%	57%	50%	70%
Constitution	1/4	2/3	2/7	0/6	2/3	3/2	2/3	12/28
%f	20%	40%	22%	0%	40%	60%	40%	30%
IF	**0/3**	**5/2**	**5/5**	**4/8**	**2/9**	**4/7**	**2/9**	**22/43**
%f	**0%**	**71%**	**50%**	**33%**	**18%**	**36%**	**18%**	**34%**
International	7/6	0/5	2/3	1/4	0/6	1/5	2/4	13/33
%f	54%	0%	40%	20%	0%	16%	33%	28%
Legislation[b]	2/4	1/7	2/5	3/4	—	4/3	1/6	13/29
%f	33%	13%	29%	43%		57%	14%	31%
Research/Stats.[c]	3/4	4/4	5/5	3/7	—	2/2	1/4	18/26
%f	43%	50%	50%	30%	50%	44%	20%	41%
Subtotal	19/23	12/21	21/26	14/31	9/18	18/22	11/29	104/160
%f 1940–1970	45%	36%	45%	31%	33%	45%	28%	39%

Year	1975	1980	1985	1990	Subtotal
Awards	3/4	6/2	7/2	7/4	23/12
%f	43%	75%	78%	64%	66%
Constitution	1/4	4/1	2/3	2/3	9/11
%f	20%	80%	40%	40%	45%
IF	**5/6**	**7/4**	**6/5**	**7/4**	**25/19**
%f	**45%**	**64%**	**55%**	**64%**	**57%**
International	4/4	3/5	5/3	4/4	16/16
%f	50%	39%	63%	50%	50%
Legislation	3/4	5/5	9/1	6/5	23/15
%f	43%	50%	90%	55%	61%
Research/Statistics	1/4	2/5	4/3	7/5	14/17
%f	20%	29%	57%	58%	45%
Subtotal	17/26	27/22	33/17	33/25	110/90
%f 1975–1990	40%	55%	66%	57%	55%
TOTAL	214/260				
%F 1940–1990	45%				

[a]The Awards Committee began as the Award Jury, then was discontinued for several years in the mid-1940s, after which it became an ALA standing committee.

[b]The Legislation Committee became a committee of the Library Administrative Division in 1956 but returned to the status of an ALA committee in the early 1960s.

[c]The Research and Statistics Committee was created in 1936 as the Statistics Committee, moved to the jurisdiction of the Library Administration Division in 1956, and became the Advisory Committee for the newly created ALA Office for Research and Development in 1965.

Table 10.1B   Comparison Of Six ALA Committee F/M Gender Ratios 1940–1990

	1940–1970	%F	1975–1990	%F	%change	Total 1940–1990	%F
Awards	26/11[a]	70%	23/12	66%	− 4%	49/23	68%
Constit.	12/28	30%	9/11	45%	+ 15%	21/39	35%
IF	**22/43**	**34%**	**25/19**	**57%**	**+ 13%**	**48/61**	**44%**
Internat.	13/33	28%	16/16	50%	+ 12%	29/49	37%
Legis.	13/29	31%	23/15	61%	+ 19%	36/44	45%
Research	18/26	41%	14/17	45%	+ 4%	32/43	43%
TOTAL	104/160	39%	110/90	55%	+ 16%	215/259	45%

[a]numbers represent female/male gender ratio, followed by percentage female

the possible part the ACONDA recommendations and the creation of women's groups within ALA may have played in this increase.

In examining possible significant variables in women's involvement in the IFC, one must look not only at numbers and percentages of females and males, but also at the other demographic factors those numbers represent, particularly those that impact differentially on women and men within IFC membership. In examining the membership of the IFC, two factors of relevance to women librarians are evident: the large number of members in administration and the small number of members in work with young people.

Women in library administration is one area that has been investigated at some length in library research literature, with findings indicating that library administration has been consistently dominated by men.[35] Among the complaints that led to the ACONDA resolutions was the charge that library administrators were overrepresented on ALA's Executive Board, Council, and in other leadership positions.[36] Likewise, in its earlier years, IFC members appear to have been chosen from a pool comprised primarily of directors, deans, and other administrators, and not reflective of ALA's actual composition in terms of status or gender. In looking at the membership of the IFC by administrative level (Table 10.2), it may be noted that top level administrators had the largest representation (more than 43%) throughout the 1940s, 1950s, and 1960s, of which few (21%) were women. During that time period, three-quarters of middle-level administrators who were IFC members were female, while 40% of members in non-administrative positions were female. In the 1970s and 1980s, although IFC members in top administrative posts continued to be primarily male (72%), members in such positions comprised only 22% of the total membership. Nearly half (48%) the IFC membership were middle-level administrators, of which 56% were female, and 57% of the IFC membership were non-administrators, of which 86% were female. Women were represented primarily at the non-administrative level during most of the decades under consideration. However, the proportion of representation from upper-, middle- and non-ad-

Table 10.2. Intellectual Freedom Committee Members: F/M Gender Ratio Listed By Administrative Status And Decade

Rank	1940s f + m =		1950s f + m =		1960s f + m =		1970s f + m =		1980s f + m =		TOTAL F + M =	
AD-1												
f + m = n	2 + 7	9	2 + 11	13	3 + 8	11	2 + 8	10	3 + 5	8	12 + 39	51
f + m = %	10 + 35	45%	7 + 37	43%	13 + 33	46%	5 + 18	23%	8 + 11	22%	8 + 25	33%
AD-2												
f + m = n	4 + 2	6	5 + 0	5	3 + 2	5	5 + 6	11	5 + 1	6	22 + 11	33
f + m = %	20 + 10	30%	17 + 0	17%	13 + 8	21%	11 + 14	25%	11 + 3	16%	14 + 7	21%
AD-3												
f + m = n	5 + 0	5	1 + 11	12	4 + 4	8	16 + 7	23	19 + 4	23	45 + 26	71
f + m = %	25 + 0	25%	3 + 37	40%	17 + 17	33%	36 + 16	52%	51 + 11	62%	29 + 17	46%
TOTAL N	11 + 9	20	8 + 22	30	10 + 14	30	23 + 21	44	27 + 10	37	79 + 76	155
TOTAL %	55 + 45	100%	27 + 73	100%	42 + 58	100%	52 + 48	100%	73 + 27	100%	51 + 49	100%

AD-1 = head administrator or dean

AD-2 = assistant/associate administrator, branch or department head

AD-3 = non-administrator

all designations according to contemporary ALA membership directories ministrative levels has changed over time, which may also be a factor in the increase of women in the IFC. Among the many charges given to ACONDA was one "to create a structure that will involve a large number of members in the programs and committee work of the organization".[37] The efforts of ACONDA to make ALA more diverse and democratic and less weighted toward those in administrative positions may be responsible in part for the marked shift in administrative level proportions in the 1970s and 1980s and the increase in the participation of women on the IFC.

Women's IFC involvement may also be related to their predominance in library service to the young. Fiepel's 1922 study reported very different selection, shelving, and checkout procedures depending on the age of the intended reader. With the exception of a few articles, such as Bedinger's 1928 essay on young people's information needs, library literature on the importance of collection diversity assumed an adult reading public. Although the collections of school libraries were being challenged during the 1940s and 1950s, the Library Bill of Rights was interpreted by some to include only the rights of adults. As a result, members of ALA's American Association of School Librarians (AASL) created the "School Library Bill of Rights," a document based on the Library Bill of Rights that spoke directly to the needs of librarians serving young people. The School Library Bill of Rights was written in 1953 and adopted by ALA Council in 1955, but it was not until 1967 that the Library Bill of Rights itself was revised to include "age" as one of the criteria by which the rights of the library user should not be abridged. This chronology raises questions about the representation from librarians serving young people on the IFC (see Table 10.3B). Very few school or public youth services librarians were appointed to the IFC until comparatively recently. Representation of youth services librarians on the IFC has been low throughout the IFC's history: school librarians were rarely appointed (the IFC included two school librarians [out of 20 appointees] in the 1940s and one school librarian [out of 30 appointees] in the 1950s), and it was not until 1962 that a public children's librarian (Augusta Baker, head of children's services at New York Public Library) was named to the IFC. Of the total of 23 youth services librarians (school and public) who were appointed to the IFC from 1940 to 1990, four (17%) were appointed before 1967, while 19 (83%) were appointed after that year. Although youth librarians have comprised only 14% of the total membership of the IFC, their numbers do account in part for the growth in female IFC membership over the years, as most type-of-library representation has stayed relatively constant over the years, while youth service representation has grown (see Table 10.3B).

Finally, it is useful to look at committee-sponsored programs. From 1952 to 1967 the committee sponsored five well-attended and publicized ALA preconferences on intellectual freedom featuring a total of 47 speakers (of which eight were female) and 38 discussion leaders (of which 24 were female). Depending on whether or not the preconference had co-sponsoring groups, the IFC of that

Table 10.3A. Intellectual Freedom Committee Members: F/M Gender Ratio Listed By Library Type And Decade

Decade	1940s	%	1950s	%	1960s	%	1970s	%	1980s	%	TOTAL	%
Public	5/3	40%	5/4	30%	3/6	38%	6/3	20%	8/3	30%	27/19	30%
Academic	1/4	25%	1/10	37%	0/5	21%	3/7	23%	8/2	27%	13/28	26%
Lib Ed	1/1	10%	0/4	13%	4/2	25%	3/3	14%	4/3	19%	12/12	15%
School	2/0	10%	1/0	3%	2/1	13%	5/1	14%	3/0	8%	13/2	10%
State	1/0	5%	1/1	6%	1/0	4%	2/3	11%	1/1	5%	6/5	7%
Special	0/0	0%	0/1	3%	0/0	0%	1/1	5%	0/0	0%	2/1	2%
Other	1/1	10%	0/2	6%	0/1	4%	3/3	14%	3/1	11%	7/8	10%
TOTAL	11/9	100%	8/22	100%	10/14	100%	23/21	100%	27/10	100%	79/76	100%
%f/m	f/m = 55/45		f/m = 27/73		f/m = 42/58		f/m = 52/48		f/m = 73/27		F/M = 51/49	

Table 10.3B.   Intellectual Freedom Committee Members: F/M Gender Ratio Listed By Age Of Population Served (Youth/Adult)

Decade	1940s	1950s	1960s	1970s	1980s	Total
School	2/0	1/0	2/1	5/1	3/0	13/2
Public (youth)	0/0	0/0	1/0	2/0	5/0	8/0
TOTAL YOUTH	**2/0 = 2**	**1/0 = 1**	**3/1 = 4**	**7/1 = 8**	**8/0 = 8**	**21/2 = 23**
%IFC	**10%**	**3%**	**17%**	**18%**	**22%**	**15%**
Public (adult)	5/3	5/4	2/6	4/3	3/3	19/19
Academic	1/4	1/10	0/5	3/7	8/2	13/28
Lib Ed	1/1	0/4	4/2	3/3	4/3	12/12
State	1/0	1/1	1/0	2/3	1/1	6/5
Special	0/0	0/1	0/0	1/1	0/0	2/1
Other	1/1	0/2	0/1	3/3	3/1	7/8
TOTAL ADULT	**9/9 = 18**	**7/22 = 29**	**7/13 = 20**	**16/20 = 36**	**19/10 = 29**	**58/74 = 132**
%IFC	**90%**	**97%**	**83%**	**82%**	**78%**	**85%**
TOTAL	11/9 = 20	8/22 = 30	10/14 = 24	23/21 = 44	27/10 = 37	79/76 = 155
	100%	100%	100%	100%	100%	100%

year was either part or all of the conference planning committee, and the gender ratio among speakers and discussion leaders generally reflected the committee's gender ratio (see Table 10.4). This was predictable, but unfortunate, as it is often in such public forums that speakers become identified with particular professional issues, and lack of representation of women on speakers' platforms may well have been among the factors informing Katz's assumption about female librarians' reticence regarding intellectual freedom advocacy.[38] IFC programming currently centers around a two-hour, high-visibility, high-turnout program at ALA's Annual Conference. Within recent years, the gender ratio of intellectual freedom program presenters has been generally balanced in terms of gender.

Women's participation in the IFC and in intellectual freedom programming has increased markedly in the years since the advent of ALA's official advocacy of intellectual freedom. A variety of factors have been identified as possible covariants in this process, particularly in the increase of women in the 1970s and 1980s. It appears that within ALA, women gain authority when administrative experience is not a prerequisite for ALA committee assignments, when the subject or service area (such as library service to young people) is one in which women predominate and are considered experts, when there is a will within ALA for appointments to be dispersed among a greater number of people, and when women are already in positions of power and may be likely to include more women in their appointments and programs. In short, the picture painted by Castagna—and implied by Katz—of male leadership and female invisibility in ALA's intellectual freedom advocacy is not supported by this examination of IFC membership and activities.

Table 10.4. ALA Intellectual Freedom Preconference Programming Gender Ratios

Year	Preconference Speakers				Preconference Discussion Leaders				Sponsor/Planning Committee			
	F	%	M	%	F	%	M	%	F	%	M	%
1952	0	0%	14	100%					2	18%	9	82%
1953	1	11%	8	89%	2	50%	2	50%	9	29%	22	71%
1955	2	50%	2	50%	22	73%	8	27%	6	67%	3	33%
1965	1	11%	8	89%	0	0%	4	100%	3	27%	8	73%
1967	4	80%	1	20%—librarians					6	54%	5	45%
	0	0%	6	100%—non-librarians								

"IT MAY WELL BE THE BASIC FACT OF THE LIBRARIAN'S SEX": WOMEN LIBRARIANS AND INTELLECTUAL FREEDOM SURVEYS, 1958–1989

Katz ends his criticism of the role of women librarians in intellectual freedom by suggesting that women are perhaps inclined to censor simply because they are women. This stereotype has an enduring place in the minds of many, and, unlike the first two under consideration, it is one about which a fairly substantial amount of quantitative research has been done.

One of the first empirical surveys of librarians' attitudes toward intellectual freedom was Marjorie Fiske's landmark study, *Book Selection and Censorship*, a report based on research conducted in California in the mid-1950s.[39] Fiske interviewed public and school librarians and found that some were quite cautious and restrictive. Others believed strongly in the importance of maintaining diverse collections despite perceived pressures from parents and community. Variables affecting librarians' attitudes included size of community, size of school, and professional involvement, with librarians in larger communities, larger schools, and with more education being less restrictive. Fiske did not comment on any clear pattern of censorship attitudes or behavior along gender lines.

Charles Busha conducted a survey in 1970 of a random sample of public librarians in the Midwest, and found a significant correlation between their attitudes toward intellectual freedom and censorship and authoritarian personality.[40] He also found that "there was a significant difference between the attitudes of male and female librarians. Male librarians agreed more with intellectual freedom principles than did female librarians; male librarians were more opposed to censorship than were female librarians; and male librarians were less authoritarian than female librarians".[41]

Michael Pope's *Sex and the Undecided Librarian*, published in 1974, is subtitled, "A study of librarians' opinions on sexually oriented literature".[42] Pope surveyed a random sample of school, public, and college librarians throughout the U.S. He found that school librarians were consistently more restrictive than other librarians, and that women were more restrictive than men, with the difference between genders being greater in school and public libraries than in college libraries.[43] Pope's results agreed with an earlier survey of 2,486 American adults on sexually oriented literature conducted by Abelson et al. for the Commission on Obscenity and Pornography in 1970.[44] Within the general population, they found a similar difference in female and male responses, with females being more restrictive toward the availability of sexual materials.[45] These findings were confirmed when Howard D. White reanalyzed their data in 1981 and concluded that "while percentages for both sexes rise or fall in the same patterns over all four variables [age, education, media consumption and recent exposure to erotica], men's are always higher than women's, indicating men's somewhat greater liberalism on the censorship issue".[46]

In 1981, Mary Lee Bundy and Teresa Stakem sent out a questionnaire to a random sample of 9% of the public librarians listed in that year's *ALA Membership Directory*.[47] The sample was predominantly white, over 30, and represented a spectrum of political views from conservative to "leftist." Librarians were asked to indicate their agreement or disagreement with the values of intellectual freedom, from general sentiments ("a chief commitment of a professional librarian should be to intellectual freedom for everyone") to specific examples "libraries should exercise caution in giving gay literature to children and youth"). There was considerable variation in librarians' responses, from 94% agreement with the first question above, to 59% agreement with the second. The researchers found that the respondents' political views were the most significant factor in their agreement with intellectual freedom principles, and that gender was not a significant variable. In fact, "The most prominent fact about the women and men in this study is how little they differ."[48]

Finally, Frances McDonald used gender as a variable in her 1989 study, *Intellectual Freedom and Censorship: Attitudes of Secondary School Librarians and Principled Moral Reasoning,* which surveyed a random sample of 450 school librarians in Minnesota, Iowa, and Wisconsin.[49] McDonald looked at the relationship between librarians' attitude toward intellectual freedom and censorship, their level of principled moral reasoning, and demographic variables. Her results showed that size of community, professional involvement, level of education, and attendance at an ALA-accredited library school were all significant variables in positive attitudes. She found no correlation between gender of librarian and attitudes toward intellectual freedom and censorship.

Although some of the surveys cited point to female librarians' greater reluctance to endorse principles of intellectual freedom and oppose censorship, the results are hardly conclusive. In examining the research over time, it appears that gender cannot be meaningfully separated from other covariants commonly associated with the work lives of female librarians. For example, Fiske, Busha, and McDonald all found that education was a key factor: "Librarians who possess more formal education have more liberal views in respect to intellectual freedom; they are also more opposed to censorship practices".[50] Length of educational career and gender are also related within librarianship, with men generally more likely than women to have advanced degrees. For example, Pope noted that 20% of the female librarians he surveyed had no MLS degree, while only 6% of the men were without an MLS degree.[51] Both Fiske and McDonald associated more restrictive attitudes with small communities, and in both studies women were more likely to work in small communities' libraries.

The studies also spotlighted personality factors not associated strictly with women so much as with people of low status, such as feelings of workplace isolation and low pay. For example, Fiske attributed librarians' acquiescence to censorship to their not feeling "strong enough as individuals or professionals to assert [intellectual freedom values] in the face of public disapproval or indifference".[52]

Librarians' comfort level with sexually oriented literature was positively correlated with familiarity, and few women in either Pope's or White's study were familiar with such materials, possibly because of the perception that erotic materials are "male territory." Finally, it must be noted that the more recent the study, the more male and female responses converged. These changes echo the changes in the IFC's gender ratio over time, and contradicts Katz's suggestion that the propensity to censor is sex-linked.

CONCLUSION AND QUESTIONS

> It is the sisters and wives and mothers, you know, Caddie, who keep the world
> sweet and beautiful. What a rough world it would be if there were only men and
> boys in it, doing things in their rough way! A woman's task is to teach them gentleness and courtesy and love and kindness.[53]

This advice was given to the title character in *Caddie Woodlawn*, by Carol Ryrie Brink. The novel, which was awarded the 1935 Newbery Medal by members of ALA's Section for Library work with Children, is a fictionalized account of the early life of the author's grandmother. Caddie is a red-headed tomboy living on the Wisconsin frontier who rides bareback, plows fields, and fixes clocks, but finally acquiesces to the requirements of Victorian ladyhood. These traditional prescriptions for female behavior operate even today when it is assumed that women are "naturally" more inclined to censor. The set of beliefs known as the Cult of True Womanhood say that it is women's work, *more* than men's, to nurture children by protecting them from controversial books, to enforce sexual purity by restricting sexual materials, to establish domesticity by creating a safe "home away from home" in the library and to submit to the authority of those who would censor the library collection. Although this view is intertwined with and reinforced by traditional female stereotypes still in operation today, women's status in U.S. society, and within librarianship, has in fact changed. These changes are reflected in the relationship between women librarians and intellectual freedom concerns, as their visibility and official involvement in intellectual freedom advocacy has increased markedly since ALA's involvement in First Amendment issues was formalized in 1939 and 1940. Gender itself does not appear to be a significant variable in beliefs or behavior around intellectual freedom in libraries.

There is, however, much territory that remains to be explored in looking for the relationship between women librarians and intellectual freedom. It has been noted that only a small proportion of female librarians are included in biographical works of U.S. librarianship.[54] Katz's "cursory examination" further points out the lack of information about the lives of women librarians who have been prominent as intellectual freedom advocates. Even though Judith Krug, as director of ALA's Office for Intellectual Freedom since 1967, is probably the single person, make or female, most often connected to First Amendment advocacy within librarianship, traditional secondary-source histories illustrate the continuing lack of coverage of women in this area. In addition to the 79 women who served on the IFC during its first 50 years, female, like male, librarians have frequently defended intellectual freedom within their own libraries. In 1950, for example, it was a woman, Elizabeth Haas of Enoch Pratt Free Library in Baltimore, who had the dubious honor of being the first ALA member to lose her library job for refusing to sign a loyalty oath. Also in 1950, it was another woman, Ruth W. Brown of the Bartlesville, Oklahoma, public library, whose dismissal—ostensibly for carrying "subversive materials" (*The Nation* and the *New Republic*)—was the first intellectual freedom-related dismissal in which ALA's Intellectual Freedom Committee was officially involved.[55] Women, like men, have also been intellectual freedom activists in their work as researchers and writers. Clearly, more biographical research is needed to make the profession more generally aware of the part women have played in intellectual freedom advocacy within librarianship.

In evaluating female librarians' activities on behalf of intellectual freedom in ALA or in other arenas, the researcher must be aware of the time and money constraints on many women's lives. The most visible proponents of intellectual freedom attend national meetings, write articles, are quoted in the press, attain advanced degrees, and serve on recognized boards or committees—all activities that take both time and money. Women, who are still viewed as having primary responsibility for "private sphere" concerns of children and housework and who still make an average of 70 cents for every dollar men earn, have, on the average, less time and less money than men. This is as true in the female-intensive library profession as it is in U.S. society as a whole. The gender gap in librarian salaries has been extensively documented, and the effect of this differential must be taken into account in obtaining an accurate picture of women's activities within ALA.[56]

Professional involvement at the state or regional level is more common for

Appendix A.   Census Figures on U.S. Librarians, 1870–1990

Year	Female	%	Male	%	U.S. Total
1860[1]					65
1870	43	20.2	170	79.8	213
1880[2]	2,732		368		3,100
1890[3]	2,764		8,453		11,217
1900	3,125	74.7	1,059	25.3	4,184[a]
1910	8,621	80.4	2,101	19.6	10,722[a]
1920	13,502	88.3	1,795	11.7	15,297
1930	27,056	91.4	2,557	8.6	29,613
1940	32,546	89.5	3,801	10.5	36,347
1950	50,670	88.8	6,390	11.2	57,060
1960	72,357	85.8	11,975	14.2	84,332
1970	99,851	81.9	22,001	18.1	121,852
1980	151,439	82.6	32,000	17.4	183,439
1990	163,359	81.3	37,522	18.7	200,881

1. In the 1860 census, the figure for librarians was not broken down by gender.

2. In the 1880 census, librarians were reported in figures for "literary persons," which also included writers.

3. In the 1890 census, librarians were reported in figures for "literary and scientific persons."

[a]"According to the Bureau of Census, the classification of catalogers in libraries with librarians' assistants and attendants in 1910 and with librarians in 1920 accounts partly for the large increase in the number of female librarians and the large decrease in the number of female librarians' assistants and attendants from 1910 to 1920."

noted in *Library Journal* 49 (1924):180.

from: Bureau of the Census. *Census of the U.S.* Washington, D.C.: U.S. Dept. of Commerce, 1890–1990.

both women and men, and, no doubt because of the lower cost in time and money, the gender gap in this arena is significantly less pronounced. Heim and Estabrook's 1980 study of ALA members reported that while there was a large gender difference regarding committees of national organizations (43% of the women versus 63% of the men were members), the gender gap narrowed at the state and regional level where 61% of the women and 72% of the men were commitee members.[57] A fuller picture of women's interest and professional investment in library intellectual freedom issues would likely emerge if women's involvement at the state and local level were investigated.

While this research has shown an increase over time in women librarians' intellectual freedom activism within the profession, some troubling stereotypes remain. Historical and survey research on librarians and intellectual freedom advocacy reveals more similarities than differences between the anti-censorship stands of women and men, but the empirical evidence—as convincing as it is— cannot in itself eradicate the lingering assumptions in the minds of those who agree with Katz's statements regarding women's "natural" willingness to censor and unwillingness to defend library materials against others' censorship attempts.

The issues that concern librarians as members of a female-intensive service profession and as First Amendment advocates are neither entirely separate nor entirely congruent. More than 90 years after the end of the Victorian age and in a field that has placed increased reliance on empirical data and studies, a belief in the Victorian Cult of True Womanhood still seems to bedevil those who would otherwise affirm their belief in gender equality. This is by no means confined to librarianship; throughout American society there are many who believe that it is women's True Nature to be submissive, domestic, nurturant, and pure. Women in librarianship continue to negotiate their way between the expectations of them as women and as librarians, and these stereotypes have a direct or indirect effect on all members of the female-intensive profession of librarianship.

ENDNOTES

[1]Bill Katz, "The Pornography Collection," *Library Journal* 96 (15 Dec. 1971): 4062.

[2]This shift in attitude and practice within the profession is documented in detail by Evelyn Geller in *Forbidden Books in American Public Libraries, 1876–1939: A Study in Cultural Change* (Westport, CT: Greenwood, 1984).

[3]Michael Harris, "The Purpose of the American Library," *Library Journal* 98 (1 Sep. 1973): 2509–2514. Dain, Phyllis. "Ambivalence and Paradox: The Social Bonds of the Public Library." *Library Journal* 100 (1 Feb. 1975): 261–266.

[4]Frederick Stielow, "Censorship in the Early Professionalization of American Libraries, 1876 to 1929," *Journal of Library History* 18 (Winter 1983): 40–41.

[5]Barbara Welter, "The Cult of True Womanhood: 1820–1860," *American Quarterly* 18 (1966): 151–174.

[6]Dee Garrison, *Apostles of Culture: The Public Librarian and American Society, 1876–1970* (New York: Free Press, 1979); Dee Garrison, "Women in Librarianship," in *A Century of Service: Librarianship in the U.S. and Canada*, ed. Sidney L. Jackson, Eleanor B. Herling, and E. J. Josey (Chicago: ALA, 1976), pp. 146–236; Suzanne Hildenbrand, "Revision versus Reality: Women in the History of the Public Library Movement, 1876–1920," in Kathleen Heim, ed., *The Statue of Women in Librarianship; Historical, Sociological, and Economic Issues* (New York: Neal-Schuman, 1983), pp. 7–27; Sharon Wells, "The Feminization of the American Library Profession, 1876–1923." (M.A. dissertation, U Chicago, 1967). It might also be noted that the founding meeting of the American Library Association in 1876 was attended by 90 men and 13 women. A decade later, the first class of Melvil Dewey's School of Library Economy was comprised of 17 women and three men.

[7]*Census of the United States.* Washington, D.C.: Bureau of the Census, U.S. Department of Commerce, 1870, 1900.

[8]Lindsay Swift, "Paternalism in Public Libraries," *Library Journal* 24 (Nov 1899): 614.

[9]Arthur Bostwick, "The Librarian as a Censor," *Library Journal* 33 (July 1908): 259.

[10]Dane Yorke, "Three New England Libraries," *Library Journal* 51 (1 Oct. 1926): 830.

[11]From its beginnings, children's services became exclusively identified as women's work. Even the professional literature of the time, which routinely used the third-person singular "he" when referring to most librarians (and certainly in reference to library directors), used "she" when referring to children's librarians. Just as women and children were linked in the home, so they were also linked in the public sphere of the library.

[12]Louis N. Fiepel, "Questionable Books in Public Libraries–I. *Library Journal* 47 (15 Oct. 1922): 857, 859; "Questionable Books in Public Libraries–II," *Library Journal* 47 (1 Nov. 1922): 909.

[13]Margery Bedinger, "Censorship of Books in Libraries." *Wilson Library Bulletin* 3 (May 1929): 623–625 (orig. appeared in *Pacific Northwest Library Association Quarterly* 1928).

[14]"The Editor's Mail," *Wilson Library Bulletin* 3 (June 1929): 691.

[15]Kunitz, Stanley J. "The Roving Eye," *Wilson Library Bulletin* 10 (Sept. 1935): 41. The "Liberal League of Librarians" correspondence ran in issues of *Wilson Library Bulletin* from September 1935 (vol. 10) to January 1937 (vol. 11).

[16]Kunitz, (Nov. 1935): 195.

[17]Kunitz, (Sept. 1936): 39.

[18]Geller, *Forbidden Books*, 188.

[19]David K. Berninghausen, "The History of the ALA Intellectual Freedom Committee," *Wilson Library Bulletin* 27 (June 1953): 813–817; David K. Berninghausen, "Intellectual Freedom in Librarianship: Advances and Retreats," in *Advances in Librarianship*, vol. 9, (New York: Academic Press, 1979), pp. 1–29; John J. Boll, "The American Library Association and Intellectual Freedom," Occasional Papers #35, (Urbana, IL: University of Illinois Library School, 1953); Edwin Castagna, "Censorship, Intellectual Freedom, and Libraries," in *Advances in Librarianship*, vol. 2, (New York: Academic Press, 1971), pp. 215–51; William S. Dix, "Intellectual Freedom," *Library Trends* 3 (Spring 1955): 299–307; American Library Association, *Intellectual Freedom Manual*, 3d ed., (Chicago ALA, 1989), pp. xii–114.

[20]Castagna, pp. 225, 227, 228.

[21]Ibid., pp. 236, 241, 243, 235.

[22]Ibid., p. 249.

[23]"1915 Handbook," *American Library Association Bulletin* 9 (Sept. 1915): 366.

[24]B. Manchak, "ALA Salary Survey: Personal Members," *American Libraries* 2 (April 1971): 409–419.

[25]Kathleen M. Heim and Leigh S. Estabrook, *Career Profiles and Sex Discrimination in the Library Profession*, (Chicago: ALA, 1983).

[26]Anita Schiller, "Women in Librarianship," in Kathleen Weibel and Kathleen Heim, eds. *The Role of Women in Librarianship 1876–1976: The Entry, Advancement, and Struggle for Equalization in One Profession*, (Phoenix, AZ: Oryx Press, 1979); Heim 1982; Heim and Estabrook 1983. ALA membership requires money and ALA involvement requires money and time, and both have often been cited as barriers to women's involvement in American public life in general and in ALA in particular. In a profession that is not well-paying to begin with, on the average women have been paid less than men in all types of libraries. In addition, ALA membership is not equally valuable to all segments of the librarian population. ALA conference attendance is important for networking and professional visibility, aspects that are particularly important to administrators, and the proportion of men in administration has been consistently higher than women throughout the time period under consideration. Heim and Estabrook's 1983 figures indicate that 50% of the men surveyed were administrators versus 30% of the women.

[27]Louise S. Robbins, "Toward Ideology and Autonomy: The American Library Association's Response to Threats to Intellectual Freedom, 1939–1969." (Ph.D. dissertation, Denton, TX: Texas Woman's University, 1991), pp. 61–63. Before Higgins' tenure, the committee was fairly inactive, but when she sought to facilitate a proactive agenda, she was eventually stymied by a lack of ALA and personal financial resources, as the IFC, like most other ALA committees, had no budget. Higgins hired her own clerical help to manage committee correspondence but finally resigned in early 1948 due to lack of time and money.

[28]Like Higgins, Boaz was a library educator, but as head of the University of Southern California's Library School, the chairship does not appear to have posed the time or money hardships that it did for Higgins.

[29]Kenyon C. Rosenberg and Daniel Suvak, "ALA Committee Membership: A Statistical Survey," *Library Journal* 98 (15 Mar. 1973): 842–43.

[30]Boris Raymond, "ACONDA and ANACONDA Revisited: A Retrospective Glance at the Sounds of Fury of the Sixties." *Journal of Library History* 14 (1979): 349–62; Dennis Thomison, *A History of the American Library Association, 1876–1972*, (Chicago: ALA, 1978), pp. 223–231.

[31]Patricia Glass Schuman, "Status of Women in Libraries: Task Force Meets in Detroit," *Library Journal* 95 (Aug. 1970): 2635.

[32]Schiller, pp. 223–256.

[33]Wiegand, Wayne A. and Geri Greenway, "A Comparative Analysis of the Socio-economic and Professional Characteristics of American Library Association Executive Board and Council Members, 1876–1917," *Library Research* 2 (Winter 1981): 309–325; Wayne A. Wiegand and Dorothy Steffens, "Members of the Club: A Look at One Hundred ALA Presidents," Occasional Papers #182 (Urbana, IL: University of Illinois Library School, 1988).

[34]Rosenberg and Suvak, pp. 842–843.

[35]Schiller.

[36]Raymond, pp. 350–351.

[37]ALA 1969 *Handbook* (Chicago: ALA, 1969): 1383.

[38]William Dix and Paul Bixler, eds. *Freedom of Communication: Proceedings of the First Conference on Intellectual Freedom, New York City, June 28–29, 1952*, (Chicago: ALA, 1954). The first ALA-sponsored preconference institute on intellectual freedom, titled "Freedom of Communication," was held in 1952. All of the 14 conference speakers listed in the proceedings were men. The IFC of that year, which appears to have planned the conference, was 18% female (2 women and 9 men). Frederic J. Mosher, ed. *Freedom of Book Selection: Proceedings of the Second Conference on Intellectual Freedom, Whittier, CA, June 20–21, 1953*, (Chicago: ALA, 1954). The second preconference, titled "Freedom of Book Selection," was held in 1953. Eight men and one woman were speakers at the conference. There were also four type-of-library discussion groups: Women led the small public library and school library groups, while men led the large public library and academic library groups. The conference was cosponsored by ALA's IFC (1 woman, 11 men), Book Acquisitions Committee (6 women, 8 men), and Board on the Acquisition of Library Materials (2 women, 3 men), whose combined membership was 29% female (9 women, 22 men). S. Janice Kee and Dorothy K. Smith, eds. "Book Selection: Proceedings of a Work Conference." *PLD Reporter #4* (Chicago: ALA, 1955). A third preconference, this one cosponsored by ALA's IFC and the Public Libraries Division, was held on the subject of book selection policies for public libraries in 1955. Instead of a series of authoritative speakers, the emphasis on member participation, with discussion groups of 12–15 members meeting during the bulk of the time alloted. The four speakers included two men and two women. Each of the 15 discussion groups had a leader and a reporter. Eleven of the leaders and 11 of the reporters (73%) were women. The planning committee for the preconference was 67% female (6 women, 3 men). "Freedom of Inquiry: Supporting the Library Bill of Rights." Proceedings, Washington, D.C., January 23–24, 1965 (Chicago: ALA, 1965). An ALA-sponsored conference on intellectual freedom titled "Freedom of Inquiry: Supporting the Library Bill of Rights," was held in Washington, D.C. in 1965. The featured speakers included eight men and one woman. Toward the end of the conference, the participants broke into four discussion groups, each led by a (male) member of the IFC. The planning committee for the conference was 27% female. Evelyn Geller, "Two Cheers for Liberty," *School Library Journal* 14 (Sept. 1967): pp. 41–45. A preconference on "Intellectual Freedom and the Teenager," jointly sponsored by the IFC and the Young Adult Service Division was

held in San Francisco in 1967. The speakers included five youth librarians (4f/1m) and six non-librarians (0f/6m). The IFC of that year was 55% female (6 women, 5 men).

[39]Marjorie Fiske, *Book Selection and Censorship: A Study of School and Public Librarians in California*, (Berkeley: University of California Press, 1959).

[40]Charles Busha, *Freedom Versus Supression and Censorship: With a Study of Attitudes of Midwestern Public Librarians and a Bibliography of Censorship*, (Littleton, CO: Libraries Unlimited, 1972).

[41]Ibid., p. 132.

[42]Michael Pope, *Sex and the Undecided Librarian: A Study of Librarians' Opinions on Sexually Oriented Literature*, (Metuchen, NJ: Scarecrow Press, 1974).

[43]Ibid., pp. 167–168.

[44]Herbert Abelson et al. "National Survey of Public Attitudes toward and Experience with Erotic Materials: Findings."In U.S. Commission on Obscenity and Pornography. *Technical Report*, vol. 6, (Washington, D.C.: Government Printing Office, 1971).

[45]Pope, p. 169.

[46]Howard D. White, "Library Censorship and the Permissive Minority," *Library Quarterly* 51 (1981): 192–207.

[47]Mary Lee Bundy and Teresa Stakem, "Librarians and Intellectual Freedom: Are Opinions Changing?" *Wilson Library Bulletin* 56 (April 1982): 582–589.

[48]Ibid., p. 588.

[49]Frances Beck McDonald, "Intellectual Freedom and Censorship Attitudes of Secondary School Librarians and Principled Moral Reasoning," (Ph.D. dissertation, University of Minnesota, 1989).

[50]Busha, pp. 85–86.

[51]Pope, p. 139.

[52]Fiske, pp. 110–111.

[53]Carol Ryrie Brink, *Caddie Woodlawn*, (New York: Macmillan, 1935), pp. 239–240.

[54]Margo Sasse, "Invisible Women: The Children's Librarian in America," *School Library Journal* 19 (Jan. 1973): 21–25.

[55]Thomison, 186; Robbins, 1991, pp. 113–114; Henderson, pp. 1810–1811. ALA's IFC requested an investigation of Brown's dismissal, which was taken on by a commit-

tee of the Oklahoma Library Association. Although Oklahoma State Librarian Ralph Hudson was the official chair of the committee, its mission was carried out by Esther McRuer (public librarian and OLA president), who formed the committee, and Frances Kennedy (Oklahoma City University librarian), who spearheaded the work and did the actual on-site investigation. Louise S. Robbins, "Anti-Communism, Racism, and Censorship in Cold War Oklahoma: The Case of Ruth W. Brown and the Bartlesville Public Library," Graduate School of Library and Information Science, University of Illinois at Urbana–Champaign. 11 Apr. 1995.

[56]Manchak; Schiller; Heim and Estabrook.

[57]Heim and Estabrook, p. 33.

chapter 11

Pratt Institute Library School:
The Perils of Professionalization

Barbara B. Brand

Historian Daniel J. Walkowitz, in a recent review, urged historians of social work to "tell a new story, a gendered narrative."[1] If historians of librarianship "tell a gendered narrative," even the well-worn subject of library education becomes a "new story." With this perpective, many topics clearly require further attention or reinterpretation.

The implicit criterion many library historians have adopted for deciding whether something merits attention and whether it should be regarded positively or negatively has been its apparent contribution to professional status. Largely for this reason, historians have neglected the three early library schools located in technical institutes. Library historian Carl White dismissed them as designed to prepare low-level workers for a class-based society.[2] When looked at from a gendered perspective, however, one of them, at least, merits attention. While the University of Illinois took over the Armour Institute School after four years and the Drexel Institute School suspended operations for eight; the Pratt Institute Library School, between 1891 and 1920, graduated over 600 students, virtually all of them women, from all over the United States and many foreign countries. They went on to perform creditably.

Because of his apparent contribution to professional status, scholars have also failed to focus critical attention on economist C.C. Williamson and his report for the Carnegie Corporation. Most library historians portray him as an unblemished hero whose negative appraisal of existing schools was correct and whose recommendations were uniformly beneficial. Williamson needs to be put in his historical context and his report and recommendations analysed critically.

Finally, the gender implications of the changes brought about by the Carnegie Corporation's large scale intervention into library education need examination. These changes, still seen as overwhelmingly positive, in fact affected many librarians negatively.

"BEST OF THE ONE-YEAR SCHOOLS"

Founded in 1887 by Charles Pratt, one of John D. Rockefeller's original partners and a self-made millionaire, Pratt Institute offered practical vocational education for both men and women. Although Pratt first envisioned an institute for the secondary technical education of artisans, foremen, designers and draftsmen, his decision to admit women immediately broadened the range of possibilities. The school's initial programs included "Domestic Art" (sewing), "Domestic Science" (cooking and nursing), and "Commerce" (shorthand and typing) for women, as well as "Industrial and Fine Arts" (mechanical drawing and wood carving) and "Science and Technology" (chemistry and electrical construction) for men. Pratt's intention to be flexible was also apparent in the design of the first building, constructed like a mill with self-supporting outside walls so that interior partitions could be easily rearranged. But if Pratt was flexible about the specific programs offered by the institute as long as they were practical, he was unwavering in his insistence on accessibility. He had gained his own limited education with great difficulty while working as a clerk and apprentice machinist, contributing to the support of 10 siblings. For this reason he firmly believed that as long as men and women could profit from the education the Institute offered, it should be open to them. No barriers such as requirements for a specific level of previous education should impede them. To avoid state regulations on degrees, the institute offered none, providing certificates or diplomas instead. To ensure his wishes were carried out he kept its administration within the family, appointing one son, Frederic B., Secretary of the Board of Trustees and Executive, and another, Charles M., President of the Board. His remaining sons: George, Herbert, John and Harold, also became trustees. Frederic B. remained chief administrator of the institute until 1937, when his son Charles took over.[3]

A library school was not part of the original plan, but the institute was coupled to a library, modeled in part on the New York Mercantile Library. Businessmen first established mercantile libraries for their employees in the early 19th century, at a time when male clerks could aspire to succeed or join their employers in managing a business. The Pratt Institute Library, like the earlier mercantile libraries, included books of general cultural interest as well as technical books.

The library opened to the Brooklyn public in 1888—predating tax-supported Brooklyn Public Library by 15 years—with Margaret Healy, another Pratt relative, as director. Healy began a training class for new staff. In 1890, she hired Mary Wright Plummer, the most promising of Melvil Dewey's students in the first class of his Columbia School of Library Economy, as assistant librarian and head of the training class. Daughter of a prosperous Chicago Quaker family, Plummer had attended Wellesley College as a special student and taught for four years before enrolling in 1887 in the School of Library Economy. In background, she resembled many of the women achievers who came into prominence at the turn of the century with "a Quaker or dissenting Protestant past; a family history of doing good; a sturdy, self-reliant mother and a supportive high-minded father."[4] An active professionalizer, she took advantage of Pratt's openness to innovation, changing the focus of the library training school from preparing staff for Pratt library to preparing librarians for a variety of public library positions.

On Healy's departure, Plummer accepted appointment as head of the library school as well as director of the library but first negotiated a year's leave in Europe. During the academic year 1894–95, Plummer, who spoke four European languages, visited libraries in Bayreuth, Nuremberg, Venice, Rome, Florence, and Paris, publishing her observations on librarianship abroad in a series of articles in *The Nation*. Contacts she made among European librarians she kept up throughout her life.

On her return she assumed responsiblity for both the library and the school. The Pratt library, in a new building featuring the first room especially constructed for children as well as a large art reference collection, became known as a model of the American free library, attracting visitors from all over the world. According to Anne Carroll Moore, Pratt's first children's librarian and later one of the leading authorities on library work with children:

> Miss Plummer's clear perception of international relationships, her scholarly tastes and her warm friendships with European librarians and writers, contributed definitely to the cosmopolitan atmosphere of the [Pratt] library and the whole institution with which she was associated. Educators from all over the world were at that time visiting Pratt Institute to gain new ideas in demonstrable terms and the free library, thanks to Miss Plummer's interpretation, proved one of the most interesting of these ideas."[5]

The Institute library school offered a year of instruction divided into three terms: two of instruction in "library economy" and cataloging followed by a third of practice work in the library. Library economy covered various techniques for organizing and maintaining libraries such as borrower registration, order-department work, classification, mechanical preparation of books for the shelves, practical charging system work, binding, and reference as well as typing and "library hand," legible handwriting for library catalogs. Cataloging, based on rules established by the American Library Association, received particular emphasis. In addition library and literary figures lectured and students took field trips to libraries, museums, binderies, and bookstores. In the spring, between the second and third terms, Plummer or the vice-director, Josephine Rathbone, escorted the students to another city, usually Boston, Philadelphia, or Washington, where they were presented to and entertained by librarians and book dealers. In 1897, for example, a class of 20, escorted by Miss Rathbone, traveled on the Fall River boat to Boston. There they visited Melvil Dewey's Library Bureau, a company making library supplies and furniture; were entertained at the Boston Book Company; had tea at the Boston Public Library; and toured libraries at Harvard, Cambridge, Wellesley, and the Museum of Fine Arts.[6]

Plummer experimented with offering a second year of specialized education. In 1898 she introduced a historical course to prepare catalogers and bibliographers for the collections of rare books that wealthy Americans were buying in Europe. The following year she introduced a course for children's librarians led by Anne Carroll Moore, the Institute's children's librarian, in conjunction with the kindergarten department of the institute. Both programs were small, enrolling only a few students. She encouraged her brother-in-law Edwin Anderson, librarian of the Carnegie Library of Pittsburgh, to take over the program for children's librarians. In Pittsburgh it flourished as a specialized Training School for Children's Librarians.[7]

Plummer found the school so fascinating that she resigned the directorship of the library in 1904 to concentrate on it full time. The trustees promoted the Applied Science Librarian, Edward F. Stevens, a graduate of Colby and the Pratt library school, to director of the library. By that time, the school faculty, in addition to Plummer and the librarians of the institute, included Josephine Rathbone and a Miss Johnson. The school enrolled 25 students a year, the largest number that could effectively be given practice in the library. The students were drawn from many states, and all had passed the stiff entrance exam as well as exams in French and German. Although most had at least some college education, Pratt policy forbade setting an educational requirement for admission. Over 95% of the students were women. The school aimed:

> To give technical training in methods of library management to carefully selected candidates, with a view to fitting them for positions as the librarians of small libraries, as heads of departments, or assistants in large libraries, as organizers or reorganizers of libraries, and as instructors of library staffs, or in library schools."[8]

In 1911 Plummer, at the urging of her brother-in-law Edwin Anderson, vice-director of the New York Public Library, resigned to take on the directorship of the New York Public Library School. Josephine Rathbone, Plummer's assistant, expected the Pratt trustees to appoint her director. Daughter of an upstate New York physician father and a southern mother, she, like Plummer, lacked a college degree, although she had attended Wellesley for one year and the University of Michigan for two as a special student. She received the Bachelor of Library Science degree from the New York State Library School in 1893 and began as assistant cataloger at Pratt the same year. If her background was similar to Plummer's, her temperament was different. Where observers characterized Plummer as dignified and reserved, Rathbone was tart-tongued and assertive. A student remembered her as "a small, trim, tailored figure, light brown hair dressed simply over a high forehead, rather plain looking but of distinguished presence."[9]

The trustees thwarted Rathbone's expectation by appointing Edward Stevens director. She remained vice-director. This remained a source of conflict between them over the nearly three decades that they continued to work together. She never accepted her subordination to him. If she could not have the title of director, she would be the director in fact. Students recollected their awareness of the feud in the "high, strained voices" in which the two conversed. A few squabbles are documented in the Pratt Archives, among them Stevens' accusations that Rathbone made unnecessary noise in the back of the classroom while he was lecturing and that she deliberately bypassed him in sending an article on the school to a library publication. Rathbone indignantly denied both charges. Students observing the two concluded that Rathbone was the real head of the school. Rice Estes, a student in the 1930s, commented, "Miss Rathbone ruled the library school. And the whole country knew it, including Mr. Stevens."[10]

The tension between them never eased. Stevens became anxious in the late 1920s that the trustees might appoint Rathbone librarian if something happened to him. "I cannot imagine entrusting to such inexperienced and oblivious hands, though temporarily, the conduct of the Library's affairs, even in the unlooked for event of the Librarian's early death. It's a man's job anyway."[11] He assuaged his anxiety by recruiting to the library a young Pratt graduate, Wayne Shirley, whom he groomed as his successor, making sure that the trustees understood his intention. The administrative structure of the school after both Stevens and Rathbone retired in 1938 continued the pattern of a male director and a female assistant.

Despite the personal animosity between them, Stevens and Rathbone shared a devotion to the institution. Stevens took great pride in the school while Rathbone claimed that the school's greatest asset was its base in the Pratt Institute Free Library, "where the students see functioning around them a library of comprehensible size, with a well-rounded, carefully-chosen selection of books, a flexible, smoothly-running organization, and a staff that sets an example of efficient work done in the finest spirit of service."[12]

Soon after she took charge, in fact if not in title, the school assumed the form it was to continue, with minor alterations, into the late 1930s. The school continued to enroll a maximum of 25 students who progressed through the three terms together. Under Plummer, the school had four full-time employees, under Rathbone it had only three; Rathbone herself, who taught reference, classification, book selection, library administration and seminars on fiction and current events; an assistant trained at Pratt, who taught cataloging, primarily; and a secretary. The staff of the Pratt Institute Free Library provided the rest of the instruction. The curriculum emphasized the techniques of library organization and maintenance originally taught in Melvil Dewey's Columbia School which was later transferred to the New York State Library in Albany. These techniques were taught with sufficient thoroughness that students could perform them immediately on being hired, or could teach them to others.

Rathbone's assistant Edith P. Bucknam (and Harriet Gooch before her) taught cataloging. According to one student, "When Miss Bucknam was through, a Pratt student could sit down in front of a pile of books, and go to work on them."[13] Students were not taught, however, that only one right way existed to do things. The same student described a mini-drama staged for many classes in Rathbone's classification course. At one meeting of the class she classified a book. At the next meeting, apparently absent-mindedly, she put the same book in a different classification. "We would call her attention to the change triumphantly, and Miss Rathbone would say, 'But that was the last time. Today I feel differently.' Thus she made the point that classification is an art, and not a science."[14]

But if library skills were important, they were not the intellectual meat of librarianship. The essence of librarianship was, as she said in numerous speeches throughout her career, "to know books and to understand the book needs of people," and to bring books and readers together in "a vital relationship."[15] Except for a seminar in fiction, Rathbone did not try to teach these directly, although she tried in various ways to encourage students to widen their intellectual horizons. She firmly believed that, "The librarian is a reading human."[16]. She furthered her vision of the educated librarian by selecting students who already had a high degree of cultural literacy, as assessed by the famous Pratt entrance examination. Widely reputed to be the most difficult library school entrance examination, between three-fourths and half of the applicants to the school failed. After the students completed library school she believed that they should continue educating themselves in libraries. In her presidential address before the American Library Association in 1932 she declared: "Work in a library is educative in itself. . . . The qualities that make for successful work with readers—as knowledge of books, imagination, sympathy, and understanding of human nature and human needs—can better be developed by work in the circulation or reference department or children's room of a good library under the stimulus of a broad-minded, inspiring chief than by study in college classrooms."[17]

Throughout the school year Rathbone attempted to assess students' personal strengths and weaknesses as well as their school performance. At the much-dreaded placement interview at the close of the year she discussed the observations recorded on the reverse of the student's official record with each student. Wayne Shirley, who followed Edward Stevens as director of both the library and the school, described these character judgements as "fantastically accurate."[18] Because Pratt still guards these student records, the flavor of the assessments of the students must be drawn from her published assessments of well-known librarians. If she gave Melvil Dewey full credit as an organizer and educator, she revealed that she had never heard him mention a book; Justin Winsor, the Boston Brahmin scholar-librarian, was so pompous she was sure his wife and daughters must "address" him rather than simply speaking to him; and the iconoclastic John Cotton Dana was like a "catfish, which by its pugnacity and energy keeps the whole barrelful [of herring] stirred up, alive and active."[19] Rathbone freely shared her student assessments with prospective employers:

> The qualities shown by each student while in the school and their subsequent careers are carefully studied in order to determine their special fitness for different kinds of work. The information thus acquired is freely and frankly at the disposal of those having appointments to make, and we are glad to be consulted when our graduates are under consideration.[20]

Unlike Plummer, Rathbone displayed little interest in curricular innovation. The changes she did make, such as the introduction of courses in book selection and storytelling between 1910 and 1920, the substitution of another modern language for German during and after World War I, and the reduction in practical work and formalizing of course hours in the 1920s, occurred largely because of outside pressures. Rather than attempting to prepare students for a variety of emerging specialities, as Plummer had, she focused on preparing them for executive positions in public libraries.

Under Plummer the school had already attracted students from across the nation and from many foreign countries. Under Rathbone, they continued coming. A regular contingent came from the Pacific Northwest, sent by graduate Mary Frances Isom, the leading professionalizer in that region. By 1921 students had come from Sweden, Norway, Denmark, Russia, Germany, Italy, Belgium, India, China, Japan, the Philippines, and the West Indies as well as from virtually all sections of the United States and Canada.[21] Stevens wrote proudly in to the trustees, "Our school is not metropolitan but more nearly cosmopolitan. We do not train for a system but for a profession, and our members come from everywhere expecting to return to their own distant environments to disseminate that which they gained at Pratt institute."[22]

Most of the students were white Protestant women, in their mid- to late twenties. Almost all had work experience, the largest number in libraries but some in teaching, social work, or office work. The men students, about five percent of the total, were less easily generalizable. For example, Herman H. B. Meyer, of the class of 1902, had a 16-year career as a mechanical engineer before entering Pratt. Truman Temple, of the class of 1916, was an upstate New York farmer, "Not in the least bucolic in speech, appearance or manner," Stevens reassured the trustees.[23] Igor Akramoff of the class of 1931 was a graduate of the Russian Naval Academy and had been an officer of the Czarist navy before the World War I.

Once students completed the library course, Rathbone placed them. In 1925–1926 she reported receiving 1,500 letters about possible positions.[24] She placed 60 to 70 graduates annually, 25 from the current class and the remainder graduates of previous classes. "Only 11% of them [our graduates] are assistants as against 21% three years ago, while the remainder are in executive positions or positions of independent responsibility."[25] The network focused around the Graduates' Association played an essential role in placement. In her report for 1915–1916 she mused, "More and more does the Vice-Director see the school as a whole, the alumni rather than the current class being the thing that is of lasting importance; the class represents the annual ring while the alumni make up the tree itself, each year growing in strength and spread of influence."[26]

A map in the school office displayed the distribution of graduates with colored pins. In her first annual report, issued in 1913, Rathbone could report a wide geographical distribution of graduates. Of the 308 graduates actively working in the field she reported, "123 are in Greater New York, 14 elsewhere in New York state, 20 in New England, 19 in Pennsylvania, 17 in the South, 68 in the Middle West, 27 on the Pacific Coast, 5 in Canada, and 3 in Europe."[27] The report for 1925–1926 showed a similar distribution with "150 of the graduates . . . in the Metropolitan district, 20 in the South, 79 in the Middle West, 26 in the far West, and something over a dozen . . . employed abroad."[28]

Rathbone belonged to multiple library and educational organizations, both regional and national. She strongly recommended that alumnae do the same. As evidence of the "professional-mindedness" of the graduates she proudly reported in 1929 that "85 per cent belong to the A.L.A. and 95 per cent belong to some library organization other than our own Graduates' Association."[29] Trips to and from meetings became "Pratt pilgrimages" enabling her to maintain contact with alumnae outside of metropolitan New York. In 1915, for example, she travelled to Chicago after the fall term; to Atlanta, Cincinnati, and Pittsburgh following the spring class trip to Philadelphia and Washington; and to Berkeley in the summer for the American Library Association annual meeting. In all these cities and places in between she stopped to visit libraries which employed Pratt graduates. "The loyalty and devotion shown made the experience a delightful one, and the chance to see our graduates at work and to discuss their problems with them on the spot was of the greatest interest and value to the visitor and cannot but react favorably on the School itself."[30] The meetings themselves served "not only to strengthen the ties between the school and its graduates by renewing friendly intercourse, but they give us opportunities of serving the graduates by introducing them to the older librarians and to other Pratt graduates, and by discussing their qualifications with librarians and library trustees seeking appointees to positions."[31]

Rathbone also maintained contact with alumnae through a detailed questionnaire sent out every three years. This triennial survey served a number of purposes: seeing that the curriculum reflected the tasks graduates were expected to perform, as well as providing both general information on library salaries and specific information on positions and salaries for placement.

Few Pratt graduates occupied the top positions in large libraries. Boards of trustees of large libraries, like school boards, and boards of trustees of large charitable organizations preferred men and Pratt graduates were overwhelmingly female. The successful careers of women directors of large public libraries—Gratia Countryman in Minneapolis, Beatrice Winser in Newark, Linda Eastman in Cleveland, Theresa West Ehlmendorf in Milwaukee, and Tessa Kelso in Los Angeles—did not markedly change the preference for men. The fact that some women were successful administrators of large libraries did not mean that administrative ability ceased being regarded as a male trait. Rossiter has described the way in which successful women scientists were defined as "exceptional," leaving the general perception that women were unsuited to science unchanged.[32] A similar mechanism may have been in place here. The jobs as heads of small libraries and middle-level "executives" in larger ones, for which Rathbone and the Pratt school prepared students, were among the better jobs realistically available to women.

CARNEGIE CORPORATION INTERVENTION

Meanwhile, in 1916, the Carnegie Corporation was preparing to take a more active role in library education. While Carnegie, himself, had granted support to a few library schools, this had never been a matter of policy. The initiator of change was Henry Pritchett, former president of MIT, executive of the Carnegie Foundation for the Advancement of Teaching, and member of the corporation's board. Pritchett's outstanding achievement as head of the Carnegie Foundation had been the commissioning of the Flexner Report, highly critical of medical education, which appeared in 1910. Abraham Flexner, a former high school teacher, visited a large number of schools, excoriating most of them in the colorful language of his muckraking contemporaries. He recommended that most of them close and that the remainder model themselves on the Johns Hopkins Medical School where his brother, Simon, held a faculty position.

Most medical historians agree that the Flexner report did not initiate reform in medical education. Flexner endorsed reforms already under way. But the report paved the way for massive foundation investments in medical education and provided a pattern for many later foundation-sponsored studies of professional education.

Pritchett believed Carnegie's practice of donating library buildings was *inefficient* (an all-purpose pejorative term popular among Progressives). As a member of the Carnegie Corporation's board, he asked Alvin Johnson, a Cornell economist, to survey libraries and prepare recommendations for the board. Ellen Condliffe Lagemann, historian of the Carnegie Corporation, believes that Pritchett wanted a Flexner-style exposé combined with a recommendation that the corporation change its course. In 1916 Johnson reported that much of the Carnegie money spent for library buildings was wasted because of "untrained and inefficient" librarians.[33]

In fact, the central problem for most Carnegie libraries was the meagerness of community financial support rather than the weakness of individual librarians. Communities receiving a Carnegie building agreed to provide an annual amount equal to 10 percent of the cost of the building for support of the library. Since the average cost of a building was $10,000, this meant only $1,000 a year for books, salaries, maintenance, and supplies. Few communities actually provided the full 10 percent.[34] Constance Bement, a Pratt graduate and library extension worker described the typical woman staffing a small Carnegie library as the "only philanthropist which her small town affords," working for a pittance or "for the good of the cause."[35]

Johnson did not recommend any further assistance to these libraries. Instead he advised the corporation to cease donating library buildings, concentrating instead on the preparation of library "experts." The corporation should also set up a central body to oversee its library activities. He later described the meeting of the corporation board to discuss the report. James Bertram, Carnegie's personal secretary and secretary of the corporation, exploded (Carnegie himself was not present). Johnson's recommendations absolutely contradicted Carnegie's intentions. "He wanted to give libraries to communities," Bertram stated, "and leave the communities absolutely free to manage them any way they might see fit. He abominated centralized, bureaucratic control. That is exactly what you want to introduce."[36] Bertram correctly expressed Carnegie's intentions, squelching any further consideration of the report at the time, but Johnson recalled that Chairman Elihu Root told him quietly: "We are all for your report . . . except Bertram . . . However, you will see, your recommendations will presently be in force."[37]

After Carnegie's withdrawal from active participation in his philanthropies in 1917, the trustees had a freer hand. The corporation ceased giving donations for public libraries in 1917 and in 1918 the trustees commissioned a new survey of library education. Bertram chose C. C. Williamson, an economist with library experience, to conduct it.

Williamson exemplified what Ross has called the third generation of American social scientists. Lacking the elite social origins of the first generation and the activist reform committments of the second, members of the third generation frequently came from humble social backgrounds and wholeheartedly adopted the university values of science and objectivity to justify their claim to social authority.[38] Growing up in rural Ohio, with parents uneducated beyond a one-room ungraded country school, even completing high school was a major achievement for Williamson. A course in stenography and typing at a local business college provided the means for further education. He attended college while working as secretary to President Charles F. Thwing, of Western Reserve University in Cleveland. After graduating, he took a similar position at the University of Wisconsin as economist Richard T. Ely's secretary and graduate student. While in Madison he cataloged Ely's private library and selected books in economics for the libraries of the University of Wisconsin and the Wisconsin State Historical Society. He briefly considered a career in legislative reference, a largely male library specialty pioneered in Wisconsin, but instead moved to New York and completed his graduate work under E.R.A. Seligman at Columbia, earning his Ph.D. in 1907. He then took a position as associate professor and head of the Economics Department at Bryn Mawr. Conflict with Bryn Mawr president M. Carey Thomas made him anxious to leave, so when Seligman recommended him for a position as head of the Economics and Sociology Division of the New York Public Library in 1911, he took it. He became head of the Municipal Reference Library in 1914. In early 1918 he resigned to take a temporary position as statistician for a Carnegie Corporation Study of Methods of Americanization study but in 1919 he returned to the New York Public Library. That same year James Bertram, formerly Carnegie's private secretary and executive of the Carnegie Corporation, asked him to conduct a study of library education.[39]

Like Johnson, Williamson believed that further Carnegie assistance to the hundreds of small libraries built with Carnegie money would be like "pouring water into a sieve."[40] He therefore ignored the library institutes, summer schools, and small library training schools which prepared women for work in many Carnegie-financed libraries, concentrating instead on the 15 "so-called professional library schools" accredited by the American Association of Library Schools, an organization of the schools themselves.[41]

Following the Flexner model, Williamson thoroughly lambasted the existing schools as not only backward, conservative, and inefficient but "an actual hindrance to the highest success in types of librarianship requiring initiative, originality, resourcefulness and large administrative capacity."[42]

Students were selected by "crude and unscientific" entrance examinations and by interviews which claimed to assess personal qualities and aptitudes for library work before any attempt had been made "to determine scientifically what personal qualities are essential" and before "accurate methods of detecting the possession of such qualities are worked out by vocational psychologists."[43]

The schools had pitifully meager resources. He estimated that annually the "sum total of the budgets of the fifteen schools ... does not exceed $150,000."[44] A number were housed in large public libraries, which he denounced, seeing "no more reason for expecting or permitting the public library of one city to train librarians for a whole state or for the whole country than for allowing the public schools of that city to use municipal revenues to train teachers for the whole state."[45]

Instructors, "about half [of whom] ... were not college graduates" wêre "untrained in teaching."[46] They lacked "fitness ... for giving instruction of high professional character."[47] The deplorable "tendency for library schools to be more or less dominated by a single personality," limited creativity in teaching.[48] In addition, Williamson found a "total lack of anything recognized as productive scholarship."[49]

Most schools claimed that their curricula prepared students for all levels and types of librarianship, but Williamson argued that they graduated "crammed with information about every conceivable subject, from incunabula to colorband filing."[50] The emphasis on library technique left students "in danger of missing the broad professional outlook, and suffering a certain deadening of initiative and imagination ... from an excessive attention to minute detail."[51] Much of cataloging and classification, courses at the "heart of the curriculum" of all the schools, could be performed by subprofessionals, he believed.[52]

The schools' pedagogical techniques were similarly inadequate. Textbooks were lacking and lectures overworked. Instructors risked "deadening [students'] initiative and enthusiasm by drilling them in the routine processes of hand work and the memorizing of rules and classes." Insisting on "a perfection in detail, they stifle[d] the indispensable qualities of enthusiasm, imagination, and initiative."[53]

In some schools Williamson found "incongruous adaptation of the methods and terminology of the university." A library school seminar was not "a group of students engaged in original research under the guidance of a scholar and investigator" but a group of "high school students engaged in acquiring a modicum of elementary information on book selection or some other subject in the curriculum under a teacher without college training or experience in research."[54] Instructors assigned practical work on "no scientifically determined basis."[55] "No clear-cut and well-defined objective" existed for field work, which was in any case "poorly supervised and inadequately analyzed."[56] Virtually the only activity of which he approved was the class trip.

He patronizingly conceded that existing schools "take themselves with the utmost seriousness and by dint of patient and devoted, if not brilliant effort do achieve results which are surprisingly large when measured by their resources in personnel and equipment."[57]

If the past was dismal, the future of library education could be bright. Williamson predicted "epoch-making advances" in library education, standardization, and certification.[58] He recommended two levels of library education to the Carnegie Corporation.

The top level was to be wholly professional, resembling contemporary graduate programs in the social sciences. Only college graduates would qualify as students. It would be housed in a university and its financial support "should receive consideration from the Carnegie Corporation."[59] Instructors would have "college training as well as special training and experience in their own field at least equal to that required in the teaching staff of the best professional schools."[60] It would prepare "workers to fill all positions requiring extensive and accurate book knowledge, advice and direction in the use of books, skill in organization and administration, and expert technical knowledge in many special lines."[61]

The actual content of the Williamson's recommended curriculum was vague. The school would not provide "the prolonged practice necessary to produce a skilled professional librarian" but would instead "lay broad and deep the foundations of knowledge, insure grasp of principles, impart an appreciation of the ideals of library service, and develop a professional attitude toward the work."[62] Pedagogically, practical work would be only for "directed and supervised observation" not for "practice in actual library work."[63]

Lower level, subprofessional training classes in large libraries would prepare women high school graduates to perform "manual labor of a purely clerical and routine nature" which the professionally-minded found "unattractive and distasteful."[64] This included "cataloguing, classification, and all kinds of record-keeping topics, including filing, indexing, alphabeting, typewriting." They would learn by means of "drill and practical work" as well as classroom instruction.[65]

To maintain the distinction between the types of education Williamson recommended a voluntary National Certification Board attached to the American Library Association, analogous to the Council on Medical Education of the American Medical Association.[66]

This bifurcated educational scheme would accomplish a number of ends. It would make library work more attractive to the professionally minded, particularly to men who avoided clerical "women's work" and looked for a clearer pathway to top positions.[67] It would provide a way of raising professional salaries since Williamson anticipated that the salaries of clerical workers in libraries could be set "even lower than those offered by commercial and private employers."[68] These workers would, in effect, subsidize the professionals. Finally, the plan would be useful in "checking the feminization of library work as a profession," both by moving large numbers of women outside professional boundaries and by attracting more men.[69]

According to Lagemann, "Williamson's prescriptions were designed to foster a bifurcation not different from that which existed between (male) school administrators and (female) teachers, and between (male) doctors and (female) nurses. It would be difficult to read the Williamson study without concluding that fostering hierarchical segmentation by gender was one of its goals."[70]

RATHBONE COUNTERS THE WILLIAMSON REPORT

The Carnegie Corporation Trustees received Williamson's report in 1921 but it was published in a revised, edited version only in 1923. Following its public release, few library educators defended themselves or their schools. They may have feared that arguing with Williamson's conclusions would label them as anti-professional, or they may have expected foundation grants to remedy the problems as had happened following foundation-sponsored reports of other professions. By denying the weaknesses, they might also be refusing the grants.

Stevens fumed privately to the trustees that Williamson was "biased and uninformed". His report was a "manifesto" "in support of preconceptions . . . by an academic mind detached from the work and failing to understand what the work attempts to do." He described Rathbone's reaction, published in the Library Journal, as "the one fearless note of response which has come from the schools under criticism."[71]

Williamson had attacked many of the features on which the Pratt educators prided themselves: a curriculum sensitive to demand, a student body selected for personal as well as intellectual aptitude, thorough coverage of the skills a graduate needed to organize and maintain a library, and openness to self-educated as well as credentialed students. It would have been uncharacteristic of Rathbone to let Williamson's criticisms stand unchallenged. She confessed that she found in the report "some of that irritating quality that participators in the fray always feel in the criticism of those who are *sur le combat.*[72]

Williamson had criticized a curriculum based on "the current demands of the librarians who employ the graduates and the experience of the graduates themselves" that he believed resulted "in excessive conservatism and conformity to custom and tradition." Instead, aggressive library educators should "be prepared to make a thorough, scientific analysis of what training for professional library work should be and build its curriculum upon its findings, instead of following tradition and imitating others."[73] Rathbone had nothing but scorn for this idea. "Fancy the criticism that would follow should the schools fail to meet the requirements of employing librarians and if the graduates discovered that their training had not fitted them to function satisfactorily under the conditions in which they found themselves!"[74]

Williamson also recommended that the schools cease trying to assess personality through interviews since "no attempt has been made to determine scientifically what personal qualities are essential. . . . Any effort to base selection [of students] on personal qualities and aptitudes for library work should be discouraged until such qualities and aptitudes are carefully and clearly defined and more accurate methods of detecting them worked out by vocational psychologists."[75] Rathbone responded, "If Dr. Williamson knew the stress library trustees and librarians laid upon 'personality' in their requests for librarians or assistants of all grades, he would understand why library school directors feel the necessity of securing students who have that elusive and indefinable but very real quality, with such empirical methods as are at hand, crude and unscientific though they be, pending the working out the aforesaid psychological tests."[76] If Williamson recommended eliminating routine work from the professional curriculum, Rathbone justified retaining some "minor record work and certain mechanical processes" in the curriculum because "high school librarians, heads of departments in the smaller libraries, and many librarians of public libraries have to do themselves or teach others to do many simple and `unprofessional' tasks."[77]

She reserved her sharpest objection for Williamson's blanket recommendation that: "Graduation from an accredited college after four years of study leading up to the bachelor's degree should now be recognized as the minimum of general education needed for successful professional library work of any kind."[78] To this Rathbone responded:

> As the representative of a school that has always stood for the exceptional person, I want to point out that in his stress on college education Dr. Williamson seems to assume that the choice is between college graduates and relatively uneducated persons fresh from high schools. As visualized by us the problem is: Shall we exclude from the school the man or woman who is really educated and who has shown fitness for librarianship tho lacking the hallmark of a degree? There are in the profession many women who have been unable to attend college but who have gained by reading, study, and contacts all that college can give—culture, trained minds, broad outlook. While this is the case, and until the profession has become so standardized that we cannot place such students advantageously, we at Pratt Institute purpose to keep an open door for them, and so far our records show that the non-college graduates with previous library experience acquit themselves quite as well as the collegians even judged by the acid test of financial recognition.[79]

Rathbone stood for a different model of professional education than did Williamson. She stood for diversity rather than unitary standards in professional education, for "organic" curriculum change rather than planning, for practice-based rather than "theoretical" education, and for preparation for a less stratified rather than a more stratified occupation.

FOUNDATION-SPONSORED REFORMS
CLASH WITH PRATT PRINCIPLES

The BEL Classifies Pratt on the Lowest Level

The Carnegie Corporation's Ten-Year Program in Library Service, announced in 1926, implemented many of Williamson's recommendations through grants totaling over $4 million. One-third went to support existing library schools. With Carnegie funding, the New York State Library School combined with the New York Public Library School and relocated to Columbia under the Williamson's deanship. One third went for the establishment of a new graduate school at the University of Chicago. The last third went to the ALA, in large part to defray the costs of a complicated new accrediting system which supplanted the system being worked out by the American Association of Library Schools, a bootstrap organization of the schools themselves.

Foundation support for ALA accreditation efforts began even earlier with foundation funding in 1923 for a Temporary Library Training Board and in 1924 for a Board of Education for Librarianship. The BEL began almost immediately to classify and rank existing library schools.

Pratt was nearly the first casualty of this new accreditation system. In October 1924, a team of five prominent librarians visited the Pratt School on behalf of the BEL: Adam Strohm, Director of the Detroit Public Library; Andrew Keogh, Director of Yale University Libraries; Harrison Craver, Director of the Engineering Societies Library; Elisabeth M. Smith, Director of the Albany Public Library; and Harriet Howe, Executive Assistant of the BEL.

In January, following the visit of the accreditation team, Rathbone sent a description of the school's purpose to Sarah Bogle, Secretary of the ALA Board of Education for Librarianship, stating:

> We have no present intention of offering other than a general, one-year course, emphasizing public library service but presenting all the more important phases of library work, and arranging to give our students practical experience in such special phases as High School libraries, village libraries, children's work, art, technical, business, medical, law library work as they may be interested in by placing them for work in different libraries in and about New York.
>
> To understand the problems of modern librarianship, and to adapt the school to them within the limits of our environment and resources; to work intensely with a limited number of students selected carefully from a relatively large number of applicants; to keep closely in touch with our graduates, promoting their interests and benefiting by their interest in the school is and has been for many years the aim and policy of the school.[80]

In June of 1925 the report of the visit was sent to both Rathbone and Stevens. The brief report criticized the fact that the director did not give full time to the school and that administrative duties were divided between the Director and Vice-Director. It criticized the instructional staff as "too small to carry the work outlined" and the school's quarters as "inconveniently located; many stairs to be climbed. There is a lack of private offices and of a separate class room, instruction now being given in the study hall." The report commented favorably on the school's clarity of purpose ("the atmosphere of the School reflects this assurance"), the "attractive and alert students," the professional library, the "active and loyal alumni association," and Pratt Library as a site for the student's practical work. "The Pratt Institute Free Library is well manned to meet the demands made upon it, and its staff is therefore able to give considerable time to the training of students."[81]

Both Stevens and Rathbone responded to the criticisms. Stevens described the administrative arrangements as ideal. "Our Vice-Director can work with

greater ease and effect that the Director assumes the ultimate responsibilities."
He denied that the quarters were inconvenient. "Two flights of stairs from the
ground, broken by easy and broad landings, whereby one is brought to the qui-
etest, lightest, and airiest section of the building, do not disturb us." One school
office sufficed and the visitors had overlooked the classroom in which students
were seated in folding chairs for flexibility. Classes held in the study hall enabled students to use "material which they keep in and upon their desks."[82]
Rathbone replied only to the criticism that, "The instructors are not sufficient to
carry the course outlined." She protested, "We *are* carrying it and have carried
it for a good many years, and on the whole to the satisfaction of our students
and graduates." She particularly demurred at the idea that more of her courses
ought to be taught by someone else. "I myself have never ended a year more
fresh and vigorous than I have this present, and I am not willing, nor do I think
it would be to the advantage of the school for me to give up the teaching of
classification, or reference work, or book selection or my class in current topics, and unless I did we simply could not keep a third teacher busy. Under these
circumstances what would you recommend?"[83] Both Stevens and Rathbone believed that the criticisms were minor. Rathbone wrote in her annual report for
1924–1925, "The school has received sympathetic consideration from the
Board. They have shown every desire to understand our special problems and
to appreciate that we must adapt ourselves to an environment that is unique, that
makes us what we are, and which we neither can nor do we desire to change."[84]

The final recommendation of the BEL, communicated to Pratt in May of
1926, did not rest on any of these criticisms, however, but on two things that
the BEL could have determined without a visit. Pratt had no educational requirements for admission and awarded no degrees. The BEL accredited Pratt
Institute Library School as a Junior Undergraduate Library School, the lowest
category. Even this was bending the rules since Pratt did not offer an undergraduate degree and had no educational requirements for admission. The BEL
was willing to do the bending only because the majority of students, 23 of 27
in the class of 1926, had at least one year of college and 19 were college graduates. The decision disappointed Stevens and Rathbone because it removed the
school from the elite rank they believed it deserved, but the ranking had few
immediate consequences.

The following year, to vindicate her claim that Pratt students had superior
academic ability, with or without a college degree, Rathbone administered two
tests obtained from the Harvard University Graduate School of Education, the
Whipple reading test and the Inglis vocabulary test. She reported triumphantly
that the results, graded by Harvard, showed not only that the collegiate and non-
collegiate groups were equal but "that the average intelligence of our class is
above that of the college graduates tested by the School of Education (indeed
there was a greater difference between our score and the college graduate score
than between that and the score of high school graduates)."[85] She publicized the

results to Pratt graduates and later used them to bolster her argument that Pratt should be classified as a graduate library school.

Subsequent events combined to increase the importance of the ranking. The first was a narrowly averted decision by the New York State Committee on Library Classification and Personnel to limit graduates of Junior Undergraduate Library Schools to the lowest two grades of a proposed five-level certification scheme. This would have made Pratt graduates, whether or not they were college graduates, ineligible for many library positions in New York State. Rathbone succeeded in persuading the committee to accept college graduation and graduation from an accredited library school for Grade 3, the largest grade. Pratt graduates with less than a college degree were still, however, barred from many positions, to her dismay.[86] The school faced "the danger of a loss of prestige and of our power to attract the quality of student we have always hitherto attracted."[87] In addition, she and the members of the Graduates' Association were fearful of the outcome of certification in other states.

Rathbone wrote a personal letter to Sarah Bogle, executive secretary of the BEL, detailing her distress:

> Don't you see that so long as the A.L.A. apparently puts Pratt in the lowest class, it will be discriminated against with such a consequent loss of prestige that we may not be able to attract the quality of student that has given us the position we have hitherto held? Already some of our western graduates are saying that they would rather Pratt closed its doors than be forced into a position of inferiority, and I am beginning to feel that unless the Board finds some way of publicly acknowledging that the school has standards that rank it among the best *one year* courses, that we owe it to our body of graduates who came to the school because they believed it to be the best one year course, not to continue if we find we can not maintain our position in the profession. Of course this is only between ourselves at present.
>
> It has not happened yet that the class has declined in *quality*, but three symptoms have manifested themselves this year that make me wonder how long we can go on without suffering. We have had fewer applications this year than for the last two or three years, we have had more withdrawals of accepted students than usual and we have no students from the Pacific coast from which direction the greatest concern about the future of the school was expressed.[88]

Strohm suggested that one way out of the dilemma might be for Pratt to award a different form of certificate to college graduates.[89] Rathbone angrily dismissed this:

> It is inconceivable to me that Pratt Institute would ever discriminate between students, who meet all the requirements of the course, on the basis of their entrance preparation, as the very foundation stone of Pratt Institute is an open door for all who are qualified to carry the work. Moreover, if the school itself were discriminated against by being apparently placed in an inferior grade, the people

influenced by this classification would not care what kind of a certificate it gave. Therefore I think there must be some change in the A.L.A. standards themselves to meet this situation.[90]

With Rathbone's encouragement the Pratt Graduates' Association went into action. The association raised money to send the president to Washington, D.C., to persuade Pratt's best-known graduate, Herman H.B. Meyer, to plead Pratt's case before the BEL. Meyer was chief bibliographer of the Library of Congress, director of the Library's Legislative Reference Service, and initiator of services for the blind and had been ALA president in 1924–1925.[91] At the association's expense, Meyer travelled to Chicago to address the BEL meeting of October 5–6, 1928. He warned that, "the low rating given the school by the A.L.A. Board of Education" threatened the school with destruction. "Because of the established policy of Pratt Institute, the school cannot function on a college graduate basis and refuse to accept fully qualified persons who do not possess a degree." He pointed out that the A.L.A. was inconsistent in promoting adult education in libraries on the one hand and in failing to recognize people who had educated themselves outside academic institutions on the other. He and the other alumni were "not asking for a lowering of the standard of scholarship" but that the Pratt Institute Library School be judged "by the work done and the quality of the output" rather than by its entrance requirements. Entrance examinations and final examinations could be set or supervised by the BEL itself to assure high standards.[92]

The BEL took no immediate action. It did, however, prepare a resolution for the ALA Council which would allow reconsideration of Pratt's ranking, which read:

> The Board of Education for Librarianship shall have authority to place in any class a library school which meets in general the requirements of that class, and whose students equal in educational qualifications those in schools accredited in that class.[93]

In March 1929, Louis Round Wilson, member of the board and librarian of the University of North Carolina, visited the school to inform Stevens and Rathbone of the proposed resolution and to look at the school again. He found:

> The work . . . admirably planned, with the result that instruction and actual practice in the department are unusually well coordinated. As a matter of fact, it seemed rather remarkable to me that the department heads could lend themselves so completely to the uses of the school. They do so at some loss of speed to the departments themselves, but to the very great profit of the library school students. It is easy to understand, after having seen the work in progress, why the Pratt students are able to go at once from the classroom to a library and begin effective operation.

The spring visits were also well planned:

> The itinerary seemed well arranged and assignments had been made carefully with reference to what each pupil was to observe and report on upon her return to the school. Altogether I was impressed with the effectiveness of the work and am convinced that the Board will not make a mistake if it secures the action from the Council contemplated in its resolution with regard to accreditation. . . . As the official visitor, therefore, I recommend that the school be accredited in line with the general resolution of the Board, provided favorable action is taken by the Council upon the resolution.[94]

The council passed the resolution on May 17 leaving the way open to invite Pratt to apply for reconsideration of its classification.[95] In September Rathbone applied for Pratt's reclassification as a graduate school, on the grounds that the majority of the students were college graduates and those who were not had demonstrated their equality in pedagogical tests, standing in class, and success in the library field.[96] This, the BEL was unwilling to grant, finally giving Pratt a category of its own, "accredited, unclassified, but with high and acceptable standards."[97]

The second factor threatening the Pratt School was the opening of a Carnegie-funded graduate library school at Columbia University in 1926, combining the former New York State Library School with the New York Public Library School. This new school provided formidable competition. The New York Public Library School and the Brooklyn Public Library School had prepared students primarily, if not exclusively, for their respective systems, leaving a secure niche for Pratt. The new school, however, offered a degree from a prestigious university. College educated students who might otherwise have chosen Pratt turned to Columbia instead. Pratt, although chartered by the state to grant degrees, had never done so. Stevens begged the trustees to "cut the Gordian knot" and award a bachelor's degree of science on completion of the library school program to students who entered with a bachelor's degree.[98] The trustees declined to change their original policy.

Columbia also graduated over 150 students annually, creating serious competition for Pratt graduates. The combination of the Depression and the increased number of graduates in the region led to Pratt's first major difficulty in placing graduates. Stevens claimed indignantly, "The tremendous overproduction of trained librarians brought about by the professional school at Columbia, ordered upon university, post-graduate, degree-conferring principles, whereby one hundred and sixty librarians are let loose annually with nowhere to go, is precisely the mass production menace which has stagnated all industry."[99]

Reminiscences of Pratt graduates of the 1930s suggest that they viewed the school more critically than earlier graduates. Wayne Shirley, of the class of 1931, described Rathbone with affection, but emphasized her peculiarities. Her pince-nez, with their habit of sliding off her nose and clattering down on the desk in front of her; the white canvas shoes she sometimes wore with a tailored suit; her fur piece, which she insisted on wearing and then forgetting at various places on the class trips, all contributed to an image decidedly at odds with the modern professional.[100] Historians have pointed out the image of deviance and eccentricity increasingly attached to single women professionals in the 1920s and 1930s.[101]

Rice Estes, of the class of 1932, was more explicitly critical:

> Miss Rathbone was a brilliant but austere woman. She reminded me in some ways of Jane Addams and of the strong intellectual, fearless professional woman of the 1920's. But she developed at the turn of the century and she stopped developing about 1920. She wouldn't change. When big new people like Williamson at Columbia and Pierce Butler at Chicago came along, Miss Rathbone ignored them and continued in the 1910 tradition. There was much complaint in our class about this.[102]

The "big new people" in library education—Williamson, an economist and Pierce Butler, a medieval historian—were both men, both highly trained in an academic specialty.

By comparison with the resources available to the new schools, Pratt's resources seemed meager indeed. Stevens told Rathbone that he continued to share her belief in library education focused on techniques of organization and maintenance. "But the millions of dollars spent in [sic] rooms and halls and desks and chairs and shelves [at Columbia] . . . beyond the dreams of any other Library school anywhere must be justified by pretensions to 'higher levels' than ours."[103]

Pratt Institute Library School should not, however, be seen simply as a weak old-fashioned school which experienced difficulty in meeting modern professional standards. Patricia Graham has pointed out the "strikingly heterogeneous array of acceptable and praiseworthy institutions" of higher education in existence between 1875 and 1925, which aided women's advancement. Pratt Institute was one of these. The Library School, with its international reputation and hundreds of loyal graduates, effectively educated and placed its predominantly female students for many years. The emergence of a new ideal-type in the mid-1920s, the research university, reduced higher education's diversity and limited the options open to women.[104]

In the late 1930s, after Frederic B. Pratt's retirement, Pratt Institute began awarding degrees and in other ways conforming to mainstream higher education. The Library School, also under new management, remained a reputable program, but never regained the prominence it had enjoyed earlier.

Williamson's plans for library education were never fully implemented. In particular, lower level programs never became popular. He had recommended a separation as clear-cut as that between doctors and nurses. Women with the requisite level of education, however, were less anxious than Williamson supposed to enter a poorly paid subprofession. Even at the time he was writing his report, public library training classes were experiencing difficulty in recruiting students. The head of one such program in the early 1920s lamented that in one year almost 500 women inquired about the school, 249 took applications, 12 filed them, 8 took the exam, and only one of the expected class of 15 actually prepared to enroll. She attributed this to "the fact that to keep body and soul together costs money and that the initial salary at the completion of the training would not cover that cost and that the range of promotion did not justify the investment in the end."[105] Such training classes either transferred to academic institutions, becoming full-fledged library schools, or went out of business.

Williamson's recommendation that most library techniques be eliminated from the professional curriculum was not implemented either. For one thing, without a clear subprofessional level, there was no place to put them. For another, the technical aspects of librarianship, particularly cataloging and classification, were publicly recognized services performed by trained librarians. In the 19th century, the relentless self-publicist Melvil Dewey created a market for librarians trained in his techniques. According to Walkowitz, professionals attempt to "create a salable commodity within a market economy."[106] Dewey succeeded in this, at least to an extent. Other professionalizing occupations struggled much longer to create such a service commodity. Social workers, for example, did not settle on casework as their central service until almost 1920. Librarians would have been foolish to remove cataloging and classification from the library school curriculum before having an equally well-recognized service to replace them.

The new Carnegie-funded schools at the University of Chicago and Columbia were the most visible result of Williamson's recommendations. Rapidly assuming preeminence among library schools, they were far less hospitable to women than Pratt had been. Over time they came to resemble the elite schools of education described by Tyack and Hansot.[107] While most of the students were women, most of the administrators and senior faculty members were men whose primary interest was preparing male students for important administrative positions.

ENDNOTES

[1]Daniel J. Walkowitz, review of *From Charity to Enterprise; The Development of American Social Work in a Market Economy*, by Stanley Wenocur and Michael Reisch, in *The American Historical Review*, 95, no. 2 (April 1990): 622.

[2]Carl M. White, *A Historical Introduction to Library Education: Problems and Progress to 1951* (Metuchen, N.J.: Scarecrow Press, 1976).

[3]Pratt Institute. Brooklyn, *Progress and Pratt Institute*, [Brooklyn, 1965] p. 7; "Pratt, Frederic Bayley," *National Cyclopaedia of American Biography*, v. 34, 154–155;

"Pratt, Charles," *Dictionary of American Biography*, v. 168–169; "Pratt, Charles," *National Cyclopaedia of American Biography*, v. 26, 72–73.

[4]Robert C. Bannister, *Jessie Bernard: the Making of a Feminist* (New Brunswick and London: Rutgers University Press, 1991), 9.

[5]Anne Carroll Moore, " Our Frontispiece: Mary Wright Plummer, 1856–1916," *Bulletin of Bibliography* 14 no.1 (January–April 1930): 2.

[6]Nasser Sharify, "The Pratt Institute Graduate School of Library and Information Science," in *The Encyclopedia of Library and Information Science*, v. 23 (New York: Marcel Dekker, Inc., 1978), 145–150.

[7]R.R. Bowker, "Memorial for Mary Wright Plummer."*Library Journal* 41 no. 12 (December 1916): 867.

[8]Sharify, "The Pratt Institute Graduate School of Library and Information Science," 149.

[9]Nordica Fenneman, "Recollections of Josephine Adams Rathbone," *Wilson Library Bulletin* Vol. 23 no. 10 (June 1949): 773–74.

[10]"Interview with Rice Estes," *GSLIS Perspectives* 2 (Spring 1976): 10.

[11]Edward F. Stevens, "Report to the Trustees, 1929–30," p. 3, Pratt Institute Archives.

[12]Josephine Rathbone, "Report to the Director, 1921–22," p. 22, Pratt Institute Archives.

[13]Wayne Shirley, "Josephine Adams Rathbone," *Wilson Library Bulletin* 34 no. 3 (November 1959): 202.

[14]Ibid.

[15]Josephine Adams Rathbone, "Creative Librarianship," *ALA Bulletin* (May 1932): 306–307.

[16]Josephine Adams Rathbone, "Some Aspects of Our Personal Life," *Public Libraries* 21 no. 2 (February, 1916): 55.

[17]Rathbone, "Creative Librarianship," p. 309.

[18]Shirley, "Rathbone," p. 201.

[19]Josephine Rathbone, "Pioneers of the Library Profession," *Wilson Library Bulletin* 23 no. 10 (June 1949): 775–779.

[20]Josephine Rathbone, "Report to the Director, 1911–13", p. 30, Pratt Institute Archives.

[21]Josephine Rathbone, "The Pratt Institute School of Library Science," *ALA Bulletin* 46 (1921): 935.

[22]Edward F. Stevens, "Report to the Trustees, 11/1/1914," p. 4, Pratt Institute Archives.

[23]Stevens, "Report to the Trustees, Nov. 1, 1915," Pratt Institute Archives.

[24]Rathbone, "Report to the Director, 1925–26," p. 22, Pratt Institute Archives.

[25]Rathbone, "Report to the Director, 1928–29," p. 20, Pratt Institute Archives.

[26]Rathbone, "Report to the Director, 1915–16", p. 21, PIA.

[27]Rathbone, "Report to the Director, 1913", p. 30, PIA.

[28]Rathbone, "Report to the Director, 1925–26," p. 23, PIA.

[29]Rathbone, "Report to the Director, 1928–29," p. 21, PIA.

[30]Rathbone, "Report to the Director, 1914–15, p. 26, PIA.

[31]Rathbone, "Report to the Director, 1916–17, p. 26, PIA.

[32]Margaret W. Rossiter, *Women Scientists in America: Struggles and Strategies to 1940* (Baltimore: Johns Hopkins University Press, 1982): 175.

[33]Ellen Condliffe Lagemann, *Private Power for the Public Good: A History of the Carnegie Foundation for the Advancement of Teaching*(Middletown, Connecticut: Wesleyan University Press, 1983): 40.

[34]Sarah K. Vann, *Training for Librarianship Before 1923; Education for Librarianship Prior to the Publication of Williamson's Report on Training for Library Service* (Chicago: American Library Association, 1961): 169.

[35]Constance Bement, "The Library Worker Speaks Out," in *The Library and its Workers; Reprints of Articles and Addresses*, ed. Jessie Sargent McNiece (New York: H.W. Wilson, 1929), pp. 217–220).

[36]Alvin Johnson, *Pioneer's Progress: An Autobiography* (New York: Viking Press, 1952), p. 238 cited by Lagemann, *Private Power for the Public Good*, p. 41.

[37]Ibid. p. 236, cited by Lagemann, *Private Power for the Public Good.* p. 26.

[38]Dorothy Ross, "The Development of the Social Sciences," in *The Organization of Knowledge in Modern America, 1860–1920*, eds. A. Oleson and J. Voss (Baltimore: Johns Hopkins University Press,): 107–137.

[39]Charles C. Williamson, "Statement Prepared for the Use of Miss Sarah K. Vann . . . June 1955," in *The Williamson Reports: a Study*, Sarah K. Vann (Metuchen, N.J.: Scarecrow Press, 1971), pp. 179–192; *Dictionary of American Library Biography*, s.v. "Williamson, Charles Clarence," by Paul A. Winckler.

[40]Charles C. Williamson, "Training for Library Work (1921)" in *The Williamson Reports of 1921 and 1923* ed. Sarah K. Vann (Metuchen, N.J.: The Scarecrow Press, 1971), p. 185.

[41]Ibid., p. 5.

[42]Ibid., p. 14.

[43]Ibid., pp. 44, 49, 50.

[44]Ibid., p. 101.

[45]Ibid., p. 122–23.

[46]Ibid., p. 55–56.

[47]Ibid., p. 53.

[48]Ibid., p. 58.

[49]Ibid., p. 99.

[50]Ibid., p. 59.

[51]Ibid., p. 14.

[52]Ibid., p. 29.

[53]Ibid., p. 62.

[54]Ibid., p. 63.

[55]Ibid., p. 79.

[56]Ibid., p. 82, 88.

[57]Ibid., p. 63.

[58]Ibid., p. 41.

[59]Ibid., p. 16.

[60]Ibid., p. 124.

[61]Ibid., p. 15.

[62]Ibid., p. 85.

[63]Ibid., p. 95.

[64]Ibid., p. 10.

[65]Ibid., p. 15.

[66]Ibid., p. 180.

[67]Ibid., p. 149.

[68]Ibid., p. 17.

[69]Ibid., pp. 230–31.

[70]Lagemann, *The Politics of Knowledge*, p. 113.

[71]Stevens, "Report to the Trustees, 1923–24," pp.3–5, PIA.

[72]"The Williamson Report: Comments from the Library Schools," *Library Journal* 48 no. 19 (1 November 1923): 900.

[73]Charles C. Williamson, *Training for Library Service: A Report Prepared for the Carnegie Corporation of New York* (New York, 1923) reprinted in *The Williamson Reports of 1921 and 1923*, ed. Sarah K. Vann (Metuchen, N.J.: The Scarecrow Press, 1971), pp. 24–25.

[74]"The Williamson Report," p. 901.

[75]Williamson, *Training for Library Service*, pp. 31–32.

[76]"The Williamson Report," p. 901.

[77]Ibid., p. 902.

[78]Williamson, *Training for Library Service*, p. 5.

[79]"The Williamson Report," p. 902.

[80]Rathbone to Sarah Bogle January 15, 1925, ALA Archives, record series 28/50/5–7

[81]ALA Board of Education for Librarianship, "Report on Pratt Institute School of Library Science, visited Oct 28, 1924," ALA Archives, record series 28/50/5–7.

[82]Edward F. Stevens to Adam Strohm June 18,1925, ALA Archives, record series 28/50/5–7.

[83]Rathbone to Strohm, June 18, 1925, ALA Archives, record series 28/50/5–7.

[84]Rathbone, "Report to the Director, 1924–25," p. 18.

[85]Rathbone, "Report to the Director, 1927–28," p. 20.

[86]Rathbone, "Report to the Director, 1928–29," p. 17.

[87]Rathbone to Strohm, Sept 19, 1928 ALA Archives, record series 28/50/5–7.

[88]Rathbone to Bogle, Sept. 21, 1928, ALA Archives, record series 28/50/5–7.

[89]Strohm to Rathbone, Sept. 26, 1926, ALA Archives, record series 28/50/5–7.

[90]Rathbone to Strohm, Oct. 1, 1928, ALA Archives, record series 28/50/5–7.

[91]s.v. Meyer, Herman H.B. *Dictionary of American Library Biography* pp. 363–64.

[92][H.H.B. Meyers], "Statement concerning the Grading of Pratt Institute Library School [presented at the meeting of the BEL, Oct. 5–6, 1928]", ALA Archives, record series 28/50/5–7.

[93]Bogel to Stevens, July 24, 1929 ALA Archives, record series 28/50/5–7.

[94]Louis R. Wilson to Anita M. Hostetter, March 28, 1929, ALA Archives, record series 28/50/5–7.

[95]Bogle to Stevens, July 24, 1929, ALA Archives, record series 28/50/5–7.

[96]Rathbone to Harrison W. Craver, Sept. 27, 1929, ALA Archives record series 28/50/5–7.

[97]Nasser Sharify, "The Pratt Institute Graduate School of Library and Information Science," in *The Encyclopedia of Library and Information Science*, vol. 23, p. 151.

[98]Stevens, "Report to the Trustees, 1928," p. 6.

[99]Stevens, "Report to the Trustees, 1933," p. 6.

[100]Shirley, pp. 201, 203.

[101]Clifford, Geraldine Joncich, "Introduction" to *Lone Voyagers: Academic Women in Coeducational Universities, 1870–1937* (New York: Feminist Press, 1989).

[102]"Interview with Rice Estes," *GSLIS Perspectives*, v. 2, p. 10, Spring 1976 (unnumbered) cited in Karlowich, Robert A. and Rhoda Garoogian, "From the Beginning: Two Pioneer Women in Library Education," *The Bookmark* v. 48 no. 1 (Fall 1989) p. 65.

[103]Stevens to Rathbone, November 14, 1935, PIA.

[104]Patricia Albjerg Graham, "Expansion and Exclusion: a History of Women in American Higher Education." *Signs* vol. 3 no.4 (Summer 1978): 761) 110.

[105]Clara W. Herbert, "Recruiting a Training Class." In *The Library and Its Workers: Reprints of Articles and Addresses,* ed. Jessie Sargent McNiece (New York: H. W. Wilson company, 1929) p. 110.

[106]Walkowitz, Review, p. 623.

[107]David B. Tyack and Elisabeth Hansot, *Managers of Virtue: Public School Leadership in America, 1820–1980* (New York: Basic Books, 1982), pp. 140–144.

chapter 12

Women's Unpaid Labor in Libraries: Change and Continuity

Cheryl Knott Malone

One hundred years ago, women's volunteer work on behalf of libraries represented strength and expansion. Philanthropic women worked in autonomous associations to create new public institutions for their communities and new public roles for themselves as activists and professionals. As historian Kathleen D. McCarthy has put it, such women "forged parallel power structures to those used by men, creating a growing array of opportunities for their sisters and themselves."[1]

Today, women's volunteer work in libraries no longer symbolizes the strength of women or the expansion of public institutions. Serving in individual institutions, volunteers work largely as rank-and-file staff members, handling routine tasks under the supervision of library employees. In the changed circumstances of the late 20th century, continued reliance on unpaid labor reveals a great deal about the status of women, the state of librarianship, and the standing of public libraries. This paper explores the evolution of women's unpaid labor on behalf of U.S. libraries, then discusses the gender dimension of those developments.

MODERN ORIGINS OF VOLUNTEER WORK

Women's work in today's libraries in the United States has its roots in the late 18th-century notion identified as "Republican Motherhood," an ideology that restricted women's civic participation to the domestic sphere where they were to produce educated sons who would make wise use of their voting rights. Despite its intended restrictions, Republican Motherhood provided justification for pursuing literacy and, more broadly, education.[2] Simultaneously, women began joining voluntary associations, those supposedly classically American entities that allowed the disenfranchised and others to act as coequals with and alternatives to the state.[3] Initial efforts were in benevolent organizations ostensibly guided by clergymen, but early on women founded and ran their own groups. Those associations eventually achieved, among other things, the establishment and maintenance of many of the public libraries in the United States.[4] American women's historical connection to education and literacy movements and to unpaid labor in and out of the home fostered a legacy of public service manifest in such activities as library work, paid or not. More directly, voluntary efforts to found and maintain libraries developed out of the social and cultural interests of the women's clubs and literary associations that blossomed in the last quarter of the 19th century.[5]

Motivation for founding libraries came from several sources: the urge to build cities complete with civic refinements, the altruistic desire to provide reading material and uplift to the general public, and the need for collections and study space created by literary clubs. One club woman wrote, "Because public amusements are fewer, and libraries less accessible, the women of the Western towns devote their energies to aiding these factors of civilization. In almost every case, an association of women in Kansas, Wisconsin, Iowa, or elsewhere, means a club for the promotion and guidance of pleasure among the young, and the collecting, studying, and circulating of good books."[6] In Michigan towns such as Manchester, Marcellus, Hesperia and Holly, Ladies' Library Associations formed subscription collections and then converted them to township libraries.[7] Further west, in the small town of Detroit, Minnesota, the Ladies Library Club established a collection, secured housing for it, then took turns serving as unpaid librarians.[8] In her 1915 overview, *Women's Work in Municipalities*, Mary Ritter Beard noted the altruistic spirit evident in the women's clubs that had founded libraries.[9]

But self-interest also figured in women's founding of libraries. One motive behind establishing libraries—as collections and as places—was the need for space in which women's intellectual activities were encouraged. For the young, single, middle- and upper-middle-class, women's colleges provided such a space. But for the majority of white, middle-class, middle-aged, married mothers, women's study clubs were the only hope for self-education. As one advocate wrote: "What college life is to the young woman, club life is to the woman of riper years, who amidst the responsibilities and cares of home-life still wishes to keep abreast of the times. . . . Club life supplies in some degree the place of higher education to those women who have been deprived of the advantages of a college course."[10] In her fictionalized account of a young mother and study club member in 1875, Helen Hooven Santmyer alluded to the difficulty of mixing domestic responsibilities with intellectual pursuits. One of the main characters, who later was instrumental in founding the town library, set to work on a paper she was to read before the club by loading the baby carriage with baby, paper, pencils, a book, and some notes and wheeling to the edge of the porch where she settled with her lap desk and the baby kicked at her papers.[11]

The hubbub of home life interfered with women's attempts at self-education. Even the home library offered no relief. The library, formerly the one masculine space in the otherwise fussy, feminized, and consumer-conscious interiors of the Victorian period[12] was being reinterpreted as family space. Candace Wheeler, an interior designer who had decorated the library in the Woman's Building at the Chicago World's Fair in 1893, wrote, "A library in ordinary family life . . . is not only to hold books, but to make the family at home in a literary atmosphere. Such a room is apt to be a fascinating one by reason of this very variety of use and purpose, and because it is a centre for all the family treasures. Books, pictures, papers, photographs, bits of decorative needlework, all centre here."[13] Whether masculine space or family area, the home library seems not to have served as the "room of one's own" Virginia Woolf considered essential for the pursuit of creative, intellectual activity.[14] It soon became obvious to the women participating in study clubs that they needed not only books to study, but also a place for studying where the books could be brought together.

Some of the wealthier and more ambitious clubs built clubhouses complete with libraries.[15] An example of the passion for clubhouse construction and the importance of books and reading to the lives of club women can be seen in the 1893 erection of the Woman's Building at the Columbian Exposition in Chicago. This two-story structure featured a library of 7,000 books by women authors and a nursery where mothers could drop off their children before touring the fair.[16] The books were for exhibit rather than use, though; the Exposition's Board of Lady Managers had directed interior designer Wheeler "to make the room comfortable and home-like, since the Board wanted the library to be a place where visitors could settle down for a while, and chat with the librarian."[17] The librarian was there to promote libraries, and the Board hoped that visitors would chat with her, especially about women writers. Thus inspired, they were to return home to found local libraries.[18]

And so they did. In 1898, the Texas Federation of Women's Club's president, Mrs. J. C. Terrell, followed the national federation's lead by announcing that the founding of community libraries was the state organization's chief mission.[19] In 1903 the Tennessee Federation of Women's Clubs operated 75 libraries open to the public in that state.[20] By 1904, when the General Federation of Women's Clubs held its seventh biennial meeting, clubs in the 34 member states ran more than 4600 traveling libraries and had established almost 500 public libraries.[21]

In Houston, for instance, club women were instrumental in securing a public library for the city around the turn of the century. In 1894, the Ladies' Reading Club successfully petitioned the private Lyceum to make its library available to non-members for home use and to move it from Market House, which was situated in an area not frequented by ladies, to a more accessible location. Consequently, when the Lyceum hired its first female librarian, she instituted a "ladies day" once or twice a month and worked hard to keep the city's various women's organizations aware of the library and its availability. Then the City Federation of Women's Clubs transformed the Lyceum into a free public library, from a male bastion to a place where women were welcome, securing funding from both Andrew Carnegie and the Houston city council. The Ladies' Reading Club paid for and oversaw the furnishing of a meeting room in the new library for the women's federation's literary clubs.[22] The Texas Federation sponsored the opening ceremony, and Katherine Finnigan Anderson evoked the library as a place for reflective thought in her sonnet to mark the occasion:

. . . come and bide
In this sequestered world of thought, aside
From every jarring sound which frets the ear
Or cumbereth the soul with anxious fear.
Enter these portals and in peace abide![23]

In the course of such work, club women stretched the boundaries circumscribing female participation in the public sphere. Their associations were vehicles for influencing community life, identifying and solving social problems, and shaping the built environment.[24] Membership afforded individual women self-confidence, support, and an expanded communications network.[25] Numerous public libraries had their beginnings thanks to the women who approached Carnegie for funding, hounded the community for support, saw to the construction of buildings, the hiring of staff, and the development of collections, and lobbied government for adequate budgets.[26] Progressive women assumed that their civic work would call to the government's attention its rightful responsibilities to sustain the kindergartens, parks, libraries, and similar needed institutions that volunteers had established.[27] What they could not foresee was that women's unpaid labor would still be necessary even after libraries became public institutions.

TRANSFORMATION OF VOLUNTEER WORK

The transformation of the locus of women's voluntary efforts from autonomous associations to established institutions coincided with a variety of developments in the middle of the 20th century. The close of World War II marked the end of a long period of want for most Americans. The economy broke growth records and shifted, by the middle of the 1950s, from a heavy-industry emphasis to the service sector as the primary source of employment. For the first time, American hospitals began to employ more people than the steel industry, automobile factories, or interstate railroads.[28] At the same time, the population boom forced the public school system to accommodate increasing numbers of new students. In the emerging service sector, women workers predominated.

In the not-for-profit arena, volunteers became integral to the provision of services.[29] The trend began in the health care industry, following the example of the Red Cross during wartime. By 1947, the American Hospital Association had added a volunteer-auxiliary division, and by 1950 an estimated half-million women were working without pay in hospitals, with that figure quadrupling by 1964.[30] Health care volunteerism served as an example for others, including educators and librarians, who continued to note hospitals' successful use of volunteers into the 1980s.[31]

By mid-century the women's club movement no longer played the highly visible role it had before. Sporadic reports of library volunteers indicated they were likely to be individuals working on behalf of a single local institution. For instance, the New Orleans Public Library in the late 1940s retained the practice of using volunteers begun during wartime personnel shortages.[32] At the San Diego Public Library, retired librarians returned to complete special projects without compensation.[33]

The initial drive for the systematic incorporation of volunteer labor into the library workplace occurred in the most feminized area of a predominately female occupation, in the school library.[34] Schools and libraries had suffered during the Great Depression and then the war as public resources went to fund crisis operations. They struggled afterward amidst debate about the propriety of federal funding for education, the apparent shortage of teachers and librarians (which ultimately helped solidify the positions of teacher's aides and library assistants), and the baby boom. The first full-blown school volunteer program began with 20 volunteers in New York City in 1956, with sponsorship by the Public Education Association and support from the Ford Foundation.[35] By 1967, the New York City school system ratio of paid to volunteer aides was 9,150 to 1,850; 17% of the system's teacher's aides were not paid for their work.[36]

The New York experience became a model for the incorporation of unpaid labor in the schools, so that by the late 1970s as many as 5 million volunteers were estimated to be working in public education.[37] School libraries benefited from the availability of such willing unpaid workers. The professionalization of librarianship and the growth of the schools had led to an increase in the number of school libraries; in 1945, there were 19,000; in 1962, a little more that 49,000; by 1974, there were almost 75,000 school libraries.[38] Despite this growth, the library profession had failed to attain consensus on the need for libraries in every public school and librarians in every library. In 1957, Mary Peacock Douglas published a book advocating the use of student assistants in school libraries.[39] In 1958, in a widely distributed American Library Association pamphlet entitled *Every Child Needs a School Library,* Mary Virginia Gaver wrote that most elementary schools had neither a library nor a librarian.[40] In its *Standards for School Library Programs* issued in 1960, the American Association of School Librarians acknowledged both the shortage of librarians and its seemingly logical outcome, the use of volunteers. AASL warned, "Volunteer student help in the library should never be exploited, and under no circumstances should it be used as a substitute for paid clerical assistance or janitorial work."[41] But a survey conducted in 1969 belied those good intentions, reporting that school-library volunteers generally performed tasks in the "preparation of materials" category of 17 activities including labeling, typing, attaching plastic jackets, and gluing pockets and date-due slips in books.[42] In 1960–1961, more than 266,000 volunteer student assistants (compared to 4,200 paid adult clerks) worked in centralized school libraries.[43]

In Houston in 1956, all of the junior and senior high schools had librarians, but the 60 elementary schools shared 10 librarians. Consequently, volunteers made up an important component of the library staff. The Houston school district reported that "since the librarian is not in the school regularly, much of the organization and administration is carried out by Parent-Teacher Association mothers, under the supervision of the Library Department."[44] Houston was not alone. Cleveland had several dozen volunteers in four school libraries in 1959. By 1967, every one of the 136 schools in Cleveland had libraries for which volunteers had raised the money, supplied the books, and provided the staff. In 1966, no elementary school in Boston had a central library, but by 1970, under the supervision of a librarian working with volunteers, virtually every school had one.[45] Volunteers painted walls; installed shelves; put up curtains, pictures, and travel posters; and processed, catalogued, and shelved thousands of books. By 1975, 90% of the school libraries and 60% of the public libraries responding to a United States Department of Labor survey reported using volunteers.[46]

The National Education Association's *School Library Personnel Task Analysis Survey* reported on the growth of school libraries after passage of the Elementary and Secondary Education Act in 1965. The act's Title II made appropriations available for library programs and materials, and as those increased, so did the number of staff members, especially the nonprofessionals. The survey found a direct correlation between size of enrollment and size of staff: "As student enrollment increased, so did the percentage of library media centers with paid staffs of four to five and six or more."[47] The survey also noted the traditional use of adult and student volunteer workers—of the 694 schools represented in the survey sample, 225 (32 percent) used adult volunteers, and 634 (91 percent) used student assistants. At higher grade levels, students replaced the adult volunteers. About half of the elementary schools surveyed used adult volunteers, but less than one quarter of the secondary schools did.[48] The statistics point to a life cycle among women volunteers, working in the schools when their children were young and later being displaced by students old enough to handle library work.

Public libraries were slower than school libraries to adopt volunteerism as a solution to budget problems and the public-relations issues that accompanied them. The pressures of the post-war baby boom forced the issue in school libraries earlier; the tax revolts of the early 1970s seem to have spawned some public libraries' volunteer programs, while the supply-side economics and private-sector initiatives of the 1980s furthered the move to unpaid staff members. Though later in coming to the widespread use of volunteers, public libraries repeated some of the patterns of school libraries. For instance, a survey of school libraries found that as paid staff size increased, the use of volunteers decreased. Of the surveyed elementary and secondary school libraries with two or three paid staff members, 71% used adult volunteers; 17% of those with four or five paid staffers did; and only 12% of those with six or more did.[49] In other words, when funding was adequate, unpaid workers were not needed. Similarly, a New Jersey survey found that public libraries with below-average budgets, fewer professional librarians, smaller collections, and shorter service hours had more volunteers on average than other libraries.[50]

THE LURE OF VOLUNTEERING

Women who joined the ranks of volunteers after the middle of the 20th century responded to factors that pulled them into the unpaid workforce. Amidst the booming economy of the 1950s and 1960s, support for hospitals, schools, and libraries typically took the bricks-and-mortar form, providing new buildings and services without necessarily ensuring sufficient staff. Even before the taxpayers' revolts of the late 1970s, some libraries chose to implement volunteer programs rather than trim their services to match local taxpayers' parsimony. A 1975 survey of libraries reported:

> The amount of labor contributed by library volunteers is modest in comparison with the hours worked by regular staff members. In most cases, library administrators appear to make a conscious effort to ensure that volunteers are not used as a low-cost substitute for regular staff. This is not always the case, however. A few libraries reported that recent budget cuts had forced staff cuts and, as a result, continuation of certain library services depended entirely on the availability of volunteers.[51]

In California, later events provided an impetus for rationalizing larger-scale use of volunteer workers. The Los Angeles Public Library employed 1,112 full-time-equivalent employees just before the Proposition 13 property-tax cut in 1978, but suffered a 10% decrease in staffing and a 40% decrease in book purchasing power after. By fiscal year 1984–1985, the first accounting of in-house and branch volunteers indicated that 1,344 individuals had provided more than 23,500 work hours for the year. That same year, the Service to Shut-ins, organized with the help of a local women's club, numbered 503 volunteers who gave almost 13,700 hours delivering library materials.[52]

The Los Angeles example was not unique. Ventura County libraries began using volunteers after the County Board of Supervisors refused to allow branch libraries to close in the Proposition 13 aftermath.[53] When the tax rollback passed, San Diego's public library lost $1 million, 40 librarians, and 30 clerks. Forty volunteers had been working for the library then; three years later, there were 150.[54] When trying to estimate the value of those volunteers, library officials calculated their hourly rate at $5 in 1983, considerably higher than the minimum wage.[55] That may have been not only a symbolic acknowledgement of the volunteers' worth, but also a real indicator of the level of work performed.

Clearly, use of volunteer workers resulted not only from management initiative or citizen assertiveness, but also from shifts in government policy. George Bobinski has traced the beginning of the end of the "Golden Age" of libraries to 1968 and the Nixon administration's desire to let libraries rely on state and local governments.[56] Many of the so-called private-sector initiatives touted during the Reagan and Bush years were in fact governmental programs offering incentives for recruiting unpaid workers to deliver public services. The need to demonstrate citizen participation and enthusiasm when proposing federal funding for local projects often translated into the use of volunteers, who provided legitimacy as well as labor.

The Library Services and Construction Act offered good examples. LSCA seed money started a volunteer program in Carroll County, Maryland, libraries in 1981, enabling the establishment of new programs with the resulting 150 hours of volunteer work per week.[57] In 1984, the Library of California set aside $2.5 million dollars of LSCA Title I funding for community-based literacy programs using volunteers.[58] Title VI of the LSCA gave grants for library-based literacy programs, a traditionally volunteer-dependent area of service.[59] Among the 1988 grant recipients was the Fremont County (Wyoming) Library, which received almost $20,000 to develop "a resource and referral center for literacy volunteers and learners."[60] LSCA Title I funds that year also supported the Kansas State Library's literacy program with a grant of $33,000 to provide, among other things, training for volunteers.[61] Library volunteer programs have started from other federally funded initiatives as well, including the Retired Senior Volunteer Program, which helped start the Pine Bluff, Arkansas, library volunteer program in 1975, for instance.[62]

Even on the local level, and perhaps more obviously, government actions affected libraries' willingness to use volunteers. In Virginia, the Prince William Public Library volunteer program traced its beginning to a Board of Supervisors decision to channel funds to police and schools rather than libraries.[63] Pennsylvania encouraged its libraries and other agencies to increase their reliance on volunteers by linking the amount of state aid provided to the amount of volunteer hours worked.[64]

Sociologists have coined the term "coproduction" to describe "the voluntary collaboration of citizens with paid employees of government agencies for the provision of public services."[65] This generally is construed as a populist democratic-participation movement, but this theory of volunteer work is diluted by realities such as stagnant budgets coupled with the same or higher levels of service. After all, how meaningful is the government-mandated use of volunteers? Nowhere is volunteer work more coercive than in the use of court-appointed "volunteers" sentenced to community service. In fiscal year 1979–1980, for example, the Leon County (Florida) Public Library reported receiving 5,982 volunteer-service hours, of which 2,221 were contributed by court-appointed workers.[66]

GENDER AS A FACTOR

The gender dimension of volunteer work in libraries is apparent in three major ways. First, gender ideology has influenced the nature and function of volunteer work. Second, the availability of unpaid women workers has shaped and been shaped by librarianship. And third, gender generally has not been considered an important philosophical or material issue, when it has been acknowledged at all.

Ideas about appropriate gender roles helped push women out of the private unpaid workplace of the home and into the unpaid workplace of public life. During the 19th century, women were considered especially fit for benevolent activity because of their assumed higher moral nature. Progressive-era women used that argument to open all sorts of avenues, particularly civic and political, to their influence. By the middle of the 20th century, men and women were still thought to occupy separate spheres. In the new context of suburban living middle-class white women, the traditional volunteer workforce, were isolated, and popular psychology condemned their supposed abundance of leisure.

Consequently, the desire for adult interaction motivated some women to join the ranks of volunteers. Guilty feelings about not contributing to the larger world propelled some stay-at-home mothers, especially those who had gone to college to prepare themselves for something more than marriage and childrearing, into the unpaid workforce. Some women did volunteer work because it kept up skills they hoped to use later in paid employment. Gender- and class-based expectations about corporate wives precluded paid employment but made volunteer work acceptable, as long as it did not conflict with domestic duties. The all-encompassing responsibilities of motherhood extended to serving as "Room Mothers" in the schools or to founding libraries for children and others to use.[67] For African-American women, participation in volunteer labor helped provide needed services that their communities otherwise would not have had.[68] In 1955 Melvin Glasser listed the main reasons for volunteering, including availability of leisure time, existence of educated women with time on their hands, decline of family-oriented recreation, desire to accomplish something, opportunity to learn new skills, use existing ones, discover new talents, and achieve recognition and status.[69] These reasons, viewed in light of the prevailing attitude that women should put their husbands and children first, revealed a great deal about the motivations that made part-time volunteer work an attractive alternative to full-time paid employment and a welcome relief from around-the-clock domesticity. One elementary-school principal went so far as to suggest that volunteer work was the antidote to what Betty Friedan had identified in *The Feminine Mystique* as housewife's malaise.[70]

Thus, volunteer work sometimes functioned to appropriate and organize whatever leisure time women had. It also offered a potentially liberating alternative to full-time paid employment and unpaid domestic duties. One volunteer recruiter wrote "that for many of today's women who . . . have led the life principally of wife and mother, a heavy volunteer commitment can . . . help to make them freer and more liberated women."[71] But, far from liberating women from the service orientation and clerical nature of most female employment, volunteer work prepared them for it. For example, three of the 66 mothers trained to be volunteers at a Connecticut elementary-school library that could not afford a paid professional in the early 1960s went back to school to become professional librarians.[72] The individuals who made such choices may have experienced them as positive steps in the transition from unpaid domesticity to the paid labor force and the promise of greater economic self-reliance. Nevertheless, volunteer work shaped vocational choices, readying many women for life in the predominately female occupations.

Statistical analyses of volunteer work show that it follows the structure of paid labor. That is, women's volunteer work is concentrated in the service industries of education, health care, and social services. For instance, during the survey week in a 1965 government study, 18% of the male volunteers reported donating their time to activities involving education compared to 34% of the female volunteers.[73] The survey also found that women were doing more volunteer work than men. Among the men, 9.5 million (85% of them in the paid labor force) had performed some volunteer work during the year while 14.8 million women, 36% of them engaged in paid employment, had.[74]

Many of those women who were not employed for pay probably hoped to use the skills learned on volunteer jobs to get paying positions later, just as volunteer recruiters told them they could. But they were preparing to enter a labor force in which duties were assigned along gender lines, with negative economic consequences for women. Women have predominated in lower-paid clerical and service occupations and in the professional fields of teaching, nursing, social work, and librarianship while men have earned more money in skilled and unskilled trades and in professions such as medicine and the law. Among women's jobs, librarianship was and remains a good choice in terms of remuneration. When compared to predominately male occupations, however, the pay lags. In 1974, for instance, within the Bureau of Labor Statistics category for professional, technical, and kindred workers, women earned $6,772 to men's $11,835 annually, a 57% gap.[75] This gender-based earnings gap, while fluctuating somewhat over time, has never come close to disappearing. In an earlier era, voluntary association activities had represented new opportunities; that was no longer the case after the middle of the 20th century.

Within this structure of occupational segregation, gender has confused the relationship of paid to unpaid library staff. Scholars who study professions and occupations have noted that in nursing and teaching, other so-called "semi-professions," the move toward professional status has been complicated, in sexist society, by the preponderance of women in the occupation.[76] In the history of American librarianship, at least since the watershed year 1876, professionalization has been a goal more than an achievement, if the voluminous literature documenting librarians' status anxiety is any indication. The tension and confusion resulting from attempts to gain professional status for a predominately female occupation are apparent in, for instance, Shera's derogatory references to "maiden aunts,"[77] a term that judges the professionalism of library workers on the bases of gender, marital status, and reproductive output. In the early years of professionalizing fervor, women, operating within the legacy of a sex role of selfless service, established and ran libraries without remuneration. Even those women who did secure paid positions in this new female field sometimes were so overworked and underpaid as to seem to be volunteers for at least part of the workday. In 1904, the head of the San Diego Public Library reported her staff's "rare devotion to their work, almost constantly working over hours even when worn by exhaustion and fatigue, and with a consciousness of salaries totally inadequate."[78]

RESISTANCE AND MANAGEMENT

One consequence of introducing volunteers into the bailiwick of women's work, then, has been the complicated interactions among women workers, some of them struggling for professional status, many of them with overlapping responsibilities, and virtually none of them receiving pay comparable to their worth. Volunteers work side-by-side with paid professional women who historically had to negotiate a place for themselves in the public arena legitimized by pay. The presence of volunteers evokes, however subtly, the traditional roles and services previously performed for no pay. Alongside the professional woman toiling for pay resides the image of the woman who asks nothing in return for her giving.

In trying to work out the relationship, paid library staff have either resisted or managed the volunteer force. When the administration at the University of California at Berkeley put forward the idea of using library volunteers in 1973, union members protested vehemently.[79] In 1975, Concerned Librarians Opposing Unprofessional Trends formed in Orange County, California, in part to resist the introduction of volunteer workers into staffing patterns.[80] Also that year, New York Public Library agreed with union demands not to use volunteers and in 1976 Leo Flanagan argued that the presence of volunteers undermined the professional status of librarians.[81] As late as 1984 Joseph Carvalho explored the problems attending the incorporation of unpaid employees into the workforce and argued that certain responsibilities and duties should be reserved exclusively for professional librarians, without suggesting exactly what those might be.[82] The topic received attention at professional gatherings as well; attendees at a 1976 conference heard one speaker warn:

> Volunteerism undermines staff morale, denigrates the work of professional staff, exploits workers, volunteers, and the public alike, disrupts the organization, and threatens the future of the institution itself. If volunteers did not leap into the breach created by failure to fund essential services . . . then funding for paid workers would be found.[83]

Despite several articulate denunciations of volunteer work, professional library literature contains proportionately few references to resistance on the part of paid employees. Instead, the professional journals have emphasized the importance of management and supervision, both to inspire cooperation in paid workers and to see that the unpaid fit in to existing hierarchical arrangements. When the women's professions suffered personnel shortages during the temporary return to the cult of domesticity that followed World War II, two-year colleges began establishing library technician programs to produce paraprofessionals who could help ameliorate the lack of librarians in the growing number of libraries. As libraries hired more and more paraprofessionals and clerical workers, more and more librarians found management and supervision to be major components of their jobs. As volunteers joined the workforce, professional librarians took on the task of managing them as well, viewing them as just another human resource.[84]

The library profession began to embrace the concept and the practice as a solution to at least some libraries' problems. Most of the articles on volunteer workers in libraries implicitly accept their presence there and focus instead on the practical problems of recruiting, training, retaining, evaluating, and rewarding these workers for whom regular paychecks were irrelevant. In 1988, a chapter on volunteers in *The Library Trustee: A Practical Guidebook* summed up at least two decades of librarians' thoughts on the subject by declaring that "Every Library Can Benefit from Working with Volunteers," cautioning that unpaid workers should not be used as replacements for paid staff and that, "Libraries need to hold out for having adequate paid staff to which can be added the work of volunteers."[85] It is not clear, though, why a library would want volunteers if it had a genuinely adequate staff to meet its mission and goals nor how it could "hold out" for better funding if it had already begun employing unpaid workers to provide services and complete routine tasks.

Judging from the burgeoning how-to literature on coordinating library volunteer programs, overseeing unpaid workers posed challenges not only for managing those workers but also for smoothing relations between paid and unpaid staff members. A school volunteer in 1965, for example, recommended that the Parent-Teacher Association recruit mothers to establish libraries in elementary and secondary schools and then work toward the employment of professional librarians in them. She went on to warn that if such mother-volunteers were successful, they should willingly give up their autonomy to defer to the supervision of the newly hired paid professional.[86] A librarian's status as a professional rests in some measure on the presence of lesser-status underlings, including volunteers. In small, one-professional libraries, the only staff members may be the volunteers. Women constitute the majority of library staff—whether paid or not—and the inclusion of volunteers adds an extra, complicating layer of what economists call labor-force segmentation, with the potential for competing interests and priorities.

The profession itself has done virtually nothing substantive to halt libraries' reliance on volunteer programs, no matter how they may undercut librarians' claims for professional status and libraries' requests for sufficient budgets. Three publications served as signs of the profession's ultimate acceptance of volunteer workers beginning in the 1970s. The American Library Association's Guidelines for Using Volunteers in Libraries, adopted in 1971 by the Board of Directors of the Library Administration Division,[87] by their very existence recognized the widespread use of unpaid workers and the potential for exploitation inherent in the volunteer movement. Ironically, the guidelines coincided with a National Organization for Women position paper linking women's service-oriented rather than activist volunteering to their exploitation in support of the status quo.[88] One of the ALA principles, that "volunteers should not supplant or displace established staff position spaces," was mitigated somewhat by another which held, "If it is essential that a minimum or basic library program be initiated or developed by volunteers, this use of voluntary persons should be considered as a temporary measure pending the employment of staff," and by a long list of the kinds of tasks volunteers could perform including such basics as "mending library materials; shelving returned materials; . . . collection of historical and archival materials; (and) . . . manning (sic) a circulation desk."[89] Because of their provenance and the resulting focus on management-related concerns, the guidelines took a practical approach typical of day-to-day administrators and supervisors rather than providing a discussion of the philosophical or ethical dilemmas raised by a volunteer presence.

Further evidence of the library profession's acceptance of volunteers came from *Library Journal,* which published special reports on the topic in 1977 and in 1983. Alice Sizer Warner and Elizabeth Bole Eddison produced the first one, which was prescriptive in nature and based not only on the authors' research but also on their own personal experiences as volunteers and volunteer coordinators. They asserted, "A special kind of spark is necessary for the basic strength of a volunteer program—a spark of belief in the inherent value of voluntary action."[90] Their report was a significant attempt to convince readers to join the volunteer movement. Six years later, the follow-up report indicated that librarians had been convinced, if not by *Library Journal,* then by budgetary vagaries and governmental policies. The second *Library Journal* special report served as a descriptive account of the widespread use of volunteers, especially in public libraries. Survey data and an appendix reproducing volunteer-management handbooks, letters, forms, and recognition awards from libraries across the country provided ample evidence that volunteer programs were no longer innovations but had become integral to the maintenance of services and collections at many institutions.[91] The late 20th-century trend in libraries is toward more volunteers and more hours worked by volunteers every year.[92]

Still, the gender dimension of volunteer work remains obscured. When President Bush spoke of "a thousand points of light," he was referring simply to "that vast galaxy of people and institutions working together to solve problems in their own backyard."[93] And when *Newsweek* followed up with a cover story on "The New Volunteers: America's Unsung Heroes," a highlighted synopsis listed facts about volunteers, including age, amount of time given, income level, and motivations, but not gender.[94] Within librarianship the management literature has ignored the implications of using unpaid women workers alongside paid. What little research has been conducted on the topic is engaged in answering important questions about volunteers other than their gender, perhaps because it is so obvious it seems foolish to pose the question.

CONCLUSION

With profound consequences, the profession in general and women in particular have participated in the 100-year transformation of women's volunteer library work from a wide-ranging, socially conscious, woman-oriented activity to a narrow, routinized, institution-specific series of tasks. Library volunteers of 100 years ago took the initiative to create a public space for themselves at a time when public libraries were still new and women had neither full public citizenship nor the vocational opportunities of today. In the 40 or so years spanning the turn of the last century, women's work in voluntary associations such as the General Federation of Women's Clubs permanently opened new avenues of female endeavor. Members learned how to organize, networked with like-minded women, and generally tested the waters of public life. After mid-century, the context, and so the meaning, of women's unpaid work changed. The continuing presence of volunteer workers in libraries signals the failure of librarians to prevent the use of unpaid workers and the failure of communities to provide adequate funding for their libraries. Volunteers thus have mediated both the budgetary and staffing shortfalls common to many libraries and the contested domain of women in the workforce.

That women's unpaid labor contributed so significantly to the development of the modern library movement is not surprising. That it continues to do so, however, is perhaps a commentary on the ultimate state of the modern library age

ENDNOTES

[1]Kathleen D. McCarthy, "Parallel Power Structures: Women and the Voluntary Sphere," in *Lady Bountiful Revisited: Women, Philanthropy, and Power,* ed. Kathleen D. McCarthy (New Brunswick, NJ: Rutgers University Press, 1990), 1. Among the books that reinforce this position are: Anne Firor Scott, *Natural Allies: Women's Associations in American History* (Urbana, IL: University of Illinois Press, 1991); Lori D. Ginzberg, *Women and the Work of Benevolence: Morality, Politics, and Class in the Nineteenth-Century United States* (New Haven, CT: Yale University Press, 1990); Barbara J. Berg, *The Remembered Gate: Origins of American Feminism: The Woman and the City, 1800–1860* (New York: Oxford University Press, 1978).

[2]Mary Beth Norton and others, *A People and a Nation: A History of the United States,* 2nd ed., (Boston: Houghton Mifflin, 1986), *Vol. I: To 1877,* 154; Mary P. Ryan, *Womanhood in America* (New York: New Viewpoints, 1975), pp. 128–129, 230–232.

[3]*Encyclopedia of American Political History* (New York: Scribner's, 1984), s.v. "Voluntary Associations," by John S. Gilkeson, Jr.

[4]Ginzberg, *Work of Benevolence,* 37; Anne Firor Scott, "Women and Libraries," *Journal of Library History* 21 (1986): 400–405.

[5]Ibid.; Theodora Penny Martin, *The Sound of Our Own Voices: Women's Study Clubs, 1860–1910* (Boston: Beacon Press, 1987).

[6]Alice Hyneman Rhine, "The Work of Women's Clubs," *The Forum* 12 (September 1891–February 1892): 522.

[7]G.M. Walton, *Libraries in Michigan: An Historical Sketch* (Lansing: Michigan State Library, 1926), pp. 10–12.

[8]*Fifth Biennial Report of the Minnesota Public Library Commission, 1907–1908* (St. Paul: The Commission, 1908), p. 18.

[9]Mary Ritter Beard, *Woman's Work in Municipalities* (New York: D. Appleton, 1915), p. 43.

[10]Ella D. Clymer, "The National Value of Women's Clubs," in ed. Rachel F. Avery, *Transactions of the National Council of Women of the United States, Assembled in Washington, D.C., February 22 to 25, 1891* (Philadelphia: The Council, 1891), p. 297, quoted in Martin, *Sound of Our Own Voices,* pp. 45–46.

[11]Helen Hooven Santmyer, *And Ladies of the Club* (New York: Berkley Books, 1985), p. 231.

[12]Cynthia Brandimarte, "Domesticity and Texas Women," paper presented at "Women and Texas History: A Conference," sponsored by the Texas State Historical Association, Austin, TX, October 4–6, 1990.

[13]Candace Wheeler, *Principles of Home Decoration* (New York: Doubleday, Page, 1908), pp. 199–200.

[14]Virginia Woolf, *A Room of One's Own* (London: Hogarth Press, 1929; reprint ed., New York: Harcourt Brace Jovanovich, 1957).

[15]Jane Cunningham Croly, *The History of the Woman's Club Movement in America* (New York: H.G. Allen, [1898]), pp. 54–57, 70, 72, 125, 137, 385, 402–404, 409.

[16]Jeanne Madeline Weimann, *The Fair Women* (Chicago: Academy, 1981), p. 369; James William Buel, *The Magic City* (St. Louis: Historical Publishing Co., 1894; reprint ed., New York: Arno Press, 1974), n.p.

[17]Weimann, *Fair Women,* p. 359.

[18]Ibid.

[19]Stella L. Christian, ed., *The History of the Texas Federation of Women's Clubs* (Houston: Dealey-Adey-Elgin Co., 1919; reprint ed., Seagraves, TX: Pioneer Book Publishers, 1986), 29–30.

[20]Tennessee Federation of Women's Clubs, *Woman's Work in Tennessee* (Memphis: Jones–Briggs Co., 1916), p. 31.

[21]Megan Seaholm, "Earnest Women: The White Woman's Club Movement in Progressive Era Texas, 1880–1920" (Ph.D. dissertation, Rice University, 1988), 175, n. 160.

[22]Orin Walker Hatch, *Lyceum to Library: A Chapter in the Cultural History of Houston* (Houston: Texas Gulf Coast Historical Association, 1965), pp. 40–41, 44, 47–49.

[23]Ibid., p. 49.

[24]Scott, *Natural Allies,* pp. 177–178.

[25]Ibid., pp. 178–180.

[26]Seaholm, "Earnest Women," p. 130.

[27]Scott, *Natural Allies,* pp. 125, 152.

[28]Cheryl Knott Malone, *Gender, Unpaid Labor, and the Promotion of Literacy: A Selected, Annotated Bibliography* (New York: Garland, 1987), pp. xiii–xiv; "Salaries and Supplementary Benefits in Private Hospitals, 1956–57," *Monthly Labor Review* 80 (September 1957): 1074.

[29]Malone, *Gender, Unpaid Labor,* p. xiv.

[30]Ibid.; Harold E. Smalley and John R. Freeman, *Hospital Industrial Engineering: A Guide to the Improvement of Hospital Management Systems* (New York: Reinhold Publishing, 1966), p. 3.

[31] "Guidelines for Using Volunteers in Libraries," *American Libraries* 2 (April 1971): 408; Eugene Arden, "Using Volunteers: Colleges Can Learn from Hospitals," *The Chronicle of Higher Education* 63 (July 1986): 613.

[32]George King Logan, "Volunteers—For Publicity," *Louisiana Library Association Bulletin* 10 (March 1947): 72.

[33]Clara E. Breed, *Turning the Pages: San Diego Public Library History, 1882–1982* (San Diego: Friends of the San Diego Public Library, 1983), p. 150.

[34]Adele B. Tunick, "Volunteer Services for Schools," *Scholastic Teacher* 87 (October 21, 1965): 10; Mary E. Shipp, "Teacher Aides; A Survey," *National Elementary Principal* 46 (May 1967): 30–33.

[35]T. Margaret Jamer, *School Volunteers: Creating a New Dimension in Education Through Lay Participation: Including the History of the First School Volunteer Program* (New York: Public Education Association, 1961), pp. 21, 91–92.

[36]Malone, *Gender, Unpaid Labor,* p. xiv.

[37]Lorna M. Wyckoff, "School Volunteers Face the Issues," *Phi Delta Kappan* 58 (June 1977): 75–76.

[38]George Bobinski, "The Golden Age of American Librarianship," *Wilson Library Bulletin* 58 (January 1984): 338.

[39]Mary Peacock Douglas, *The Pupil Assistant in the School Library* (Chicago: American Library Association, 1957).

[40]Mary Virginia Gaver, *Every Child Needs a School Library* (Chicago: American Library Association, 1958).

[41]American Association of School Librarians, *Standards for School Library Programs* (Chicago: American Library Association, 1960), pp. 20–21.

[42]National Education Association Research Division, *School Library Personnel Task Analysis Survey* (Chicago: American Association of School Librarians, 1969), p. 76.

[43]Mary Helen Mahar, *Statistics of Public School Libraries, 1960–61* (Washington, DC: U.S. Department of Health, Education, and Welfare, 1961), p. 9.

[44]*A Handbook of Facts about the Houston Independent School District* (Houston: Forum on Public Education, 1956), p. 25. The use of multi-school librarians augmented by volunteer mothers continued for years; see Eloise Norton, "School Libraries and Volunteer Help," *Peabody Journal of Education* 43 (July 1965): 18–20.

[45]Morris D. Caplin, "An Invaluable Resource: The School Volunteer," *The Clearing House* 45 (September 1970): 12.

[46]United States. Department of Labor. Bureau of Labor Statistics. *Library Manpower: A Study of Demand and Supply* (Washington, DC: U.S. Office of Education, 1970), p. 10.

[47]NEA, School Library Personnel, p. 15.

[48]Ibid., p. 16.

[49]Ibid.

[50]Tzvee Morris, "Library Volunteers," *New Jersey Libraries* 8 (October 1975): 4–7, cited by Loriene Roy, "Volunteers in Public Libraries: Issues and Viewpoints," *Public Library Quarterly* 5 (Winter 1984): 34.

[51]29. BLS, *Library Manpower*, p. 10.

[52]Virginia Walter, "Volunteers and Bureaucrats: Clarifying Roles and Creating Meaning," *Journal of Voluntary Action Research* 15 (January–March 1986): 23–25.

[53]"Proposition 13 Spurs Use of Volunteers in Ventura," *Library Journal* 104 (May 1, 1979): 996.

[54]Breed, *Turning the Pages*, pp. 145, 150.

[55]"San Diego Volunteers Rate $5 an Hour," *Library Journal* 108 (August 1983): 1420.

[56]Bobinski, "The Golden Age," p. 343.

[57]"LSCA-Funded Volunteer Program Catches on in Carroll County," *Library Journal* 107 (March 1, 1982): 500–501.

[58]*The Bowker Annual of Library and Book Trade Information*, 31st ed. (New York: R.R. Bowker, 1986), p. 246.

[59]Gary E. Strong, "Adult Literacy: State Library Responses," *Library Trends* 35 (Fall 1986): 243–261.

[60]*The Bowker Annual Library and Book Trade Almanac*, 34th ed. (New York: R.R. Bowker, 1989), pp. 254–255.

[61]*Bowker Annual*, 34th ed., p. 267.

[62]Alice Sizer Warner, *Volunteers in Libraries II*. LJ Special Report #24. (New York: R.R. Bowker, 1983), p. 6.

[63]Mary Jo Detweiler, "Volunteers in Public Libraries: The Costs and Benefits," *Public Libraries* 21 (Fall 1982): 80.

[64]Warner, *Volunteers in Libraries II*, p. 7.

[65]Walter, "Volunteers and Bureaucrats," p. 22.

[66]Lois D. Fleming, *Volunteer Service Manual, Leon County Public Library* (Tallahassee, FL: The Library, 1981), p. 9, reprinted in Warner, *Volunteers in Libraries II— Exhibits* (microfiche accompanying report).

[67]Alice Sizer Warner and Elizabeth Bole Eddison, *Volunteers in Libraries*. LJ Special Report #2. (New York: R.R. Bowker, 1977), pp. 8–11; Herta Loeser, *Women, Work, and Volunteering* (Boston: Beacon Press, 1974), pp. 91–131; United States. Department of Labor. Manpower Administration. *Americans Volunteer*. Manpower/Automation Research Monograph No. 10. (Washington, DC: Government Printing Office, 1969), pp. 9–10.

[68]Wendy Kaminer, *Women Volunteering: The Pleasure, Pain, and Politics of Unpaid Work from 1830 to the Present* (Garden City, NY: Anchor Press, 1984), pp. 78–79, 121–122.

[69]Melvin A. Glasser, *What Makes a Volunteer?* Public Affairs Pamphlet No. 224. (New York: Public Affairs Committee, 1955), pp. 4–6.

[70]Robert F. Hillenbrand, "An Elementary Principal Views the Feminine Mystique," *National Elementary Principal* 46 (May 1967): 531–535.

[71]Loeser, *Women, Work and Volunteering*, p. 29.

[72]Ann Strayer Burkhardt, "The Trained Volunteer and the Elementary Library," *American School Board Journal* 150 (March 1965): 15–16.

[73]*Americans Volunteer,* p. 33.

[74]Ibid., pp. 27, 31.

[75]U.S. Department of Labor. Employment Standards Administration. Women's Bureau. *The Earnings Gap Between Women and Men* (Washington, D.C.: Government Printing Office, 1976), p. 8.

[76]Amitai Etzioni, ed. *The Semi-Professions and Their Organization: Teachers, Nurses, Social Workers* (New York: Free Press, 1969), v–ix; Barbara Melosh, *"The Physician's Hand": Work Culture and Conflict in American Nursing* (Philadelphia: Temple University Press, 1982), pp. 3–13; Susan Reverby, *Ordered to Care: The Dilemma of American Nursing, 1850–1945* (Cambridge: Cambridge University Press, 1987), pp. 1–7; Kathleen Weibel and Kathleen M. Heim, *The Role of Women in Librarianship 1876–1976: The Entry, Advancement and Struggle for Equalization in One Profession.* (Phoenix: Oryx Press, 1979), xiii; Anita R. Schiller, "Sex and Library Careers," in *Women in Librarianship: Melvil's Rib Symposium,* eds. Margaret Myers and Mayra Scarborough (New Brunswick, NJ: Rutgers University Press, 1975), pp. 11–20; Dee Garrison, *Apostles of Culture: The Public Librarian and American Society, 1876–1920* (New York: Free Press, 1979); Suzanne Hildenbrand, "Revision versus Reality: Women in the History of the Public Library Movement, 1876–1920," in *The Status of Women in Librarianship: Historical, Sociological, and Economic Issues,* ed. Kathleen M. Heim (New York: Neal Schuman Publishers, 1983), pp. 7–27.

[77]Jesse Hauk Shera, *The Foundations of Education for Librarianship* (New York: Becker and Hayes, 1972), pp. 108, 137.

[78]Breed, *Turning the Pages,* p. 38.

[79]Suzy Hagstrom and Steve Rubenstein, "Library Eyes Volunteer Plan," *The Daily Californian,* April 19, 1973, p. 20.

[80]Ellen Levine, "Volunteerism in Libraries," *Bay State Librarian* 69 (Summer 1980): 11–14.

[81]Leo Nelson Flanagan, "Some Second Thoughts on Survival in the Seventies: or Two Views of the Volunteer Dilemma," *Catholic Library World* 48 (October 1976): 112–114.

[82]Joseph Carvalho III, "To Complement or Compete? The Role of Volunteers in Public Libraries," *Public Library Quarterly* 5 (Spring 1984): 35–39.

[83]Leslie Trainer, "METRO Workshop on Volunteers in Libraries Sparks Controversy, Offers Practical Advice," *American Libraries* 7 (December 1976): 666.

[84]Malone, *Gender, Unpaid Labor,* op. cit.

[85]Rashelle Schlessinger Karp, "Volunteers in Libraries," in *Advances in Library Administration and Organization: A Research Annual,* Vol. 5, ed. Gerard B. McCabe and Bernard Kreissman (Greenwich, CT: JAI Press, 1986), p. 15. For a more balanced and informed review of the literature, see Roy, "Volunteers in Public Libraries," pp. 29–40.

[86]Kathleen Roedder, "The PTA—Library Supporter," *The Instructor* 75 (November 1965): 83.

[87]"Guidelines for Using Volunteers in Libraries," *American Libraries* 2 (April 1971): 407–408.

[88]Pat McCormick, "NOW Task Force on Volunteerism," *Ms.,* February 1975, p. 73.

[89]"Guidelines," pp. 407–408.

[90]Warner and Eddison, *Volunteers in Libraries,* p. 38.

[91]Warner, *Volunteers in Libraries II.*

[92]*The Bowker Annual of Library and Book Trade Information,* 27th ed. (New York: R. R. Bowker, 1982), pp. 21–22; *The Bowker Annual of Library and Book Trade Information,* 28th ed. (New York: R.R. Bowker, 1983), pp. 15–16.

[93]President George Bush, June 22, 1989, quoted in "The New Volunteers," *Newsweek,* July 10, 1989, p. 36.

[94]"The New Volunteers," p. 37.

Cited Authors

Subject Index

About the Contributors

Clare Beck is Government Documents Librarian at Eastern Michigan University, University Library 309, Ypsilanti, Michigan 48197 (email: lib_beck @emuvax.emich.edu). Her degrees are from the University of Chicago (B.A., history), the University of Denver (M.A., librarianship), and Eastern Michigan University (M.A., social science). An active member of the American Library Association, she was a founding member of the Government Documents Round Table and serves on the Committee on the Status of Women in Librarianship. She is also a member of the Michigan Academy of Science, Arts and Letters at which she has presented papers on diverse topics. She has published articles on the history of women librarians in *Library Journal* and *College & Research Libraries*. She is preparing a full-length biography of Adelaide Hasse.

Barbara Brand is head of the Interlibrary Loan/Document Delivery Department and Women's Studies/Africana Studies subject specialist at Melville Library, State University of New York at Stony Brook, Stony Brook, New York 11794-3300 <bbrand@ccmail.sunysb.edu>. She received an M.A. in library science from the University of Wisconsin in 1965 and has held a variety of public-service library positions: Columbia University, University of North Carolina, the District of Columbia, and Seattle Public Library. She also held an administrative position at the University of Washington School of Librarianship before earning a doctorate in higher education administration from the University of Washington in 1978. She has published articles and presented papers on the history of women's professions, particularly librarianship, social work, and public health. She is an active member of the American Library Association, the American Society for Information Science, and The Special interest group on Women in Education of the American Educational Research Association as well as regional professional associations. In 1985, she received a National Endowment for the Humanities travel to collections grant, and, in 1987, a SUNY Conversations in the Disciplines Grant to fund a university conference on censorship. While at the University of Washington, she helped to develop a grant to support a regional Career Development and Assessment Center for women librarians.

Helen H. Britton (A.B. in Ed., Leland College, now closed; M.A., University of Iowa; M.A.L.S., University of Michigan) is librarian emerita, California State University, Long Beach (CSULB). She has been a college English instructor and assistant professor, a public librarian, and a university librarian, who has served in a variety of positions, including administrative appointments. She has practiced librarianship in the Free Library of Philadelphia; Louisiana State Library; the Thompson Memorial Library, Ohio State University; the Sterling C. Evans Library, Texas A&M University; the M. D. Anderson Library, University of Houston; and the University Library, California State University, Long Beach. At the latter library, she held positions as an assistant library director for reference and instructional services and as an associate library director. Her most recent prior publications were "Interactions: A Library Faculty Matrix Organization and a Public Policy and Administration Policy," in *Reference Services and Public Policy*, edited by Richard D. Irving and Bill Katz, New York, Haworth Press, 1988: and "Dorothy Porter Wesley: A Bio-Bibliographic Profile," in *American Black Women in the Arts and Social Sciences*, 3rd edition, revised and enlarged, by Ora Williams, Metuchen, NJ, Scarecrow Press, 1994.

Geraldine Joncich Clifford is professor emerita in the School of Education at the University of California, Berkeley. She received her bachelor's and master's degrees from the University of California at Los Angeles and her doctorate at Teachers College, Columbia University. She has served as director of the system-wide University of California Education Abroad Program Study Center for Australia and New Zealand. Her numerous honors include receipt of a Guggenheim Fellowship, a Spencer Foundation Grant for research and a Rockefeller Humanities Fellowship. In 1992 she received the Willystine Goodsell Award for contributions to women and women's issues in educational research. Among her numerous papers and essays, "Women's Liberation and Women's Professions" in *Women and Education in American History: Essays from the Mount Holyoke Sesquicentennial Symposia* (1988) is especially noteworthy. Her books include *"Equally in View": The University of California, Its Women and the Schools* (1995), *Ed School: A Brief for Professional Education* (with James Guthrie) (1988) and the edited collection *Lone Voyagers: Academic Women in Coeducational Universities, 1870–1937* (1989). She is currently preparing for publication *"Those Good Gertrudes": The Woman Teacher in American History*.

Georgia Higley is a reference librarian in the Serial and Government Publications Division, Library of Congress, Washington, D.C. 20540 (email:ghig @loc.gov) where her specialties are European Union documents and American state publications. She received her M.S.L.S. from the University of North Carolina at Chapel Hill, where she was selected for the Library of Congress Intern Program and for membership in Beta Phi Mu. She holds an M.A. degree in English and B.A. degrees in English and History from George Mason University. At the Library of Congress, she was a founder of the Reference Forum Steering Committee, a staff organization devoted to reference issues, serving as one of its first co-chairs. She is also co-moderator of a reference listserv for the Library. She is to present a paper at the 1996 meeting of the American Studies Association on Cherokee Nation newspapers.

Suzanne Hildenbrand teaches cataloging and online bibliographic retrieval in the School of Information and Library Studies at the State University of New York at Buffalo, 381 Baldy Hall, Buffalo, New York 14260 <LISHILDE@UBVM.CC.BUFFALO.EDU>. She received her bachelor's degree in history at Brooklyn College of the City University of New York, her master's degree in Library Service at Columbia University, and her Ph.D. in the History of Education at the University of California at Berkeley. She has been a high school librarian and a cataloger in academic libraries, and has served overseas with the United States Information Agency. Her publications include "Promoting Participation: Libraries and Women's Role in American Society," in *The Role of Libraries in the Democratic Process* (1996); "Women in American Libraries: The Long Road from Contributions to Transformation," in *Leidenschaft und Bildung* (1992); and selected entries including "Origins of Public Library Services to Children, 1876–1910," in *Women's History in the United States: A Handbook* (2nd. ed., forthcoming). She edited *Women's Collections: Libraries, Archives and Consciousness* (1986) and has served on the Committee on the Status of Women in Librarianship of the American Library Association.

Christine Jenkins is a member of the faculty of the Graduate School of Library and Information Science, University of Illinois, 410 DKH, 1407 W. Gregory Dr., Urbana, Illinois 61801-3680 <jenkins@alexia.lis.uiuc.edu>. She teaches courses in youth services, young adult literature, gender issues, and LIS foundations and history. She received her M.L.S. from the University of Wisconsin (UW–Madison) in 1973 and worked for 13 years as a school library media specialist in the Ann Arbor Public Schools before returning to UW-Madison for doctoral studies in the School of Library and Information Studies. She also has a master's degree in children's literature from Eastern Michigan University.

Her research interests center around women, young people, libraries, reading, and intellectual freedom, both current and historical. She has published articles in *Booklist;* the *Journal of Youth Services in Libraries; Feminist Collections, Libraries, Erotica and Pornography* (1991); and the *Encyclopedia of Library History* (1994). She is an active member of the American Library Association in the areas of youth services and intellectual freedom, having served on the 1989 Caldecott Committee and as a director of the Intellectual Freedom Round Table and chair of the ALSC Intellectual freedom Committee.

Glendora Johnson-Cooper is Associate Librarian in the Oscar A. Silverman Undergraduate Library (UGL) at the University of Buffalo, Buffalo, New York 14260 (gjcooper@acsu.buffalo.edu). As Collection Development Coordinator, she is responsible for the allocation of the UGL serial and monographic budget. Her research interests include racial and ethnic diversity within academic libraries, historical and contemporary contributions of African American Librarians, and library residency programs designed to attract librarians of color. An active member of the Black Caucus of the American Library Association, she assisted in planning the program for the First National Conference of African-American Librarians. She is Project Manager of the University Libraries Residency Program.

Linda Lewis is Associate Professor at the University of New Mexico General Library, Albuquerque, New Mexico 87131-1466 <llewisa@unm.edu>. She received her bachelor's degree in history and her master's degree in library science from the University of Oklahoma. She began her professional career as a humanities reference librarian and is now head of the Collection Development Department. Her publications include contributions to *European Immigrant Women in the United States: A Biographic Dictionary* (1994) and *Reader's Guide to Science Fiction* (1989) and "Bibliographic Computerized Searching in Psychology," in *Teaching of Psychology* (1986). She is interested in the history of women in the Southwest. With two associates, she began researching the lives of women in the history of New Mexico, which resulted in her work on Julia Asplund.

Anne Lundin is an Assistant Professor on the faculty of the University of Wisconsin-Madison, School of Library and Information Studies, where she teaches courses on children's literature, youth services, storytelling and collection development.

She graduated from Ohio Wesleyan University and received a master's degree in English from the University of Michigan and a master's of library science from Louisiana State University. Her PhD in library science is from the University of Alabama.

Her background includes 15 years as an English teacher in many diverse places with diverse populations, and five years as curator of the de Grummond Children's Literature Research Collection at the University of Southern Mississippi. The de Grummond, the second largest such collection in the country, consists of original manuscripts, illustrations and rare books.

Lundin has recently published a monograph entitled *Teaching Children's Literature* (McFarland, 1995) and has published extensively in journals such as *The Lion and the Unicorn, Children's Literature in Education, Library Quarterly, Collection Building*, and *College and Research Libraries*. She is on the Newbery Committee for 1995 and on the board of the Center for Print Culture at the University of Wisconsin-Madison.

Her research interests are historical: in the importance of children's books as literature and print culture; in the foundational work of early children's librarians in establishing the field and a paradigm of service in the reviewing and coverage of children's literature in Victorian periodicals; and in the influence of Kate Greenaway, Randolph Caldecott and Walter Crane as the late-19th century pioneers of the modern picture book.

Cheryl Knott Malone is a doctoral student and lecturer in the Graduate School of Library and Information Science at The University of Texas at Austin. She also works as a reference librarian and bibliographer for history, government, American studies and Australian studies at UT's Perry-Castaneda Library. Recipient of a Fulbright Senior Scholar Award in Library Science for travel to research collections in Australia, she serves as editor of the Australia and Oceania section of the *Guide to Reference Books*, 11th ed. (Chicago: American Library Association, in press). She compiled *Gender, Unpaid Labor, and the Promotion of Literacy: A Selected, Annotated Bibliography.* (New York: Garland Publishing, 1987), and her book reviews have appeared in *American Reference Books Annual* and *Libraries & Culture.* Her research interests include the role of women in establishing public libraries in the United States as well as the history of library services to African-Americans.

Joanne Passet earned a B.A. from Bluffton College, an M.A. from Bowling Green State University, and an M.L.S. and PhD. from Indiana University. She is the author of *Cultural Crusaders: Women Librarians in the American West, 1900–1917* (1994) and co-author, with Mary Niles Maack, of *Aspirations and Mentoring in an Academic Environment* (1994). Her articles have been published in the *History of Education Quarterly, Libraries & Culture, Library & Information Science Research,* and *Library Quarterly.* She has taught at the University of California, Los Angeles, and at Indiana University. She is currently working on a second doctorate, in women's history, at the University of Wisconsin-Madison, where she has received a Gerda Lerner Fellowship.

Clara L. Sitter received her bachelor's degree at the University of Oklahoma in American Studies, her master's in Library Science from the University of Texas at Austin and her doctorate in education from the University of Colorado at Boulder. Her current position is Instruction Coordinator in Public Services at the Consortium Library at the University of Alaska, Anchorage. Her earlier professional experience has been varied and includes teaching librarianship as well as library service in high schools and colleges. Experience in the Rare Books Library at the University of Texas at Austin stimulated her interest in Fannie Ratchford.

Sitter has numerous publications including *Handbook for Alaska K–12 School Libraries* (1995), *Plugging into the Electronic Library* (1995), and *The Vertical File and Its Alternatives* (1992). She has been active in professional organizations and in professional programs. She has, for example, offered workshops on the electronic resources now available to university faculty, and on using ERIC for students and faculty. In addition she has participated in a workshop on reference skills and in an institute for Alaska School Librarians. She displays an active interest in public educational affairs and in intellectual freedom, speaking and writing often on these topics. She has served on the Alaska Committee for the White House Conference on Libraries.

Sitter's current research interests include local history, library history and library instruction. Her research in progress includes work on Anchorage place names and information resources in education.